THE HISTORY OF AUSTRALIA

The Twentieth Century

THE HISTORY OF AUSTRALIA

The Twentieth Century

Russel Ward

HARPER & ROW, PUBLISHERS
New York, Hagerstown, San Francisco, London

This work was first published in Australia under the title *A Nation for a Continent: The History of Australia 1901-1975.*

FIRST U.S. EDITION

LIBRARY OF CONGRESS CATALOG CARD NUMBER: 77-11795

ISBN: 0-06-014514-5

78 79 80 81 82 10 9 8 7 6 5 4 3 2 1

CONTENTS

Contents

ILLUSTRATIONS

MAPS

ABBREVIATIONS

(Basic references cited in the footnotes)

A.E.	Australian Encyclopaedia
A.J.P.H.	Australian Journal of Politics and History
C.A.	Commonwealth Acts
C.P.D.	Commonwealth Parliamentary Debates (to 1961)
C.P.D. – H.R.	House of Representatives (from 1962)
C.P.D. – S.	Senate (from 1962)
M.A.D. I	Modern Australia in Documents 1901-1939
M.A.D. II	Modern Australia in Documents 1939-1970
S. I	Australian Federal Politics and Law 1901-1929
S. II	Australian Federal Politics and Law 1929-1949
S.M.H.	Sydney Morning Herald
V. & P.	Votes and Proceedings of the House of Representatives (from 1901)

ACKNOWLEDGEMENTS

Every historian who ever lived stands on the shoulders, or sometimes in the shadow, of predecessors, colleagues and students, especially the general historian who must build on the published work of others as well as on research work of his own. This book owes a great deal to living and dead writers whose work is referred to in the footnotes and the bibliography.

I am especially grateful to friends who have helped hugely with criticism, advice and encouragement and with the typing, collation and checking of the manuscript and appendices: particularly Miss Alison Affleck, Mr Terry Hogan, Dr Noel McLachlan, Dr Ron Mendelsohn, Mrs M. Pittendrigh, Dr Tom Tanner, Mrs Jillian Oppenheimer, Associate-Professor A. T. Yarwood and Mr Tim Bass who must be the best publisher's reader in the world. I must thank also my wife Barbara and our children for giving me time and peace in which to write.

Russel Ward
University of New England, Armidale, 1977

The author and publisher wish to thank Mr Vane Lindesay for invaluable help in the selection of illustrations and the following for permission to reproduce copyright material on the pages listed:
The Herald and Weekly Times Ltd (*Melbourne Punch, Herald, Argus*): 3, 151, 170, 184, 196, 209, 221, 227, 277, 286, 320; John Fairfax & Sons Ltd (*Sydney Morning Herald, Smith's Weekly, Sun*): 88, 100, 304, 313, 371, 392; News Ltd (*Labour Daily*): 179; Tribune: 257; Australian Consolidated Press (*Bulletin*): 131, 164, 299, 332; David Syme & Co. Ltd (*Age*): 395, 417; Mr Bruce Petty: 361, 382, 412, 417; Mr Paul Rigby and News International: 347; Janet Glad and Curtis Brown (Aust.) Pty Ltd: 51, 109, 219, 235.
Mr Phillip Burgoyne: 365.

PROLOGUE

Though this book surveys the history of Australia in the twentieth century, it seems necessary to write a few preliminary words about Australian prehistory and history up to 1900, and particularly about the origins and nature of the federal Constitution.

Australia came into existence as a national state on the first day of the twentieth century. Geologically speaking it is the oldest continent though it was the last, except for Antarctica, to be discovered by Europeans. However, human beings had lived in it for at least 35 000 years.

The indigenous inhabitants, the Australian Aborigines, have dark brown, nearly black, skins, but in many other physical characteristics they resemble Caucasoid rather than Negroid or Mongoloid peoples. Their hair, for instance, generally grows prolifically and is neither lank and straight as among Mongoloids, nor frizzy as among Negroids, but wavy as among Europeans. Very young children occasionally have blond hair. Speech studies have shown that practically all of the 300 or so Aboriginal languages belong to one linguistic family which has no connection or affinities whatever with any other language in the world. The Aboriginal people are classed by some ethnologists as a special species within the Caucasoid group and by others as a fourth, distinct, 'Australoid' race of mankind.

The Aborigines lived for tens of thousands of years with a Stone Age technology and a purely food-gathering economy. Like the Kalahari Bushmen of South Africa, they had not learnt to practise any form of agriculture or to keep any domestic animals — except for the wild dog or *dingo* which was sometimes used in hunting. Consequently they generally built no houses or villages of even a semi-permanent character, but moved about according to the seasons in pursuit of wild game and edible plants, camping here or there perhaps for a few nights, perhaps only for one. They hunted and lived in extended family groups or hordes, each numbering on the average about forty or fifty. Neighbouring hordes would meet at traditionally hallowed places from time to time to carry out tribal ceremonies. Each of the larger tribal groups possessed a common language and occupied a traditionally defined territory. Indeed almost every aspect of Aboriginal life was governed by tradition or immemorial custom.

Lacking the arts of agriculture and husbandry, they also lacked any form of storable wealth and, hence, commodities to fight over. Perhaps this fact helps to explain why they were among the least political and least warlike peoples known to history. Hordes and tribes had no chiefs or headmen and no authority structure other than that which attached 'naturally' to the older and wiser males, who administered tribal custom while being themselves bound by it. Breaches of traditionally proper behaviour were punished, often by death, and personal quarrels occurred as frequently as among other human beings, but there is no evidence that Australian Aborigines practised or even understood the civilised institution of warfare. When ill-used by Malay or other visitors to the northern coast, or by the European invaders after 1788, the Aborigines fought back; but no tribe seems ever to have conceived the idea of exterminating or enslaving another or annexing its territory. There are many references to inter-tribal 'wars', but eye-witness accounts make it clear that these meetings resembled ritualistic international sporting fixtures rather than battles. Two tribes would meet by arrangement at a traditionally appointed place. The women would hurl insults and the men would throw spears at each other, nimbly dodging the missiles, sometimes for hours, before someone was hit. Then, whether the man was wounded or killed, the 'war' was over for the season and both tribes joined in a great dance or corroboree until the next meeting a year or so later. The peaceful nature of the Aboriginal race did nothing to protect them from the white invaders: rather the reverse.

Dutch sailors charted roughly much of the northern, western and southern coasts of Australia from 1606 onwards, but showed no disposition to settle. James Cook, greatest of modern English navigators, discovered the eastern coastline and claimed it for Britain in 1770. In 1788 the British Government sent a fleet, laden with convicts and their guards, to found a settlement at Botany Bay, where Cook had spent some weeks eighteen years earlier. The commanding officer, Captain Arthur Phillip of the Royal Navy, decided instead to unload his cargo eight or nine kilometres away in Port Jackson where Sydney now stands. In the next fifty years other settlements were

Melbourne Punch, 14 May 1925

THE NIGGER—AND THE WOODPILE

(Concern at the disappearance of the Australian forests grows apace—and at the sitting of the Church Congress lamentations were heard about the treatment of the aborigine).

The Last of the Tribe: "My word, pretty soon no place in Australia for us Aussies!"

made at different points on the coastline, sometimes to found a new penal station for convicts, sometimes to 'forestall the French' and sometimes simply with a view to profit. Among these settlements five flourished mightily and became the capitals of separate colonies: Hobart (1803 Tasmania), Brisbane (1824 Queensland), Perth (1829 Western Australia), Melbourne (1835 Victoria) and Adelaide (1836 South Australia). In all the Aboriginal inhabitants were detribalised, dispossessed and destroyed by the white invaders. Even Christian and other philanthropists among the latter found it impossibly difficult to understand a people who had no concept of private, as opposed to tribal or collective property. Sometimes Aborigines were shot or poisoned like troublesome animal pests; more often they succumbed to European diseases and to spiritual sickness caused by separation from their tribal lands. Anthropologists have estimated that in 1788 there were probably about 300 000 Aborigines in Australia and that this number had been roughly constant for many thousands of years. By 1900 there were left only about 60 000 people of pure Aboriginal descent.

Transportation of convicts to eastern mainland Australia virtually ceased in 1840 and shipments to Tasmania ended in 1853. At the request of the colonists themselves convicts were sent to Western Australia from 1850 to 1868. Long before this, wool-growing had become the staple industry of the whole country, though South Australia early developed an export trade in wheat also. In 1851 the discovery of fantastically rich goldfields in New South Wales and Victoria gave a strong impulse, directly or indirectly, to the prosperity of all the colonies. Gold also attracted a great influx of migrants, mainly British, who swelled the colonial demands for self-government. By 1856 full responsible government on the British parliamentary model had been established in New South Wales, Victoria, South Australia and Tasmania. Queensland received self-government on its separation from New South Wales in 1859, and Western Australia in 1890.

When the six colonies obtained self-government, they were completely separate entities politically, and nearly all colonists thought this situation good. In many ways the colonies had closer connections with Britain than they had with each other. Fifty or a hundred kilometres away from the colonial capitals population was so sparse, and roads so bad or non-existent, that the easiest and quickest way to travel between them was usually by sea. When the colonies began to build railways in the 1850s and 1860s, it did not seem to matter that they chose different gauges, for few people envisaged the possibility of the lines ever joining. Yet even at that time there was an underlying cultural unity among the invaders throughout the continent. New South Welshmen and Victorians, Western Australians and Queenslanders, South Australians and Tasmanians shared the same English speech and essentially the same amalgam of British culture, traditions, habits, religions and institutions. Despite much inter-colonial rivalry, all tended to think of themselves first as Australians — or as British colonists in various parts of Australia. From the very beginning of each colony 'overlanders' had taken stock and ideas from one to the other — except for Western Australia and Tasmania whose sole feasible means of communication with the other colonies was by sea. When some of the empty space between the colonial centres was filled with settlers and country towns, when transport and communications brought the colonies closer together, it was natural and convenient for them to join in some form of union — just as it had been necessary for them to develop separately, for practical reasons, in the early years of settlement.

By 1872 all towns of any size on the continent were in telegraphic communication with each other and with Great Britain. By 1888 the four capital cities in the major eastern colonies — New South Wales, Victoria, South Australia and Queensland — were joined by railways. Inter-colonial customs duties and other barriers to the growth of trade began to worry practical men, while idealists and chauvinists began to have visions of a united Australian people taking the leading place among the countries of the southern hemisphere. In 1889 the Premier of New South Wales, Henry Parkes, issued what federationists referred to as a 'clarion call' for the federal union of the colonies. For the next eleven years politicians and many interested citizens produced propaganda and took part in a series of conferences on the issue. The federal Constitutions of the United States of America, Canada and Switzerland were studied by some and discussed freely by all.

The most intractable problem was that of reconciling State rights with the democratic rule of the majority. Each of the six colonies was to be a constituent State of the new nation, but they were by no means equal in population. New South Wales and Victoria together contained about twice as many people as all four of the other States. If the new federal Parliament were to decide issues by majority vote, would not the rights and interests of the smaller States always be at the mercy of the two south-eastern giants? The solution in essence was borrowed from the Constitution of the United States: the Lower House was to represent numbers and the Upper House States. Thus New South Wales with 1 370 000 people in 1901 would elect 26 members to the House of Representatives while Tasmania with 174 000 people would elect only five. In the Upper House or

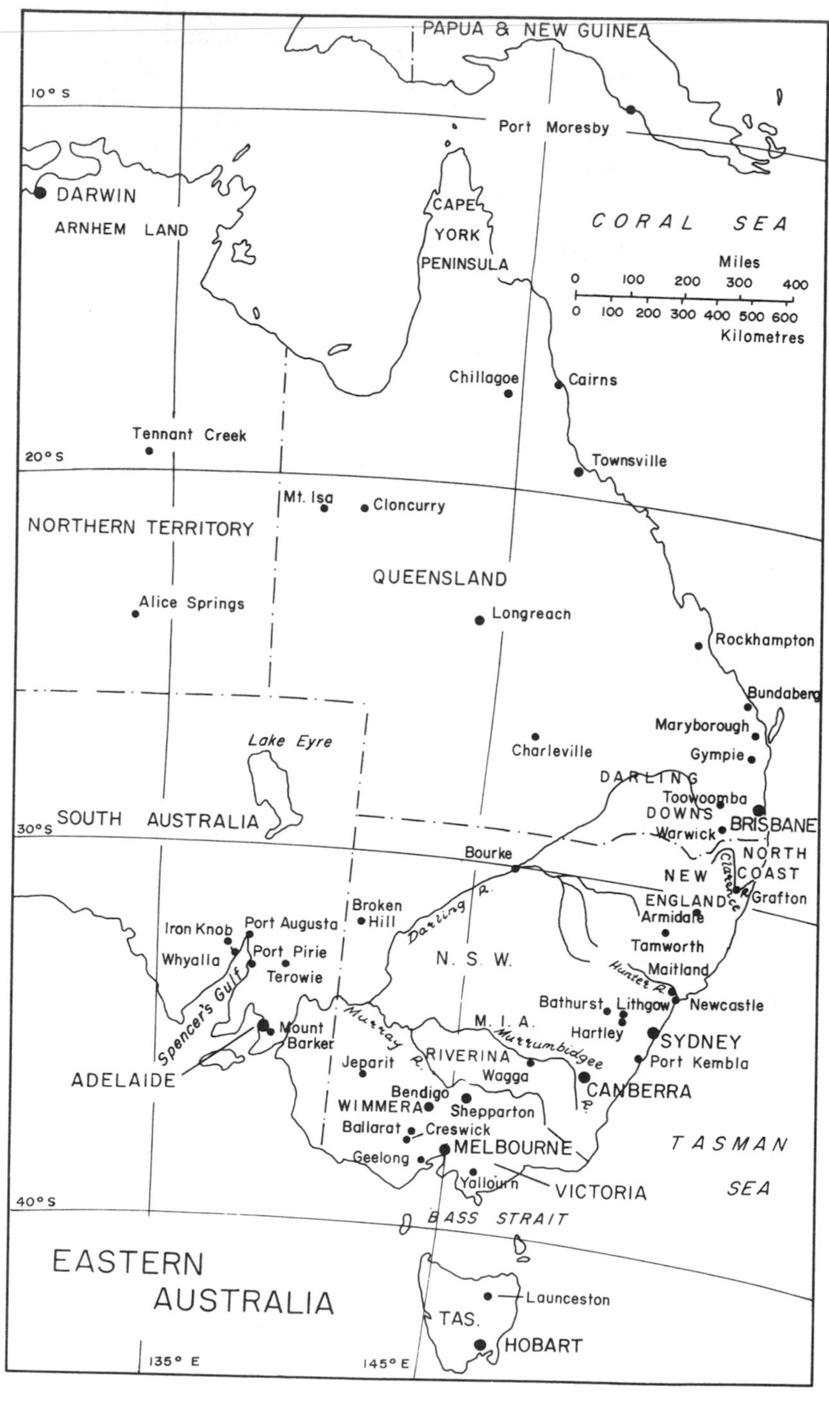
PAPUA & NEW GUINEA
10° S
Port Moresby
DARWIN
ARNHEM LAND
CAPE
YORK
PENINSULA
CORAL SEA
Miles
0 100 200 300 400
0 100 200 300 400 500 600
Kilometres
Chillagoe
Cairns
Tennant Creek
20° S
Townsville
Mt. Isa
Cloncurry
NORTHERN TERRITORY
QUEENSLAND
Alice Springs
Longreach
Rockhampton
Bundaberg
Maryborough
Gympie
Lake Eyre
Charleville
DARLING
DOWNS
Toowoomba
BRISBANE
Warwick
30° S
SOUTH AUSTRALIA
Bourke
NORTH
COAST
NEW
ENGLAND
Grafton
Clarence R.
Broken Hill
Darling R.
Armidale
Tamworth
Iron Knob
Port Augusta
Whyalla
Port Pirie
Terowie
N. S. W.
Maitland
Hunter R.
Newcastle
Bathurst
Lithgow
Hartley
Spencer's Gulf
Mount Barker
Murray R.
M. I. A.
Murrumbidgee R.
SYDNEY
Port Kembla
ADELAIDE
RIVERINA
Jeparit
Wagga
CANBERRA
Bendigo
WIMMERA
Shepparton
Ballarat
Creswick
MELBOURNE
TASMAN
SEA
Geelong
Yallourn
VICTORIA
40° S
BASS STRAIT
EASTERN
AUSTRALIA
Launceston
TAS.
HOBART
135° E
145° E

Senate, however, the States were to have equal representation, electing six senators each.

In the year 1900 the British Parliament passed an Act establishing the six Australian colonies as States of 'one indissoluble Federal Commonwealth under the Crown of the United Kingdom'. The States retained their own parliaments and all their powers except those specifically handed over to the new Federal Government. These Commonwealth powers include the right to impose taxation and to grant old age and invalid pensions (in addition to State taxes and pensions); exclusive power over customs and excise duties, defence, naval and military matters, external affairs, immigration and emigration, posts and telegraphs, census and statistics, lighthouses and coastal navigation, trade and commerce between the States or with foreign countries, currency and coinage, weights and measures, patents and copyrights, banking and insurance, and territories such as Papua, the Northern Territory or the Federal Capital Territory itself. Since customs and excise duties had provided a major proportion of every colonial government's revenue, it was agreed that for the first ten years the Commonwealth Government should hand back to the States three-quarters of its receipts from these sources. A valid Commonwealth law takes precedence over State laws inconsistent with it. The Commonwealth Parliament may make minor alterations to the Constitution but any important 'structural' change can be made only if a Bill passed by Parliament is then approved at a referendum by an absolute majority of the electors and by a majority of the electors *in a majority of the six States*. Any or all of the States may also refer, or hand over, specific powers to the Commonwealth if their parliaments wish to do so.

Like those of the States, the Commonwealth Parliament was modelled on that of Westminster. Constitutionally it consisted of the Monarch, a Senate and a House of Representatives, just as the parliament of each State consisted of the Monarch, an Upper House known as the Legislative Council and a Lower House known as the Legislative Assembly. However, the Legislative Councils were elected on a restrictive property franchise in all States except Queensland and New South Wales whose Councils consisted of members nominated for life terms by the Queen's representative, the State Governor. Thus the State Upper Houses usually acted as guardians of conservatism against the popularly elected Assemblies. In the new Commonwealth Parliament, however, both Houses were to be elected by the same voters — all those entitled to vote in elections for the Legislative Assembly in their State. In practice this meant adult male franchise except in the case of South Australia and Western Australia which had given the vote also to adult females in

TIMOR
10°S
TIMOR
SEA
Bathurst I.
DARWIN
ARNHEM LAND
Joseph
Bonaparte
Gulf
Pine
Creek
Katherine
Admiralty Gulf
INDIAN OCEAN
Wyndham
Ord R.
Victoria River
Downs
Derby
Fitzroy R.
Broome
Fitzroy
Crossing
Halls Creek
Port Hedland
De Grey R.
GREAT SANDY DESERT
20°S
Exmouth Gulf
Marble Bar
NORTHERN
TERRITORY
Fortescue R.
North
West
Cape
WESTERN
Ashburton R.
GIBSON DESERT
AUSTRALIA
Lyons R.
Gascoyne R.
Carnarvon
SOUTH
AUSTRALIA
Murchison R.
GREAT VICTORIA DESERT
Mt. Magnet
Laverton
Geraldton
Abrolhos Islands
Menzies
Moora
Coolgardie
Kalgoorlie
30°S
Goomalling
Norseman
PERTH
Freemantle
GREAT AUSTRALIAN
BIGHT
Bunbury
Katanning
Esperance
Cape Leeuwin
Albany
Miles
0 100 200 300 400
0 100 200 300 400 500 600
Kilometres
WESTERN
AUSTRALIA
115°E
40°S
125°E

1894 and 1899 respectively. Since members of the first Commonwealth Parliament felt it was invidious to have South and Western Australian women with a vote, but not those in other States, they extended the franchise in 1902 to all adult native-born or naturalised British subjects (including women) who had lived in Australia for at least six months. The same Act, however, disqualified persons of unsound mind, attainted of treason, under sentence of imprisonment for one year or more, and *Aboriginal natives of Australia*, Asia, Africa and the Pacific Islands (not including New Zealand) — except for a handful of such persons already enrolled as voters for the State parliaments.[1] At the time of federation nearly all (white) Australians, like other people of European descent, believed that 'coloured people' were innately, genetically inferior to whites. Nevertheless, Federal Parliament was, almost from the beginning, considerably more democratic than those of the States.

As we have seen, members were elected to the House of Representatives from constituencies containing approximately the same number of people, except that no original State, however lightly populated, could have fewer than five seats in the Lower House. For elections to the Senate each State was regarded as a single constituency returning six members. Members of the House of Representatives served normally for a three-year term, but senators for six years. Only half the senators faced the electors at each election so that there might be an in-built element of experience and continuity in the parliament. The Constitution expressly provided that the number of senators should always be, as nearly as possible, half that of the members of the Lower House. For the first forty-eight years of Commonwealth government there were thirty six senators, six from each State and, seventy-five 'full' members of the House of Representatives. In 1922 whites in the Northern Territory were given the right to elect a representative who, however, had no vote except on matters of purely local interest to his constituency. In 1949 the Federal Capital Territory was also given a member with similarly restricted voting rights. In 1966 both members were given full equality with their fellow representatives. Those who framed the Constitution took great pains to give the Senate maximum powers consistent with majority rule, because they believed that it would be the guardian of State rights. In fact it has not worked out like that. The cry of State rights is heard almost as often in one House as in the other, and divisions in both Houses, from the beginning, have usually been along party and almost never along State lines.

Under the Constitution the Governor-General, representing the

[1] *C.A.*, 1912, vol. 1, Commonwealth Franchise Act, No. 8 of 1902.

Queen, has the power to call together and prorogue both Houses and to dissolve the Lower House. The House of Representatives may not last for more than three years from the date of its first meeting after an election, though it may be dissolved and another election called by the Governor-General on the advice of the Prime Minister at any time. Legislation may be initiated in either House and they have equal rights except in the area of 'money bills', which may be initiated only in the Representatives. The Senate may not amend taxation or appropriation bills raising money for 'the ordinary annual services of the government', and it may not amend any bill in such a way as 'to increase any proposed charge . . . on the people': but it has power to 'request' the Representatives to make specified amendments in such bills. In practice the Senate has used this power to 'request' changes so vigorously that it has amounted to a complete power of amendment. The Representatives may not 'tack' other measures on to money bills. If the Senate 'rejects or fails to pass' a bill that has been twice passed by the Representatives, at an interval of at least three months, the Leader of the Government may ask the Governor-General for a 'double dissolution' and a new election. If the new Houses after the election still cannot agree, the deadlock is resolved by a simple majority vote at a joint sitting of both Houses.

Following American practice the Constitution also provided for the establishment of a High Court of Australia. This tribunal was to act as a court of appeal from the Supreme Court of each State, but it was also to carry out the special function of arbitration on disputes between States, or between any of them and the Commonwealth. Thus the High Court came in fact to exercise considerable political power through its decisions as to the explicit meaning of many rather generally-worded clauses of the Constitution. Keen as they were on Australian nationhood, the founding fathers were equally keen on retaining some tangible constitutional links with Britain; and so they provided for an appeal in certain cases, from the High Court of Australia to the highest law court in the British Empire, the judicial committee of the Privy Council.

One of the most contentious issues was the practical one of choosing a national capital. In 1901, Melbourne and Sydney, with just under half a million people in each, were vastly larger than the other State capitals. Sydney was the oldest European settlement in the continent, but Melbourne was more centrally situated among the six States. Jealousy between them was intense. Finally delegates to the last constitutional convention agreed to a compromise: that an entirely new capital city should be built. It should be in the State of New South Wales though at a distance of at least 100 miles (160 kilometres) from Sydney; but pending its construction the

Commonwealth Parliament should meet in Melbourne. The Victorian Government generously made its handsome parliamentary building in Melbourne available to the new Commonwealth legislators — for twenty-six years, as it turned out. Since Melbourne was to have the Parliament, Sydney obtained the honour of mounting the inaugural celebrations.

Chapter 1

A NATION FOR A CONTINENT

c. 1900 — 1903

Inauguration and political groupings — People and resources — The arts, nationalism and imperialism — Legislation and White Australia

INAUGURATION AND POLITICAL GROUPINGS

On Tuesday 1 January 1901 steam trains, steam and electric trams, steam ferries, and innumerable horse-drawn buses and cabs carried Sydney's holiday crowds to Centennial Park to witness the political birth of the Australian nation. It was the first time in the history of the world, many delighted to note, that the boundaries of a nation-state had coincided with those of a whole continent. Rain fell early in the morning but cleared by eleven when a procession with bands and banners began its march to the ceremonial site. Buildings, telegraph poles and streets were decked as never before with bunting and triumphal arches. The vast crowds were light-hearted and happy. They cheered the 200 mounted police who led the procession, they cheered the thirty-three Railways Bandsmen in black and silver uniforms who followed them, and they cheered even more vociferously the shearers and other bush workers who came next. It is interesting that the trade-union section of the procession took precedence over the military and other components, including a contingent of volunteers back from the South African War. In 1901 the symbolic exemplar of the national character was apparently still the bushman rather than the soldier or 'old digger' who took over the role after the Great War of 1914-18. Next day the *Sydney Morning Herald* wrote:

> There were few indeed but paid a hearty tribute of admiration to the representative shearers who headed the procession — men that could be sent anywhere to do anything, from shearing to soldiering — men who would give a good account of themselves in any company in the world . . . all mounted on good bush horses . . . fine-looking back-blocks men with a certain freedom of bearing and suggestion of capability that was very effective.

Prominent politicians were also cheered with rather undiscriminating enthusiasm. Edmund Barton, the leading New South Wales federationist, who had been chosen barely a week earlier as caretaker Prime Minister pending the calling of the first federal elections, was cheered lustily. So was his fellow-minister, Alfred Deakin, the leading Victorian federationist; but so was Sir William 'Big Bill' Lyne, the consistently anti-federationist premier of New South Wales; while George Reid, the New South Wales Freetrade leader whose inconsistent attitude to the federal question had earned him the nickname of 'Yes-No' Reid, was cheered to the echo. However all the dignitaries arrived safely at Centennial Park where the first Commonwealth government was to be sworn in by the newly arrived Governor-General, John Adrian Louis, seventh Earl of Hopetoun and Marquess of Linlithgow. An ornate, open-sided, stone pavillion had been built especially for the occasion. Lady Lyne, wife of the State Premier, in black gown, black and purple bonnet and white gloves, was among the first to welcome the vice-regal party on its arrival at one o'clock. In a resonant, formal voice, an official then read the Queen's proclamation and her commission of Hopetoun as Governor-General. Few in the vast crowd of about two hundred thousand spectators could hear what was said, but most could see figures moving in the pavillion. In his resplendent uniform, topped by a hat from which sprouted what the vulgar termed 'horse feathers', the Earl repeated his oath of allegiance and the oath of office. He then swore in as executive ministers of the interim Government Edmund Barton, Alfred Deakin, Sir William Lyne, Charles Cameron Kingston of South Australia, Sir James Dickson of Queensland, Sir John Forrest, Premier of Western Australia and Sir George Turner, Premier of Victoria. Neil Lewis of Tasmania and Richard O'Connor of New South Wales were then sworn in as ministers without portfolio. The main business before them all was to arrange for the first federal election on 29 and 30 March.

At the turn of the century political groupings were not as clear-cut as they became nine years later. To contemporaries the main political bone of contention seemed to be fiscal policy rather than any division between left and right, radical and conservative. Thus the two major political parties were known as the Freetraders and the Protectionists. Both were thoroughly bourgeois groupings and both contained liberal-minded and even radical members as well as conservatives; but on balance, at any rate in federal politics, the Protectionists stood somewhat to the left of the Freetraders and for this reason they were sometimes known as Liberal Protectionists or even simply Liberals. Freetrade policies naturally drew strong support from pastoralists (or 'squatters' as they were still commonly called) and wholesale and retail traders, importers and exporters; while manufacturers and often their employees, and nationalists usually supported protection.

To some extent the two major groupings were divided geographically by the Murray River. In colonial days Victoria had pursued a protectionist policy from 1861 onwards, while New South Wales had remained more or less faithful to free trade. Thus, by the time of federation, manufacturing industry was much stronger in Victoria than in any other colony, while in New South Wales 'revenue tariffs' continued to rise as revenue from land sales declined in the 1880s and 1890s. In Australian history conservatives have always tended to stress loyalty to Britain and the Empire, or even to 'great and powerful friends' overseas like the United States of America, while radicals and progressives have tended to stress local Australian nationalism. Here was another difference between the two major parties: as the logic of their fiscal beliefs implied, Freetraders tended to stress imperial unity and patriotism while Protectionists placed more emphasis on fostering local Australian nationalism and independence within the Empire. It must be remembered also that both parties would have been more accurately described as loose groupings of men having common views on the fiscal question. Neither party had developed the unity, discipline and continuing close-knit, extra-parliamentary structure which we associate with political parties today.

The political scene was further complicated by the existence of a third party, the Labor Party — a social-democratic party based initially on the trade unions like the British Labour, the French Socialist and the German Social-Democratic Parties. However, since about 1890, when it first won seats in the legislatures, the Labor Party had been relatively much stronger and more influential in the major colonial parliaments than its counterparts were in any other country in the world. By sitting on the cross-benches and giving, in return for legislation desired by the Labor movement, support to Freetrade or Protectionist governments, the colonial Labor parties had already achieved much by 1901. Indeed, in the opinion of a brilliant young French scholar who studied Australian society in 1899, the colonies then already led the world in 'welfare state' measures such as factory, labour, land and pension legislation. Albert Métin stressed that this progress sprang from the generally liberal tone of colonial society and politics, almost as much as from the political and industrial efforts of the Labor movement. He was impressed by the colonists' scorn for political theorising and their strongly empirical, practical approach. Above all he stressed the moderation, the loyalty to the monarchy, and deep respect for religion of most Australian Labor people. Though they had achieved so much more than their French or British counterparts, they had, he thought, also became thoroughly bourgeois in the process.

The Labor Party was a much more closely-knit and well-disciplined organisation than either of its more conservative rivals. From the time of Labor's début, indeed, the other parties, if only in self-defence, were forced to strengthen their organisations more and more. Even so, Labor politicians, in or out of parliament, enjoyed considerably more independence than they do today. Even to write or speak of the Labor Party in the federal sphere at this time is, strictly speaking, incorrect. Labor members elected to the first Commonwealth Parliament owed their allegiance to their respective State Labor organisations, which sometimes laid down differing policies. Labor did not acquire any kind of central (federal) organisation until 1902, and even then no continuing, central, authoritative body existed until a Federal Executive Committee of the Party was established in 1915. Since they held strongly conflicting views on free trade and protection, Labor members were free to vote as they liked on fiscal issues. On other matters, however, every Labor member had to vote in the way determined by the majority vote of all Labor members of Parliament meeting privately in Caucus before each parliamentary session.

Cutting across all these political patterns was the personal factor. Politicians without very strong belief in either free trade or protection, or the rights of the workers, might join one group or another because of their liking or admiration for the party chief. Thus Sir John Forrest, for eleven years Premier of Western Australia until February 1901, was conservative in most ways and a 'moderate' Freetrader, but his close friendship with Barton and Deakin, the Protectionist leaders, assured him of a place in their Cabinet.

As leader of the interim Government, Barton gave his policy speech at Maitland in the Hunter Valley. Son of William Barton, sharebroker and estate agent, Edmund Barton was born in Sydney in 1849. Educated at Sydney Grammar School and the University of Sydney, he obtained his Master's degree with honours in Classics in 1870 and was called to the Bar in 1871. He built up a successful legal practice but from 1879, when he was elected to the Legislative Assembly of New South Wales, he devoted most of his energies to politics, being a most distinguished Speaker of the House for four years from 1883. When Sir Henry Parkes, acknowledged leader of the federal movement in New South Wales, was finally defeated politically in October 1891, he sent for Barton and asked him to take over the leadership of the movement which Parkes no longer had the strength to carry. A sound lawyer and a successful man-of-the-world, Barton was perhaps too much of a dilettante to reach, despite his deep commitment to federalism, the very first rank in politics. A future conservative prime minister, R. G. Menzies, said of him:

> A rich and beautifully modulated voice, a handsome and dignified appearance, exquisite courtesy, embracing both deference to his colleagues and genuine consideration for counsel, a clear sense of relevancy, a scholarly diction: all these things Barton possessed and practised.[1]

He was also a *bon viveur* and a keen club-man, known to some by the nickname of 'Toby Toss-Pot'.

His policy speech was sober, even equivocal, rather than exciting. He stressed the 'machinery' measures which the Government was already engaged upon and promised, if returned to power, that he would press on with the taking over from the States of their customs, defence and postal organisations. He also promised to establish a High Court to police the federal system as provided for in the Constitution. He was the first federal politician, though by no means the last, to promise unification of the different State railway gauges. He thought the Commonwealth should take over from the States responsibility for old age pensions, if and when money became available. Hedging most obviously on the fiscal issue, he said that most of his cabinet colleagues were protectionist, but that for the time being at least, customs and excise duties must be regarded primarily as a source of revenue, indeed as the only source of revenue for the federal government which should never, except in the gravest national emergency, impose direct taxation. At the same time he contrived to imply that this modest level of customs imposts would be high enough to provide adequate protection from foreign competition to those industries which needed it.

G. H. Reid was generally regarded as the Freetrade leader, but since no federal Freetrade party yet existed, he was not in a position to speak for those who were to be his followers after the election. He travelled the eastern States speaking energetically on scores of platforms and extolling the virtues of free trade as a policy. He opposed Commonwealth old age pensions because of the expense that would be involved, and he exercised his considerable wit in criticism of the cloudiness and pomposity that often marked Barton's speeches.

Labor candidates lacked clear federal leadership even more than the Freetraders. From their speeches it is clear that they expected to

[1] John Reynolds, *Edmund Barton*, Sydney, 1948, p.vii.

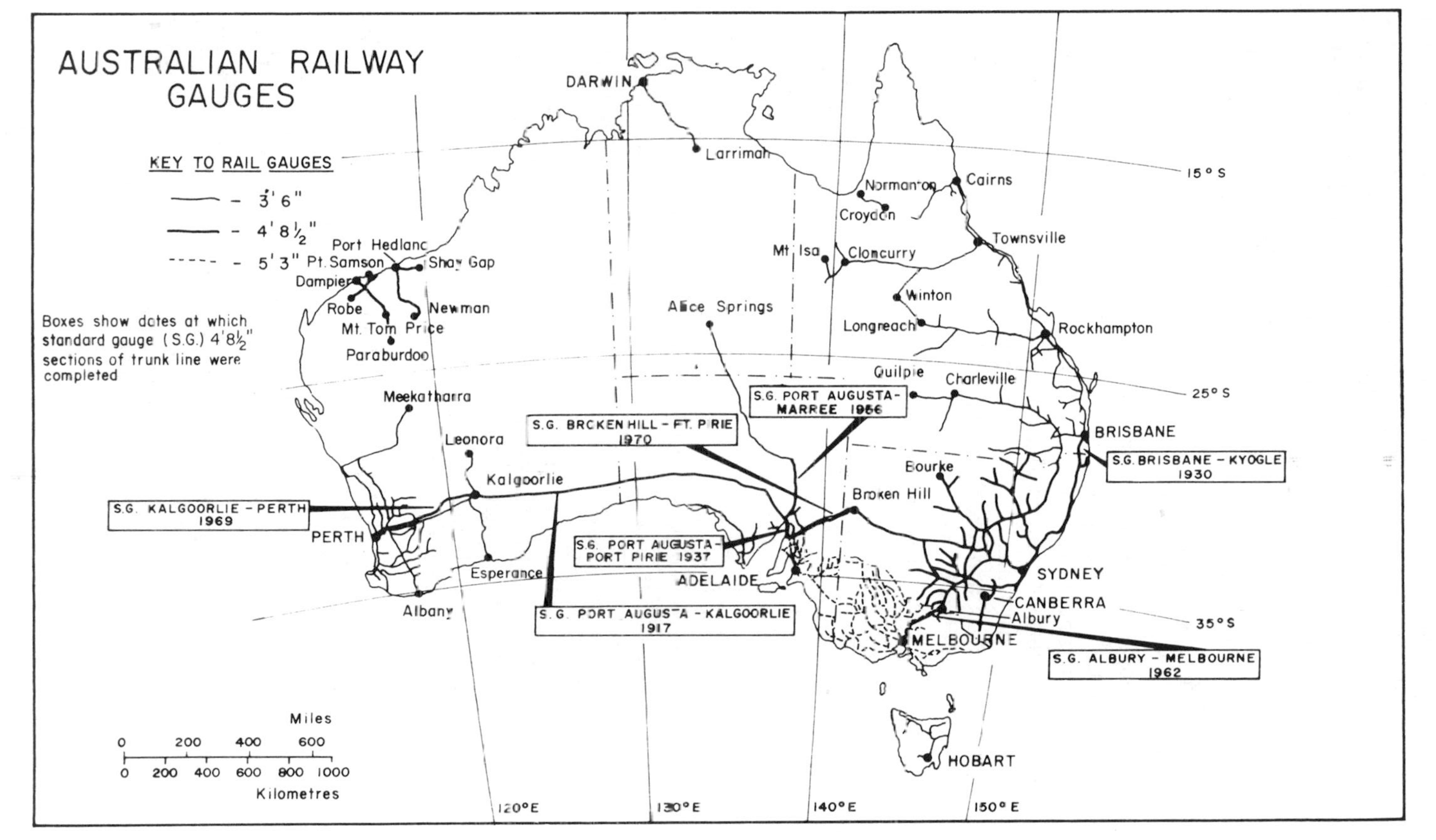
AUSTRALIAN RAILWAY GAUGES
KEY TO RAIL GAUGES
- 3'6"
- 4'8½"
- 5'3"
Boxes show dates at which standard gauge (S.G.) 4'8½" sections of trunk line were completed
DARWIN
Larrimah
Port Hedland
Pt. Samson
Shay Gap
Dampier
Robe
Newman
Mt. Tom Price
Paraburdoo
Meekatharra
Leonora
Kalgoorlie
PERTH
Esperance
Albany
Alice Springs
Mt Isa
Cloncurry
Normanton
Croydon
Cairns
Townsville
Winton
Longreach
Rockhampton
Quilpie
Charleville
BRISBANE
Bourke
Broken Hill
ADELAIDE
SYDNEY
CANBERRA
Albury
MELBOURNE
HOBART
S.G. KALGOORLIE - PERTH 1969
S.G. BROKEN HILL - PT. PIRIE 1970
S.G. PORT AUGUSTA-MARREE 1956
S.G. BRISBANE - KYOGLE 1930
S.G. PORT AUGUSTA-PORT PIRIE 1937
S.G. PORT AUGUSTA - KALGOORLIE 1917
S.G. ALBURY - MELBOURNE 1962
15° S
25° S
35° S
120° E
130° E
140° E
150° E
Miles
0 200 400 600
0 200 400 600 800 1000
Kilometres

form only a small group on the cross-benches of parliament and to trade with the major parties support in return for concessions, as they had been doing so successfully in the colonial parliaments. They also believed, even at this early date, that the Constitution must be amended to give more power to the Commonwealth Government, if it was ever to be an effective instrument of social reform.

The one policy on which all parties were in agreement was that the national parliament must begin by passing laws to restrict the immigration of 'coloured' persons so as to ensure a 'White Australia'. Nearly all candidates favoured this policy but some did so more strongly than others. Generally speaking, the more democratic, the more radical, the more 'progressive' a person was in other ways, the more strongly racist he was likely to be.

The elections produced a situation which was to characterise the next three parliaments up to 1909. Of the three parties, or groupings, none had a majority or a hope of forming a government, unless it could win the support of one of the others. To the first House of Representatives 32 Protectionists, 27 Freetraders and 16 Labor members were returned. In the Upper House there were 11 Protectionists, 17 Freetraders and 8 Labor senators.[2] Thus the Labor Party held the balance of power in both Houses. Its leader was J. C. Watson, member for the New South Wales constituency of Bland. Since Barton and all the ministers of his interim cabinet had gained seats in the parliament, and since he had reason to expect general support from Labor, there was no need for any further swearing-in ceremonies and the Protectionist Government continued in office with Barton as Prime Minister and Deakin as Attorney-General. Lyne was Minister for Home Affairs, Turner Treasurer, and C. C. Kingston Minister for Trade and Customs. Forrest was Postmaster-General for a few weeks and then became Minister for Defence. Minor portfolios were held by a Queensland Senator, J. G. Drake (Postmaster-General from 5 February 1901), N. E. Lewis and Sir Philip Fysh (Ministers without Portfolio) and Senator R. E. O'Connor (Vice-President of the Executive Council).

It was Melbourne's turn to provide the stage for the next ceremonial occasion. In the vast Exhibition Building on 9 May the first Commonwealth Parliament was declared open by the Duke of Cornwall and York, second legitimate son of Edward VII, later to succeed to the Imperial throne as George V. The leading Australian

[2] Here, and subsequently when election results are given, the figures often differ slightly from those in Appendices IV and V, pp. 442-43. Generally, figures in the text reflect the number of votes usually commanded by the major parties, while those in the Appendices give in more detail the affiliation of members, in some cases with purely temporary splinter-groups of one or two.

ARRIVAL OF THE NEW BABY

Bulletin, 1900 — *Nurse Barton: "He ain't much to look at now. But wait till he grows!"*

artist of the day, Tom Roberts, fixed the scene for posterity in a painting, innumerable copies of which were to adorn government offices and educational institutions. In the evening the royal couple, the politicians and a vast crowd of other citizens reassembled in the same building to hear a concert. The high point of the night was the singing of *Australia* by the 'divine Nellie Stewart', a native-born singer and actress held in affection by Australian play-goers for over fifty years. Lord Tennyson, eldest son of the poet and Governor of South Australia, noted in his diary that 'the Cabinet Ministers forget to bow when passing before Royalty'.[3] It might have been ignorance rather than forgetfulness.

PEOPLE AND RESOURCES

What was the condition of the country the new ministers had to rule? In 1901 the population of Australia was 3 772 000 — about half that of greater London or New York City at the time. Nearly 80 per cent were Australian born and most of the remainder had been born in the British Isles. In New South Wales, Victoria and South Australia between a third and a half of the people lived in the capital cities, though only about 20 per cent did so in the other States. Metropolitan populations were growing faster than those of the country districts. This reflected the fact that secondary and tertiary industries were growing in importance though manufacturing was still confined mainly to the processing of food and other primary products. Wool-scouring, boot and shoe-making, canning of meat and fruit, timber-milling, brick-making, flour-milling, biscuit-making and so forth employed many people in Sydney and Melbourne but fewer in Adelaide and other capitals. Some clothing was manufactured in Victoria behind her protective tariff wall but the vast bulk of the wool-clip was sent overseas and some of it re-imported as fine English cloth. There were also a number of factories producing ploughs, harrows and other agricultural implements. Yet there was little or nothing in the way of a machine-tool or precision engineering industry and, although Australian iron-ore and coal deposits were soon to be counted among the richest in the world, there were only the embryonic beginnings of a 'heavy' metal industry. The country's prosperity still depended mainly, indeed overwhelmingly, on her primary industries — pastoralism, agriculture and mining. Australia, men said then and for long afterwards, 'rode on the sheep's back'.

That, in 1901, was the rub, for there were only about half as

[3] J. A. La Nauze, *Alfred Deakin*, Melbourne, 1965, 2 vols, vol. 1, p. 229.

many sheep's backs to ride upon as there had been seven years earlier. Falling wool prices and grossly over-optimistic speculation during the 1880s in land and building, especially in Melbourne, led to the onset in 1890 of the most terrible business depression the colonies had known. In 1893 most banks failed, closing either permanently or temporarily for a period of 'reconstruction'. Only nine of twenty-eight banks in the whole country remained open continuously and honoured their obligations in full: only ten of sixty-four financial institutions which accepted deposits weathered the storm. Most collapsed completely. The situation was worsened by a series of great strikes involving for the most part pastoral and transport workers.

Things would have been worse still but for the discovery of fabulously rich goldfields in Western Australia at this time. During the 1890s the populations of Victoria and South Australia actually decreased while that of the western colony more than trebled. In 1903 Australia as a whole again briefly became the leading gold producer in the world, and in the same year was completed a 560-kilometre water pipeline linking Kalgoorlie, the major gold-mining town, with Mundaring Weir near Perth. Nevertheless recovery in the eastern colonies was painfully slow and it was further retarded by a natural disaster. Between 1895 and 1902 there occurred the longest and most severe drought in Australian history. There were 106 000 000 sheep in the whole country in 1894. By 1902 this number had been reduced to approximately 55 000 000 and it did not reach the 1894 figure again until 1928. The effects of the drought were exacerbated by a plague of rabbits which competed with the remaining livestock for what little herbage there was.

Thus, when the Commonwealth began, the staple export industry was at the very nadir of its fortunes. The depression had been so severe that the colonial governments had for the most part suspended their assisted immigration schemes. Factors which helped the slow climb back to prosperity were the boom in gold-mining noted above and a more solidly-based growth in base metal mining at Broken Hill in New South Wales and elsewhere. Sugar-growing on the Queensland coast flourished mightily and there was a sharp increase in exports of frozen beef to Europe, a trade that had become technically possible only from 1880. Above all the wheat-growing industry, based on the multiplication of government railway lines in suitable areas, boomed at this time, total production increasing from 26 000 000 bushels (950 000 cubic metres) in 1891 to 103 000 000 bushels (3 750 000 cubic metres) in 1913.

Despite drought and depression, the standard of material living for the mass of white Australians (and New Zealanders) was probably higher than for their counterparts anywhere else in the world at the time. The first motor cars had been marvelled at, but few people thought that the internal combustion engine would ever replace the horse for most work. Telephones were becoming common among the rich and in business-houses, and most people used the government telegraphic service, at least on great or tragic occasions in their lives. Coach services using horses supplemented the railway system in country areas but the inland river-steamer traffic on the Murray-Darling system was in decline, strangled by the rapid railway expansion. Most large towns of any size were lit, at least partly, by electricity, but electric irons, stoves, vacuum cleaners, washing machines, refrigerators and other domestic labour-saving devices were yet to be invented for the most part and were certainly unknown to most Australian housewives. Only the well-to-do could afford ice-chests and to employ domestic servants, and proportionately many more people did their own housework than in Europe. Perhaps the clearest indication of the relatively high standard of living was the well-established and thoroughly characteristic pattern of home life. In city and country alike nearly every family lived in a house on a separate block of land large enough to contain at least some garden and outhouses. About half the householders owned, or were in process of buying their own homes. Even in the inner areas of Sydney and Melbourne the number of people living in terrace houses or in tiers of two or more storeyed blocks of flats was relatively small, and minute compared with the norm in European and North American cities. From these homes men, and some women, went out in the morning to work, in most cases a 48-hour week.

About three-quarters of the people were Protestants and about one-quarter Roman Catholics, generally of Irish descent. About 40 per cent were members of the Church of England. Some 13 per cent were Methodists and 11 per cent, mainly of Scots descent, Presbyterians. Most of the remainder belonged to other dissenting Protestant sects such as the Baptists and the Salvation Army. Because Irish men and women in the nineteenth century were generally much poorer and less well educated than English or Scots people, Irish immigrants and their descendants in Australia were disproportionately numerous in unskilled and semi-skilled occupations. For this reason, and because it claimed to be the standard-bearer of Australian nationalism rather than of Empire loyalty, the growing Labor Party attracted the support of most Catholic people. Keen Anglicans tended to be very conservative and empire-minded people, but for many of those who put themselves down as Church of England in the decennial censuses, religion was a rather perfunctory, nominal matter having little effect on their lives. Some of the dissenting sects, particularly Methodists and Baptists, acted as though salvation depended on the complete abolition of dancing, gambling, drinking and the Roman Catholic Church. On Sundays, in addition, all sports, amusements and pastimes were forbidden to good nonconformists. Persons holding this gloomy, puritanical attitude to life came to be known by the peculiarly Australian name of 'wowsers'. Methodism provided the backbone of Australian wowserism and, since Catholics were usually Labor voters, dissenters of all kinds tended strongly to vote for conservative parties which were not above angling for the 'wowser vote'. Though as puritanical as Methodism in sexual matters, Catholic teaching on drink, gambling and Sunday sport was generally much more permissive. Of course there were many teetotallers among Labor politicians and many high-living men of fashion among conservative ones but these 'exceptions' did not much affect the general pattern of party loyalties.

Since government systems of 'free, compulsory and secular' education had been introduced by 1880 in all colonies save Tasmania (1885) and Western Australia (1893), most citizens were at least literate in 1901, though some old people, particularly among manual workers and some younger people brought up in the far outback, still signed their names with a cross. Most Aboriginal children received no formal education. The few who did were taught by white missionaries or by managers, often themselves only modestly literate, on segregated government reserves for Aborigines. However, the State educational systems took responsibility for most white children only up to the age of thirteen or fourteen. There were then very few high schools (State secondary schools) — none in South Australia and none in Western Australia for instance — and entry to them was highly competitive. For the most part secondary education was still the preserve of those children whose parents could afford to pay high fees at independent schools, usually owned by the major churches. Governments provided some technical and trade schools at secondary level. Universities existed in Sydney, Melbourne, Adelaide and Hobart, but not in Brisbane or Perth. Their students, except for a very few brilliant scholarship holders, were drawn almost exclusively from among the children of the bourgeoisie.

THE ARTS, NATIONALISM AND IMPERIALISM

Despite this quite modest provision of higher education, the arts were flourishing in 1901. Indeed an upsurge of national sentiment in literature and painting during the 1880s and 1890s had played some part in bringing about federation. In Australia from the very beginning there had been two kinds of culture and patriotism existing side by side. Educated, middle-class people, very often even when they and their parents were Australian-born, tended to continue thinking of themselves as Britons living, perhaps temporarily, in Australia. Naturally they continued also to regard Britain as the source of all culture and refinement, with the result that, when they produced works of art, these tended to be somewhat anaemic imitations of British models. Before about 1880 practically all Australian literature and painting was British in style and spirit, even when the writer or artist was consciously striving to portray Australian reality. On the other hand the masses were often unable, or unwilling, to keep up connections with the British Isles ('Home' in the minds of most Australians in the nineteenth and early twentieth centuries). Moreover most enjoyed a much higher standard of living than they could usually have hoped to achieve in Britain. Naturally they came, much more rapidly and completely than did middle-class people, to think of themselves first as Australians and to relate to the material environment around them rather than to the 'old country' on the other side of the world. They produced little or no formal art, but long before 1850 they had created a new way of pronouncing the English language and a body of oral literature — ballads, folk-songs and stories — thoroughly Australian in spirit and subject matter. In the period from about 1880 to 1914 many journalists, writers and artists discovered this popular culture and, in doing so, discovered how to write in an Australian idiom for an Australian audience. For the first time large numbers of middle-class people began to identify with their native land and its ways, though most saw themselves as belonging to a country which, however independent, remained very much a part of the British Empire. Avowed republicans, though probably relatively more numerous in the 1890s than ever before (or afterwards until the 1970s), comprised only a small minority of the population.

The new nationalism, and the literature which helped to inspire it, were fostered by a famous Sydney weekly newspaper, the *Bulletin*, which during the 1890s carried on its title page the motto: 'Australia for the Australians'. From its foundation in 1880 until 1914 it was an extremely well-written, lively journal, which increasingly expounded nationalist, radical and white racist ideas. It also published Henry Lawson, A. B. ('Banjo') Paterson, Joseph Furphy ('Tom Collins') and nearly all the other leading writers and black-and-white artists of the time — whether their politics were radical or not. During the Great War (1914-1918) the *Bulletin* changed course and became extremely conservative, even reactionary, politically; though it continued to discuss and publish some of the best Australian writing. The best of Lawson's short stories, of Paterson's popular ballads, and Furphy's great novel, *Such is Life*, challenge comparison with the best works in their respective *genres* ever done in English. At the same time Tom Roberts, Arthur Streeton and others were painting Australian life and nature in a new and exciting way. It is hard now to imagine the shock of self-recognition which these works caused when they first came out; but it is important to remember that the experience was not shared by everybody. Even at the height of the nationalist euphoria at the turn of the century, at least a large minority of the population retained a colonial, or British imperial, outlook, and in the sphere of international relations most Australians took it for granted that whatever Great Britain did was right and to be supported with all their might.

This is best illustrated by Australia's attitude to the Boer War (1899-1902). When the first Commonwealth Parliament was elected in 1901, volunteers had already been dispatched by the six Australian colonies to serve under British commanders in South Africa. The new national government, in taking over the colonial defence departments, enthusiastically carried on with voluntary recruiting. Like the undeclared war in Vietnam sixty-five years later, the conflict in South Africa was a 'dirty colonial war' in which the imperial aggressor was universally held to be in the wrong by every power in the world except some of its own closest allies and client-states. There was considerable liberal (and Liberal) opposition to the war in England itself, but probably less, proportionately, in Australia. The *Bulletin* opposed the war — and lost some circulation as a result. Some courageous intellectuals spoke out against it. George Arnold Wood, first Professor of History in the University of Sydney, was publicly censured by its governing body, the University Senate, for his anti-war views. In Victoria and South Australia a few nonconformist liberals like H. B. Higgins, Rev. A. Rivett and Rev. Dr Charles Strong spoke out clearly, but dissent was strongest, though not usually most articulate, in the Labor movement.

Even so, when the Commonwealth Parliament debated the issue in January 1902, all except six Labor members and one Radical Protectionist, Higgins, voted to support Britain by all available means. Before the war was over more than 15 000 Australian troops had embarked for South Africa. Nearly all were mounted men who, to the surprise of their British commanders, fought better on the whole than the British regular soldiers. They nearly doubled the number of cavalrymen on the British side, thus making possible the decisive manoeuvres which finally defeated the Boers.

Another illustration of Australian loyalty to the mother country

Bulletin, 1902

THE PRIME MINISTER CHRISTENS THE BABY

was provided by the so-called Boxer Rebellion against the presence of Europeans in China, which broke out in June 1900. Immediately about 500 naval volunteers from New South Wales, Victoria and South Australia went to serve with the British contingent. For about nine months they carried out police duties in Tientsin and Peking. G. E. Morrison[4], the Australian-born son of the first headmaster of Geelong College, was the China correspondent of the London *Times* during these troubles. He noted in his diary having witnessed, with some disgust, the great British soldier, Lord Kitchener, stealing from the Imperial Palace for his private collection priceless Chinese *objets d'art*.[5]

If Australians themselves had been asked at this time what accomplishments most distinguished them from the people of other nations, most would have pointed, with some justification, to their sporting prowess. Since their history was so short and peaceful, they had no great military, or naval or even political heroes to idolise, no ancient monuments of their own civilisation in their own land, and no great departed writers or artists holding up the mirror to their own past. Thus some romanticised dead bushrangers as symbols of national sentiment and all, including those who were tone-deaf, raved about the voice of Dame Nellie Melba, the great opera singer, who was then bewitching concert-goers throughout the world. The pioneering age was scarcely over, however, and pioneering inevitably sets more store by physical strength and skill than by the loftiest mental or spiritual attainments. Great sportsmen, sportswomen and racehorses, then or now in Australia, are generally more widely known and honoured than great soldiers, statesmen, or even Nobel Prize-winners.

Since the first test cricket-match in 1876, Australia had beaten the mother country more often than not at the game and in the year of federation two great South Australian cricketers, Joe Darling and Clem Hill, again led the national team to victory over the Englishmen. Other popular sports were football, horse-racing, boxing and tennis. New South Wales and Queensland played Rugby football, but in the four southern States a national football game, peculiar to Australia, grew up from the mid-nineteenth century onwards. Most popular of all perhaps were various kinds of water sports — yachting, boating, rowing, sculling, and swimming. It seems odd that this should be so in the driest continent on earth, until

[4] Morrison had the kind of toughness Australians like to think is a national characteristic. In 1882, aged 20, he walked alone, roughly along Burke and Wills's tracks of 22 years earlier, from the Gulf of Carpentaria to Melbourne: about 3000 kilometres in 123 days.

[5] Cyril Pearl, *Morrison of Peking*, Sydney, 1967, pp. 199-200.

one remembers that the vast majority of the people have always lived on or near the coast. Henry Searle, born at Grafton on the Clarence River in New South Wales, became champion sculler of the world in September 1889. When he died on his return from Europe three months later, Sydney streets were more crowded than they had ever been before — even on the occasion of the first royal visit in 1867. Swimming had always been immensely popular in Australia but in the early years of federation advances were made in the sport which affected it throughout the world.

At the Paris Olympic Games of 1900 the Australian, F. C. Lane, became world champion swimmer over 200 metres and two years later became the first human being to swim 100 yards (90 metres) in 60 seconds. His team-mate in 1902, R. T. ('Dick') Cavill, broke many other world records and was the first man to use the 'crawl' stroke in championship swimming. Cavill had learnt it in the 1890s in Sydney from Alick Wickham, a boy who had learned it in the Solomon Islands. The fastest mode of swimming in the world had, of course, been practised for centuries by Polynesians and Melanesians. It is perhaps unfair that it should be known to the world as the 'Australian crawl'. The art of surfing — of riding in to the beach on breaking waves, with or without some kind of board — was learnt in Australia in the same way. There was almost no bathing on open ocean beaches in the nineteenth century, partly because it was forbidden between the hours of 6 a.m. and 8 p.m. by an old colonial ordinance in New South Wales. In 1902 W. H. Gocher, editor of a Manly (Sydney suburban) newspaper, openly defied the law and was not prosecuted. Bathing in the surf quickly became popular but another Pacific Islander, Tommy Tanna, who worked as a gardener's boy at Manly, had to show white Australians how to ride the breakers. By 1910 Sydney surfers had formed voluntary Surf Life-Saving Associations, invented life-saving gear and formulated examinations for members. By 1960 well over 100 000 persons throughout Australia had been saved from drowning by these voluntary bodies. The first person rescued by the life-savers' reel and line in 1907 was, as it happened, the ten-year-old Charles Kingsford Smith. Surfing became an extremely popular sport, almost a cult, in Australia and spread thence throughout the world.

Cycling on the recently invented bicycles was immensely popular among all classes and, like surfing and swimming, it was indulged in by both sexes. Wowsers balefully denounced mixed bathing and some, including the Pope himself, warned that cycling was destructive of female virtue and modesty: but mixed bathing and cycling only became more fashionable. One of the most popular songs of the day, in Australia as in the rest of the English-speaking world, went:

Daisy, Daisy! Give me your answer, do!
I'm half crazy all for the love of you.
It won't be a stylish marriage
I can't afford a carriage;
But you'll look sweet, upon the seat
Of a bicycle built for two!

LEGISLATION AND WHITE AUSTRALIA

The first Commonwealth Parliament was probably of a higher calibre than any that have succeeded it. The prestige of the first national Parliament attracted to it many of the best men from the State parliaments — something which has not happened so obviously since. The vast majority of all members had had previous parliamentary experience. Of the seventy-five members of the House of Representatives, fifty-eight had sat in colonial parliaments, twenty-two had been ministers, and no fewer than ten had been premiers of their colonies, some, like Forrest, for many years. One venerable figure, W. H. Groom of Queensland, provided a living link with convict times. Transported as a lad in the *Hashemy* in 1849, he worked on the goldfields after his emancipation and was elected first mayor of Toowoomba in 1861. In the following year he was sent by the Darling Downs electors to the Queensland Parliament of which he remained a member until his resignation in 1901 to contest the federal seat for the district. He was Speaker of the Queensland House of Assembly from 1883 till 1888. South Australia, however, had the honour of providing the first Speaker of the House of Representatives. F. W. Holder, a Methodist lay preacher and journalist, had a distinguished career in the South Australian Parliament from 1887, becoming Premier from December 1899 until his resignation to contest a federal seat. He was elected unopposed to the Speaker's Chair and knighted in 1902. He did much to maintain the generally dignified tone of debate in the early years of federal government.

This was helped too by the wide consensus among members, and in the country, about the major tasks of the first Parliament. As the Prime Minister had foreseen, most of its acts were concerned with establishing the 'machinery' of the new national government — the Commonwealth Public Service Act, the Posts and Telegraph Act, the Defence Act, the Judiciary and High Court Procedure Act, the Patents Act, and so on. In most cases there was little room for disagreement about the principles embodied in such bills, and debate was usually confined to matters of detail, or emphasis or timing: but the same was true of the one great body of substantive legislation with which Barton's Government concerned itself, the bills establishing the White Australia Policy.

In the second half of the nineteenth century all the colonial governments had, from time to time, enacted laws forbidding or hampering the immigration of non-European peoples, particularly Chinese, to Australia; but the legislation had not been very effective because the six governments had seldom been able to agree on the same action at the same time. Queensland particularly had been reluctant effectively to ban coloured immigration because its prosperity depended quite heavily on the coastal sugar-growing industry which, in turn, was believed to depend upon the exploitation of indentured Melanesian labourers. Between 1847 and 1904 nearly 60 000 Islanders generally known as *Kanakas* (from a Melanesian word for *man*) were imported into Queensland. The recruiting agents, commonly known as *black-birders*, often employed deceit, violence or murder to obtain their complement of Kanakas. Once landed in Queensland, conditions for the Kanakas were better than on the recruiting ships, thanks to the colonial government's protective legislation; but even so their death-rate was several times higher than that of the white population. In law the Kanakas were free men who undertook, for a consideration, to work for a fixed term, usually three years, for a white sugar-planter. In fact their condition was not very different from that of the slaves on cotton plantations before the American Civil War. Yet the Anglican Bishop of Brisbane could say to the Synod in 1892:

> It is a good thing [the Kanakas] should be here with us; and when they have become, as many have, Christian churchmen, it is well that our white people should have before them the good example in discharge of religious obligations which is set them by their coloured brethren.[6]

Some other clerics denounced the Kanaka trade. A creditable humanitarian desire to end this disgraceful traffic in human beings was one of the motive forces of the White Australia Policy. A stronger one was the desire of Australian working-men and women to be protected in the market-place from the competition of cheap, semi-servile foreign labour. Strongest of all was naked and unashamed racism, colour prejudice — call it what you will.

It is fair to remember that Australians of a century ago were not uniquely wicked or ignorant. The period from about 1870 till the Great War marks the high tide of European, not just British, imperialism. During it practically every white-skinned person, in the Americas as well as in Europe and elsewhere, believed passionately in the 'natural', 'innate', genetic superiority of the 'White Race'. Had not Darwin demonstrated the 'survival of the fittest' in the

[6] *C.P.D.*, vol. 5, p. 6931.

animal kingdom? The Social Darwinists, by a mis-application of his teachings, demonstrated to the satisfaction of nearly all save coloured people, that 'native' peoples were doomed to subjection or destruction at the hands of the superior White Race. When scientists and learned men spoke thus, it is not surprising that most ordinary people took the further step of believing in the innate superiority of German or French or Anglo-Saxon 'blood' — within the agreed general superiority of the white peoples.

For Australians of Irish (and Welsh, Cornish and Highland Scots) descent, rhetoric about the virtues of the Anglo-Saxon race presented a problem. E. W. O'Sullivan, New South Wales Minister for Public Works from 1899 to 1904, to whom Sydney owes its great Central Railway Station, was one of those who solved it by referring always to the 'Anglo-Celtic Race'. Granted the ubiquity of these racist delusions among Europeans everywhere at the time, it is easy to understand why Australians acted on them more decisively than most. From the beginning much of their history had been conditioned by distance — distance, above all, from their homeland and, in a broader sense, from Europe, the source of their material and spiritual culture.[7] With a population minute compared with that of their Asian neighbours, it is understandable that they felt threatened, particularly when the power of Japan began to be manifest around the turn of the century. Certainly almost every member who spoke on the subject began by saying how serious, and pregnant with future consequences, the matter was.

The White Australia Policy was not embodied in any single parliamentary Act. In fact 'White Australia Policy' is merely a form of words widely used before and long after 1901, to describe majority Australian attitudes towards the immigration of coloured people. The policy was first given nation-wide legal force by two Acts and a single clause of a third Act of the first Commonwealth Parliament. Chronologically the first of these was Clause 15 of the Posts and Telegraphs Bill; the second was the Immigration Restriction Bill, and the third the Pacific Island Labourers Bill.

The Posts and Telegraphs Bill was naturally one of the first 'machinery' measures introduced by the Government and had no apparent relevance to the White Australia Policy. In mid-June 1901, however, during the second reading, Western Australian Senator Staniforth Smith suggested that the Bill should be amended to provide that *all* ships in receipt of a mail subsidy from the Commonwealth, whether they were registered in Australia or not, should be compelled to employ only white labour. Staniforth Smith,

[7] Geoffrey Blainey, *The Tyranny of Distance*, Melbourne, 1966.

a radical Protectionist who later joined the Labor Party, was perhaps the most rabidly racist member of either House. Three weeks later Senator T. Glassey of Queensland moved such an amendment to Clause 15 of the Bill which dealt with the Postmaster-General's power to make contracts for the carriage of mails. Glassey was an independent (ex-Labor) member. His amendment was defeated, but during the debate on the Bill in the committee stage in the House of Representatives, William Morris Hughes, another Labor man and a future prime minister, moved a similar 'white mails' amendment to Clause 14. When this clause was recommitted to the House in September, Hughes withdrew his amendment because Barton had rewritten Clause 15 to include provision for 'white mails'. Thus amended under Labor pressure, the clause (and the Bill) passed both Houses and became law.

The Immigration Restriction Bill, the main law designed by the Government to give effect to the White Australia Policy, was introduced in the House of Representatives in August. Barton's drafting of the Bill had been influenced by the Conservative British Colonial Secretary, Joseph Chamberlain, who was most anxious that the proposed Australian legislation should not give offence to Indian and other coloured subjects of the Empire or to the Japanese with whom Britain was negotiating an alliance. Barton accordingly put into the Bill the device of an education test, such as the colonial government of Natal had adopted in 1897 to keep out Indian immigrants. The Bill required that *any* applicant for admission to Australia *might* be required by an officer of the Commonwealth Customs Service to write out fifty words of English as dictated by that officer. It was understood by everyone, and often openly stated in the debate, that the test would be applied to all coloured applicants for admission and to no one else. The Government hoped, forlornly, as might have been predicted, that Asian and African people would innocently mistake the form of the Bill for its substance and so would not take offence.

No such disingenuous, if polite, fiction would do for the Labor Party. Its supporters feared or despised coloured people on racist grounds as passionately as any Protectionist or Freetrader of them all; but they had more cause than did middle-class people to fear them on economic grounds also. As the radical Protectionist member H. B. Higgins put it:

> In the determination of this question we should not look for the judgment of those who merely know what it means from behind a brandy-and-soda and a long cigar in a city club.[8]

[8] Michael V. Moore, 'Unequal and Inferior: the White Australia Policy in the First Commonwealth Parliament' (B.A. Hons thesis, University of New England, 1962), p. 89.

In the Victorian furniture trade and sometimes elsewhere during the previous fifty years, the presence of Chinese had had the effect of lowering wages and making fewer jobs available for white workers. Accordingly during the second reading debate on the Bill, J. C. Watson, leader of the Labor Party in the Representatives, gave notice of an amendment that would substitute for the dictation test a form of words explicitly excluding from Australia 'any . . . aboriginal native of Asia, Africa or of the islands thereof'. After long and passionate debate, Watson's amendment was defeated. It was then argued that the dictation test in English might keep out cultivated European migrants while it would allow a bi-lingual Japanese or an American Negro into the country. After further debate the Bill was amended to allow for a dictation test in any European language and sent on to the Senate.

There Labor tried again. In Committee the South Australian Labor Senator, Gregor McGregor, moved an amendment almost identical with Watson's. At this stage the amendment was defeated by a clever manoeuvre of some Opposition Freetrade senators — not because they cared greatly about which form the Bill was to take, but because they hoped to force Labor members to treat with them and so, perhaps, to bring down the Government. The Opposition manoeuvre misfired. Alarmed at the possibility of the Bill's being held up indefinitely, Labor senators in a body swung behind the Government and passed the Bill in the form in which it had come up from the Representatives.

It is important to realise that, despite the contentious oratory of the debates, virtually all members in both Houses were at one, as were their electors, in the determination to exclude coloured aliens. The argument was simply over the method by which exclusion for all time was to be accomplished. Was the polite but hypocritical subterfuge of the dictation test to be used, or were black, brown and yellow people to be told rudely, if honestly, that they were unwelcome in Australia because of the colour of their skins? The Imperial Government, the Australian Government and many Freetraders, because generally their British connections were stronger than those of the Protectionists, wanted the dictation test. Labor wanted to call a spade a bloody shovel.

Many Australians, moved perhaps by a creditable desire to see the best in their ancestors, have maintained that the provisions of the Immigration Restriction Act were arrived at mainly or even wholly for economic reasons. Alas, it was not so. It is true that nearly all speakers on the Bill mentioned the economic threat of cheap coloured labour and the need to protect the high (white) Australian standard of living. Many made much of these arguments; but all speakers, implicitly or explicitly, made even more of racist arguments

PIEBALD POSSIBILITIES — A LITTLE AUSTRALIAN CHRISTMAS FAMILY PARTY OF THE FUTURE

about the 'innate inferiority' of coloured people, the need to guard against 'contamination', to preserve 'the purity of the blood' and so on. Some of the more thoughtful and better-educated members like Alfred Deakin, the Protectionist Attorney-General, pointed also to the vast cultural *difference*, not necessarily involving inferiority or superiority, between Australians and Oriental people like the Chinese and Japanese, and used this as an argument for exclusion; but even these members never denied the supposed fact, or protested against the innumerable assertions, of the 'innate inferiority' of coloured people. Deakin was careful to avoid publicly asserting these ideas and his main speech on the Bill has been often quoted from, and more often paraphrased, to show that Australians at the beginning of the century did not hold racist beliefs. Here is the nub of what Deakin actually said:

> For my part, I have been careful from the first not to attempt to justify this Bill, and the exclusiveness of feeling which it represents on the score of any moral or other inferiority on the part of those whom we desire to exclude. Whether or not there exists such inferiority is a matter for argument and dispute elsewhere. I have frankly stated from the first that the exclusiveness on the part of the Australian people is perfectly independent of the mental and moral status of the Japanese, when measured by the only standards that can be properly applied to them, namely, those of their own race and of their own history . . . these people do differ from us in such essentials of race and character as to exclude the possibility of any advantageous admixture or intermarriage if we are to maintain the standards of civilization to which we are accustomed. . . . Our civilization belongs to us, and we belong to it; we are bred in it, and it is bred in us. It fits us and is our means of progress and advancement. These people have their own independent development, their own qualities, and also the civilization, forms of life and government, which naturally attach to them.They are separated from us by a gulf which we cannot bridge to the advantage of either.[9]

It will be seen that even the sensitive and scholarly Deakin harboured racist feelings, however urbanely disguised — 'these people do differ from us in such essentials of race and character as to exclude the possibility of any advantageous admixture or intermarriage . . .' The sentiments of the Prime Minister are less often quoted: yet there is no doubt that they expressed the feelings of nearly all members of both Houses. Barton said:

> I do not think either that the doctrine of the equality of man was really ever intended to include racial equality. There is no racial equality.

[9] *C.P.D.*, vol. 5, p. 5819.

> There is that basic inequality. These races are, in comparison with white races — I think no one wants convincing of this fact — unequal and inferior. The doctrine of the equality of man was never intended to apply to the equality of the Englishman and the Chinaman. There is a deep-set difference, and we see no prospect and no promise of its ever being effaced. Nothing in this world can put these two races upon an equality. Nothing we can do by cultivation, by refinement, or by anything else will make some races equal to others.[10]

Many other members expressed the same views more brutally. W. M. Hughes, in his usual vituperative style, said, 'We object to these people because of their vices, and of their immorality, and because of a hundred things which we can only hint at'.[11] C. C. Salmon, a Victorian Protectionist, spoke of our having 'here in Australia an admixture of the best and choicest of the white races', and of the necessity of protecting its 'purity'.[12] The egregious Senator Staniforth Smith admitted that the Japanese were a very well-educated nation, but went on to state that 'the Caucasian races cannot mingle with the Mongolian, the Hindoo, or the negro' since half-castes lost fertility and their progeny, if any, were 'always wretched and miserable'.[13]

In both Houses only one member unequivocally opposed the Bill root and branch. This was an arch-conservative Freetrader from New South Wales, Arthur Bruce Smith. Fourth son of William Howard Smith, a wealthy shipping magnate, and for some time managing director of the family firm, Bruce Smith was a barrister and an 'independent' politician of the old school. Pompous in manner and prolix in style, he nevertheless made the most sensible speech on the Bill. He emphasised the importance to Australia of the British connection and the imperial ideal of the equality of all citizens under the law. He praised the 'old-fashioned virtues' of the Japanese and said it was humiliating to inform the world that Australians were afraid to come into contact or competition with them. He denounced the nonsensical talk of 'racial purity' and informed the House that there was 'no race on the face of the earth that is of a more mixed character than the British race . . . The Chinese and the Japanese and the Indians are in the strict sense of the term, purer as a race'. Finally he said that the legislation was unnecessary because the Asian population of Australia was decreasing already (which was true) and he accused fellow members of trying 'to make political capital by appealing to some of the worst instincts in some of the more credulous

[10] *C.P.D.*, vol. 4, p. 5233.

[11] *C.P.D.*, vol. 4, p. 4823.

[12] *C.P.D.*, vol. 4, p. 5066.

[13] *C.P.D.*, vol. 6, p. 7246.

of the people'. Bruce Smith even had the melancholy pleasure of the man who accurately prophesies woe. 'The debate on this great question . . . ' he said, 'and the results of this debate will constitute a sort of mirror in which we, as a people, can be seen by other nations'.[14]

Seventy years later opinion leaders in all the nations of the earth knew about the White Australia Policy. Sometimes it was the only thing they knew about Australia and nearly all, except those in the Union of South Africa and Rhodesia, found it repugnant. Another Freetrade member, D. N. Cameron from Tasmania, echoed Smith's views. However, he added that he could quite see why working men might favour the Bill — an indirect way of advancing economic arguments for it. With the exception of Smith, all members who spoke on the Bill gave racist or socio-cultural or economic reasons, or some combination of the three, as arguments in support of the White Australia Policy. Careful examination of the debates leaves no doubt about the relative weighting given to these three reasons. A Queensland Labor Senator, J. C. Stewart, was not quite right about the priorities when he said, 'for racial, social, and economic reasons we cannot permit [coloured people] with safety to enter [Australia]'.[15] The real order was racial, economic, social.

Unlike the Immigration Restriction Bill, the Pacific Island Labourers Bill provoked real and determined opposition and it was finally passed in the Senate only by quite a narrow margin. The Bill provided that no more Kanakas could be brought into Australia after 1904, that all Kanakas in Australia had to be repatriated to their native islands by the end of the year 1906 and that the deportations were to take place gradually so as to minimise inconvenience for the white planters. In the event bloodshed, which had stained the traffic for so long, continued during the repatriation process, for it was always troublesome and sometimes impossible to find which particular island a Kanaka had been taken from. Those who were landed on an island not their own were often maltreated and sometimes murdered by its inhabitants.

Logically every member of either House who had supported the passage, on racist grounds, of the Immigration Restriction Act, should have supported the Bill for deporting the Kanakas: but special and powerful minority interests were involved in the latter proposal. The profitability of the coastal Queensland sugar industry appeared to depend upon the continuance of a supply of cheap and docile Kanaka labour. The promise of a federal bounty to sugar-growers to make up for the loss of the Kanaka work force, did

[14] *C.P.D.*, vol. 4, pp. 5153-65.

[15] *C.P.D.*, vol. 6, p. 7331.

nothing to appease them. Those who profited directly or indirectly from the sugar industry, many conservatives with money to invest and some men with Queensland squatting interests, were prominent in opposition to the Bill.

The second reading was moved by Barton in the House of Representatives on 2 October 1901. R. Edwards, a Queensland Protectionist, immediately moved a number of amendments aimed at weakening the Bill and postponing for as long as possible the date of its final implementation. He received little support, however, and the Bill was sent up to the Senate on 8 November. There the opposition was much more formidable. It was led by Senator John Ferguson, a Queensland Freetrader who was also President of the Central Queensland Separation League, a body supported mainly by sugar-planters and others whose prosperity depended on that industry.

Some of the speeches on the Bill make astonishing reading today. In the House William Knox, Freetrade member for the Melbourne seat of Kooyong, quoted from a learned work called *Control of the Tropics* by Benjamin Kidd, which proved that white men were innately unsuited for field work in tropical countries and that the offspring of white men who did such work would be anaemic and impotent. Freetrade Senator J. T. Walker, of New South Wales, approvingly quoted a *Daily Telegraph* report on a certain Dr Spencer who 'simply pointed out the notorious fact that the British race is unable to propagate itself within the tropics — a fact so well established by ethnologists that I should have thought it unnecessary to draw attention to it nowadays'.[16] Protectionist Senator Dobson, of Tasmania, read from a leading article in the *Hobart Mercury* of 2 December 1901 which explained to members that blacks had 'a second liver [and a] protective pigment in their skins, a fact so notorious that it [could] only be ignored by blind politicians and cranky Labor members'.[17]

Ferguson moved two amendments similar to those moved by Edwards in the House. One, known popularly as the 'colour-line amendment', sought to confine the operation of the Bill to that part of Australia south of the Tropic of Capricorn. Like other amendments, and despite or perhaps because of the weighty arguments mentioned above, it was defeated, but only by sixteen votes to ten. Royal assent to all three Bills we have been considering was received by January 1902 and so, for better and for worse, the White Australia Policy was written into the law of the infant Commonwealth.

[16] *C.P.D.*, vol. 6, p. 8234.

[17] *C.P.D.*, vol. 6, p. 8263.

Other achievements of the Barton Government may be briefly summarised. Late in 1901 a public competition produced a flag for the nation, featuring both the Union Jack and the Southern Cross, which constellation had been associated with local Australian sentiment from very early times. Indeed in 1851 the Australasian League for the Abolition of Transportation, which was active in all the eastern colonies, devised a flag for itself which was substantially identical with the national flag of 1901 except that the latter included, in addition to the Cross, a single large six-pointed star to symbolise the six States. The flag of the republic of Victoria, hoisted briefly by the Eureka rebels in 1854, had also featured the Southern Cross though not, of course, the Union Jack.

The tariff question was settled in an exhausting series of debates. The outcome was necessarily a compromise which satisfied neither Freetraders nor Protectionists. Since the Government had undertaken to impose no taxes except in the fields of customs and excise, it had obviously to raise sufficient revenue from these sources for its own needs after three-quarters of receipts had been handed over to the States. Thus even Freetraders recognised that some tariffs on imported goods were necessary, but they constituted the largest group in the Senate and were determined that customs duties should be kept as low as possible. Manufacturers and lobbyists besieged members with pleas for particular interests. In the event the tariffs of 1902 ranged from 5 per cent to 25 per cent on a whole range of imported goods and it began to appear that protection was to be the policy of the Commonwealth.

In 1903 the Sugar Bounties Act gave, as promised, compensation to planters who employed only white labour. In the same year the Defence Act did little more than establish two principles: one, that the military forces were to consist principally of citizen soldiers and not of a professional standing army, and two, that citizen soldiers were not to be compelled to serve outside Australia. The Government also brought forward a Bill to establish a federal Arbitration Court but was baulked by a bitter Victorian railway strike in May. This persuaded Labor and some other members that the proposed arbitration Act should include power to adjudicate in industrial disputes concerning government employees as well as those working in privately owned industries. Estimating that it would not be able to pass the Bill without accepting some such unpalatable amendment, the Government shelved the legislation.

Not long before the second federal election Barton resigned to take one of the three positions on the newly established High Court Bench. He had (presumably) recommended himself for a knighthood in the preceding year. Another political knight, Sir

Samuel Griffith, a leading figure in the drafting of the federal Constitution and for several years Premier of Queensland, was made Chief Justice. The third initial appointment to the High Court Bench was that of R. E. O'Connor, Barton's friend and Government leader in the Senate. Thus was established at the very beginning of the High Court's existence, the tradition that appointments to it might be political in nature, and often palpably were. Alfred Deakin, the Attorney-General, the leading Victorian federalist and a friend of Barton's, succeeded him as Protectionist leader and Prime Minister.

Chapter 2

THREE ELEVENS IN THE FIELD
c. 1904—1908

Deakin, Watson, Reid and arbitration — 'New Protection' and the Basic Wage — Nationalism and imperialism — White Australia and defence

DEAKIN, WATSON, REID AND ARBITRATION

Alfred Deakin, second Prime Minister of Australia, is generally thought to have been also the greatest. Certainly he was one of the most likeable. Except for three periods totalling twenty-two months, he was in office from September 1903 until April 1910, and whether in office or not he did more than any other man to shape the Australian way of life for the following fifty years or so.

Born in 1856, the son of an accountant, he spent seven years at Melbourne Grammar School before doing Law at the University there. As a young man he wrote verse and prose, publishing two small books: indeed, throughout his life he continued to write voluminously in diaries about his 'inner life', being at heart more interested in philosophy, literature, history and the supernatural than in practical affairs. At the university he gave more attention to writing than to law and he became a first-class journalist. He met and became a *protégé* of the liberal-minded David Syme, proprietor of the Melbourne *Age*, then certainly (and still, arguably) the most influential daily newspaper in Australia. Syme and his paper had virtually converted Victoria to Protectionism and they continued fervently to preach that faith for the Commonwealth after federation. In the last two decades of the nineteenth century Syme was known in Victoria as King David, and it was said that no Victorian government could be elected without his approval. When the *Age* commended Deakin to the colonial electors he was sent to the Legislative Assembly in 1880. At the age of 27 he became Solicitor-General, Commissioner for Public Works and Minister of Water Supply in the Service-Berry Government. In the last portfolio he was instrumental in launching the first serious and large-scale irrigation programme in Australia. He continued to sit in the Victorian Parliament until he resigned in 1900 to enter the federal legislature.

Despite his consuming intellectual interests, Deakin was easily the most successful practical politician in the national Parliament until his retirement in 1913. Tall, black-bearded and dignified, he had a commanding, some said a 'mesmeric', presence. He was recognised as the finest orator of his day: yet his greatest political skill was his ability to win over opponents with tact and charm in informal conversation outside the debating chamber — a faculty recognised even by his political enemies when they nicknamed him 'Affable Alfred'. His liberalism was deep and genuine, as was his fervent but sanely balanced Australian nationalism. In both these respects he had much more in common with the Labor leader, Watson, than with the Freetrade chief, Reid, or most other non-Labor politicians. Whether as Prime Minister or in opposition, he used generally to travel daily on a bicycle, or with other workers on the cable tram, between his Melbourne suburban home and Parliament House: a fact which shows something about Deakin's character but also about the simplicity of Australian life before the Great War. At Imperial Conferences he more than held his own with British Prime Ministers, but refused a knighthood and returned home unaffected by much flattery and fêting in London. The worst that can be said of him is that, as the anonymous Australian correspondent of the London *Morning Post*, he reported favourably on his own political activities.

In the election campaign at the end of 1903 the main issue was industrial arbitration. After the disastrous strikes of the early 1890s, when the colonial governments had not hesitated to use the power of the state against employees, most Labor voters believed that arbitration courts, armed with some coercive powers, *vis-à-vis* both employees and employers, would help them in the struggle for what they regarded as wage-justice. On the other hand most conservatives thought that the same institutions would help to avoid or suppress strikes and maintain industrial peace. The activities of State wages boards and arbitration courts, which had been set up in most of the colonies in the 1890s, gave some warrant for both beliefs.

In his policy speech at Ballarat Deakin promised to set up a Federal Arbitration Court with power to adjudicate in industrial disputes occurring in more than one State, but he would not allow State government employees to come under the proposed Court's jurisdiction. Though in favour of higher tariffs, he proposed to accept a 'fiscal truce' for the time being. Not so Reid, the Freetrade leader who, Canute-like, demanded reductions in the tariff of 1902. Watson, for Labor, agreed with Deakin over the tariff and also over the establishment of a Federal Arbitration Court which, however, he held must have jurisdiction over all workers including State employees.

Another facet of Labor's electioneering is of some interest as exemplifying that party's early stance as the standard-bearer of local

Australian nationalism as opposed to British Imperial loyalty. At the Imperial Conference of 1902, Barton and his Defence Minister, Forrest, had agreed to pay a subsidy of £200,000 a year towards the upkeep of a Royal Naval Squadron to be stationed 'normally' in Australian waters — though it might be moved anywhere at will by the British Admiralty. Watson criticised the Deakin Government for having made this arrangement, arguing that Australia should have a navy of its own, independent of British control.

In the elections of December 1903 Labor increased its strength in both Houses at the expense of both the other parties. In the Representatives there were 26 Protectionists, 24 Freetraders and 25 Labor members: in the Senate the figures were 9, 13 and 14 respectively. The Protectionist Government was sure enough of Labor support to continue in office, but it was at this time that Deakin made his famous speech ruefully comparing the political situation with a cricket match: 'What kind of a game of cricket . . . could they play if they had three elevens instead of two, with one playing sometimes with one side, sometimes with the other, and sometimes for itself?'.[1] The first major Government measure to be brought forward was the Arbitration Bill. The debate on it was long, bitter and confused. On 2 April 1904 a future Labor prime minister, Andrew Fisher, moved an amendment extending the scope of the proposed Court to include State government employees. Some Protectionists and Freetraders voted with Labor and the amendment was carried thirty-eight to twenty-nine. Deakin at once resigned and the Governor-General called on Watson to form the first Commonwealth Labor Government.

Born of English parents in Valparaiso, Chile, in 1867, John Christian Watson was taken to New Zealand in childhood, educated at the State school in Oamaru and apprenticed to the printing trade. At the age of 19 he made his way to Sydney where he worked as a compositor. In 1893, when only 26 years old, he was elected President of the Sydney Trades and Labour Council and soon afterwards of the Australian Labour Federation. In 1894 he presided over the New South Wales Labor Conference which framed the 'solidarity pledge', the promise thereafter binding on all Labor parliamentarians to vote on issues as directed by majority decision of Labor members meeting in Caucus. He was a member of the New South Wales Parliament from 1894 until his election to the Federal Parliament in 1901. He was only 37 years old when he became Prime Minister and Treasurer of the Commonwealth. A neat, quietly-spoken man of moderate height, he held himself well

[1] J. A. La Nauze, *Alfred Deakin*, Melbourne, 1965, 2 vols, vol. 2, p.363.

and looked straight at people through eyes of 'a clear sapphire blue'. He was a 'moderate' Labor man, renowned for his sincerity, tact and good manners. Conservatives who met him were sorely puzzled to think how such a sane, decent fellow could have acted as midwife at the birth of the 'solidarity pledge' they regarded with such horror. That Deakin and he had the greatest respect and liking for each other is clear from their private letters. In fact Deakin promised him 'every consideration' in his impossible task of governing Australia with majorities against him in both Houses.

'Every consideration' was not enough. In less than four months the Labor Administration foundered, as the Protectionists had done, on the rock of arbitration. The House actually passed the Bill (containing power to hear disputes involving State government industrial employees) through the committee stages, but the Government was committed to a clause instructing the proposed Court to give preference to trade-union members. This proposal was defeated 36 to 34 by a group of Protectionists and the Freetraders. Watson resigned and was succeeded by a very different type of man.

Son of a Presbyterian parson, George Houston Reid was born in Scotland in 1845, came to Melbourne with his family as a child of seven, and went to work as a clerk in Sydney when only thirteen. He entered the New South Wales public service in 1864 rising to be private secretary to the Attorney-General. In 1875 he published *Five Essays on Free Trade*, a work awarded the gold medal of the Cobden Club. Later in life he read nothing but light novels. He became a successful barrister and sat in the New South Wales Parliament from 1880 till federation, being Premier of the colony, with Labor support, from 1894 to 1899.

Reid's character is something of an enigma. Some believed him to be a genuine liberal inspired by progressive ideas: others thought him the complete opportunist, ready to espouse any policy that promised to bring him place and power. Probably he became more cynical and less idealistic as he grew older. Certainly he was a most astute, flexible and vain politician. He was enormously fat, affected a monocle, and regarded himself as a lady's man. Cartoonists sometimes represented him as a pig. He was a vulgarian not above exploiting his physical appearance to gain a laugh from the crowd. He was a tremendously effective platform speaker, affecting a slow drawl which enabled the dullest in the audience to follow his arguments. A cultivated English visitor characterised him as 'Reid, the uncultured, the popularly humorous, the finely vulgar'.[2] In his

[2] C. P. Trevelyan, *Letters from North America and the Pacific 1898*, London, 1969, p.176.

autobiography he wrote, 'a thinner skin, a keener sense of shame, a less resolute endurance, a more diffident estimate of my abilities might have spoilt my chances for life', but even Reid's thick hide must have been punctured by a retort he once drew upon himself in the Commonwealth Parliament. Baiting a radical Protectionist member, Isaac Isaacs, who glowered at him from the opposite front bench, he sneered: 'The Right Honourable minister looks as if he would like to eat me'. Isaacs replied instantly: 'The Right Honourable member has forgotten my religion'.[3] Yet this incident was remembered partly because it was rarely indeed that Reid was worsted in a contest of wits. Deakin despised and distrusted him and thought him 'resolutely selfish': but he furnished the democratic politician's final proof of personal integrity when he died in London in 1918, a poor man.

Reid became Prime Minister of Australia in August 1904, backed by all Freetrade members and a conservative group of Protectionists led by Allan McLean who became Minister for Trade and Customs. This was the third minority Government to hold office, if hardly power, within the year and it was clear from the start that it could not survive long. Isaacs, Lyne and a number of Protectionist radicals at once agreed with the Labor Party to bring the ministry down as soon as possible. However, Reid's political skills were such that he managed to hold onto power until the end of the parliamentary session in December. Ironically, the only really significant piece of legislation to be passed was the Conciliation and Arbitration Bill which had been initiated by Deakin and supported by Labor. The Act set up a Court of Conciliation and Arbitration with coercive powers to deal with interstate industrial disputes. It was to be presided over by a judge nominated from among the members of the High Court bench. Soon afterwards the High Court ruled that the new industrial Court could have no power to deal with State employees. Nevertheless the establishment of a Federal Arbitration Court in 1904 was, in its long-term effects on Australian society, one of the most significant events in the nation's history. Increasingly it tended to set precedents — and to set the pace — for State industrial boards and tribunals. Because it could only deal with accredited spokesmen for the workers in an industry, it inevitably stimulated the growth of trade unions, which were still suffering from the effects of the great strikes and the great depression of the 1890s. Estimated trade-union membership in Australia stood at 97 174 in 1901. By 1914 it had risen to 523 271. Moreover, as we shall see, the Court

[3] L. F. Fitzhardinge, *William Morris Hughes*, vol. 1, Sydney, 1964, pp.124-5.

soon established what was then a new thing under the sun — that a minimum wage should be guaranteed by law for even the least skilled workers in the country.

Naturally the Reid-McLean Government received little credit for the enactment of what was essentially the idea of its opponents. As Prime Minister, Reid put off the evil day for as long as possible by arranging that Parliament should not re-assemble for a full six months — until 28 June 1905. Two days later his Government was defeated by forty-two votes to twenty-five. 'I think,' said Watson, more caustically than was his wont, 'we shall all welcome the disappearance of a Ministry that has neither achievement in the past, policy in the present, nor prospects in the future to justify its existence'.[4] Each of the three elevens had had a brief, and largely abortive, innings. For the next three years, from July 1905 till November 1908 political life was more stable and fruitful. The Protectionists remained in office with steady Labor support — so steady that, although the Protectionist vote fell quite steeply in the general election of December 1906, the Deakin Government carried straight on with its programme. At this election Protectionists won only 17 seats in the Representatives and Labor twenty-six. Reid tried, with some success, to frighten electors by painting alarming pictures of the 'extremism' of the Labor Party. He described it as a 'socialist tiger' seeking whom it might devour. He, his Freetrade followers and some other conservatives went to the electors under the label of 'Anti-Socialists'. They gained 32 seats.

'NEW PROTECTION' AND THE BASIC WAGE

'New Protection' was the issue which dominated the years of the second Deakin Administration, just as arbitration had dominated the previous period. Deakin had agreed to the fiscal truce as a necessary practical expedient, but a temporary one. Since the first Parliament, experience had converted most Labor members into Protectionists and Deakin believed that, in the new political situation, a further measure of tariff protection for nascent Australian secondary industries was attainable as well as desirable. The 'new' part of the proposed legislation had an irresistible appeal for most Labor members and voters. In the past tariffs had helped the Australian manufacturer simply by placing a high duty on competitive goods from abroad, but there was no guarantee that the workers in his factory were not being exploited by their employer. The New Protection legislation sought by various means to ensure that workers

[4] *C.P.D.*, vol. 25, p.41.

LOOK BACK AT ANGER: *"Hop" on Arbitration*

Bulletin, 21 February 1891

BEDFELLOWS—BUT SLEEPING WITH ONE EYE OPEN

in protected industries shared in their employers' tariff-based prosperity. In some cases firms could be excused payment of some excise duty if the Government was satisfied that they paid fair and reasonable wages: in others high import duties, for example on imported harvesters and other agricultural machines, might be greatly reduced if the Government thought the protected Australian manufacturers were not paying fair wages or were selling their goods at too high a price. The 'Old' Protection had safeguarded the interests of the manufacturers. It thus made payment of good wages possible. The 'New' Protection sought to make them actual. The newly created Court of Conciliation and Arbitration was given the task of deciding what were and what were not 'fair and reasonable' wages. In the first half of the twentieth century no Australian judicial decision aroused such widespread interest or had such important consequences, as that which resulted from the New Protection legislation.

The first President of the Commonwealth Arbitration Court had been Barton's friend, R. E. O'Connor, but he resigned after little more than a year in the position. His place was filled in 1906 by Henry Bournes Higgins who, with Isaac Isaacs, had been appointed by Deakin to fill the two extra places on the High Court Bench created by the Judiciary Act of that year. The son of a Methodist minister, Higgins was born in County Down, Ireland, in 1851 and came to Melbourne with his family in 1870. He studied law and built up a successful legal practice before entering Victorian politics in 1894 as the member for Geelong. In 1901 he was elected to the Commonwealth Parliament for the seat of North Melbourne and, though not a member of the Labor Party, he served as Attorney-General in the Watson Government of 1904. Like Isaacs he was, in Parliament, a radical Protectionist. Naturally they brought with them to the High Court a liberal bias which contrasted with the conservative bent of Griffith, Barton and O'Connor. Higgins worked immensely hard and in all his dealings was a man of absolute rectitude. He was extremely, almost painfully, idealistic; dignified, gentle and courteous in manner under even the most trying circumstances. Even those who disagreed with him most strongly, never questioned his sincerity or the purity of his motives. He married a sister of 'Chinese' Morrison.[5] Their only child was killed in the Great War.

Soon after Higgins's appointment to the Court he was faced with an application from H. V. McKay, proprietor of the Sunshine Harvester works near Melbourne, to certify that the wages paid his

[5] See p. 27 above.

employees were 'fair and reasonable'. McKay needed such a declaration from the Court in order to gain exemption from excise duties imposed under the New Protection legislation. Higgins examined workers and housewives on their views of living costs, as well as official statistics. On 8 November 1907 he refused McKay the desired exemption on the ground that wages paid by his firm were not fair and reasonable. They were insufficient he held, in words that will always bear quoting, to meet 'the normal needs of the average employee regarded as a human being living in a civilized community'.[6] With this yardstick a fair and reasonable wage, he held, would be seven shillings a day, or £2 2s od for a normal six-day week of 48 hours. He affirmed that he had not inquired into the capacity of the industry to pay such a wage, but had reached the figure of £2 2s od solely by consideration of the needs of an unskilled labourer with (on the average) a wife and three children to support. The immediate effect of what came to be known as 'the Harvester Judgment' was that the minimum wage for all workers under Commonwealth Arbitration Court awards rose by about 27 per cent. The long-term result was that such a minimum or 'basic' wage, calculated on the above basis, became for the following sixty years a fundamental feature of Australian life. Workers with any degree of specialist training or skills were of course paid more than the basic wage, which itself was adjusted annually or more often, to keep pace with the cost of living. When the length of the standard working week was reduced — as in 1948 from 44 to 40 hours — the value of the basic wage was not reduced and thus was in effect increased by the provision of more leisure and more overtime payments.

The Harvester Judgment also, in a sense, secured the substance of what the New Protection Acts aimed at, even though they were all disallowed by the High Court. Deakin had wanted to ensure that workers in industries protected by Commonwealth tariffs received reasonably good wages. By a majority judgment of 3 to 2 the Court held that the legislation was invalid because the Constitution gave the Commonwealth no power to fix wages or conditions of labour or to interfere with industrial relations within each State. Not surprisingly the majority consisted of the three more conservative judges with the radicals, Higgins and Isaacs holding that the legislation was completely valid. The leading authority on Australian constitutional law, Professor Geoffrey Sawer, believes the minority judgment was probably the sounder.[7] However that may be, it is clear that the New

[6] *M.A.D.* I, p.112.
[7] *S.I.*, p.83.

Protection Acts brought about the Harvester Judgment, which established a legally enforced, reasonable, minimum wage not only for workers in protected industries but in all industries. Living conditions were improved also by the passage in 1908 of the Invalid and Old Age Pensions Act. Continually foreshadowed by preceding Governments, this Act marked the beginning of direct Commonwealth action in the field of social security. Pensions were payable to British subjects, excluding Aborigines, at the age of 65 and recipients were subject to a means test.

It should be noted that the High Court's ruling did not and could not affect the validity of the tariffs established by the New Protection legislation, but only of the accompanying provisions relating to conditions of labour in protected industries. The Freetraders fought bitterly but unavailingly, for the great majority of Labor men were already convinced Protectionists when the parliamentary debate on the tariff began in August 1907.

NATIONALISM AND IMPERIALISM

New Protection was written into the Labor Party's platform, binding on all members, at its annual conference in 1908 in Brisbane. As in 1902 the result was something of a compromise: Freetraders believed the tariff of 1908 ruinously heavy while Protectionists thought it not really protective enough. Nevertheless the tariff of June 1908, which embodied a 5 per cent preference for British goods, was genuinely protective of young Australian manufacturing industries. What is more important, it established two principles which were to hold generally for the next sixty years or so. Protection, regardless of the party in office, was to be the fixed fiscal policy of the Commonwealth and, as the tariff level rose, it generally incorporated some degree of preference for British commodities. It is sad — or ironical — that the paladin of Protection, David Syme, did not live to see the consummation of his life's work. He died in February 1908 while the protection debate was still raging.

Syme, the great economic nationalist, had considered the 5 per cent preference to British goods of no importance. Not so Deakin. He was at once the greatest Australian nationalist and the greatest imperialist in the Commonwealth Parliament, his only rival in this respect being W. M. Hughes, easily the ablest man in the Labor Party though not then its leader. To both men, as to most of their fellow citizens up till the Second World War, positive and unquestioning loyalty to Throne and Empire was in no way inconsistent with an equally fervent loyalty to Australia: rather, it was a condition of it. For most, but not all people, national and imperial

LOOK BACK AT ANGER: *Imperial Preference*

Bulletin, 30 May 1903

INTER - EMPIRE FREETRADE (i.e., PREFERENCE TO NIGGER - LABOR PRODUCTS)

THE BRITISH LION: *"Here, my young friend, is a little gift I have for you. I'm going to give preference to your goods and you to mine, and we'll all be one—one Empire, one Throne, one Tariff."*

LITTLE BOY FROM MANLY: *"That's all right, John, but what about the other paw and your friends there."*

patriotism were complementary, not contradictory. As Deakin and Hughes saw it, nationhood demanded that Australia should create its own defence forces so that Britain could be assured that, as Hughes said, 'whatever may come, we shall render a good account of ourselves here both on land and on sea'.[8] Membership of the Empire and involvement in Britain's wars had been taken for granted by most citizens ever since N.S.W. had sent a contingent of volunteers to the Sudan War in 1885. A naively patriotic letter to the press on that occasion had been signed 'Little Boy from Manly' (the Sydney sea-side suburb). For the next thirty years or more the 'Little Boy from Manly', dressed in a sailor suit, served in *Bulletin* and other cartoons as the symbol of young Australia, often making to John Bull and others innocently devastating remarks of the type, 'The Emperor has no clothes'.

Equally it was taken for granted that Australian relations with foreign countries could normally be conducted only through Great Britain and by the grace and favour of the British diplomatic service. As his own Minister for External Affairs in his first two administrations, like Hughes in the short-lived Watson Government, Deakin was deeply concerned with changes in the balance of power in the Pacific — so deeply that in 1904 and 1905 he negotiated directly with the Japanese Consul-General in Australia over the application to Japanese nationals of the Immigration Restriction Act. Generally, nevertheless, Australian nationalism, at the diplomatic level, consisted in making Australian views very plain to Britain and in seeking to influence British policy. In both exercises Deakin was more successful than most of his successors in the External Affairs portfolio have been.

The nature of Australia's independence within the Empire was dramatically illustrated in the Commonwealth's first year by Britain's declaring its readiness to hand over British New Guinea. In November 1901 Parliament passed an Act authorising the Government to accept responsibility for the administration of one of the most 'backward' colonial areas in the world. In the British, south-eastern portion of the island, as in the rest of it, head-hunting and cannibalism were common practices and many tribes had never set eyes on a European. The territory was totally undeveloped, lacking almost completely any such amenities as roads and bridges, and hundreds of quite distinct languages multiplied the problems of government. A more immediate difficulty was that, as Deakin said, 'owing to pressure of other responsibilities, Parliament was quite unable to give to the questions affecting Papua the careful attention

[8] *C.P.D.*, vol. 14, p.2318.

they required'. Britain handed over control in March 1902 and for the next six years Papua was governed — or largely left to its own devices — by a series of temporary and makeshift arrangements. Confusion was compounded by bad blood between the remaining British colonial service personnel and the incoming Australians.

One of these latter was a 43-year-old member of a very remarkable Australian family, John Hubert Plunkett Murray. He went to Port Moresby in August 1904 as Chief Judicial Officer to replace a young Queenslander who had suicided dramatically at the foot of the flag pole in front of the administration building. Murray's grandfather came to Australia in 1817 as paymaster of the 48th Regiment. His son Terence in 1837 was granted good grazing land near the present capital city of Canberra. The splendid house he built on this grazing run, Yarralumla, now serves as the residence of the Governor-General. Terence Murray became a leading figure in New South Wales, succeeding W. C. Wentworth as President of the Legislative Council from 1862 until his death in 1873. He was knighted in 1869. His eldest son, J.H.P. Murray, was born in 1861. The second son, Gilbert, born in 1866, went to England at the age of 11 and became a brilliant classical scholar and Regius Professor of Greek at Oxford from 1908 to 1936. Young Hubert Murray was educated at Sydney Grammar School and proceeded to Magdalen College, Oxford, in 1881. There he became amateur heavyweight boxing champion of England and graduated with double first class honours in Classics and 'Modern Greats'. He then studied law in London and returned to Sydney in 1886, becoming Parliamentary Draftsman and later Crown Prosecutor. He served with distinction in the Boer War and then was appointed to his judgeship in New Guinea, which was officially renamed Papua in 1906.

Deakin was under considerable pressure from the Labor Party to appoint an Australian as Lieutenant-Governor of Papua and the party's man for the job was the Western Australian Senator Staniforth Smith who, perhaps because of his remarkable views on genetics, was supposed to be an expert on 'native races'. Deakin withstood this pressure and one of his last acts as Prime Minister in his second Administration was to appoint Murray as Lieutenant-Governor of Papua in November 1908. It is hard to imagine that there could have been a better man for that job at that time. He implemented Deakin's policy which was also his own. When asked in Parliament whether white or black interests were to be preferred in the case of a clash, Deakin answered forthrightly: 'Yes, in our opinion, Papua belongs first to the Papuans. Their well-being is to be studied in most respects even before that of men of our own colour'.[9] Murray's resolute defence of Papuan interests against the encroachment of settlers, traders, miners and beachcombers, made him unpopular at first with many whites, but by the end of his long reign he was respected, often revered, by nearly all, irrespective of race. His rule was paternalistic and benevolent. During it the whole country was brought under control with extraordinarily little violence or bloodshed. His achievements were immense if one remembers that no Australian government ever provided a tenth of the finance necessary for Papua's needs. From 1901 to 1906, for example, Parliament voted an annual sum of £20,000 — just double the salary of the Governor-General of Australia. Most members of parliament were happy to leave Murray to devise and implement his own policies in a country about which they knew little and cared less. One measure of his success is the fact that he continued in office for thirty-one years and died in harness, aged 79, in Samarai in 1940 while on a tour of inspection.

The complex nature of the imperial relationship was also exemplified by Deakin's activity over the New Hebrides. This large group of Pacific Islands lay some six or seven hundred kilometres north-east of New Caledonia, which France had annexed in 1853. In the last quarter of the nineteenth century Queensland *blackbirders* hunted there for Kanakas, British and Australian missionaries preached the word of God mainly in the Presbyterian version, and a wealthy Australian company, Burns Philp and Co., traded for copra, sandalwood and other island products. At the same time, naturally, French interests were penetrating the archipelago. Following the annexation of British New Guinea under Australian pressure in 1885, Deakin, then a leading Victorian politician, had pressed for the annexation of the New Hebrides at the Imperial Conference of 1887. All he achieved was the establishment of a joint Anglo-French naval commission which exercised some loose control over the islands and had the effect of warning other powers off.

As a federal politician speaking for the whole of Australia, Deakin returned to the attack. He feared French designs on the islands: he was urged incessantly by the Presbyterian missionaries, and only less vehemently by Burns Philp and Co., to annex them. In 1901, the Barton Cabinet proved that Australia had indeed become a sovereign state by engaging in the dirty business, always justified by 'national interests', of spying. Two agents, paid secretly out of Commonwealth funds, were sent to the New Hebrides to spy on the French and report on the situation — which they did. For the next six years Deakin bombarded the Imperial Government with increasingly

[9] *C.P.D.*, vol. 33, p.3345.

clamorous demands for annexation. His Majesty's Government, engaged from about 1904 onwards in bringing about a détente with France, was not impressed. It negotiated on the issue without even keeping the Australian Government fully informed of what was happening. Deakin was very angry at being misled, but could do nothing except protest — which he kept on doing. The Anglo-French Convention on the New Hebrides was signed in October 1906. It merely confirmed and elaborated the agreement of 1887 for joint control, known officially as the Anglo-French Condominium, but often called by both French and British island residents the 'Anglo-French Pandemonium'. Deakin may have consoled himself with the thought that, without his determined and long-continued intervention, Britain might well have ceded complete control of the islands to France.

The experience may also have increased Deakin's anxiety to establish formal diplomatic relations with London, so that an Australian representative should be on the spot to press his Government's views on the Imperial Government. For many years before 1901 each colony had appointed such a representative, known as its Agent-General, and these colonial ambassadors continued to represent their States in London after federation: yet the Commonwealth still had no such representative in 1906. The need had always been obvious and indeed most sessions of the Commonwealth Parliament had discussed the question; but action was continually postponed because of jealousy between persons and parties as to how the representative in London should be chosen and who he would be. The enabling Act was finally passed by Deakin's third 'Fusion' Government in September 1909, and G. H. Reid knighted and sent to London as Australia's first High Commissioner. No doubt Deakin chose Reid partly in recognition of his long and distinguished public service, but partly also as a reward for his having stepped down from leadership of the Freetrade Party some months before in order to make the Fusion Government possible. No doubt too he was glad to have Reid, whom he had always disliked, removed to the far side of the earth.

In a few minutes during the last hours of the 1907 session of Parliament, Deakin obtained £5,000 for a national purpose, the long-term outcome of which was far more important than the whole New Hebrides archipelago on which he had expended so much time and trouble. The distinguished Professor of Geology at the University of Sydney, Edgeworth David, had written asking Deakin for help in equipping the British Shackleton expedition, which was about to leave for the South Polar regions. Three young Australians were going with Shackleton. One of them was Douglas Mawson, whose own later explorations in Antarctica did much to give Australia a valid claim to nearly half of that continent.

WHITE AUSTRALIA AND DEFENCE

Deakin's fervent nationalism ensured that he was always concerned with the problem of Australian defence, though he handed the portfolio to colleagues in all his governments. At first Parliament was apathetic on the subject. In 1901 more than three generations had passed since Britain had been involved in a serious war for survival — as opposed to innumerable colonial wars which she usually won, and none of which ever posed a serious threat to her existence. All Australians knew that Great Britain had been incomparably the most powerful country on earth since the Battles of Trafalgar and Waterloo at the beginning of the nineteenth century. Above all, they knew that Britannia ruled the waves, as they vehemently asserted in song whenever inspired by patriotism or alcohol. They also knew Australia to be an island, however large. It was hard for them to believe seriously in the possibility of Britain's defeat in war and so of an invasion of Australia. True, there had been French 'threats' and Russian 'threats', and the German 'threat' in New Guinea since 1883: but all of them had proved to be illusory or transient or at most dormant. No semblance of an actual attack on Australia by a foreign power had actually occurred, and it was hard to think that one ever would as long as the British Navy remained supreme. It was all very well for those who liked soldiering to form volunteer companies and even sail off to the Sudan or South Africa for fun or glory, but it was not very well to pay higher taxes for serious, permanent and large-scale defence establishments. The first federal Parliament reflected truly the national feeling when it refused to take any considerable steps towards setting up an Australian army or navy. Yet three factors at the turn of the century were already beginning to change the massive apathy with which most people regarded the subject of Australian defence: the new fact of political nationhood, the rise of Germany and the rise of Japan.

The need for a co-ordinated system of continental defence had been one of the main arguments in favour of federation. The mere fact of its achievement provided a potent spur towards the organisation of national defence forces. What sort of independent nation was it that had no army or navy worth mentioning? At a more realistic level, Deakin and many others must have asked themselves how they could expect to have any real influence on Imperial policy, for example in the New Hebrides dispute, while Australia was content to leave virtually the entire burden of defence to the mother country. Such considerations were weighty enough to cause W. M. Hughes, J. C. Watson and some other Labor members to advocate compulsory military service and the creation of an Australian navy right from the beginning of the Commonwealth. They received little support however, inside and outside Parliament, except from a few retired military or naval officers: and the aims of the two groups were temporarily parallel rather than identical. Labor men wanted a citizen army strictly for home defence: conservatives usually wanted it to be used overseas in Imperial wars also.

Support for compulsory military training grew steadily, however, during the Commonwealth's first decade. The new century ushered in a period of obviously worsening relations between the great European powers. Commercial, strategic and military rivalry between Britain and Germany built up tension to a level never reached by similar British rivalry with France or Russia since the end of the Napoleonic Wars. The armaments race gathered momentum. From 1901 Germany set out to build a navy equal to Britain's. The launching of the first dreadnought in February 1906 intensified rivalry and fear. The conclusion in 1904 of the *Entente Cordiale* with France made it seem almost certain that Britain would be drawn into the next European war. All these signs and portents affected Australian opinion and increased support for defence projects, particularly among conservatives.

The rise of Japan, however, was very much more influential. Her victory over the moribund Chinese Empire in 1894-95 had demonstrated that Japan was becoming a power to be reckoned with, but most Australians were not unduly impressed. After all, they felt, the Japanese had only beaten another 'coloured' nation. There was nothing unexpected or alarming in that. The British Government assessed the situation more realistically. In 1902 it ended nearly a century of isolationist policies by signing a Treaty of Alliance with the rising power in the East. Each state undertook not to enter separate agreements with other powers without consulting its ally, to remain neutral if its ally were attacked by one other power, but to come to its aid if it were attacked by two or more other powers. The alliance was renewed in 1905 for ten years and again reaffirmed, in 1911, for four years. It was obviously a great addition to British security. It helped to 'contain' Russia, still the 'traditional' nineteenth century enemy of Britain, and it enabled the Royal Navy to concentrate in Atlantic, Mediterranean and Home waters where the German threat was greatest. One small Pacific Squadron of Royal Naval vessels was still to be based in Australian ports, but it could be ordered to sail anywhere at any time by the Admiralty in Britain. By making Japan an ally the treaty should have made Australia feel more secure, but it

Bulletin, 1902

THE MOTHERLAND'S MISALLIANCE

"London, 12th February — The Foreign Office has announced the conclusion of a treaty of alliance between Great Britain and Japan."
BRITANNIA: "Now my good little son, I've got married again; this is your new father. You must be very fond of him."

did not. Very naturally many Australians had a guilty conscience about the rigour and passion with which they supported the White Australia policy. They believed, rightly, that 'coloured' people must resent it bitterly, and they saw that the only 'coloured' people with the industrial and military technology to give effective expression to their resentment were the Japanese who were, moreover, a great deal nearer to Australia than the Germans or Russians. They feared and distrusted Japan no less because she had become an ally of Britain. Some, in fact, feared her more. There were many radical nationalists who feared that the alliance might in fact cause Britain to condone, or at least not to oppose wholeheartedly, Japanese pressure on Australia. Hughes put the majority feeling plainly in a speech in the Representatives in 1906:

> The fact that we should now rely on the Japanese for the maintenance of British supremacy in eastern seas is not calculated to inspire with confidence those who have the ideal of a White Australia, and all that this term connotes.[10]

The greatest single stimulus to the growth of militarism in Australia before the Great War was the Russo-Japanese War of 1904-05. For generations Australians, like other people of European descent, had grown accustomed to thinking of themselves as innately and unalterably superior to 'coloured' people or 'natives'. Yet in this war Japan routed a great European power, and one moreover with much greater reserves of manpower than she could muster herself. Those who had shrugged off the Japanese victory over China ten years earlier were gravely shocked. From the beginning of the war Japanese troops *and* their weapons, training and technology proved superior on every front; but many Australians clung to the belief that no Asian nation could possibly master the highly technical art of war at sea. Then on 27 May 1905 the Imperial Japanese Navy, with trifling losses, annihilated the Imperial Russian Navy in the Battle of Tsushima Straits.

Officially Australia was unmoved or even pleased by the news. Was not Japan Britain's major ally? Most newspaper and other conservative comment was favourable or at least untroubled. But popular and unofficial feeling, often strong even among conservative spokesmen, was deeply anti-Japanese. Proponents of White Australia had always known that Japan, ally or not, was a nearer and potentially graver threat to their security than any or all European nations could ever be. Now, they felt, the threat was no longer

[10]*C.P.D.*, vol. 32, p.2582.

potential but actual. Henry Lawson expressed the real feelings of most of his countrymen in a bad poem published in the *Bulletin* on 15 June 1905:

While the crippled cruisers stagger where the blind horizon dips,
And the ocean ooze is rising round the sunken battleships,
While the battered wrecks, unnoticed, with their mangled crews drift past—
Let me fire one gun for Russia, though that gun should be the last.

. . .

'Tis the first round of the struggle of the East against the West,
Of the fearful war of races — for the White Man could not rest.
Hold them, IVAN! staggering bravely underneath your gloomy sky;
Hold them, IVAN! we shall want you pretty badly bye-and-bye!

Fighting for the Indian empire, when the British pay their debt,
Never Briton watched for BLUCHER as he'll watch for IVAN yet!
It means all to young Australia — it means life or death to us.
For the vanguard of the White Man is the vanguard of the Russ!

In Britain the increased danger of war had inspired the formation of a National Service League as early as 1901. Its president was the Duke of Wellington, its stance was high Tory, and its object was to bring about conscription for military service. No British Labour man would have anything to do with such policies. Opposition to compulsory military service, especially in peacetime, had long been a settled tradition among English-speaking peoples. Yet in Australia, as we have seen, Hughes and some other Labor leaders, as well as a few extreme conservatives, had continually advocated compulsion even in the first Commonwealth Parliament. They were moved by isolation, distance from possible allies, and a much greater degree of racial hatred and fear than British Labor leaders had cause to harbour. Deakin strongly supported their efforts to strengthen Australia's defence forces, but at that time he baulked at compulsion. Tsushima changed his mind and that of thousands of others.

On 5 September 1905 about fifty men gathered in the plushy atmosphere of Sydney's Australia Hotel to found the Australian National Defence League. Captains of commerce, ex-military and naval officers, eminent academics, church dignitaries and belted knights rubbed shoulders with W. M. Hughes, J. C. Watson, E. J. Brady, editor of the Sydney *Worker*, the President of the Trades Hall Association and other Labor leaders. Colonel G. R. Campbell and W. M. Hughes were elected as honorary co-secretaries. The meeting agreed that the League's aim was to do everything it could to secure:

> Universal compulsory training (military or naval) of the boyhood and manhood of Australia for purposes of National Defence, the military training is to be on the lines of the Swiss system, and the naval training on the lines of the British Royal Naval Reserve, modified to suit the local circumstances.[11]

We may be sure that the Labor men were instrumental in having the reference to 'the Swiss system' written into the League's constitution. They all had bitter memories of the 'great strikes' of the 1890s when the colonial Governments had not hestitated to use troops as strike-breakers. Professional soldiers, or volunteers who loved the glamour of bright uniforms, might be so used again by any government: but most radical nationalists believed — or persuaded themselves to believe — that an army based on universal conscription could never be used to intimidate citizens, precisely because it consisted of *all* citizens, or a cross-section of all citizens, under arms. Most would be 'workers' who could never be persuaded to fire on their striking brethren, but who would vigorously defend their homes against foreign invaders. Probably most Labor proponents of compulsion sincerely held this innocent belief, despite a host of evidence to the contrary which was available in 1905, and more which has become available since. It is doubtful whether Hughes did.

Within a few months the National Defence League was publishing a very effective monthly propaganda journal, *The Call*. It was brilliantly edited by the indefatigable Hughes and illustrated by the greatest cartoonist of the day, Norman Lindsay, who was, and remained till his death in 1970, a bigoted racist. *The Call* was sent gratis to all federal politicians and, to judge by the growth of the League, it had considerable influence inside as well as outside Parliament. In September 1906 Deakin declared himself converted to the Labor policy of building a strong Australian Navy, instead of continuing to pay the subsidy of £200,000 per annum to the Royal Navy. Later that year the campaign for compulsion received further impetus from what became known as the 'California Schools Crisis'.

In October 1906 the San Francisco Board of Education capitulated to pressure from white American racists and resolved to segregate Japanese, Chinese and Korean children, who had previously attended common schools with white class-mates, in separate special schools. This was seen by the Japanese as the culmination of a series of insults heaped on them by Californians. It precipitated the most serious crisis up to that time in Japanese-American relations and there was talk of war on both sides of the

[11] L. F. Fitzhardinge, p.221.

Pacific. Public opinion in Australia was probably more inflamed by the implications of the crisis than it was in the United States, outside the State of California. E. J. Brady's comment in the *Worker* of 17 January 1907 was typical of radical nationalist feeling:

> And, once more, the lesson for Australia is, Johnny, get your gun! Also, build ammunition and ordnance factories. Get your people taught to shoot, and generally in a position to put the national back to the wall and fight the wildest wild-cat fight in history; for if he doesn't fight the U.S.A. tomorrow, the chances are the Jap will be picking a quarrel with us the day after tomorrow.

When the crisis subsided President Theodore Roosevelt decided to send the American Battle Fleet to cruise in the Pacific 'not so much [as] a threat to Japan as a demonstration for the benefit of Japan'.[12] Australians generally were delighted and so was Alfred Deakin.

It seems likely that most voters were converted to a belief in compulsion during 1907. Probably, at any rate, Deakin thought they were; for his own long-standing hesitation over military conscription ended. At the end of the parliamentary session just before the Christmas recess, he outlined to the House his Government's new defence plans. The Commonwealth was to create its own local defence navy, consisting of nine submarines and three destroyers, in addition to providing a thousand Australian seamen for the locally stationed squadron of the Royal Navy. Compulsory military training was to provide a nation-in-arms in case of emergency. All able-bodied men between the ages of eighteen and twenty were to be given two or three weeks' instruction annually in rifle-shooting, drill and other warlike arts. Furthermore factories would be set up to make Australia self-sufficient in small arms and ammunition. Generally speaking, liberal and radical opinion applauded the Prime Minister's plan but conservatives and left-wing Laborites were opposed. Military conscription in peacetime they felt to be a shocking break with British tradition. It had not been done 'at Home': therefore it was wrong. On the other hand the Fourth Commonwealth Political Labor Conference, held in Brisbane in July 1908, by 24 votes to 7 wrote Compulsory Military Service into the party's platform.

Meanwhile Roosevelt continued with his scheme for a Pacific cruise by the American Grand Fleet. The British Government, as Japan's ally, was displeased, even alarmed at the possibility of Japan's being provoked into hostility. At the first port of call, in

[12] Thomas A. Bailey, *A Diplomatic History of the American People*, New York, 1955, p.572.

Trinidad in the British West Indies, the British Governor carried out his instructions from the Colonial Office and received the visitors with glacial coolness. From Deakin's point of view in Australia, however, the American cruise was something to be encouraged by every possible means. As the only great 'white' power in the Pacific, the United States should be encouraged to help Australia and to keep an eye on the Japanese. Deakin asked a most unhappy and reluctant Colonial Office to invite the United States fleet to visit Australia; and he forced the Office's compliance by first writing to the American Ambassador in London, and the Consul-General in Australia, asking them to advise the President to accept the official invitation when it came. Australians were enraptured when they heard the news. Britain had abandoned to Japan the main burden of protecting her interests in the Pacific. The United States might replace Britain as a protector. In anticipation of the visit the popular and influential Sydney *Bulletin* on 7 May changed its front page motto from 'Australia for the Australians' to the wider, but equally racist, slogan 'Australia for the White Man'.

The sixteen great battleships, gleaming in their white paint, steamed into Sydney Harbour on 20 August 1908. It was a fine, sunny day in early Spring. Sydney's welcome could fairly have been described as hysterical — or, in some respects, blasphemous. The *Sydney Morning Herald* published a poem by C. E. W. Bean, later to be the official historian of Australia's part in the Great War, which hailed the 'Anglo-Saxon race', which of course included Americans, as God's chosen people. Norman Lindsay painted for the *Lone Hand* a special cover, which showed a great *white* hand reaching down from the sky. It offered to Australia as a great gift a gleaming American battleship, flying 'Old Glory' and ploughing through troubled seas. Newspapers reported that greater and more enthusiastic crowds thronged the streets than on any previous occasion in the nation's history, except for that of the Commonwealth's inaugural celebrations. Innumerable dinners, dances, picnics and private invitations were tendered to the officers and men of the ships and innumerable speeches were made. Admiral Sperry, the American commander, had to speak in reply as many as thirteen times a day. The theme of all the oratory was more or less openly racist. Indeed it was Australians who immediately christened the ships 'The Great White Fleet'. Until the visit Americans themselves had referred to them as the Battle Fleet or the Atlantic Fleet or the Grand Fleet. After a week in Sydney the ships sailed on to Melbourne where the saturnalia was repeated. Before the fleet left for Japan, 221 sailors deserted. Many became prominent Australian citizens.

The visit did much to strengthen support for Deakin's defence Bill. When Parliament re-opened on 16 September, the Governor-General congratulated senators and members 'upon the brilliant success attending the visit to these shores of the great Fleet of the United States'.[13] Thomas Ewing, Deakin's Minister for Defence, introduced the second reading of the Bill. In the ensuing debate Reid tried to discredit the Government by branding the Laborite, Hughes, as 'the real author of the conscription scheme': which he was. Old Sir John Forrest, a survivor from the heroic age of Australian exploration, spoke against compulsion on the ground that it was un-British. Nevertheless the Bill would probably have been passed if political changes had not brought the Government down. As Reid's remark implied, the small number of Protectionist ministers had long relied on Labor support to retain office. Naturally the more numerous Labor members chafed at the situation and wished again to savour the delights of place. Moreover, the recent Brisbane Labor Conference had banned any further parliamentary alliances with non-Labor groups. In November 1908 Andrew Fisher, who had succeeded Watson as leader of the Labor Party, withdrew his support from the Deakin Ministry and was sworn in on the 13th as Prime Minister of another minority Labor Government. Before the year was out, however, Sydney had become the scene of yet another demonstration of racial prejudice and passion, more remarkable in some ways than that occasioned by the visit of the Great White Fleet.

In the Commonwealth's first decade Sydney and Melbourne, though not the other State capitals, were becoming great commercial and manufacturing cities with large slums, poverty, organised crime and all the other evils apparently inseparable from life in a metropolis. Both were infested with larrikins, youths addicted to mischief, hooliganism and often crime. Larrikins affected a singular and ostentatious style of dress, almost amounting to a uniform, and organised themselves in rival gangs or 'pushes'. These were most troublesome and numerous in the last quarter of the nineteenth century and the first quarter of the twentieth. They fought with the police and each other and baited respectable citizens, but they were tolerated and even romanticised by popular opinion. Paterson, Lawson, Furphy and most of the new nationalist writers of the 1890s romanticised bushmen, bush life and bushrangers. With the rapid growth of the cities writers began in the twentieth century to write of city life as well — particularly of 'low life' in the slums and among the 'pushes'. Louis Stone, a Sydney schoolteacher, wrote the first worthwhile novel of larrikin life in an Australian city, though his

[13] *V. & P.*, 1908, vol. 1, p.2.

Jonah was not published until 1911. Similarly C. J. Dennis, a Melbourne journalist and poet, was writing verses about larrikins and city life before they were collected and published in 1915 as *Songs of a Sentimental Bloke*. This book was enormously successful and Dennis, sometimes known as the Laureate of the Larrikin, published many more verses along the same lines. The 'Sentimental Bloke', like most of his countrymen of the time, was passionately addicted to sport, especially racing and boxing.

An actual Melbourne larrikin, John Wren, won a great deal of money when *Carbine* won the Melbourne Cup in 1890. He used it to build up an illegal gambling business in a back lane in the suburb of Collingwood. For many years from 1893 onwards John Wren's totalisator operated in these premises, which were heavily barricaded and guarded. He relied more on bribery and corruption than force, however. Some members of State and federal parliaments were in his pay, as well as large numbers of policemen. By the time of his death in 1953 Wren had acquired great influence in the Labor Party, particularly its Victorian Branch, and with the Catholic Archbishop of Melbourne, Dr Daniel Mannix. He re-invested his profits in horseracing and the promotion of cycling, boxing and other sporting contests. In these latter fields, however, he was far outstripped by a Sydney rival.

Hugh D. McIntosh was an extremely able, tough, ambitious and acquisitive young man who became a powerful entrepreneur, businessman and newspaper magnate. In about 1909, when he and Wren were fighting each other ruthlessly for the control of Australian boxing, by complete chance they shared a two-berth sleeping compartment one night on the Sydney-Melbourne express. The tough McIntosh later recorded his astonishment when the tougher Wren 'knelt down on the floor of the carriage and said his prayers'.[14] As a lad McIntosh worked in the newly opened Broken Hill mines and in a variety of other jobs including that of chorus-boy in several stage shows. By the time he was 25 in 1901 he had made a fortune by catering to the great Australian hunger for meat pies. He bought the pies from a number of bakeries and organised a small army of vendors to distribute them for him at Sydney's racecourses, beaches, sports grounds and parks. By 1915 he wielded such influence that the Labor Premier of New South Wales, W. A. Holman, admitted to a Labor conference that he was 'absolutely bound' to him.[15] By 1908 he was promoting vaudeville shows and sporting contests and

[14] Niall Brennan, *John Wren, Gambler*, Melbourne, 1971, p.244.

[15] Peter Loveday, 'New South Wales', *Labor in Politics . . . 1880-1920* (ed. D. J. Murphy), St. Lucia, 1975, pp.88-91.

he had erected at Rushcutter's Bay, on the site of a market garden, a huge un-roofed, timber boxing-stadium, then the biggest of its kind in the world. Australians were still as keen as ever about sport and, at that time, particularly about boxing. Indeed sporting mania reached its peak in the years before the Great War. McIntosh was confident of recouping his expenditure on the stadium many times over.

On 24 August 1908 the first officially recognised world title-fight to take place in Australia was staged in McIntosh's stadium. A crowd of 17 000 people paid for tickets to see the reigning heavyweight title-holder, Tommy Burns of Canada, knock out his Australian challenger, Bill Squires, in the thirteenth round: but this bout was only a curtain-raiser for what was to follow. In 1908 there had never been a black champion boxer because white champions had always refused to fight against black or brown men. A bout between black and white pugilists in the United States, then the headquarters of professional boxing, was as inconceivable as it would be in the Union of South Africa today. Yet there was a black champion of the world, Jack Johnson of Galveston, Texas. Both he and Burns had suffered only three defeats each in some sixty fights, with opponents of their own colour. McIntosh decided to bring them together.

Burns had repeatedly refused to meet Johnson, but he could not refuse the then record offer McIntosh made him of £6,000 win, lose or draw. Johnson, the black man, had to accept £1,000 plus expenses. No boxing match before or since has ever attracted such interest. The well-known author, Jack London, came to cover the story for some American newspapers. For the first time in Australian history, three or four women (including Mrs London) were admitted to a prize-fight. On 26 December, Boxing Day, 800 kilometres away in Melbourne's Collins Street, traffic was brought to a halt by the milling crowds jostling each other in an attempt to see round-by-round bulletins as they were posted up outside a newspaper office. Johnson was five inches (thirteen centimetres) taller and two stone (thirteen kilograms) heavier than Burns. When he stepped into the ring a storm of booing almost drowned some very faint clapping. Burns received from 20 000 throats a deafening ovation that continued for five minutes. He was beaten in the first round, but Johnson continued to punish him until police put an end to the spectacle in the fourteenth round and McIntosh declared Johnson the winner on points.

Not all Australians followed the fight with the same feelings, though most did. Next day, a Sunday, Rev. Henry Worrall preached in the Bendigo Methodist Church. He described the events at Rushcutter's Bay as a 'carnival of savagery . . .' 'After all the boasting and bragging and betting', he said, 'those twenty thousand raving white Australians beheld their white champion beaten by the despised black man. Racial hatred has been set on fire . . .' Most who read his remarks dismissed them as the croakings of a wowser and a spoilsport; but even the parson himself may have been moved closer to support for compulsory military training, to judge by the implications of another part of his sermon:

> God grant that the defeat on Saturday may not be a sullen and solemn prophecy that Australia is to be outclassed and finally vanquished by these dark skinned people.[16]

[16] Keith Dunstan, *Sports*, Melbourne, p.203.

Chapter 3

LABOR IN POWER

c. 1909 — 1913

The Fusion and the Constitution — Labor comes to power — Labor initiatives — Compulsory voting — Defence and peacetime conscription — Social progress: political stagnation

THE FUSION AND THE CONSTITUTION

Although its implications were not immediately obvious, the swearing-in of the Fisher Labor Government of 1908-09 heralded a new era in Australian politics. Fisher's decision to cease keeping Deakin and his liberal Protectionists in power was the first step in a series of events which, in six months, substituted a two-party system for the 'three elevens' situation that had complicated the first eight years of national government.

Fisher, unlike Watson before him, did not have the job of choosing his own ministers. The Labor Party Caucus decided that it should elect those who were to become cabinet ministers, though the Prime Minister then allotted portfolios among them as he thought best. This procedure has been followed ever since by Australian Labor governments. Fisher chose the ambitious and irrepressible Hughes as his Attorney-General, but even Hughes's fiery energy, in the few weeks left before the Christmas recess, was unable to accomplish anything much beyond the tidying-up of some business left over from the second Deakin Administration. At this time there were actually not three party groupings but four in the federal sphere. Joseph Cook had succeeded Reid as the leader of the conservative Freetrade Party and Sir John Forrest was the unofficial leader of an independent group, most of whom had deserted Deakin's Protectionist Party because of its reliance on Labor support. It was clear to Deakin that he would never again be able to govern with firm Labor backing. During the long parliamentary recess he therefore constructed a coalition consisting of virtually all federal politicians except the Labor members and four radicals among his own followers.

When Parliament reassembled at the end of May, he thus found himself at the head of a united 'Fusion' of all politicians whose ideas were to the right of his own, and opposed to the Labor Party on his left. As he said himself in a letter to his sister, 'behind me sit the whole of my opponents since Federation'.[1] It is not surprising that Labor people as a matter of course, but also a great many others, saw his action as a betrayal of his long-held principles and felt that he would do anything to get office. A new level of bitterness and rancour disfigured the federal Parliament at this time. 'Big Bill' Lyne, who had been Minister for Trade and Customs in Deakin's second Administration, was left out of the Fusionist Cabinet. He never forgave his old leader, greeting him when he entered the chamber with roars of 'Judas!'. W. M. Hughes, however, was the master of vituperation. At the end of a long speech he took up Lyne's suggestion:

> I heard from this side of the House some mention of Judas. I do not agree with that; it is not fair — to Judas, for whom there is this to be said, that he did not gag the man whom he betrayed, nor did he fail to hang himself afterwards.[2]

The Fisher Government was dismissed in a few days and the Fusionist Cabinet sworn in on 2 June 1909. Portfolios were allotted not so much on merit as on the necessity to 'balance' the claims of the different groups which had formed the Fusion. Deakin of course became Prime Minister of his third Government. His old friend Forrest was Treasurer and Cook Minister for Defence. For the first seven weeks bitterness was such that debates were continually interrupted by interjections. Lyne had sworn to hound Deakin to his political grave. He was particularly disruptive and Parliament accomplished little. On 22 July 1909, in a speech on the tariff, Lyne made a particularly savage attack on Deakin, which provoked interjections and recriminations from both sides of the House. The storm raged all night with the much-respected Speaker, the South Australian Sir Frederick Holder, moderating the tumult more effectively than any other member could have done. At five o'clock in the morning he fell forward on to the floor. Those nearest heard him mutter 'Dreadful! dreadful!' as he lost consciousness to die in his room a few hours later. Members were quietened somewhat by this dramatic incident.

In 1909 federal government 'machinery' was still being set up. Interesting Acts of this sort passed by the Fusion Government were the Seat of Government Acceptance Act, the Coinage Act and the

[1] J. A. La Nauze, *Alfred Deakin*, 2 vols, Melbourne 1965, vol. 2, p.573.
[2] *C.P.D.*, vol. 49, p.175.

High Commissioner Act. The first finally fixed on the Canberra district, in the foothills of the Southern Alps in New South Wales, as the site of the future federal capital. The second authorised minting of an Australian silver and bronze coinage to replace the British coins in use up to 1909. The third made it possible to provide G. H. Reid with the much-prized job of Australian envoy in London, in reward for his action in stepping down from the leadership of the Freetraders to make way for Cook — which deed, in turn, because of Deakin's hatred of Reid, had made the Fusion possible. Labor members vigorously opposed the passage of the High Commissioner Bill precisely because they suspected the job was to be Reid's. The Fusionists also amended the Commonwealth arbitration process by a further Act providing penalties for employers who dismissed employees because of activity in trade unions, and for employees refusing to work for employers because of their activity in employers' associations.

Early in 1909, while Parliament was in recess during Fisher's first brief Administration, Germany had announced the building of thirteen dreadnought battleships to be completed by 1912. The news gave rise to something like panic in Britain and accelerated the armaments race. The Admiralty at last consented to the Australian plan, initiated by Labor and more latterly pressed forward by Deakin, for building its own fleet — provided that the Australian ships would come under central Admiralty control in time of war. The Naval Loan Act authorised the Government to build with loan money in the United Kingdom a fleet consisting of one heavy battlecruiser, three light cruisers, six destroyers and three submarines. Labor and a few independent members opposed the legislation because they wanted the estimated cost of £3,695,000 to be met from revenue and the ships to be built in Australia.

The Defence Act of 1909 passed into law the principles which had been canvassed during Deakin's second Prime Ministership; yet its passage in September was not so much a triumph for him as for W. M. Hughes, the tireless Labor member for West Sydney. Since the first Federal Parliament met in 1901 he had campaigned ceaselessly inside the House and outside for universal compulsory military training. At first he had been almost alone, even in his own party, but time and events had conspired with Hughes's arguments, and with the guilty fears engendered in men's hearts by their commitment to the White Australia Policy, to convert almost all politicians — though not so many of their electors — to a belief in conscription for home defence. The Act provided for this and for the continuance of voluntary enlistment for any overseas service. There was little opposition in Parliament. Hughes criticised the Bill because

PRELIMINARY TO OUR DEFENCE

it did not go far enough. Some conservatives among Cook's followers were successful in shortening the compulsory training periods which had been canvassed in the previous year. They wished to minimise inconvenience to employers who might prefer profits to the loss they expected to sustain while their employees were being trained in their patriotic duties. In any case the actual details of the Act were subject to alteration when it came to be implemented. Deakin had invited the leading Imperial soldier, Lord Kitchener, to visit the Commonwealth to report on the state of its defence forces.

Deakin himself regarded the Financial Agreement of August 1909 between the Commonwealth and the States as the greatest achievement of his third Administration. Those who know how hard it has been, before and since, to secure *any* agreement between the Commonwealth and all of the States, must agree with him. Under the 'Braddon clause' of the federal Constitution, the Commonwealth was to hand over to the States three-quarters of its receipts from all customs and excise duties, but only for the first ten years. From the end of 1910 the Commonwealth Parliament was free, under the clause, to determine without reference to the States what moneys, if any, it should grant them. There had been many previous conferences about the problem but all had been abortive. At the Melbourne Conference in August, Deakin, Cook and Forrest met the State Premiers and secured their agreement to a scheme whereby the States would be paid twenty-five shillings per head of population annually from Commonwealth revenues. The meeting was held behind closed doors, but it seems that the Premiers, as the price of their assent, demanded that the agreement be written into the Commonwealth Constitution. Accordingly Deakin brought before Parliament a Constitution Alteration (Finance) Bill which, in the end, was passed by only one vote. Labor members, and a good many of those who usually supported the Fusion Government, did not object strongly to the twenty-five shillings *per caput* payment but they thought it little short of madness to make this specific arrangement virtually unalterable for all time by writing it into the Constitution. The purchasing power of money had been so stable for so long that few members worried about the possibility of inflation. A related measure giving the Commonwealth power to take over State public debts incurred since Federation, the Constitution Alteration (State Debts) Bill, was passed without opposition.

Under the Constitution both Acts, to be effective, had to be approved by an absolute majority of people and by a majority of the electors in a majority of the six States. Both questions were accordingly put to the people in a referendum, held concurrently with the general election for the fourth Commonwealth Parliament, which took place on 13 April 1910. The State Debts proposal was approved and the Constitution thereby amended accordingly, but the proposal to make payment of twenty-five shillings per head to the States a part of the Constitution in perpetuity was narrowly defeated. Nevertheless, successive governments made this in fact the basis of their relations with the States until post-World War I inflation began to be seriously felt in 1927. The election of 1910 gave a decisive victory in both Houses to the Labor Party. It is pertinent to ask why.

LABOR COMES TO POWER

It is a truism to notice first that social-democratic parties, professing to stand especially for the interests of employees in capitalist societies, were born, grew in influence and sometimes achieved power in western European societies generally (including Australia and New Zealand but not the United States of America) between about 1890 and 1940. There are many obvious and associated reasons for this — the growth of free, universal education systems in the second half of the nineteenth century, the increasing need for a literate and educated workforce in increasingly complex technological societies, the formulation and spread of socialist ideas, and so on; but before the Great War the Australian Labor parties, at both Commonwealth and State levels, advanced further and faster than other such reformist parties elsewhere.

The basic reason for this is that Australia was a new country in which social-democrats, radicals and reformists had relatively little to push against. There was no hereditary aristocracy, no established or state church, no traditionally sanctioned and entrenched conservative class as in older countries. Extreme conservatives were a self-appointed minority who differed usually from their neighbours in wealth, but less often in taste, manners, refinement, education or 'breeding'. Indeed many well-known Australian reactionaries notoriously lacked such attributes, while many radicals and liberals, like Deakin, Higgins, Holder and Watson possessed them. As a distinguished British visitor, John Martineau, said of the late colonial period, Australian 'society is like English with a thick slice cut off the top and a thin slice off the bottom'.[3] There were few members of the Fusion or Liberal Party in 1909, for instance, who would not have been more at home in the contemporary British Liberal Party than in the Conservative Party. The fact that the whole political spectrum stood further to the left than in other countries around the turn of the century is evidenced by the then common description of Australia,

[3] Geoffrey Serle, *The Rush to be Rich*, Melbourne, 1971, p.6.

not usually in irony, as 'the working man's paradise'. The term was freely used even in the 1890s, before Labor had been able to form even a minority government anywhere;[4] and it was applied equally to New Zealand which led all the Australasian colonies in welfare-state legislation, but which was slowest to develop strong political Labor activity.

This interesting difference springs partly perhaps from the different composition of the two populations. In New Zealand about 12 per cent of the people were Roman Catholics. In Australia as a whole the Catholic population was double that. The vast majority of them were people of Irish descent and by 1910 nearly all Australian Catholics were Labor voters. This is not to say that the Labor Party in Australia is, or ever was, a Church party on the European model or a party controlled by the Catholic Church: it is to say that, until a decade after the Second World War, Labor politicians, whether Catholic or Protestant or even agnostic, could usually rely on 'the Catholic vote'. Catholic opinion leaders, lay and clerical, usually assumed that Labor was the party through which they might exercise political influence. There were many reasons for this.

First, as Catholic spokesmen themselves used constantly to point out in the nineteenth century, most Irish-Australians were wage-earners in unskilled or semi-skilled occupations. When the Labor Party, with its gospel of ameliorating the conditions of the masses, began soliciting votes in the 1890s, it was as natural for most Catholics to comply as it was for many Protestant manual workers: and this they did, despite early exhortations to the contrary by some members of the Catholic hierarchy. At first many senior clerics feared, or assumed, that Labor would be atheistic, communistic, revolutionary and even anti-clerical. Thus the two Catholic papers published in Sydney, the *Freeman's Journal* and the *Catholic Press*, both opposed Labor until 1901 when they began to support it. Some clerics, however, including the most senior of all, Moran, Australia's first cardinal, strongly supported the Labor Party almost from its inception. Having satisfied themselves that it was essentially a law-abiding reformist body, with not the smallest intention of taking to the barricades, they pointed out to the flock that many of Labor's social policies coincided with the ideas for social justice propounded by Pope Leo XIII in his 1891 encyclical *Rerum Novarum*. They believed that social justice demanded the restoration of 'state aid' to church-controlled education. Labor was as opposed to state aid as every other political grouping, but most Catholics hoped that perhaps

[4] Anderson Dawson was Premier in the first (minority) Labor Ministry to take office anywhere — in Queensland from 1 to 7 December 1899.

one day they might have enough influence to bring about a change in the party's policy. They could see little hope of influencing the other parties very much on this or other issues.

Labor's nationalist stance also attracted the support of Irish-Australians. From the very beginnings of settlement, people of English or Scottish descent often thought local Australian patriotism was 'disloyal' because, they felt, it tended to weaken loyalty to Britain and the Empire. For Irish Catholic people, with their bitter memories of English rule, the growth of Australian nationalism was to be encouraged for this very reason. Their spiritual leaders fostered the tendency for Irish-Australians to be more nationalist than anyone else because they felt attachment to the new land might help to mollify the bitter, often seditious, feelings towards Britain so many continued to harbour. Even the Catholic Englishman who became Archbishop of Sydney, John Bede Polding, at the mid-century was already urging his Irish-descended flock to forget old-world hatreds by becoming loyal sons and daughters of their new land. In doing so, he coined, or at least used, the slogan 'Australia for the Australians' some thirty years before the *Bulletin* flew it at the masthead. Labor's nationalist stance embraced a cooler and more critical attitude than that of conservatives towards Imperial adventures in general, and overt and avowed support for the cause of Irish Home Rule. Moreover, Labor leaders stressed their party's neutrality in religious questions — a neutrality which tended in practice to be friendly to Catholics because they were still, to some extent, a disadvantaged minority, often discriminated against by employers in the competition for work, and in some other ways. Add to this that the more conservative political parties were generally quite strongly Protestant in their orientation and increasingly influenced by the nonconformist 'wowser vote', and it is hardly surprising that by 1910 the alliance between the Catholic Church and the Labor Party was firmly established.

In the election campaign of early 1910 Fisher promised that Labor, if elected, would impose direct Commonwealth taxation for the first time: not, one would have thought, a very popular measure, even though it was to take the form of a land tax designed to 'break up the big estates'. He formally committed Labor to a protectionist fiscal policy and advocated the creation of land and sea defence forces 'made in Australia'. The Fusionist Party spoke with differing, and sometimes flatly contradictory, voices on many issues as its component parts had not yet composed all their differences. Deakin wished, for instance, that his followers should be known as the Liberal Party, but many of them disliked the name because of its past association with Deakin's Protectionist Party and most continued, as did the newspapers, to refer to themselves as Fusionists. Under these circumstances the result should not have been surprising. Labor had been gaining support steadily since the inception of the Commonwealth.

In 1901 it received 13.5 per cent of the votes cast for the Senate, 30 per cent in 1903 and 39 per cent in 1906. Indeed it was the fear of Labor victory in the 1910 election which had driven the Protectionists and Freetraders into their marriage of convenience and, seemingly, disgust at this manoeuvre among some electors played a part in the Labor victory. In the election on 13 April Labor obtained just over 50 per cent of all votes cast for the Senate and all 18 Senate seats being contested, giving a House of 22 Labor to 14 Fusionist senators. In the Representatives Labor won 41 seats and the Fusion thirty-one. There were three independents of whom two usually supported Labor and one the Fusion. In a speech a few days after the election, Cardinal Moran publicly exulted that 'the wowsers' had been beaten. It was the first time in the history of the Commonwealth that there was a Government with an absolute majority in either House, let alone in both; and it was the first time in the history of the world that a social-democratic party had achieved such a position.

The new Prime Minister, Andrew Fisher, was an ex-coalminer who had emigrated from his native Ayrshire in Scotland to Queensland in 1885. He was then 23 years old. He continued to work at his trade in Australia. He was soon elected to an offical position in the Miners' Union and in 1893 was sent by the electors of Gympie to the Queensland Parliament, being Secretary for Railways and Public Works in the short-lived Dawson ministry of 1899. At the first federal election he won the seat of Wide Bay and held it until his retirement fifteen years later. Though he had read well in politics and economics, Fisher was a self-educated man whose greatest admirers would hardly have called him brilliant. Indeed his party colleagues had elected him to the leadership on Watson's retirement, passing over the mercurial Hughes, for quite other qualities. He was cautious, shrewd, slow-thinking, but sensible in his canny Scottish way and above all patently sincere, hard-working and dependable. His public speaking was clear and vigorous. He believed that the moderate, reformist Labor ideals he held so sincerely were best for the whole nation as well as for its working class. A remarkably handsome man, clean-shaven but for a heavy moustache, he easily maintained the dignity of the prime-ministerial role. Unlike Deakin, he actually enjoyed dressing for formal occasions in top hat and frock coat. Motor cars were becoming more common and Fisher ordered a Renault for official use. Not for him the greater dignity of simple tram-travel which had sufficed for Deakin. Fisher was Treasurer as well as Prime Minister.

His most interesting Cabinet colleagues were Hughes, the Attorney-General, Senator G. F. Pearce, Minister for Defence, Frank Tudor, Minister for Trade and Customs, Senator McGregor, Government Leader in the Senate, and the Minister for Home Affairs, King O'Malley.

The economic outlook favoured the new Government. Since 1906 seasons had been generally good and the man on the land had prospered accordingly; but the building and manufacturing industries were expanding even more rapidly. Between 1901 and 1913 the total national production doubled in value — at a time when the value of money remained practically constant. Despite the growth of secondary industry in the capital cities, most people retained the traditional belief in the overwhelming importance of primary production, and State Governments spent much money on building more railways to service the wheat industry. They also devised schemes for providing small settlers with land and expert advice on easy terms, and all State Governments revived the assisted migration schemes which had been largely abandoned during the great depression of the 1890s and the great drought of 1895-1902. Indeed, the feeling among working people that they were not getting their just share of the country's increasing wealth was one of the reasons for the Labor victory. Many workers resented their taxes being used to bring out poor British migrants to compete on the labour market when the estimated unemployment rate was still 5.6 per cent of trade union membership. Amid the returning prosperity there was much industrial strife.

During the previous year the powerful Broken Hill Proprietary Company had locked out its mine workers for several months in an attempt to lower their wages. The men went to arbitration and Mr Justice Higgins brought down a judgment favourable to them, only to have it set aside, on appeal by the Company to the High Court. In the Hunter River coalfield there was a bitter miners' strike from November 1909 till a month before the election, when it was settled, largely on the employers' terms and mainly by the efforts of the ubiquitous W. M. Hughes.

It is small wonder that some militant workers began at this time to heed the teachings of the Industrial Workers of the World. Commonly known as the I.W.W. or 'the Wobblies', and founded in Chicago in 1905, they differed from most revolutionary Marxists in the heavy stress they placed on strike action and violence. In their view politicians, parliaments, courts and arbitration were all created by the capitalists to trick or terrify the workers. Salvation lay in strengthening and extending trade union activities until there was only 'One Big Union', which would then overthrow the state and set up a workers' government. For about fifteen years from 1907 the I.W.W. was a good deal more influential in Australia than in the land of its origin, certainly more so than such doctrinaire left-wing sects as the Socialist Labour Party. Nevertheless the extent of its influence should not be exaggerated — as it invariably was by all kinds of conservative spokesmen who saw 'Wobblies' lurking furtively behind every strike. Naturally the new Government went further in legislation on industrial relations and social welfare than Deakin's Governments had been willing to, though it cannot be said that, in the long run, strikes decreased as a result.

LABOR INITIATIVES

The Conciliation and Arbitration Act of 1910 formally gave the Court power to fix the minimum wage, to give preference to trade union members 'other things being equal', and to call *compulsory* conferences of the parties to an industrial dispute. It extended the Court's jurisdiction to cover domestic servants and pastoral and agricultural workers, while another Act brought to all public servants employed by the Commonwealth the possibly questionable benefits of arbitration. Other laws provided compensation for workers injured in federal employment or in federal territories and for seamen engaged in interstate trade. The new social service legislation which, at the time, most angered conservatives was the Maternity Allowances Act of 1912. Thereafter mothers were paid a 'baby bonus' in a lump sum at the birth of each child. There was to be no means test and many wowsers felt that the measure would put a premium on what they called 'immorality'. Even more shocking to traditionalists were Labor's land tax and banking legislation. Most newspaper editors, bankers, squatters and merchants, but not apparently the majority of voters, saw both as rampantly 'socialist' measures; but with the large Government majority in both Houses they were unable to negate or weaken the relevant bills.

The Land Tax and Land Tax Assessment Acts of 1910 imposed a graduated scale of taxation on the unimproved capital value of all land in the Commonwealth above the value of £5,000. The avowed aim was to 'break up the big estates' and so, indirectly, to help more 'small men' to settle on the land. This had been the stated aim of almost all colonial land legislation since 1861. What was new and upsetting to conservatives was the method, that of direct Commonwealth taxation of land, and the fact that it was done by a Labor Government. They need not have worried so much. The impost had very little effect on the rate of subdivision of big country properties. Indeed the owners of city land were soon more affected by it than country proprietors; but it did provide a continuing, relatively painless and very welcome source of revenue to the Government and all its successors. Labor's banking and financial measures, since they were seen to affect everybody and not just rich landowners, proved even more alarming in prospect and sensible in practice. Some of the distress in conservative breasts sprang from the widespread belief, at least partly erroneous, that Labor's financial bills were the brainchild of the Minister for Home Affairs, King O'Malley, probably the most bizarre character ever elected to the Commonwealth Parliament. The Commonwealth Bank Bill, in particular, was loudly claimed by him.

No one knows exactly when or where O'Malley was born, but it was probably between 1854 and 1858, of Irish parents, and in Canada or the United States. He grew up in the latter country and worked for some time in a bank of which an uncle was the manager. He tried his hand at several other kinds of business and migrated to Australia in the late 1880s. After a short stay in Queensland he set up as a land agent in Adelaide. In 1896 he was elected to the State House of Assembly on a remarkable platform which included the banishing of barmaids from hotels, the provision of lavatories in South Australian trains and the legitimisation of bastard children whose parents subsequently married. What is more remarkable, all three aims were achieved. Although South Australia produces most of the wine in Australia, for more than fifty years after O'Malley passed that way the sinful stuff had to be served by men dressed like undertakers in black alpaca coats. Trains still have lavatories and unmarried parents may still legitimise their offspring by subsequently marrying each other.

O'Malley was elected as an Independent to the first federal Parliament for a Tasmanian seat which he held till 1917. He soon joined the Labor Party, not so much because he agreed with its policies as because he hoped to use it to forward some of his own schemes. He habitually addressed other males, no matter what their status might be, as 'brother', and liked to be known himself as 'the bald-headed eagle of the Rocky Mountains'. He boasted that, in order to avoid taxation in the United States, he had created a mythical religious organisation, 'the Waterlily, Rock-bound Church of the Redskin Temple in the Chickasaw Nation'.[5] In short, O'Malley was something of a confidence-man and more than something of a buffoon. He irritated Hughes, himself an expert in

[5] *A.E.*, vol. 6, p.401.

playing to the gallery, and infuriated the staid Fisher who set such store by the dignity of the Government; but he was also intelligent, courageous and persistent. If some of his hobby-horses, like his total condemnation of alcohol, were idiosyncratic, others, like his advocacy of a Commonwealth Bank, were both wise and practical.

There is continuing controversy about O'Malley's part in the bank's founding. There is no doubt that he was the first person to put such a plan to the Labor Party — at the Brisbane conference of 1908 — that he continued vociferously to push the proposal forward and, until he died in 1953, to claim credit for its achievement. There seems to be little doubt either that the actual form of the legislation, and still more the uses to which the newly-established bank was actually put, owe more to Fisher and Hughes, acting on 'expert' technical advice, than to the 'bald-headed eagle'. Set up in 1911, the Commonwealth Bank carried out all usual trading and savings bank business on a competitive basis with the private banks. It was managed by a single governor, appointed by the Government and nominally responsible to Parliament, and it was immediately and continuously successful. It never attempted, as O'Malley and some other left-wing Laborites would have liked, to drive the private banks out of business, and it did not for many years assume most of the functions of a central state bank; but it was instrumental in the issuing for the first time of a single national currency which considerably increased the financial strength of the Commonwealth. The Commonwealth Treasury issued banknotes against a minimum gold reserve of 25 per cent of the notes in circulation. Notes issued by private banks were driven out of existence by the imposition of a tax on them.

Because of its large and stable majority, the Labor Government enjoyed power as well as office. It was therefore able to implement several useful, national, non-party measures, some of which had been promised by many preceding governments but never carried out. It actually started the building of the national capital at Canberra. As Minister for Home Affairs O'Malley called for designs from all over the world. The competition was won by a great American architect, Walter Burley Griffin, and Canberra, in 1976 a city of about 200 000 people, was built basically to his design. In its early days 'giggle-juice', as O'Malley called all alcoholic beverages, was banned from the Federal Capital Territory and residents had to travel about eleven kilometres to the neighbouring New South Wales town of Queanbeyan for a drink.

In 1911 the Commonwealth also took over from South Australia the administration of the Northern Territory, over one million square kilometres of country, most of it desert or semi-desert. It has been estimated that the area supported about 35 000 Aboriginals before the arrival of European settlers from about 1860 onwards. In 1911 there were perhaps half that number left, many of them still living the traditional tribal life, but some working for European pastoralists and mining prospectors among the 3310 people of European, Asian or mixed descent. South Australia had constructed in 1872 the overland telegraph line to Darwin which first gave Australia instant communication with Britain and the rest of the world; but the State had not the human or financial resources to develop the area, and was glad to hand over responsibility to the Commonwealth. The Fisher Government built 320 kilometres of railway link (still uncompleted) between Darwin and the South under the Pine Creek to Katharine Railway Survey Act of 1912. It also actually began the construction of the famous trans-continental railway line between Port Augusta and Kalgoorlie which, when finished in 1917, linked Western Australia with the rest of the Commonwealth. Sir John Forrest, the conservative 'father' of Western Australia, and the larrikin radical, O'Malley, must for once have been equally pleased by the same thing. In 1913 the Commonwealth completed the process of taking over mail services from the States by issuing the first Australian postage stamps to replace those issued by each State.

Despite its control of both Houses Labor was not able to go as far as it wished along the road to the complete welfare state. The Commonwealth Constitution, or more accurately the interpretations of it already pronounced by conservative-minded judges, strictly limited federal power over trade, commerce, wages and prices, conditions of work and other matters of vital interest to social reformers. The Workers Compensation Act of 1912, for instance, could apply only to the Commonwealth Government's own employees and to all employees in Commonwealth territories (then Papua, the Northern Territory, and the Federal Capital Territory) but not to the vast majority of citizens. To remedy this situation the Fisher Government passed eight Constitutional Amendment Bills through Parliament only to have all its proposals rejected by the people at two subsequent referenda.

The first question asked for Commonwealth power over all (not just interstate) trade, commerce and industry, power to control all wages and conditions of employment, to arbitrate on all industrial disputes and to control all business combinations and monopolies. The Fusionists campaigned against the proposals, fearing that Labor would use them if they were granted, to centralise control in federal hands and to 'socialise' the country. The second question asked electors specifically for the power to nationalise monopolies. The referendum was held on 16 April 1911 and resulted in a decisive negative in all States except Western Australia — which favoured both proposals. Perhaps this was an augury of things to come. Six months later, in October, West Australians elected their first majority State Labor Government led by John Scaddan.

Perhaps, too, the Government thought, people had voted 'No' to be safe, because they were confused about the different and quite complex powers asked for in the first question. Something might yet be won if the electors were given an opportunity to vote on each requested power separately. Accordingly the people voted at another referendum held concurrently with the general election of May 1913. Substantially the same powers were asked for but in six questions instead of two. Again the answer was 'No', but there were substantial 'Yes' majorities in Queensland, South Australia and Western Australia. The latter two States had elected their first majority Labor Governments in 1910 and 1911 respectively. Queensland was to do so four years later. Since the circumstances of this State election finally affected all Australian elections, we shall examine it in some detail.

COMPULSORY VOTING

Compulsion to vote at parliamentary elections has been universal in Australia since 1942 when South Australia adopted the practice. It is almost unknown in other democratic countries and, indeed, seems to most people in the world an undemocratic practice. Most Australians accept it as a matter of course, exhibiting, in this and other ways perhaps, what some observers have called a faith in 'compulsory democracy'; but how did it come about?

Towards the end of 1914 a Liberal Government was ruling Queensland but a State election was due in May 1915. The recent federal election of September 1914 had shown a strong 'swing' to Labor in Queensland and many other portents seemed to suggest that the State's first majority Labor Government might be returned. Liberal politicians generally believed that, while many of their supporters did not trouble to vote, nearly all Labor supporters did because, thought the Liberals, the Labor Party was so much more tightly disciplined and well organised than their own extra-parliamentary organisation was. In desperation they passed two electoral laws, one designed to keep as many potential Labor voters as possible away from the polls and the other to drive their own supporters to them. In 1913 the Queensland electoral law was amended to require that, to be placed on the electoral roll, a citizen had to have a permanent home in the electorate and live continuously in it for two months prior to the election. This Act effectively disfranchised a great many shearers, fencers, cane-cutters, carriers, prospectors, stockmen and other nomadic rural workers who usually voted Labor. Then in November 1914 J. G. Appel, the Home Secretary, introduced another Bill requiring all registered electors to cast their votes under pain of being fined up to £2. The leader of the 'Country Liberal' Party, Lieutenant-Colonel C. D. W. Rankin, said during the debate:

> We are going to have compulsory legislation and compulsory voting . . . because [as things are] . . . the dishonest exercise of the franchise by one individual might bring . . . such a terrible catastrophe as putting a Labour [sic] Government into power.[6]

Reading between the lines of the debates it is clear that the Labor politicians did not object particularly to the introduction of compulsory voting as such. They may even have suspected it would be to their advantage, despite the contrary belief of the Liberals. They did, of course, object most strenuously to the amendment of 1913. The discreditable manoeuvres did not have the result the Liberals hoped for. Queensland's first majority Labor Government was elected in May 1915 with T. J. Ryan as Premier, and Labor stayed in power until the great Depression; but compulsory voting had come to stay. The voters never objected to being driven to the polls and it saved all political parties and politicians a great deal of money, time and effort, which otherwise had to be spent in 'getting out the vote'. It was introduced in Commonwealth elections in 1924, in Victoria in 1926, in New South Wales in 1928 and in South Australia in 1942, by anti-Labor governments. Labor administrations introduced it in Tasmania in 1928 and in Western Australia in 1936.

DEFENCE AND PEACETIME CONSCRIPTION

In its first year of office the Fisher Government resolved the decade of argument about national defence forces by implementing the long-standing Party policy for the creation of a separate Australian Navy and the not so long-standing policy for the introduction of compulsory military training for home defence. The relevant bills were introduced by the Minister for Defence, G. F. Pearce, who had been one of Hughes's earliest converts to the idea of compulsion.

The son of a blacksmith, Pearce was born at Mount Barker in the

[6] G. Atkin, *The Introduction of Compulsory Voting in Queensland, 1914* (B.A. Hons thesis, University of New England, 1967), p.18.

Mount Lofty Ranges near Adelaide in 1870. After some elementary schooling he became a farm-boy at the age of twelve and was then apprenticed to a carpenter for five years. He became a fully qualified tradesman in the depth of the depression of the early 1890s. As there was no work to be had he joined the gold rush to Western Australia, like so many other South Australians (and Victorians) of the time. He had no luck at gold-digging but found plenty of work at his trade. He became a prominent figure in the young Western Australian Labor movement and was elected to the Senate at the first federal election of 1901. He remained a senator, though not a member of the Labor Party, until he lost his seat in 1937. Pearce began as a most 'moderate' Labor man and, like nearly all humans, grew more conservative as he grew older. He greatly admired Deakin and learnt much from him about literature as well as from wide reading of his own. Sensible, humane and quietly spoken, he was yet an effective public speaker, ably seconded by his wife who sometimes, at open air meetings, silenced persistent interjectors by attacking them from the rear with her umbrella.[7] He also had the foresight to establish an aviation training school at Point Cook, Victoria, before the outbreak of the Great War. This was in effect the beginning of the Royal Australian Air Force. He was knighted in 1927.

The Naval Defence Act of 1910 established a Naval Board, responsible to the Minister for Defence, to administer the new fleet. Ships had already been ordered. The destroyers *Parramatta* and *Yarra* arrived from Britain in September. By the time war broke out in 1914 the Royal Australian Navy comprised these and the *Warrego*, shipped out in parts and assembled in Sydney, the light cruisers *Melbourne* and *Sydney*, two submarines and a battle cruiser, the flagship *Australia*. The navy was popular with almost everybody. It was manned entirely by volunteers, enlisted for periods of at least some years' continuous service. There was in it nothing at all of the element of compulsion on which the citizen army was based.

The Fusion Government's Defence Act of the previous year had not been put into operation pending Lord Kitchener's report on Australian military defence. This was submitted in February and its recommendations differed surprisingly little from those of the 1909 Act except for one important addition. Kitchener strongly recommended the establishment of a military staff college along the lines of the United States' West Point Academy. For the rest, his recommendations were that, with the exception of certain categories such as clergymen, magistrates, policemen, members of parliaments,

[7] The writer's maternal grandfather, who went to Western Australia at about the same time and for the same reasons as Pearce, twice witnessed such incidents.

and those with religious objections to bearing arms, all physically fit Australian males were to undergo compulsory military training as follows:

Age Group	*Name*	*Period of Training per Year*
12 to 14	Junior Cadets	120 hours
14 to 18	Senior Cadets	16 days or equivalent
18 to 20	Recruit Trainees	16 days, 8 of which to be in camp
20 to 25	Trained Soldiers	6 days in camp
25 to 26	Trained Soldiers	Muster Parade only

The prestige of the Imperial war-lord was so immense that there was never any real doubt of his recommendations being implemented. The only substantial change concerned the military staff college. Kitchener had recommended that cadets should be charged a fee of £80 per annum. Even Hughes baulked at this *élitist* idea, and Labor egalitarianism ensured that entry to the Royal Military College at Duntroon was free (though competitive), and that cadets were paid a living allowance sufficient to support a young man from even the poorest family. Inside and outside Parliament most articulate people had come to support compulsion. A great many reasons, or rationalisations, were advanced, not least among them the ancient platitude that military training makes men out of boys and gentlemen out of larrikins; but the greatest single underlying reason undoubtedly was fear of Japanese (or other Asian) reaction to the White Australia Policy. As Pearce said in the Senate, though the Labor Party believed in international arbitration, they were realists. He continued:

> Is Japan or China prepared to arbitrate with us about our Immigration Restriction Act? And, even if they were prepared to arbitrate on that question, of course, we are not.[8]

A few left-wing Labor members like the recently elected Victorian, Frank Anstey, were obviously unhappy about the Bill, but none made any real attempt to oppose its passage. So Australia became the first English-speaking country in the world, at least in modern times, to enforce compulsory military service in peacetime, and the Fisher Government the first Labor government ever to do this.

Events during the next three years showed that the Government had misjudged popular feeling. Nearly all members of Parliament,

[8] *C.P.D.*, vol. 56, p.1672.

newspaper editors, and other leaders of public opinion, including a good many trade union officials, were in favour of compulsion but it was soon evident that a great many Labor voters and quite a number of more conservative people were not. Except for the legal compulsion on parents to send their children to school, Australians had not known such regimentation since convict times — and then, as a contemporary observer put it, 'nothing [could] induce them to enter into the army, nor take office in the police.'[9] Penalties fixed under section 135 of the Act were very severe. The minimum fine for evasion of his military duties by a boy or man was £5, and this could be increased up to £100 at the discretion of the magistrate. In 1912 £5 was more than a basic-wage earner received for two weeks' work. Complaints flowed in to members of Parliament and in 1912 Pearce amended the Act so as to make £5 the maximum fine: but this had no effect in stemming the tide of evasion, criticism and protest.

Tens of thousands of ordinary citizens broke the law but articulate and organised opposition came almost entirely in the first instance from two kinds of people: radical socialists and Christian pacifists. Broken Hill and Newcastle, scenes of the recent bitter industrial troubles, were centres of working-class disaffection. Some of those who voiced opposition were members of the Labor Party, some of various revolutionary sects like the I.W.W. and some members of no particular organisation. The first two parents to be charged with preventing their sons from registering for training were both radical socialists. Henry Holland was editor of the Sydney *International Socialist* and a leading trade-union militant well known in both the Newcastle district and Broken Hill. Alfred Giles was a journeyman butcher in the latter city. Holland vigorously proclaimed his own guilt, stating publicly that:

> . . . it amounts to teaching boys to do murder for a class purpose . . . Roy [Holland's son] has no choice whatever in the matter, and while he is under 21 years of age I shall firmly refuse to allow him to take any part whatever in the abominable military crimes . . .[10]

He was fined the maximum of £100, or three months' hard labour, but left for a lecture tour of New Zealand without paying or going to prison. Perhaps the Government was glad to be rid of him. He became leader of the New Zealand Parliamentary Labor Party

[9] E. S. Hall to Sir George Murray, *Historical Records of Australia*, I, 14, p.580.

[10] T. W. Tanner, *The Introduction of Compulsory Military Training in Australia* (Ph.D thesis, University of New England, 1968), pp.391, 392.

from 1919 till his death in 1933. Giles went to gaol but was released on a technicality, in an appeal to the Supreme Court of New South Wales, brought by the Broken Hill Branch of the Australian Miners' Association.

The Rev. A. Madsen, a Victorian Methodist minister, and several members of that Society of Friends, usually known as Quakers, which has consistently opposed war since the seventeenth century, were also fined but preferred to serve gaol sentences. At Easter 1912 a number of Adelaide Quakers took the initiative in forming the Australian Freedom League to oppose compulsion. Branches were formed in all States and they became increasingly influential in all sections of the community. Still, it is a surprise to find that the person elected President of the New South Wales Branch at its inaugural meeting on 24 May 1912 was none other than Colonel James W. Macarthur-Onslow, M.L.A., Commanding Officer of the First Light Horse Brigade of New South Wales and a great grandson of John Macarthur of Camden, a founder of the Australian wool industry.

It is hardly less surprising to find thoroughly respectable middle-class organisations like the South Australian branches of the Women's Christian Temperance Union and the Young Women's Christian Association, joining the campaign against compulsion. Lady Holder, widow of the first Speaker of the House of Representatives, led a deputation of women's organisations to protest to the Prime Minister when he visited Adelaide in May 1913. South Australia was the centre of activity against the Defence Act, probably because of the heavily nonconformist nature of its population (about 55 per cent compared with about 30 per cent for Australia as a whole in 1911). It was also the Australian centre of wowserism. Some of the opposition to compulsory training sprang from parents' fears that their boys would be corrupted in the army by drink, gambling and profligacy. In the three years from 1 July 1911 to 30 June 1914, 27 749 prosecutions were launched under the Defence Act. Most resulted in fines for those charged, but 5732 persons were punished by imprisonment in military gaols. There can be little doubt but that the compulsory military training would have been dropped if war had not broken out in 1914.

SOCIAL PROGRESS: POLITICAL STAGNATION

The Great War showed, among other things, the stage reached in the development of communications technology. Motor vehicles were used for ambulances and sometimes for other purposes such as the transport of high-ranking officers, but common soldiers had to walk

Smith's Weekly, 1930

WOWSERS

or travel by bicycle or train. Cavalry units were still used in the Middle East, the Ukraine and other theatres of war but not after the first few months of fighting in France. Horses were used to haul heavy artillery pieces into position and for all other heavy work. Similarly, in Australia during the pre-war years taxis were beginning to displace horse-drawn cabs, but heavy or bulky goods were still moved by horses and wagons. Private cars were becoming common among the rich, but in the country nearly all farm and station work was still done by horses. In the outback motor vehicles were barely beginning to replace coaches for the transport of passengers and mails. When the war began aircraft of any kind were still rare in Australia, although, as we have seen, George Pearce had had the foresight to begin an air arm of the Defence Department. The first air-race in Australia, from Botany to Parramatta (two Sydney suburbs) and return, took place in June 1912 between an Australian, W. E. Hart, and an American known as 'Wizard' Smith. Hart won by default. It was a very windy, turbulent day and Smith refused to take off.

Telephones and typewriters were hardly novelties any longer. The Commonwealth Post Office installed its first automatic telephone exchange at Geelong in 1912. Typewriters, usually operated still by male clerks, were invading most business offices. Gramophones were still something of a novelty. Wireless telegraphy came to Australia during those years, though it affected people's daily lives not at all until after the war was over. Between 1910 and 1914 the Government constructed several stations, at Sydney, Perth and other points on the coast, capable of maintaining communication with ships at sea. One of the earliest practical uses of wireless took place in connection with the Australian Antarctic Expedition of 1911-1914 led by Dr Douglas Mawson, the young man who had served his apprenticeship to Polar exploration with Shackleton.

Born in England in 1882, Mawson came to Australia with his parents as a child. Educated at the University of Sydney, he carried out a geological survey of the New Hebrides when only 21 years old in 1903. Two years later he was appointed to a lectureship in Mineralogy and Petrology at the University of Adelaide, where he remained for the rest of his life — apart from the years spent in field work and Antarctic exploration. While still quite young he was appointed to the Chair of Geology. He married a daughter of G. D. Delprat, a Dutch mining engineer who became managing director of the Broken Hill Proprietary Company in 1898. In 1911 he organised an Australian-New Zealand Antarctic expedition, finance being provided by the Commonwealth Government, some State Governments and private donations including a munificent one from Samuel Hordern, proprietor of a large Sydney department store.

Macquarie Island is a bleak, rain-soaked piece of land about 1600 kilometres south of Tasmania and the same distance north of the opposite coast of Antarctica. In December 1911 a five-man party established there a wireless and meteorological station to keep in touch with the explorers. The expedition surveyed about 1600 kilometres of the continent's coastline and penetrated about 500 kilometres inland to the South Magnetic Pole. On one journey B. E. S. Ninnis disappeared into a crevasse with the sledge and practically all of the provisions. Exhibiting tremendous stamina and willpower, Mawson just managed to walk back to the base but the third member of the party died of exhaustion. Between 1929 and 1931 Mawson led a combined Australian-New Zealand-British expedition to the Antarctic. Frank Hurley's photographs provide a magnificent pictorial record of both expeditions and Mawson published *The Home of the Blizzard*, a considerable piece of literature as well as a record of exploration.

In 1911, however, the name of Norman Brookes meant more to most Australians than that of Douglas Mawson. The son of wealthy parents, he was sent to Melbourne Grammar School where be became a tennis champion. In the 1890s this did not mean much. Tennis was regarded as a rather milk-and-water game for genteel people, not to be compared with manly sports like boxing, football, cricket, rowing and so on. In 1900 an American, Dwight F. Davis, gave a handsome trophy for international competition by amateur tennis teams. Australians hardly knew of the existence of the Davis Cup until Norman Brookes and a New Zealander, Anthony Wilding, won it for Australasia in 1907. Under the rules the final round must be played in the country currently holding the Cup. When the match took place in 1908 tennis was no longer in public estimation a second-rate sport. In fact contemporaries compared the occasion with the annual running of the Melbourne Cup. The vast crowd of spectators included the Governor, the Chief Justice and the Premier of Victoria, Sir Thomas Bent, the coarse-grained, fervently nationalist son of an ex-convict from Penrith, New South Wales. Brookes and Wilding beat the American challengers in 1908 — and 1909 and 1910 and 1911. By that time Australians considered themselves the world's greatest tennis-players.

When the Fisher Government's three-year term of office drew towards its close early in 1913 it is probable that Brookes's name meant more also to most Australians than that of Joseph Cook. Since stepping down from the Prime Ministership in 1910, Deakin's health had failed. Gradually the deputy-leader of the Fusionists, Joseph Cook, assumed leadership of the Opposition which, by 1913, had become generally known as the Liberal Party. Cook was one of the first of a long line of Labor politicians who, prompted by conscience or self-interest, deserted their party for what was often a more distinguished career in the ranks of its enemies. Thereafter they were usually regarded by radicals in Australia as 'Labor rats' and by conservatives as unusually honest and far-seeing politicians. Born in Staffordshire, England, in 1860, Cook, like Fisher, was a coalminer. He began work at the age of nine, migrated to New South Wales as a young man, and worked for about five years in the mines at Lithgow before being elected to the Legislative Assembly in 1891 as the Labor member for Hartley. When in 1894 a party conference demanded from all candidates a pledge that they would vote in parliament as decided by the majority of Labor members in Caucus, Cook refused, left the party and was soon made Postmaster-General in George Reid's Freetrade Government. He entered Federal Parliament in 1901 as the member for Parramatta and held the seat for twenty years. We have seen how he succeeded Reid as leader of the Freetraders and then succeeded Deakin as leader of the Fusion-Liberals. He was perhaps a competent debater: otherwise there is no reason to dissent from Professor F. Alexander's characterisation of him as 'a dull, heavy plodder', lacking any suggestion of wit or brilliance.[11] The two ex-coalminers led their respective parties into the election campaign of May 1913.

Fisher promised to increase still further protective tariffs for Australian industries. It was no longer politically feasible to advocate reduction of tariffs but Cook, who had been a Freetrader before he became leader of the Liberal Party, promised to set up a Tariff Board to examine and report upon any proposed new duties. However, the election itself was overshadowed in the public mind by the referendum proposals which were being voted upon on the same day, 31 May. As we have seen, the electors rejected Labor's request for greater Commonwealth powers. They rejected also, though only by the narrowest of margins, the party which had proposed them: and so a dull, heavy plodder became Prime Minister of Australia for a little over a year. He chose the old Western Australian conservative, Sir John Forrest, as his Treasurer and an ex-Premier of Victoria, known as 'Iceberg' Irvine, as his Attorney-General.

The Cook Liberal Government achieved very little during its term of office because, like so many of its predecessors, it was a government that held place, but hardly power. In the House of Representatives it held 38 seats to the Labor Party's thirty-seven. Thus, after providing a Speaker and a Chairman of Committees, the Government had only equality with the Opposition and every

[11] F. Alexander, *Australia Since Federation*, Melbourne, 1972, p.18.

July 17, 1913.

POLITICAL ODDMENTS.

The merest glance at the New Federal Ministry inspired one with the idea that, compared with their predecessors, they were a team of able men, capable of doing their duty.—Daily paper slobber.

An impression of the Front Treasury Bench, House of Representatives, July 9, 1913.—(Left to right) Little Willie, Mister Groom, Penny-Stamp Wynne, Irvine (the cool strong man), Sir Bigjohn, Paddy Glynn (the humorist), and Mister Cook (who supplies the necessary gloom).

The Worker, 17 July 1913

contentious bill depended on the casting vote of the presiding officer. Worse, from the Liberals' point of view, was the position in the Senate where Labor had 29 seats to the Government's seven. Thus the few laws enacted were generally of an essentially non-party, administrative nature, like the Norfolk Island Act, which transferred responsibility for the island to the Commonwealth from New South Wales. Since 1856 it had been inhabited by some descendants of the *Bounty* Mutineers moved by the British Government from Pitcairn Island, which was no longer large enough to support the population.

The Government sought to resolve its difficulties by a 'double dissolution' of both Houses of Parliament. Section 57 of the Constitution provides that if a bill, twice passed by the Representatives with an interval of more than three months between the two third-readings in the Lower House, be twice rejected by the Senate, the Governor-General may, on the advice of his Prime Minister, dissolve both Houses and hold a new election to resolve the deadlock. The Liberals therefore devised a bill which they thought the Labor majority in the Senate would be certain to reject, but which would embody a principle popular with the electorate at the subsequent election. The Government Preference Prohibition Bill sought to revoke Labor's recent legislation of preference to unionists in granting Government and some other employment. It was duly rejected by the Senate. Cook asked the Governor-General for a double dissolution which, after some hesitation on the latter's part, was granted on 4 June 1914.

At first the issues raised in the election campaign were rather reminiscent of those in its predecessor. Fisher promised more social services, including government assistance for orphaned children, higher protective tariffs where necessary and government or co-operative organisations to assist primary producers with credit and marketing arrangements. Cook proposed preferential voting arrangements and a system of proportional representation for the Senate. Stealing a plank from Labor's platform he also proposed constitutional amendment to give the Commonwealth power to deal with oppressive monopolies. He wanted to change the method of controlling the Commonwealth Bank, to put the Post Office under a Commission, and so on. But all such questions were brushed aside by the outbreak of the Great War on 4 August 1914. Virtually everyone took it for granted that Australia would be at war as an integral part of the Empire. In a much-quoted speech made in Victoria four days before war broke out Fisher said, 'But should the worst happen after everything has been done that honour will permit, Australians will stand beside our own to help and defend her to our last man and shilling'. Cook was expressing, though less eloquently, similar sentiments on behalf of the Liberal Party. The main, almost the only, election issue became, 'which Party do you want to entrust with Australia's destiny during her first great war?'. The electors answered by a majority vote for Labor candidates in every State of the Commonwealth. The Fisher Government was returned with 42 seats in the Representatives to 32 for the Liberals and one Independent. As a result of the double dissolution all 36 Senate seats had been contested. Labor won 31 of them.

Chapter 4

AUSTRALIANS AT WAR

c. 1914—1919

The first A.I.F. and Anzac — Events on the home front — Conscription for overseas service? — Politics, war and the second referendum — Monash, Hughes and Versailles

THE FIRST A.I.F. AND ANZAC

In the *Official History* of Australia's part in the Great War, Ernest Scott wrote that at its outbreak 'the two party leaders . . . were in harmony upon the vital issues of the hour, and the henchmen on both sides were in complete agreement with them'. Other historians have generally repeated Scott's picture of all the people and politicians of Australia being initially united in support of the war effort. If this were true it would be quite astonishing that a majority of Australians, sometimes described by their opponents as 'pro-German', should have voted, little more than two years later, against conscription for overseas service. It is true of course that all Liberal politicians, a majority of Labor politicians and a large majority of the people wholeheartedly supported the war; but there was a minority, very small at first, of Labor men inside and outside Parliament and of men and women who voted for them, which, though by no means pro-German, opposed the war itself on revolutionary Marxist, or Christian pacifist or humanitarian grounds. As the war dragged on, as casualty lists mounted, as living standards at home deteriorated — and as Britain became embroiled in the bloody suppression of the Irish nationalist movement — this minority gained more and more support, though it never approached majority status.

There were five Labor members of the House of Representatives — King O'Malley, Frank Anstey, W. G. Higgs, J. Matthews and F. Brennan — and three Queensland senators, Ferricks, Mullan and Stewart, who from the beginning made no real secret of their anti-war views. In October 1914 the most outspoken of them, one of John Wren's *protégés*, Frank Anstey, passionately denounced King Albert of the Belgians and the war itself, as a sordid struggle between rival groups of capitalists for the commercial and industrial supremacy of the world. 'What a mockery to call this curse of war the upholding of civilization,' he concluded.[1] The fact that four of the five dissident members of the Lower House, including Anstey, were re-elected in 1917, shows that quite a large number of people agreed with, or at least complacently tolerated, these anti-war views. In the first months of the war, however, their influence on events was almost negligible. The Governor-General, Sir Ronald Munro-Ferguson, cabled London describing the 'indescribable enthusiasm and entire unanimity throughout Australia' for the Empire's cause.[2] Most contemporary observers would have agreed with this assessment.

On 7 August, three days after the formal beginning of hostilities, the Cook Government received a cable suggesting that Australian forces might destroy or seize three German wireless stations in the Pacific — at Rabaul in German New Guinea, at Yap in the Caroline Islands and at Nauru. A mixed naval and military force of about 1500 men was hurriedly assembled, and joined by a citizen-force battalion which had volunteered in Townsville. These North Queenslanders never reached New Guinea however, because the stokers on their transport refused duty. Apparently they belonged to the small minority of dissenters opposed to the war. After only eleven days training on Palm Island, in the Barrier Reef near Townsville, the remainder of the force, escorted by H.M.A.S. *Australia* and three destroyers, reached New Britain and captured Rabaul. Two Australians were killed and five wounded in the token resistance. On 17 September the German Governor signed a capitulation promising not to resist British occupation of all German possessions in the Pacific except Samoa. The German island of Nauru, fantastically rich in phosphates, was occupied on 6 November. Britain's Japanese allies had been even quicker to occupy Yap — and other German Pacific possessions north of the equator.

On the same day that the German surrender was signed in Rabaul, the third Fisher Labor Government was being sworn in in Melbourne. As before, Fisher was Prime Minister and Treasurer, Pearce Minister for Defence and Hughes Attorney-General. After little more than a year, however, in October 1915, Fisher retired to the calm of the High Commissionership in London and Hughes became Prime Minister; but long before this Hughes's ability and his demonic energy had made him the main force in the Government.

Born in London to Welsh parents in 1864, William Morris Hughes claimed to have had no knowledge of the English language until he was six. He received a good secondary education, was a

[1] *C.P.D.*, vol. 75, p.148.

[2] F. K. Crowley (ed.), *A New History of Australia*, Melbourne, 1974, p.312.

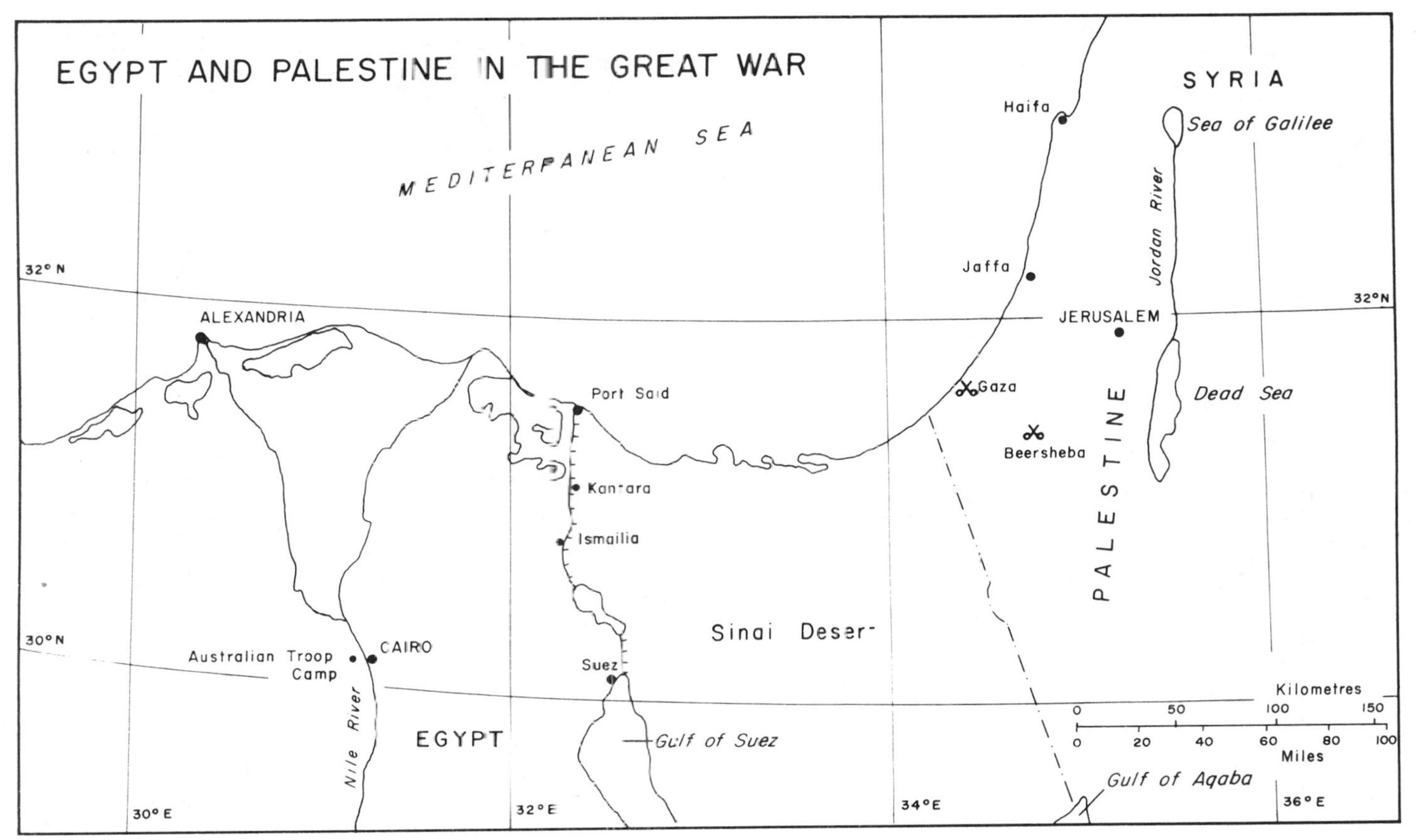
EGYPT AND PALESTINE IN THE GREAT WAR
MEDITERRANEAN SEA
SYRIA
Sea of Galilee
Haifa
Jordan River
Jaffa
JERUSALEM
Dead Sea
Gaza
Beersheba
PALESTINE
ALEXANDRIA
Port Said
Kantara
Ismailia
Sinai Desert
Australian Troop Camp
CAIRO
Suez
Nile River
EGYPT
Gulf of Suez
Gulf of Aqaba
Kilometres
0 50 100 150
0 20 40 60 80 100
Miles
32° N
30° N
32°N
30° E
32° E
34° E
36° E

student teacher for a time and left for Australia, the 'land of opportunity' at the age of twenty. For a few years in the 1880s he 'roughed it' in Queensland and New South Wales, working as, among other things, a fettler on the railways, drover, boundary-rider, seaman, pantry-man, fruit-picker, shearer, actor, tally-clerk, and steward. By 1890 he was the proprietor of a shop in the Sydney waterside suburb of Balmain, where he sold second-hand books, locks, umbrellas and other goods. During the 'great strikes' of the early 1890s he became secretary of the Wharf Labourers' Union and later president of the nation-wide Waterside Workers' Federation. He was one of the founders of the Labor Party in New South Wales and was elected to the Legislative Assembly in 1894, before transferring to the Commonwealth Parliament in 1901. Meanwhile he found time to study law and became a King's Counsel in 1904. He was a convinced and consistent believer in centralising power in the federal government and, as we have seen, at once the greatest Labor man, the greatest Imperialist, the greatest nationalist and the greatest militarist in the country. Even Hughes's energy could not indefinitely sustain all these policies, mutually contradictory as they were in some respects, but when the break came during the war it was his party and not himself that lost place and power. Skinny and gnome-like in appearance, from his Queensland days onward he suffered from chronic dyspepsia and deafness — which exacerbated his already irascible nature. Unscrupulous, sardonic, immensely able and immensely witty, he became a legend in his own lifetime. Even his worst enemies were half-charmed by his murderous wit, the sheer effrontery of his opportunism and the broad larrikin streak in his character. He enlivened the House of Representatives continuously from 1901 till his death at the age of 88 in 1952. Except for the legendary nineteenth-century bushranger, Ned Kelly, and the greatest Australian politician of the twentieth century, R. G. Menzies, no other Australian, not even any sporting hero, is so well remembered, if not exactly honoured, as 'Billy' Hughes.

The outgoing Liberal Government had already placed the Australian Navy at the disposal, for the duration of the war, of the British Admiralty and had offered to recruit, train and equip an expeditionary force of 20 000 men. Such was the enthusiasm for the war that this target was reached by the end of August and over 50 000 volunteers were in training by the end of the year. Some joined to defend Britain and the Empire and some to defend Australia in the fields of France, but none seem to have thought it possible that the interests of the two countries might not be identical. Many of these early volunteers rushed to the recruiting offices because they regarded the war as a great adventure in which they wished to share, and they feared it might be over before they could reach the scene of battle. One man rode his horse 740 kilometres to Oodnadatta and thence travelled by train to enlist in Adelaide. Rejected there he took ship to Hobart, was rejected again, but finally succeeded in passing the medical examination in Sydney. By the end of the war more than 330 000 volunteers had actually sailed for Europe or the Middle East as soldiers in the Australian Imperial Force. The total number of enlistments, including those in the Australian Flying Corps but excluding those in the Navy, was 417 000 — out of a total Australian population of approximately 820 000 men of military age in 1914.

The first commander of the A.I.F., as the expeditionary force soon came to be known, was Major-General Sir W. T. Bridges who had served with distinction in the Boer War and had been, since 1911, first commanding officer of the military training college at Duntroon, near Canberra, where a small professional staff for the Citizen Army was taught. At the outset he established the principle that Australian troops were to retain their own identity throughout the conflict and not to be distributed among larger British units as they had been in South Africa. Showgrounds and sportsfields were commandeered and training camps set up near the capital city in each State. The men were armed with ·303 rifles produced at the Government's small arms factory in Lithgow, New South Wales, and dressed in heavy boots, khaki puttees, trousers, tunic and the slouch hat with the left-hand brim swept back and pinned to the crown, which was thereafter to be the distinguishing mark of the Australian soldier. In the training camps they learnt to fight, as the future was to show, and they learnt, under protest, to drill, to present arms and so on, but some never learned to salute — a manoeuvre they regarded as undemocratic and demeaning. They formed the most democratic army, though not quite in the way envisaged for so long by 'Billy' Hughes, to exist since tribal days. Four years later in France a British soldier serving in a unit on the Australian flank wrote in his diary that they

> were the roughest of the rough, had no discipline at all, but were among the finest fighters in the world.[3]

Thirty-eight ships, loaded with about 20 000 troops, met in the beautiful natural harbour of King George's Sound at Albany in Western Australia. On 1 November they steamed out to sea,

[3] Michael Moynihan (ed.), *People at War 1914-1918*, Melbourne, 1973, p.130.

OFFICER [recently transferred]: **In the unit I came from batmen WERE batmen!**
FED-UP BATMAN: Well, yer can't be sure of any dam' thing in this outfit. Sometimes yer find an officer IS an officer; sometimes 'e's a plain —.

Smith's Weekly, 1933

escorted by H.M.A.S. *Sydney*, H.M.A.S. *Melbourne*, and a British and a Japanese cruiser. The men had been destined for England and the Western Front, but Turkey had just entered the war as Germany's ally. Lord Kitchener, now Britain's Secretary of State for War, asked that the 'colonial' force should be diverted to Egypt. As Agent-General in London, G. H. Reid cabled his fears that many men would be disabled by sickness if they sailed straight from Australia into the middle of an English winter: and so they were diverted to Egypt — for training and to strengthen Britain's hold on the Suez Canal. On the way a message from the wireless station on the Cocos Islands informed the convoy that the German raider, *Emden*, was sending a landing-party ashore. *Sydney* raced to the scene and destroyed the *Emden*, which had sunk scores of thousands of tons of allied shipping in the three months of war. It was a small victory — *Sydney* could outrange and out-speed the *Emden* — but it was Australia's first, greeted with unrestrained jubilation all over the country.

In Egypt the main Australian camp was placed at Mena, almost in the shadow of the Great Pyramid, which the troops climbed — and defaced by scratching their names on the uppermost stones. After the first few days of sightseeing they grew bored and bloody-minded with the flies, the heat, the desert and the repetitive training drills. They had come to fight, not for this. They broke camp *en masse*, got drunk and raced through the streets of Cairo on donkeys or pirated tram-cars. It was not uncommon for more men to be absent without leave from a unit than to be on duty. They sneered at the inhabitants as 'Gyppos' and at Egypt as the 'land of sin, sand, shit and syphilis'. On Christmas Eve 1914 they stole the motor car of their British commanding officer, General Birdwood, from outside his headquarters and took it to their camp. A few days before they left for Gallipoli a rumour spread that some Australians had been stabbed in the Wasser, Cairo's brothel district. There followed immediately a vast riot. Harlots, bullies, beds and furniture were thrown into the street and several buildings were fired and demolished. British military police attempted to arrest the Australians but retreated baffled. One account says an Arab boy was run down by a car-load of rioters. At last on 1 April all leave for the Australian and New Zealand Army Corps was cancelled. The First Lord of the Admiralty, Winston Churchill, had devised a plan for forcing the entrance to the Black Sea.

By the first months of 1915 the war on the western front had settled down to something like a position of stalemate. From Switzerland to the North Sea, all through the fair fields of France, the rival armies had dug a continuous double line of trenches, from which they shot at and raided each other. About seven million men died, but the position remained virtually unchanged for nearly four years. From the first days of the war Russia, the main ally of Britain and France, was under severe pressure from the central Powers on her west and from Turkey in the south. The only ice-free, all-weather ports through which munitions and other supplies could be shipped to Russia were on her Black Sea coast, and these could be reached only if the allies could force the Straits of Constantinople and, it was hoped, in the process knock Turkey out of the war. British and French forces were to land at Helles at the foot of the Gallipoli Peninsula and the Australian and New Zealand Army Corps under Bridges was to land sixteen kilometres to the north. The two armies were then to join, crushing the Turkish defenders between them, and so the Allies were to dominate the peninsula and the entrance to the Sea of Marmara. It was a good plan but in the event one that failed from insufficient allocation of resources and a good measure of bad luck.

In the half-light of early dawn on 25 April 1915 thousands of Australia's best and bravest young men scrambled on to the beach in what was to be known thereafter as Anzac Cove. In the face of murderous Turkish fire from prepared positions at the top of the ridge, they clawed their way up the steep hillside and dug in. By the end of the day they had gained a beach-head about 800 metres deep and withstood a heavy Turkish counter-attack, led by the man who was to modernise Turkey after the war, Mustapha Kemal; but they had suffered over 1000 casualties. Among the dead was Captain J. P. Lalor, a grandson of the miners' leader at the Eureka revolt in 1854. About a month after the landing on 19 May thousands of Turkish soldiers attacked the Australian positions. They lost over 10 000 men killed or wounded for 160 Australian dead and 468 wounded. A few days later an eight-hour truce was arranged to bury the Turkish dead. The soldiers fraternised, exchanging cigarettes, photographs and jokes. Thereafter 'Johnny Turk' or 'Jacko' was held in respect, even a sort of affection, by the Australians as a brave and resourceful soldier who played the game hard but fair. After eight months of slaughter, for no appreciable military gain, the Anzacs were ordered to withdraw. More than 10 000 Australian and New Zealand soldiers, including General Bridges, as many French and nearly three times as many British troops had been killed.

The Anzac withdrawal constitutes one of the most successful stratagems in the history of warfare. For three days not a shot was fired from the Allied trenches. Thereafter periods of vigorous and noisy military activity were alternated with further, though shorter, periods of silence — to which the enemy became quite accustomed.

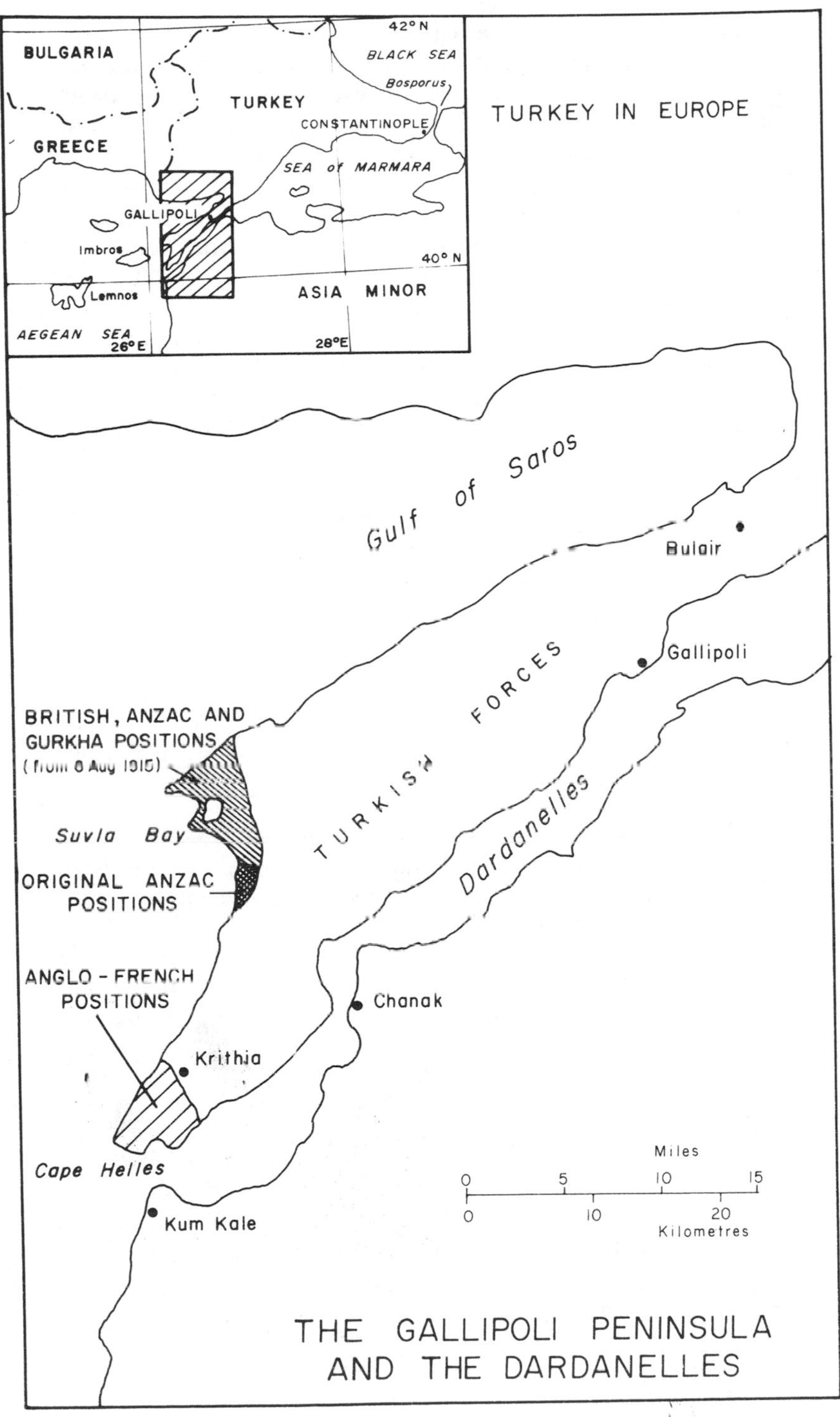

THE GALLIPOLI PENINSULA
AND THE DARDANELLES

In two nights just before Christmas 1915, 20 000 men were embarked in transports and shipped away under cover of darkness. A rearguard of about 1 500 men retreated from trench to trench on the second night, firing as they did so, and also embarked safely, leaving behind them a few rifles rigged to fire intermittently, some land-mines and booby-traps. The whole operation cost only two casualties. So history was made by a glorious failure. At Anzac Cove Australians had shown the whole world — and themselves — that they could fight as well, or better, than the men of any other nation, including England itself: something most of them would not have believed before 1915. Profane, drunken and undisciplined they remained, but they had passed the test of battle with first class honours. The British commanding officer in Egypt, General Sir John Maxwell, wrote privately in October 1915 to his compatriot, the Governor-General of Australia:

> The men are splendid as fighters, the best the world has seen! No words can overpraise them. In the trenches their discipline is excellent, for they see the reason why! but here in Egypt . . . the men do not see the necessity for either training or restraint.[4]

At home grief and pride struggled for mastery in many breasts. Enlistments in the A.I.F., which had slackened in the early months of the year, shot up again after the news of Anzac. A Navy chaplain, Father Gibbons, summed up what had happened, writing in retrospect that:

> the events of Anzac morning were written in red fire in the brains of the men who took part, in black and bitter grief in the hearts of the bereaved, and in gold across the consciousness of the new nation of Australia born that morning.[5]

Or a new nation had been baptised in blood, as some had it. But for all the pride and posturing, the war had ceased to be a great adventure. Soldiers abroad and civilians in Australia knew, after Anzac, that a long, bitter struggle lay ahead.

EVENTS ON THE HOME FRONT

At home the Government had passed, in the first months of the war in 1914, two very important Acts which armed it with emergency powers for the duration of the war and six months thereafter — the

[4] W. L. Gammage, *The Broken Years*, Canberra, 1974, p.124.

[5] Mary Wilson, 'The Making of Melbourne's Anzac Day', *A.J.P.H.*, vol. 20, no. 2 (August 1974), pp.197-209.

Trading with the Enemy Act and the War Precautions Act. The first, with the Enemy Contracts Annulment Act of the following year, made it a criminal offence to trade in any way with enemy firms or persons and gave the Government power to proclaim as such, transactions it deemed to be in breach of the legislation. The second Act and successive amendments to it was so wide in its scope as virtually to clothe the Government with dictatorial powers. It authorised the Governor-General in Council, in effect the Government of the day, to make regulations 'for securing the public safety and the defence of the Commonwealth'. Such regulations had the force of law, but were not usually subjected to parliamentary examination. Members accepted the assurance of the Attorney-General, W. M. Hughes, that these sweeping powers were necessary in the unprecedented wartime situation. Some of them, and of their constituents, later had cause to regret their acquiescence. Regulations under the Act established a strict censorship of newspapers, letters and other forms of communication, and penalised 81 specific offences such as exhibiting a red flag, showing disloyalty to the British Empire, or spreading rumours likely to cause alarm. In the Royal Hotel at Tumbarumba, New South Wales, a drunken countryman said it was a capitalists' war and should be fought by the capitalists. He was fined £100, a labourer's wage for about nine months, and would have been sentenced in addition to six months' gaol but for the fact that his son was in the trenches at Gallipoli.

The Commonwealth's power to do almost anything it wished by regulation, under the general authority of the War Precautions Act, was confirmed by an important High Court decision in June 1916, in what came to be known as the 'bread case'. Under the federal Constitution all power in matters of defence belonged to the Commonwealth so that, in wartime, it seemed likely that the national government could override State rights in almost any field by pleading the overriding exigencies of national defence. The Labor Party had been by no means chastened by the referendum defeats of 1911 and 1913. A 1915 Interstate Party conference decided on yet another attempt to secure the federal powers twice refused by the people. However Hughes persuaded the party that it would be better to have the State Premiers 'refer' to the Commonwealth the desired powers, mainly control over prices and business. What is even more surprising, he also persuaded the Premiers to refer most of the powers for the duration of the war and one year thereafter. Then the agreement was nullified by attacks on it from some of the undemocratically constituted State Upper Houses. The Commonwealth meanwhile had fixed the price of bread by regulation under the War Precautions Act. The validity of the regulation was challenged in the High Court by a master baker but upheld by the Court, Mr Justice Isaacs stating that, if any connection whatever with national defence [in wartime] could be established, 'the Court must hold its hand and leave the rest to the judgment and wisdom and discretion of the parliament and the Executive it controls'.[6] This decision meant that the national government, as the framers of the Constitution had probably intended, was virtually omnipotent in wartime.

Labor policy had long been to pay for defence out of current taxes rather than by borrowing, but it became obvious early in the war that no amount of taxation would cover the enormous expenditure involved. Though the State governments were all behind the war effort, they showed little inclination to curtail their spending on internal development and public works. So the Commonwealth borrowed heavily, both in Britain and from its own citizens, and also introduced a range of new taxes. Some economy was achieved by avoiding competition on the London money market. Soon after Hughes took over as Prime Minister on 27 October 1915, all States except New South Wales agreed that the Commonwealth should be responsible for all overseas public borrowing. New South Wales fell into line in 1918. Over £180,000,000, an immense sum in those days, was raised from internal loans. Much of it was subscribed in instalments by quite poor men and women. When war broke out Commonwealth revenue came from only two sources, customs and excise duties and the land tax on large estates. Customs and excise continued to provide funds and the incidence of land tax was increased sharply, lands held under lease from the Crown becoming liable, as they had not been before the war. Death duties were imposed for the first time; deceased persons' estates, if more than £ 1,000 in value, were taxed on a sliding scale of from 1 per cent to 15 per cent. An entertainment tax imposed a levy of one penny on admission charges of between sixpence and a shilling to all public entertainments such as the moving-picture shows — which were becoming extremely popular. Most drastic of all, as it seemed at the time, was the imposition of a Commonwealth income tax, with steeply graded rates, on all who earned more than £156 a year — that is, about £20 more than the basic wage at the time. The tax on £156 was just under £12.

To the miseries of higher taxation and other wartime hardships, there was added another for the citizens of all States except Queensland and Western Australia — six o'clock closing of hotels and other licensed premises. Nonconformist churchmen and women

[6] Zelman Cowen, *Isaac Isaacs*, Melbourne, 1967, p.168.

and been pressing for the prohibition of alcohol and, failing that, the curtailment of drinking hours, for many years before the war broke out. In every State the Women's Christian Temperance Union was a formidable propagandist body which applied pressure to politicians of all parties though, as we have seen, non-Labor parliamentarians were usually more amenable to the demands of the temperance advocates. The war greatly strengthened the temperance campaign. Many people felt that abstinence from alcohol was a small sacrifice to make when soldiers were giving their lives on the battlefield. Just how greater sobriety among civilians would contribute to victory was not always clear, but after King George V announced, at the beginning of April 1915, that he was becoming a total abstainer for the duration of the war, it seemed disloyal not to follow suit. As always in matters relating to the 'wowser vote' at that time South Australians led the way. Even before the King's announcement, on 27 March 1915 they had voted by almost 2 to 1 for six o'clock closing of hotel bars. In Victoria the Government shut the bars at six o'clock by a Temporary Restriction Bill in 1915 with amendments a year later. 'Temporary' proved in fact to mean fifty years. Tasmanians also voted for six o'clock closing in a plebiscite.

In New South Wales the Holman Labor Government bade fair to withstand the pressure for early closing, but its hand was forced as a result of the mutiny by A.I.F. men in training at Liverpool Camp near Sydney. The commanding officer rashly increased hours of drill to just over forty a week. On 14 February 1916, 5000 troops refused duty, broke camp and were joined by some 10 000 other soldiers from nearby camps. They looted two hotels in Liverpool, commandeered trains to Sydney and spent the day drinking, rioting and looting in the city. One soldier was shot dead by military pickets at Central Railway Station. Within a few days the men all returned to duty, and the old hours of drill were restored; but the temperance forces naturally used the incidence to reinforce their arguments. The plebiscite was arranged for 6 June 1916. On the preceding day confused reports of the Battle of Jutland reached Sydney and the Anglican Archbishop Wright announced, 'In this solemn hour of the Empire's need every true patriot should vote for 6 o'clock closing'.[7] A large majority did.

Six o'clock closing or not, the health of the Australian economy still depended principally on that of the wheat and wool industries. The health, and indeed the existence of Britain, depended on getting these and other basic supplies through the German submarine blockade. In 1914 a severe drought almost destroyed the wheat

[7] *S.M.H.*, 8 June 1916, p.10.

crop, but in the following year both total yield (6 188 000 cubic metres as opposed to 910 000 cubic metres in 1914) and yield per hectare were records. Because of shipping shortages and other wartime disruption of established patterns of trade, private wheat-broking firms were unable to cope with the situation. Plagues of mice and weevils attacked the millions of bags of wheat awaiting transport at wharves and railway sidings. In 1917 the number of mice destroyed was measured in hundreds of tons. So the Commonwealth and State Governments combined to set up a Wheat Board which purchased the crop from the growers and took responsibility for selling it overseas. The British Government bought vast quantities of wheat and other primary products: in fact it contracted, for the duration of the war, to buy all the beef and mutton Australia could spare from 1915 onwards and all the wool from 1916 — in which year the Government established, by yet another regulation gazetted under the War Precautions Act, a Central Wool Committee to handle the clip. Shipping, however, remained a problem.

It was at least partly solved by the resourceful Hughes. Hard-pressed by the German submarine campaign, Britain had set up a Shipping Control Committee to make the best possible use of her merchant fleet. Hughes pressed for more ships to be allocated to the Australian run, but the Committee, and the British Government, were adamant. The same ship could bring more than four times the quantity of cargo from North America, in four return voyages, as it could in one return voyage from Australia. Hughes shouted and Fisher, as High Commissioner in London from October 1915, pleaded in vain. Then, during his London visit, made mainly for quite other purposes, in early 1916 Hughes secretly bought fifteen tramp steamers for the Commonwealth Government. Appalled at this larrikin way of gaining a point, the British Government nevertheless could do nothing but acquiesce. By this deal Hughes had the satisfaction also of implementing a long-standing item of Labor policy — the establishment of a Government enterprise to compete with privately-owned firms. The ships formed the nucleus of the Commonwealth Shipping Line and in two years had earned in net profits more than the £2,000,000 which Hughes had paid for them, despite the fact that the Line charged lower rates than those of private steamship companies.

The continuing shipping shortage and the sudden cessation of trade with Germany inevitably acted as a stimulus to Australian manufacturing industry. There were severe shortages at first. Germany then led the world in certain branches of industry such as chemicals, optics and electronics. Almost all headache pills and powders, for instance, had been imported from Germany. A

BORN IN AUSTRALIA

UNEMPLOYED FROM FREETRADE ESTABLISHMENT:
"Now, why the deuce should the war put me out of a job?"

Bulletin, 1914

Victorian chemist named Nicholas was the first to find an alternative formula for Bayer aspirin tablets. He set up an 'Aspro' factory in Melbourne and outside it a country mansion known to local residents as 'Headache Hall'. By the end of the war ships, dynamos, typewriter-ribbons and other products previously imported — nearly 400 articles altogether — were being manufactured in Australia.

The most important expansion was the manufacture of iron and steel and the associated base-metal industries. When war broke out a small blast furnace at Lithgow was producing about 130 000 tons of pig-iron per year. By 1919 total Australian production was approaching one million tons, most of it smelted by Australia's most powerful commercial enterprise, the Broken Hill Proprietary Company Limited, or the B.H.P. as it is universally known. Founded in 1885 to exploit the fantastically rich silver-lead-zinc ores at Broken Hill in western New South Wales, the company branched out into coal and iron mining and the treatment of base-metal ores generally. In 1897 it set up smelting works for its ores at Port Pirie on Spencer's Gulf in South Australia. Not far from Whyalla, a port on the opposite western side of the Gulf, extremely rich surface finds of iron ore were made. In 1911 the company decided to move into the field of iron and steel manufacturing. Its manager G. D. Delprat, obtained expert advice from America and began the series of interlocking operations which is still the basis of B.H.P.'s strength. The company's own ships carry iron ore from Whyalla to its steelworks at Newcastle and Port Kembla in New South Wales, and return with coal from its mines near these cities to feed its smelting works at Port Pirie and, more recently, its ship-building industry at Whyalla. The decisive steps were taken during the war with the establishment of the B.H.P. iron and steel works at Newcastle.

Unfortunately for national unity, working people did not receive a fair share of this war-induced prosperity. Despite governmental efforts to control them, prices rose much faster than wages. If we take an index figure of 1000 to represent the real purchasing-power of wages in 1911, this figure fell to 948 in 1914, 854 in 1915 and did not again rise to 1000 or over until 1921. Hughes and the majority of his cabinet colleagues had swept aside all thought of further social reforms until 'after the war'. As we have seen, Hughes's agreement with the State Premiers to take control of price-fixing for the duration of the war, was rendered partly ineffective by the Legislative Councils in some States. The Labor movement regarded this as a betrayal and a series of strikes, from December 1915 onwards, demonstrated its belief that the working class was being asked to pay for the war while capitalists were making even bigger profits than usual. Among the innumerable offices held by Hughes was that of president of the Waterside Workers' Federation — whose members struck for higher wages despite his pleas. Broken Hill silver-lead miners, coalminers and shearers all carried out successful strikes in 1916. In some degree they were moved by disillusionment with the war, as well as by purely industrial grievances: and this at the time when the re-grouped and reinforced A.I.F. divisions were moving into the hell of trench warfare in France. National divisions and antagonisms were greatly exacerbated by the Prime Minister's growing belief that it was necessary to impose military conscription for overseas service.

CONSCRIPTION FOR OVERSEAS SERVICE?

Taking up an invitation to dominion prime ministers to discuss the war situation with the British Cabinet, Hughes spent the second quarter of 1916 in Britain. As we have seen, he bought much-needed ships for Australia and made arrangements for the sale of wheat, wool and other products to Britain, but he also visited the troops in France, attended a Paris Economic Conference as a member of the British Delegation, and made innumerable speeches on the theme 'Wake up England!'. Amazingly, the British liked being instructed by a colonial. His fiery speeches, his abrasive scorn for diplomatic niceties, his fiendish energy and his burning patriotism appealed to many as being typical of the young fighting nation 'down under'. His criticism probably helped to bring about the replacement of the indecisive Asquith by 'Billy's' more dynamic fellow Welshman, Lloyd George, later in the year. Hughes was offered, but declined, a seat in the British War Cabinet. He was fêted by duchesses and, more importantly, saluted by the British press as a great statesman. He was given the freedom of London and nine other cities, and a gratifying number of university honorary degrees. All this was faithfully reported in the Australian press and Hughes came home on 31 July 1916 to a hero's welcome — but also to a gathering political and social storm.

During his barn-storming tour Hughes had become convinced that conscription must be introduced in Australia, as it had been in January 1916 in Britain. People were already deeply and bitterly divided on the issue. Universal service leagues, anti-conscription leagues and other propaganda bodies had been seeking to influence opinion for nearly a year. In the eastern States trade-union organisations and the Labor Party had declared against any form of conscription and the latter body had specifically warned its members,

BILLIWOG

NO WAR IS COMPLETE WITHOUT ONE

Bulletin, 1918

including the Prime Minister and the New South Wales Premier, W. A. Holman, against having anything to do with pro-conscription bodies. Labor parliamentarians were hopelessly divided on the issue, but no politician could count heads more accurately than Hughes, and he knew that the majority was unalterably opposed to him. Legal opinion held that conscription could be simply introduced, without debate, by regulation under the War Precautions Act. Alternatively Liberal support for a conscription bill was certain and this would have ensured its passage through the Representatives, though not through the Senate, where there was an absolute majority of anti-conscriptionist Labor members. Either course of action would obviously split the Labor Party and probably lose Hughes the Prime Ministership. Faced with this dilemma he decided on a plebiscite in the hope that a large popular majority for conscription would force his anti-conscriptionist colleagues, or a sufficient number of them to keep him in power, to change their minds and their votes. It seems that the Labor Cabinet agreed to the plebiscite proposal by only 5 votes to 4 and the Labor Parliamentary Caucus of 73 members by a bare majority of one.

The conscription referendum campaign divided the nation into rancorously hostile groups. Generally speaking the rich and respectable supported conscription while the poor opposed it. All the daily newspapers and the still influential weekly *Bulletin* were for it. Most trade-union journals and the pamphlets of revolutionary or radical sects like the I.W.W. were against it. The need for conscription was trumpeted from almost every Protestant pulpit in the land. In Melbourne the Church of England Synod unanimously resolved that Almighty God was on the side of the Allied Powers and that therefore conscription was morally necessary. The Deity must have been puzzled to find a great many Catholic priests, led by the Coadjutor Archbishop of Melbourne, Dr Daniel Mannix, recently arrived from Ireland, exhorting their flocks to a contrary view. During the campaign Britain was still engaged in suppressing the Irish rebellion of Easter 1916 and, though some Catholic bishops let it be known they were in favour of conscription, Mannix, most of the priesthood and nearly all lay Australians of Irish Catholic descent were stirred to a degree of Anglophobia by these events on the other side of the world. Like a great many other Australians, Frank Anstey, the English-born agnostic, the most outspokenly anti-war member of the House of Representatives, believed that the Irish Catholic vote was decisive in defeating the conscription referendum. Long afterwards he wrote in an undated letter to a friend

> My dear Harry, You know and I know that if there had been no Easter week in Ireland in 1916 and no murder of poor Jim Connelly and his

> associate leaders there would have been no hope of defeating conscription in Australia. Before that date the Irish were as War mad as the English but Easter week stirred the Paddy.[8]

Others thought that the rank and file of the Labor movement and people with international pacifist ideas like Anstey himself were the decisive factor in favour of 'No'. Others again put it down to 'the women's vote' and still others to the devilish machinations of the I.W.W. Few at the time blamed or praised the Prime Minister for swelling the number of 'No' voters, but his reckless vilification of all opponents certainly provoked, or frightened, some potential supporters into the opposition camp.

As the campaign progressed Labor's opposition to conscription hardened — except in Western Australia where the State Branch of the party decided to allow members to support either side. In September Hughes and Holman were formally expelled and a few days later a few hundred Maltese immigrants arrived in Sydney. The *Worker* inflated the number to a thousand and presented the incident as a capitalist plot to undermine working conditions — and the White Australia Policy — by introducing cheap labour while Australian workers were away fighting in Europe. For some time Hughes was jibed at by opponents as 'William Maltese Hughes'. The referendum was to be held on 28 October. The Government ordered young men to report for military training under the home service scheme on the second day of that month and Hughes threatened relentless prosecution of defaulters. Opponents believed the men were being called up, in anticipation of a 'Yes' vote, for drafting into the A.I.F. Frank Tudor and two other Cabinet ministers resigned.

Hughes's trump cards were played in the last two months of the campaign. From the beginning conscriptionists had done everything possible to identify all opposition with the revolutionary violence advocated by the tiny band of I.W.W. members. In September some I.W.W. activists were arrested and charged with forgery of bogus five-pound notes. On 4 October, two days after the call-up, three more I.W.W. men were charged with the murder of a police constable. Finally on 10 October, only eighteen days before the referendum, and in the glare of tremendous publicity, twelve I.W.W. men were charged with treason — in fact with conspiring to burn down Sydney. 'I.W.W. Assassins Want You to Vote No', screamed one newspaper headline: but the people did vote 'No' on 28 October. A few months later the 'I.W.W. Twelve' were found guilty and sentenced to terms of imprisonment ranging from five to

[8] *Anstey Papers*, Australian National University Archives.

The Worker, 5 October 1916

THE "CASE" FOR LABOR
(By W. M. Hughes).

fifteen years. In 1920, after the war, a Royal Commission of Inquiry appointed by a New South Wales Labor Government, found that ten of them had been 'framed' and they were released from gaol.

Under Hughes's Military Conscription Referendum Act voting was made compulsory — for the first time in any Australian poll except for that conducted in Queensland the previous year. There was an overall 'No' majority of 72 476 in a total poll of 2 247 590 votes. New South Wales, South Australia and Queensland had small 'No' majorities. Western Australia, where the Labor Party had taken a neutral stand on the issue, returned a very large 'Yes' majority. Despite Hughes, Holman and a good many other Labor politicians, the Labor Movement and most Labor voters had voted 'No'. The men of the A.I.F. voted 'Yes', but by a surprisingly small margin. It seems likely that most front-line soldiers voted 'No' despite official urging to the contrary but most of those still in training voted 'Yes'.[9] Ian Turner has shown that in fact the result was probably determined in the farming electorates which usually voted conservative.[10] With a good season behind them and a shortage of labour exacerbated by the call-up of 2 October, most farmers voted, contrary to their usual behaviour, with the mass of manual workers for no conscription.

POLITICS, WAR AND THE SECOND REFERENDUM

Naturally the anti-conscriptionists were elated at their unexpected success. When the Labor Caucus reassembled on 14 November a Queensland member moved a vote of no-confidence in Hughes. Seeing that the numbers were against him, the Prime Minister dramatically called on his supporters to follow him out of the room. George Pearce, the Minister for Defence, and twenty-three others did so, leaving behind forty anti-conscriptionist Labor men who confirmed the Prime Minister's expulsion from the party and elected Frank Tudor, a Victorian, as the new parliamentary Labor leader. Conservatives said the Labor Party had 'blown out its brains', while Labor supporters likened Hughes and his comrades to rats deserting a sinking ship. Knowing they could rely on Liberal support, Hughes and Pearce immediately formed a new, 'National Labor' Party, minority Government, which proceeded to pass an Unlawful Associations Act outlawing the I.W.W. This repressive law was greatly strengthened a year later. The minority Government was short-lived. The Liberals demanded some of the sweets of office as

[9] Lt.-Col. P. P. Abbott, C.M.G., *War Diary*, vol. 2, 2.2.1916-11.6.1917, p.183 (owned by descendants).

[10] I. A. H. Turner, *Industrial Labour and Politics: 1900-1921*, Canberra, 1965.

the price of their support. Backroom discussions led to the Liberal Party being renamed, or re-formed, as the National or Nationalist Party (at first the terms were used interchangeably), which embraced Hughes and his ex-Labor followers in its membership. On 17 February 1917 a new Nationalist Ministry was sworn in. Hughes, now leader of the Nationalist Party, remained Prime Minister and Attorney-General, and Pearce Minister for Defence. Three other ex-Labor men found a place in the new Cabinet and six ex-Liberals including Cook as Minister for the Navy and old Sir John Forrest as Treasurer.

By this time the sixth Commonwealth Parliament was approaching the end of its three-year span, as was the Parliament of New South Wales in which Holman, showing the way to Hughes, had become the first 'Nationalist' Premier. The referendum result seemed to augur badly for the Nationalists and both leaders cast about for some means of prolonging the life of their parliaments. Public opinion was hostile to any such manoeuvre, however, and Holman, after some delay, was forced to the polls. The Nationalists won a comfortable victory, thus encouraging Hughes to follow suit. He felt constrained, however, to promise that if elected the Nationalists would not introduce conscription except with the people's permission after another plebiscite. In the general election of 5 May 1917 the Nationalists had a landslide victory — 53 seats in the Representatives to 22 for Labor. The Nationalists won all 18 Senate positions which were being contested, giving them 24 seats to 12 in the Upper House. Obviously the referendum 'No' vote had been a vote against conscription, but not against the vigorous prosecution of the war — to which the 'Nationalists' were dedicated much more strongly than the rump Labor Party. Analysis of the results shows that many farmers — and others — who had voted 'No' returned to their normal conservative allegiance. All ministers were re-elected and so the Hughes Cabinet continued in office unchanged, except that Senator Millen, previously Vice-President of the Executive Council, was given a new portfolio of Repatriation. Littleton Groom, son of W. H. Groom, and previously a Minister without Portfolio, replaced Millen.

During the early part of the referendum campaign, most but not all of the A.I.F. were fighting in France. After Gallipoli all troops had been withdrawn to Egypt for rest, regrouping, reinforcement and further training. In the northern Spring of 1916, between March and June, the four infantry divisions were shipped to France, while the Australian and New Zealand Light Horse units stayed in the Middle East under the command of General Harry Chauvel, knighted in the following year, a bush-bred boy from Tabulam in the Clarence River district of New South Wales. He and his horsemen served under Allenby, the British General in command of the whole Middle Eastern area. At first their task was to defend Egypt and the Canal against Turkish attacks but early in 1916 they went on the offensive and began the long task of driving the Turks out of Sinai, Palestine, Syria and, finally, out of the war in October 1918 before the German capitulation. By then Chauvel's small force of Anzac cavalry had grown to an army of five divisions, the Desert Mounted Corps, which included British, French and Indian units as well as Australians and New Zealanders. It was the largest body of cavalry ever employed under a single commander in modern warfare. The decisive Battle of Gaza which turned on a successful charge by the Australian Fourth Light Horse Brigade on a double line of Turkish trenches at Beersheba, began on 27 October 1917. The men galloped over three kilometres, under heavy fire, before jumping over the trenches and dismounting to fight the defenders hand to hand. It was Chauvel's faultless planning and synchronisation of the work of his scattered columns which continually surprised and finally overwhelmed the enemy.

In France three Anzac divisions were used in the first Battle of the Somme which began on 1 July 1916. Five weeks later 23 000 of the Australian soldiers were wounded or dead. The Somme, like Bapaume, Bullecourt, Messines, Ypres, Passchendaele, Villers Bretonneux and so many other French battlefields, became and remained a household place-word in Australia, more familiar to all than the names of many rivers or towns in their own country. There is no point in listing them all or giving details of the fighting. In a welter of mud and blood extending from Switzerland to the North Sea men killed and maimed each other daily for a few metres of ground, which changed hands again the next day or the next month. The slaughter continued for four years, because the strategists and generals on both sides could think of no better way of defeating the enemy than to bleed him to death by the exhaustion of the supply of his young men and his industrial output. When American manpower and wealth were thrown into the scales on the Allied side in 1917, the final result became inevitable.

By this time the Australian soldiers had bestowed on themselves a nickname which was to remain with them and their sons' sons in other places and other wars. They called each other 'diggers', partly, in all probability, from memories of the goldfields and Eureka Stockade, and partly from the prodigious amount of digging done by the men of all the armies engaged in the Great War.

Because they were volunteers, and because they never learnt to obey orders automatically but continued to think for themselves

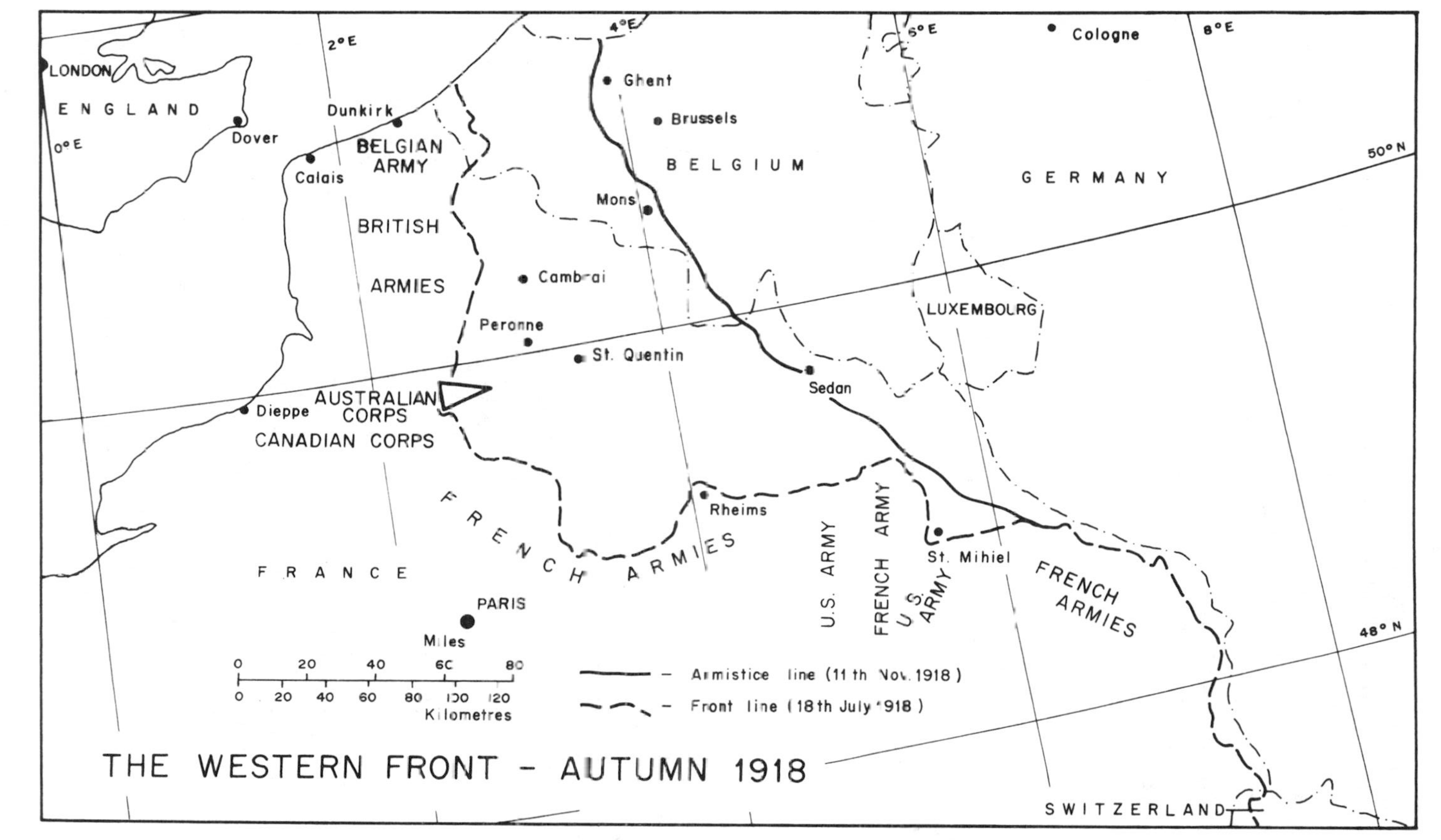

THE WESTERN FRONT - AUTUMN 1918

even, or especially, when in action, the Australians were second to none as brave and resourceful fighters. Indeed they soon won a reputation as the best shock-troops on the Allied side, and were used accordingly. Of 330 000 troops sent overseas, 59 258 were killed in action or died of wounds, and another 173 815 were wounded. These figures give a total casualty rate of 68.5 per cent, a much higher figure than that for other troops involved. The comparable figures are New Zealand 58 per cent, United Kingdom 52.5 per cent, Canada 51 per cent, France 55 per cent and Germany 54 per cent.[11]

Censorship and patriotism assured that the fighting in France was presented to the Australian people in the rosiest possible light. Every murderous affray might be shown as the possible beginning of the end, but the ever-increasing toll of dead, wounded and missing could not be hidden. Encouraged by the 'No' vote and appalled by the seemingly endless slaughter, pacifists, socialists and radicals of all kinds redoubled their efforts. War-weariness increased, especially among working people who were most affected by rising prices, shortages and deteriorating living standards. In mid-1917 Labor Party branches in all States except Western Australia and Tasmania passed resolutions blaming the capitalist economic system for the war and calling for a negotiated peace. Then on 2 August in New South Wales began the greatest strike in Australian history. The State Government introduced more stringent rules into its Railways and Tramways workshops, rules which the men saw as a threat to their working conditions. They struck, but they were motivated as much by general frustration and war-weariness as by the new rules. Within a few days lorry-drivers, miners, wharf-labourers and seamen had joined them. The Federal and State Governments declared that the strike had been fomented by enemy agents and, of course, by the I.W.W., so many of whose leaders had been in gaol throughout the year. They recruited 'free' labour and commandeered all stocks of coal, coalmines, motor and horse-drawn vehicles and some classes of ships: they arrested on charges of conspiracy three leading members of the strike committee, a New South Wales member of Parliament, A. W. Buckley, and some of the maritime unions' leaders. The trials were held long after the strike was crushed and none of the men were convicted. Those who had taken part in it were victimised. One of them, the future Prime Minister, J. B. Chifley, was dismissed but reinstated, on appeal.

On the western front the immolation of the civilised world's best

[11] A. G. Butler, *The Australian Army Medical Services in the War of 1914-1918*, vol. 3, Canberra, 1943, pp. 869, 881.

young men continued. On 6 November the third Battle of Ypres, no more decisive that its predecessors, ended with 38 000 Australian casualties. The next day news of the Bolshevik revolution in Russia reached Australia and Prime Minister Hughes announced that a second conscription referendum would be held on 20 December. The precise proposal was that voluntary recruiting should continue but that, if fewer than 7000 men a month came forward, the deficit should be made up from conscripted, fit, single men between the ages of 20 and 44, chosen by lot. Over the year the voluntary enlistment rate had dropped steadily from about 5000 to about half that number per month. The campaign was briefer, but even more envenomed than the first. There was no limit to exaggeration and vilification of opponents by both sides. A conscriptionist leaflet entitled *The Anti's Creed* read in part:

> I believe that our women should betray the men
>   who are fighting for them.
> I believe it was right to sink the *Lusitania*.
> I believe that Nurse Cavell got her deserts.[12]

An anti-conscription journal suggested that if conscription were implemented so many men would be killed that Australian women would have to marry 'Chinese, Japs and Hindoos'.[13]

The Prime Minister himself set a deplorable example of intemperance. His misuse of censorship powers went so far, on one occasion, as to attempt the muzzling of the anti-conscriptionist Premier of Queensland. At the end of 1917 Queensland was the only State with a Labor Government. The Premier, T. J. Ryan, was easily the ablest Labor politician of the day. Despite wartime difficulties he had made Queensland the most advanced 'welfare state' in the Commonwealth at the time, providing employment in a wide range of public works, setting up State enterprises to lower the price of many commodities by competition with private enterprise, and making an eight-hour working day mandatory for all. When Ryan spoke at length in Parliament against conscription, Hughes ordered the postal authorities not to handle the issue of Hansard containing the transcript of the Premier's remarks. Ryan repeated them in public outside Parliament and was promptly charged, under the War Precautions Act, with making false statements about the war effort, but was acquitted with costs given against the Commonwealth. Leaving Queensland, Hughes addressed a crowd at the Warwick

[12] J. M. Main, *Conscription: the Australian Debate 1901-1970*, Melbourne, 1970, p.91.
[13] I. A. H. Turner, *Industrial Labour and Politics*, Canberra, 1965, p.163.

railway station, where he was hit by a rotten egg aimed by a citizen of Irish extraction, one Patrick Brosnan. The Queensland police sergeant on the platform refused to arrest Brosnan, but he was in fact charged, and duly fined ten shillings and costs, three days later.

This incident so inflamed the Prime Minister that he immediately gave orders for the creation of a Commonwealth police force, the first of a number of quasi-secret police organisations such as A.S.I.O., the Australian Security Intelligence Organisation. Like such clandestine bands of men in other civilised lands, they are charged with the duty of spying on other countries and on enemy agents in their own; but again, as elsewhere, they have been much more effective in inhibiting change or progress by spying on and threatening radicals, intellectuals, trade unionists and critical persons among their fellow citizens. The explosion of the addled Warwick egg on Mr Hughes's hat marked, in a sense, the beginning of the end of Australia's age of innocence.

When the votes were counted it was found that the 'No' majority had increased substantially. Victoria had joined the other three largest States in voting against conscription and available evidence suggests that the 'No' majority of the men in the trenches had also increased. Most certainly bitterness had increased too. An incident that occurred three weeks after the second plebiscite in the main street of Armidale, New South Wales, must have been repeated, with variations, all over Australia. On 2 January 1918 an Irish Catholic townsman, T. H. Murphy, painter and paper-hanger, discussed the result with a Protestant dentist, R. C. R. Simpson. Murphy observed that he had voted 'No' himself though he had volunteered several times. 'Well', replied Simpson, 'I am of the same opinion as others. I think Conscription was defeated by the three C's: the cowards, the ——— and the Catholics of this country.' A week later the pair exchanged further compliments. Simpson repeated his insults. Murphy replied in kind and a fistfight ensued in front of the Post Office.[14]

During the campaign Hughes had repeatedly emphasised that he and his ministers could not carry on the government without the power to conscript and that they would not attempt to do so. He had promised in the most explicit terms that if the referendum were defeated he would resign. After the Christmas break he and his ministers did so on 8 January 1918; but those who had innocently supposed that the second 'No' vote spelt the end of the Hughes Government, grossly underestimated his charlatanism and

[14] D. J. Martin, *A Country Town at War* (B.A. Hons thesis, University of New England, 1976), pp. 108-10. The second 'C', deleted in press reports, was referred to in following Court proceedings as 'a very vulgar reference to women'.

unscrupulousness. Since he remained the leader of the majority Nationalist Party, and since he gave no advice to the Governor-General to call another election, Hughes and his entire Cabinet, in a ceremony aptly characterised by one historian as a 'solemn farce', were sworn into office again two days later.

MONASH, HUGHES AND VERSAILLES

Meanwhile there was no diminution in the rate at which the belligerents' human and material resources were being used up on the western front; but by the third quarter of 1918 American supplies of men and munitions were making themselves felt. Germany was nearly exhausted and, to some, appeared to be moving towards revolution as Russia had done a year earlier. On 1 January 1918, in response to repeated pressure from Hughes, all five Australian divisions in France were formed into a single Corps under the popular English commander General Birdwood, who had been with the Australians since Gallipoli. In May, however, Birdwood was promoted to command of the British Fifth Army and replaced as Australian Corps Commander by the greatest soldier Australia ever produced.

Son of a Jewish gold-rush immigrant from Eastern Germany, John Monash was born in Melbourne in 1865 and educated at Scotch College and the University of Melbourne where he graduated in the three faculties of Arts, Engineering and Law. He built up a successful civil-engineering practice but spent much time training as a soldier in the Citizen Forces, having reached the rank of colonel when war broke out. He commanded the Fourth Infantry Brigade on Gallipoli and had much to do with the masterly planning of the withdrawal. As Corps Commander at the Battle of Hamel on 4 July 1918 he first showed what could be achieved by the carefully planned co-ordination in an attack of tanks, aeroplanes, infantry and artillery. Monash and his veteran Australian divisions played a key part in the final victorious assault on the Hindenburg Line. His planning was so successful because he understood his countrymen and made use of their capacity for independent action and improvisation, instead of trying to suppress it. Between 27 March and 11 November 1918, though constituting less than 10 per cent of the British Army, they defeated thirty-nine enemy divisions and they captured 23 per cent of the prisoners and 21.5 per cent of the ground recovered from the enemy.[15] After the armistice of 11 November 1918 Monash was given the difficult task of organising the repatriation of all Australian soldiers who survived. After 1920,

[15] W. L. Gammage, *The Broken Years*, Canberra, 1974, p. 204.

as general manager of the State Electricity Commission of Victoria, he developed the rich brown-coal deposits at Yallourn in Gippsland, giving the State a cheap and efficient supply of power and fuel. He became President of the Australian and New Zealand Association for the Advancement of Science and Vice-Chancellor of Melbourne University. In war and peace he was modest, courteous, quiet-spoken and scholarly, with a considerable knowledge of literature and music. His *Australian Victories in France*, published in 1920, reflects these qualities and shows the great pride and affection he felt for his men. His life helps to explain why there is probably less anti-Semitism in Australia than in other English-speaking countries.

While Monash was engaged in bringing the diggers home, the Prime Minister, at the apex of his career, was exulting in his role at the Versailles Peace Conference of 1919. By sheer force of personality the tiny, abrasive little man often elbowed aside Lloyd George or the great President Wilson of the United States, to occupy the centre of the world stage. His hard-headed approach to defeated Germany endeared him to the French Prime Minister Clemenceau, nicknamed by his countrymen 'The Tiger'. When he arrived at Versailles Hughes had long been using a hearing-aid, a device which he would ostentatiously switch off if he considered the speaker of the moment foolish or boring. He kept it switched on, no doubt equally ostentatiously, when Clemenceau was speaking. The latter wrote later of Hughes as 'the noble delegate from Australia, with whom we had to talk through an electrophone, getting in return symphonies of good sense'.[16] President Wilson, who worked for moderation and humanity in the framing of the peace treaty, found Hughes's communications cacophonous. Exchanges between the two men have passed into Australian folklore. The best remembered (true) anecdote tells of one of the many occasions on which Wilson found it difficult to believe that such a diminutive man, from such a sparsely populated, remote and unimportant country, could be so troublesome and influential as he in fact was. Wilson felt constrained to remind Hughes that he spoke for a nation of 120 million people, the population of the United States at the time. Instantly Hughes replied in his rasping voice that he spoke for a country which had contributed sixty thousand dead to the Allied cause — more men killed in action in fact, as he did not need to remind Wilson, than the United States had suffered in the whole war.

Notwithstanding all his playing to the gallery, the incredible Welshman served Australia well at Versailles. He insisted that he (and Joseph Cook who was completely overshadowed by him)

[16] *A.E.*, vol. 5, p.26.

should represent Australia as a belligerent nation in its own right, not merely as part of the British delegation. The point was made when he signed the treaty separately on behalf of Australia. We shall see that for the following twenty years a succession of conservative governments was content, in the field of foreign relations, almost to revert to Australia's earlier quasi-colonial status; but Hughes did set the precedent for independent action within the Empire. He was elected vice-president of the Reparations Committee and used all his rhetorical powers to press, unsuccessfully, for the heaviest possible reparations from Germany. Although he had, like most of his successors for twenty years, little faith in the League of Nations, he made Australia a founding member of that body. He successfully implemented his countrymen's and his own racist passions by defeating a Japanese proposal to have a declaration of racial equality embodied in the Covenant of the League. He feared that even such an abstract expression of principle might threaten the sacrosanct White Australia Policy. For the same reason he had the gravest reservations about the Japanese mandate over the former German Pacific Islands north of the Equator, the Caroline, the Marshall and the Mariana Islands, but in this he was overruled by Britain. He was therefore all the more truculently insistent on securing the substance, though not the form, of sovereignty for Australia over the former German possessions south of the equator. The League's C Class mandate was virtually a device for securing Australian control of immigration and trade in north-eastern New Guinea, New Britain, New Ireland and all other formerly German possessions north of the Papua border, south of the Equator and between longitude 141° and 160° east. The phosphate-rich island of Nauru remained under Australian occupation till 1921 when it was granted as a mandated territory jointly to Britain, New Zealand and Australia — though Australia continued to provide the administration.

Lionised by vast crowds when he returned to Australia in August, and fondly christened 'the Little Digger' by returned soldiers, Hughes decided to call the next federal election early while the tide of popular feeling ran so strongly in his favour. He did so and was duly returned to office on 13 December 1919 though, as we shall see, changes in politics and in the temper of the electorate brought about his fall from power during the following Parliament early in 1923. Though it was not very obvious in 1919, the war had wrought vast changes in the outlook of Australians. First of all, as Hughes had reminded Wilson, 60 000 of them were dead, and, because of the system of voluntary recruitment many, probably most, of these were among the very best, bravest and most idealistic of their generation: men who might have given a lead to their countrymen in many walks of life, had they lived. It is not surprising that, without them, Australian life for the next twenty years was much more staid, cautious and conformist than during the first twenty years of the Commonwealth. One Australian historian, R. M. Crawford, has characterised the period as 'the mean decades' and another, C. M. H. Clark, as 'the age of the survivors'.

Before the war, as we have seen, majority sentiment favoured the development of a vigorous nationalism, however brash and disfigured by racist illusions it may have been, and of social experimentation which made Australia, at that period, the most advanced welfare state in the world. National patriotism and social progress seemed to many only two aspects of a single policy, which was to make Australia the ideal democratic state of the common man — the White Australian common man, of course. The policy was implemented by Deakin and his radical Protectionists and the Labor Party in a working partnership up till 1909, and thereafter by the Labor Party alone with the conservative Fusionist Liberal Party in Opposition. All things seemed possible, including the preservation till judgment day of a lily-white egalitarian, Australian democracy. The war itself, at first, was a great adventure not on any account to be missed. Four years of slaughter at the front and rancorous division at home changed all that beyond recall. War would never again be thought of as a glorious adventure: at best, rather, as a grim necessity. Although belief in the innate superiority of white over black or yellow or brown men survived, belief in the supreme virtue of the Anglo-Saxon (or Anglo-Celtic!) 'races' did not. The Turks were decent and the Germans tough.

The self-appointed guardians of the national tradition, the Labor Party, and the nation itself, split over the conscription issue. About half of those eligible to serve with the colours did so and about half did not. For the next twenty years ex-servicemen and their dependants scorned those who had been anti-conscriptionists. Labor, which had led the nation into the war, emerged from it as the party identified in the minds of its opponents with the I.W.W., anti-conscription and sedition at home, and with support for the Irish national rebellion and even bolshevism and revolution abroad: in short, as the party of 'disloyalty' to Britain and the Empire. The anti-Labor Party, strengthened by the accretion of Hughes, Pearce and many other ex-Labor men and women, emerged from the war as the party of loyalty to Britain and the Empire, though whether it had taken over with Labor deserters custody of local Australian nationalism, is less certain. Hughes's emphatic nationalist gestures at Versailles were applauded by Labor opinion but criticised and even disavowed as vulgar and, in effect, anti-British posturings, by influential sections of his own Nationalist Party and its supporters.

The truth is that the war had shown the mother country to be so much less omnipotent than the men of the early Commonwealth had believed her to be. The moral was that Australia, though much more important in her own right than before, was also much more totally dependent on her junior partnership with Britain — or some other distant protector. However proud of their newly blooded Australian identity they might be, most people felt, more passionately than before the war, that national survival depended on Imperial unity and British protection; and so in the sphere of national, that is Commonwealth, government, majority sentiment between the wars generally favoured the conservative, anti-Labor political groupings (under whatever name) which had always tended to place loyalty to Britain above local patriotism. During the war, and specifically over the question of conscription, the influential Sydney *Bulletin*'s policy changed from radical nationalism to conservative imperialism.

Majority opinion changed in the same way at the same time. The old digger replaced the bush-worker as the symbolic embodiment of the national identity. In most ways the change was not great. Both idealised stereotypes emphasised 'masculine', 'frontier' virtues and vices — mateship in a hard, male world where survival depended on mutual loyalty, initiative and endurance, where 'tall poppies' were brought low and men were aggressively egalitarian, where mental and spiritual powers were scorned but 'practical' skills prized, where 'white men' swore habitually but drank and whored only when they could — on leave or on the occasional spree: but there were two marked differences. The 'noble bushman', insofar as he was a political being, was a radical and an Australian nationalist like the men in Lawson's stories. The 'old digger', insofar as he was a political being, was a conservative and an Austral-British imperialist like thousands of local and national leaders of the Returned Soldiers' League.

Chapter 5

MARKING TIME
c. 1920—1928

Society and communications — The Country Party, rehabilitation and the R.S.L. — Industrial militancy — Hughes, Bruce and the eighth Parliament — Bruce, men, money and markets — Bruce and the trade unions

SOCIETY AND COMMUNICATIONS

The surviving diggers returned in 1919 to a homeland where, for some months, people wore white cotton face-masks in the streets. Like the rest of the world Australia was suffering from a severe epidemic of pneumonic influenza which attacked children and young adults rather than their elders. Schools, hotels, picture shows, racecourses and other places where infection might be transmitted were closed, but the disease claimed about 12 000 lives. In most other ways Australia seemed to have changed very little from what the returned soldiers had known five years earlier, though some important developments were apparent by the end of the decade.

In 1920 the total population was rising towards five and a half million, if anything, owing to the pre-war assisted immigration programmes, more predominantly British by descent than it had been at the time of federation. More than half of Australia's total overseas trade, both import and export, was still conducted with the United Kingdom and other Empire countries and more than three-quarters of all overseas public and private investment flowed from the same source. In all these respects the United States was the country next most important to the Australian economy, but it stood a long way behind, accounting in 1920 for only 22 per cent of Australian imports and 7.5 per cent of exports. A tiny proportion of the South Australian wheat crop was carried away each year by the last large commercial sailing ships to ply the seas, a small fleet based on the Aaland Islands in the Baltic Sea. Nearly all passengers and cargo were carried in coal-fired steamships, the larger vessels being of up to 20 000 tons displacement, but from the 1920s most new ships were oil-burning motor vessels. Every drop of mineral oil used in Australia had to be imported from abroad.

The internal combustion engine was driving horses off the roads.

In 1924 the last Cobb and Co. coach was replaced by a 'service-car' in western Queensland and more people began to use cars both in the cities and the bush. By 1929 motor lorries and trucks had displaced drays and carts practically everywhere, though horse-drawn delivery carts owned by bakers, butchers and other tradesmen were still to be seen in the cities. In the wheat-belt most farmers were still using horse-teams for ploughing, drilling and harvesting, though by 1929 tractors were almost as often to be seen in the paddocks. Camel teams and motor lorries were both common in the dry interior. Steam locomotives still hauled virtually all the trains in Australia except for those on the suburban railway systems of Melbourne and Sydney which were electrified between 1919 and 1929. Cable trams still ran in Melbourne but were supplemented by an electric system with overhead wires, such as served all the other capital cities and even a few country towns like Ballarat and Bendigo in Victoria and Kalgoorlie, centre of the goldfields in Western Australia. Sydney's green, yellow and grime-coated trams were larger, noisier, and more numerous than those elsewhere. Very often they ran in joined pairs, leading an English visitor to compare them with copulating butterflies. Sydney travellers, more realistically, made them a synonym for noise, rush and forcefulness — in a popular slang expression, 'going through like a Bondi tram'. Steam and horse trams were no more. Private or governmental motor-bus services supplemented the trams in all cities. By 1929 all inner-city road surfaces and many main roads elsewhere had been sealed with bitumen to cater for motor vehicles.

The greatest advances in transport were made in aviation. With its vast distances, scattered population and normally clear, sunny weather, no country in the world provides better flying conditions than Australia, nor has made more use of aeroplanes. Most of the aerial pioneers were pilots in the Australian Flying Corps which operated one squadron in Palestine and three in France. During the whole war they destroyed 276 enemy aircraft for a loss of 60 of their own. In 1919 the South Australian brothers, Ross and Keith Smith, won the £10,000 prize offered by the Commonwealth Government for the first British aircraft manned by Australians to fly from London to Australia. They flew a Vickers-Vimy machine, now housed as a relic at Adelaide airport, and took 28 days. In 1921 other ex-A.F.C. men, Major Norman Brearley and Charles Kingsford-Smith, began operating the first regular commercial airline in Australia, flying between Geraldton and ports on the north-west coast up to Broome. In the previous year another wartime pilot, Hudson Fysh, and his partners began a service between Charleville and Cloncurry which they registered as Queensland and Northern

Territory Aerial Services Ltd (Qantas Ltd). This line prospered and expanded vastly, moved into the international flying sphere and was wholly acquired by the Commonwealth Government in 1947. Up till 1976 it had one of the best safety records in the world, having lost only seven passengers in one flying accident in 1951.

In 1928 Qantas contracted with the Presbyterian Australian Inland Mission to maintain an aeroplane and pilot on call at Cloncurry to start the celebrated Flying Doctor Service. Before that year people in the far outback, who were victims of serious accidents or critical illnesses, usually died before they could be carried, often for hundreds of kilometres, to a hospital. After 1928, thanks to Rev. John Flynn's vision, a doctor and nurses flew to the patient within hours. In 1928 H. J. L. Hinkler, a boy from Bundaberg in Queensland, broke the Smith brothers' record by flying from London to Darwin in fifteen and a half days. This was also the longest solo flight ever made up to that time. Perhaps the greatest of all breakers of aerial flight records was Charles Kingsford-Smith. In the same year, 1928, in the twin-engined 'Southern Cross', he and his crew, Charles Ulm, N. Litchfield and T. McWilliams, made the first trans-Pacific flight from the United States to Australia via Hawaii and Fiji, the first trans-Tasman crossings from Australia to New Zealand and back again, and the first non-stop trans-Australia flight of 3360 kilometres. 'Smithy' was knighted in 1932 but was killed three years later aged only 38, when his aircraft crashed in the Bay of Bengal en route from England to Australia. By the end of the 1920s all the capital cities in Australia and many country centres were connected by regular, reliable air services.

Cities and towns universally were lit by electricity, gas or wood or coal fires still being used most often for cooking. Radio receiving sets were quite common by the end of the decade, but manually-wound gramophones and, to a lesser extent, pianolas, were the major means of providing light music and entertainment in the home. As elsewhere in the western world, in the 1920s women enjoyed a degree of social and sexual freedom unknown to earlier generations. Some explained it as a reaction to the deprivations of the war years and/or as women taking equal rights for themselves because of the sterling contribution they had made to the war effort. Others pointed to a falling-off in church-going and the ready availability of relatively reliable contraceptive devices. Whatever the reason, women cut their hair short in a 'bob' or a 'shingle'. They smoked cigarettes in public and drank cocktails. They danced the Foxtrot and the Charleston to the music of gramophone records. They went swimming and surfing in bathing suits that exposed more and more of the body. For the first time in the history of Christian civilisation, they showed their

"*Before we were married he used to call me an angel.* **Now he** *doesn't call me anything.*"

"*Perhaps he doesn't want to hurt your feelings.*"

"*Not he—it's my private opinion that he isn't game.*" *Bulletin*, 1927

legs in the streets as dresses grew shorter and shorter, finally rising above the knee in about 1927. Under their skirts the more daring 'flappers' discarded long bloomers for short 'scanties', and rolled their stockings down to the knees so as to expose a good deal of naked thigh when they moved, or sat down, or stepped into a motor car, or rode pillion on a motorcycle behind young men. They sang a popular 'rag-time' dance tune:

Don't let people tell you that it's shocking
To wear your sweetie's picture on your stocking!
Laugh at Ma! Laugh at Pa! Give them all the ha-ha-ha!
Roll 'em low and show your pretty knees!

Yet with all this freedom the 'wowser' influence in Australian life hardly lessened. In most States hotels continued to close at six o'clock and petty criminals continued to cater for the thirst of the ungodly in 'sly-grop shops' after that hour. Gambling was illegal except on a licensed racecourse and John Wren's Collingwood Tote had been closed by the police in 1907; but every town had one or several clandestine 'two-up schools' for those who played the game, and any number of illegal 'S.P. bookies' (starting price bookmakers) who usually operated by telephone. In every town and suburb 'picture palaces' were built to show Charles Chaplin, Mary Pickford and other 'stars' of the silent screen, and in every bush hamlet the local School of Arts or district hall would screen films at least once a week: but Commonwealth and State governments applied a rigidly puritanical censorship to films and indeed, to all books, pictures, gramophone records and other material entering the country from abroad. A few silent films of good quality were made locally, by Raymond Longford and others, before Hollywood established its virtual world-monopoly of the industry. Indeed the first 'feature film' ever made anywhere is said to have been a popular life of Ned Kelly, now lost. Longford's *Sentimental Bloke* and *On Our Selection* survive.

The first Australians too were existing in just the same way as before the war. Some lived on the white man's charity on government or church mission-stations or reserves. More eked out an existence as itinerant fringe-dwellers in the 'black's camp' on the outskirts of country towns, working sometimes at fruit-picking or other unskilled tasks. In the far outback tribal remnants provided much of the labour on cattle and sheep-stations, both in the paddocks and the homestead; but usually they worked for rations and a derisory fraction of the wage demanded by white men and women for the same work. Only in the Kimberley District, in

Arnhem Land, parts of Cape York Peninsula, and in the desert areas of Central and Western Australia were there still a few thousand Aboriginals all told, who preserved some semblance of their own tribal culture: and these, sometimes, were still dealt with in the old way by the white invaders.

In 1927 in the East Kimberley District and in 1928 in Central Australia, there occurred the last large-scale massacres of Aboriginals, in both cases as had been usual in the past, at the hands or with the connivance of, the police. These were the last cases of the kind only because (white) public opinion — after more than a century — would no longer tolerate such deeds and in both cases governments were forced to institute inquiries. In the Kimberleys case the Royal Commissioner, G. T. Wood, found that Aboriginals had killed a white man called Hay on Nulla Nulla Station and that two constables, two 'special' constables, Hay's partner and seven armed Aboriginals had set out to arrest the murderers. Instead they had caught, chained together and murdered at least eleven Aboriginals, burning the bodies in their campfires. The Rev. E. Gribble at the neighbouring Forrest River Mission gave evidence that about thirty of his regular Aboriginal visitors disappeared at the time. There was also evidence that Hay's partner, a man named Overheu, had subsequently murdered an Aboriginal employee who had witnessed the slaughter. Every bar-fly in the port of the district, Wyndham, knew the facts but no witness could be found to attest them in court. The murderers went scot free.

THE COUNTRY PARTY, REHABILITATION AND THE R.S.L.

During the war a very important political realignment had taken place — not much remarked upon at the time amid the emotional conscription campaigns, the sound and fury generated by the Prime Minister[1] and the overriding issue of the conflict itself. This was the emergence, once again, of a third political party, this time the Country Party. From 1919 onwards if there were not, in Deakin's phrase, three elevens in the field, there were at least two and a half. With the benefit of hindsight it is easy to argue that the Fusion of 1909 rendered inevitable the growth of a new third party to replace, in some respects, the defunct Freetraders. As we have seen, the Freetraders were in reality absorbed by the Protectionists and not vice versa, despite the fact that the Protectionists were very much in

[1] Especially during his time as 'National Labor' Prime Minister, Hughes, accurately enough, made continual use of the slogan 'Win the War'. The *Bulletin*, equally continually paraphrased this as 'Win by Jaw'.

the minority at the time of the Fusion. Within two or three years the 'fused' Liberal Party tariff policy had become indistinguishable from that of the sometime Protectionists: but the pastoralists, farmers, merchants and importers who had usually supported the Freetrade Party were not converted to protection. Graziers and farmers still wanted to buy the cheapest and best possible supplies — agricultural machinery, fencing wire, rabbit traps, tools, flour, tea, sugar and so on; and importers still wished to supply them at prices uninflated by high tariffs, ideally at prices unaffected by any customs or excise duty at all.

As the years passed after 1909 it became only too evident that the Liberal Party was totally committed to a high protection policy for Australia's developing secondary industries, and that the Labor Party was equally keen on protection, perhaps more so. Moreover it was clear that an increasingly large majority of the Australian people were protectionist. Even importers and merchants could pass on the high costs of protection simply by increasing their prices, but the primary producer could not, since he was mainly dependent on the competitive, but fluctuating, prices for wheat, wool and frozen meat in the world market. What was the unfortunate countryman to do ? From 1900 onwards he joined, in greater numbers than ever before, a number of sectional pressure groups — farmers' unions, pastoralists' associations, dairy-farmers' co-operative societies and so on. By the end of the war several of these bodies were active in each State. They had different names and constitutions but essentially the same set of grievances and aims.

They all believed that protection, at any rate the kind of protection being implemented by the two major parties, was bad for their members' pockets and so for the country generally. Despite Hughes's herculean and successful efforts to market their produce during the war, they blamed him — and both the parties he had led — for interfering with 'private enterprise' and the free flow of the market, for 'socialising' tendencies in fact. More cogently they blamed him for keeping low by legislation the price of wheat and other farm products on the domestic market, in order, as they saw it, to benefit the city masses. They resented Labor's attempts to 'break up the big estates' with its graduated land tax and to improve wages and conditions for rural workers. At the same time they feared and distrusted the Liberal-inclined bankers and merchant financiers in the cities who handled their produce, bought and sold their properties and lent them money on mortgage. Above all, they (and a good many city-dwellers) believed devoutly in the ancient myth, by no means peculiar to Australia, that country people, especially small freeholders, are innately nobler, braver, more industrious, and above all more deserving, than those who inhabit the sinful, sophisticated and effete cities. Their rhetoric constantly stressed the 'independence' and 'enterprise' of the man on the land; but in accordance with the perennial Australian tradition of omni-competent government action, the last thing they really wished for was to be left alone. On the contrary they wanted differential government action to aid, comfort and subsidise primary producers. Some have seen this policy as a kind of rural socialism: if so, it was one designed to benefit rural landowners rather than wage-earners. Generally speaking, Country Party politicians have been more conservative than their Nationalist (or United Australia Party or Liberal) brethren.

The movement began in Western Australia, possibly because that State lost most by passing over its customs and excise taxing powers to the Commonwealth. In 1912 several bodies came together to form the Farmers and Settlers' Association of Western Australia. By 1914 it had created an independent Country Party which won eight seats out of a total forty-nine in the State election of that year. In the same way farmers' parties were established in Queensland in 1917, in Victoria in 1918 and in New South Wales in 1920. In 1918 delegates from State rural bodies set up an Australian Farmers' Federal Organisation which devised a common platform for the 1919 Commonwealth election. The State bodies nominated some candidates of their own, and the A.F.F.O. others, in addition to some Freetrade-inclined Nationalists whom it 'endorsed'. In the event this group of rural candidates, which soon came to be known as the Country Party, won eleven of the seventy-five seats in the House of Representatives.

It should be noted that this was the first federal election to employ the system of preferential voting which had been introduced in Queensland in 1892, in Western Australia and Victoria in 1911, in New South Wales in 1926 and in South Australia in 1929. Since 1907 Tasmania had employed the complicated Hare-Clark system of proportional representation, which was adopted also in 1948 for elections to the Commonwealth Senate. Under preferential voting a candidate is declared elected without more ado if he obtains an absolute majority of all valid first preference votes cast. If no candidate does so, then the candidate with the smallest number of first preference votes is eliminated from the count and his second preference votes are distributed to the remaining candidates. The second preferences of the remaining candidate with the lowest total vote are then distributed and so on until the candidate preferred by the majority of voters is elected. The system was actually first used federally in the Corangamite by-election of December 1918, which was won by a 'Farmers' candidate'. It had been introduced by the Nationalist Government a few months earlier in a bid to 'buy off' opposition from the nascent Country Party forces. As long as 'first-past-the-post' voting prevailed, both Nationalists and Country Party candidates hesitated to stand against each other, lest they should 'split' the conservative vote and hand the seat to Labor.

It is also worth noting that for over sixty years the Country Party has been able, generally speaking, to retain the support of different and in some ways, rival, country interests. In the nineteenth century one of the major political and social cleavages in Australia had been that between 'squatters' and 'free-selectors' or 'cockies', between wealthy pastoralists on the one hand and struggling wheat farmers on the other. Yet since the Great War the Country Party has been able to reconcile the interests of both groups and, in many areas, of dairy farmers, orchardists and mining magnates as well. Because of the deep conservatism, already noted, of most leading figures in the Country Party, it has worked always in conjunction with the major anti-Labor Party in the federal sphere and in most of the States, but it is not bound to do so. In the Victorian Country Party, for instance, small farmers are relatively much more influential and wealthy pastoralists less so than elsewhere, with the result that the Country Party has often made political alliances with Labor in that State. Because it frankly represents the interests of a minority, the party has never been able to contemplate governing in its own right. It is, moreover, a regional party. That is to say that, while it commands very strong support in some rural areas, it has seldom managed to shake the grip of the two major parties on other, sometimes quite similar, country districts. The North and South Coasts of New South Wales, for example, both depend largely on dairy-farming, timber-getting and tourism. In terms of electoral support the North Coast is easily the greatest Country Party stronghold in Australia, while the South Coast more often returns Nationalist (or U.A.P. or Liberal) or Labor members to both federal and State parliaments.

Personal factors have something to do with it of course. The man who did more than any other two or three persons to create the Country Party in eastern Australia and then to lead it for a generation, was born in 1880 at Grafton on the Clarence River on the North Coast of New South Wales. Grandson of a town clerk and son of a mayor of Grafton, Earle Christmas Grafton Page was educated at a local state school before going on to Sydney High School and winning a scholarship to Sydney University. He came top of the matriculation class at the high school when he was only fifteen and also topped his final year in medicine at the age of twenty-one. Two years later, with two partners, he set up practice in South

Grafton and established a private hospital there. Acquiring something more than local renown as a first-class surgeon and general practitioner, he became quite rich, investing his money in farming and pastoral properties both in the Clarence district and farther afield. In 1908 he bought one of the first motor cars to be seen in the district, a 20-horsepower Itala, made adjustments so that it could be used for an ambulance, and drove it round the mud tracks of the area on his professional calls. In 1913, at the age of 33, he was elected to the South Grafton Council as an alderman. During the next two years he became a prominent political figure, mainly by his work in reviving the long-dormant 'New State' movement for separation of the North Coast and New England tablelands region from New South Wales.

This agitation ceased almost completely when Page joined the A.I.F. He was away for sixteen months and spent a good deal of that time examining water conservation and hydro-electric schemes in Egypt on his way to the front and in Canada on his way home. He worked as a medical officer in a casualty clearing station in France. In his autobiography he implies that he was invalided out of the army, but gives no clue as to the nature of his illness. Back in Grafton he threw himself again into politics, inspiring and co-ordinating the agitation of various farmers' organisations which were creating the Country Party. In the election of December 1919 he was sent to the Commonwealth Parliament as member for Cowper, the electorate of which Grafton is the focal point. Page was once characterised by a political opponent as 'a giggling bush doctor'. Indeed he had an affable, jolly personality and he understood his bush constituents so well that he continued to sit as member for Cowper until 1961; but he was also immensely energetic, astute, ambitious and calculating. Frank Green, for many years Clerk of the House of Representatives, who knew him well, wrote:

> the only way to conduct an argument with Page with any hope of success was in writing, because in verbal argument he talked with great rapidity, followed each short burst with: "You see, you see, you see". And while the opponent was trying to see, Page would move on to another point with the assumption that the previous issue had been completely settled in his favour.[2]

A man with such splendid gifts was bound to rise to the top in politics. From the time of his election he was easily the most influential of the eleven new Country Party members. They formally elected him to the leadership of the group in April 1921.

[2] Frank C. Green, *Servant of the House*, Melbourne, 1969, p.103.

Most diggers did not enjoy such a short war, such an interesting passage home and such immediate success on their return to civilian life as Dr Page, though practically all were repatriated in time to vote, if they wished, in the election which sent him to Parliament. As Minister for Repatriation, one of those who had left the Labor Party with Hughes, Senator E. D. Millen, had the difficult task of finding congenial work for the surviving heroes. The immediate post-war years were prosperous by then contemporary standards. Even so, with an unemployment rate of about 8 per cent in 1920, not all of the returned men were happy to be civilians again. Adjustment was specially difficult for those who had joined the A.I.F. at 18 (or even younger in the case of some who had lied about their age), for they had known nothing but childhood and war. One way of helping to cope with the problem was the granting of preference in employment to returned soldiers. The federal Government and all State governments except that of Queensland, legislated for soldier preference. Queensland's Labor Government retained the previously established, but conflicting, principle of preference to trade unionists. In practice neither law meant very much except in the case of jobs in a government service. Private employers could not efficiently be forced to hire any but those they regarded as the best applicants for a job: but the legislation did much to ensure that the bitter divisions of the war years continued. Tens of thousands were both returned soldiers and trade unionists, but this fact did little to soften the hostility between many old diggers and those whom they often regarded as 'shirkers'.

Many men simply returned to their old jobs. In the case of clerical workers this was not so easy to do because women, employed sometimes at less than half the male rate, had invaded offices, banks and shops during the war. Thousands of others were trained, or re-trained, in trades or professions at government expense. Others were given money to buy houses or businesses of their own, or to bring out 'war brides' from Britain or France or even Palestine. The most popular calling was farming. As we have noticed in connection with the growth of the Country Party, the *mystique* of the land was still very strong. In the 1920s Australian governments and people alike still generally thought of primary production as more satisfying to the individual, and more important to the nation, than any other way of making a living. And so the benevolent Commonwealth Government provided money, loans, fertilizer, land and machinery for nearly 40 000 returned soldier-settlers — many of whom had had no previous experience on the land whatever. It is not surprising that there were more failures than successes among them.

In 1916 there was founded a voluntary organisation which

The Worker, 10 February 1916

THAT PROMISE.

"Melbourne women have been invited to enter the hitherto exclusive Chamber of Finance as bank clerks."—News item.
"Many returned soldiers complain that the promise of employers to keep their jobs open has been broken."—News item.

BANKER (to returned soldier): "Yes, yes; possibly I DID say something about keeping your position vacant, but it has lately been capably filled by a charming young woman (to whom wages are no object); and I feel sure that you, as a soldier, will not be so unchivalrous as to ask me to discharge her to reinstate YOU!"

thereafter did a great deal for returned men and the dependents of those who did not return. The Returned Soldiers' and Sailors' Imperial League of Australia, universally known as the R.S.L., held its first Federal Congress in Brisbane. Membership was, of course, restricted to servicemen who had actually served in a theatre of war overseas. At first few returned soldiers joined, but after a few years membership stabilised at something a little less than a half of those eligible. This proportion, however, is very much higher than in similar ex-servicemen's organisations in Britain, the United States or any other comparable country except New Zealand. From the beginning the League worked frankly as a pressure-group seeking to influence public opinion and governments in favour of returned soldiers' interests, and almost from the beginning it was given recognition and semi-official status by governments. In October 1918, for instance, the Minister for Defence, Senator Pearce,

> issued an order notifying all [Commonwealth Government] departments that the League was to be recognised as the offical representative body of returned soldiers, and complaints coming from the League, in theory, at any rate, must have immediate attention.[3]

Generation after generation the League watched most successfully over the interests of soldiers' widows, orphans and of returned men, whether they belonged to the League or not. It saw that governments provided suitable education for the children of dead heroes, that their mothers were given adequate pensions, and that free medical attention, pension rates and so on for returned men were as good as they could possibly be in a hard world. It also built thousands of R.S.L. club rooms and halls to cater for the social life, and often for the post-six o'clock thirst, of members and friends.

The R.S.L. played a major role in making the anniversary of the Gallipoli landing into an Australian National Day. Primarily as a result of its efforts, the Victorian Parliament in 1925 passed 'An Act to constitute Anzac Day a Public and Bank Holiday and for other purposes'. By the end of the decade the day was celebrated with tremendous emotion in all States. On the morning of 25 April each year old diggers, many in their faded khaki uniforms and all with campaign ribbons and medals clanking on their chests, marched to services of remembrance, usually held in the open air before the war memorial in every city, town and hamlet. Younger people particularly, were exhorted to cherish their country, to honour the fallen and to be prepared, if necessary, to make similar sacrifices themselves on the altar of patriotism. The characteristics, real or

[3] G. L. Kristianson, *The Politics of Patriotism*, Canberra, 1966, p.12.

supposed, of the Australian soldier were held up for emulation by the rising generation. Partly in reaction to the sober solemnity of these proceedings, people tended to spend the afternoon and evening in merrymaking. In public houses and streets and squares old soldiers drank together, fought their battles over again and, in the face of the law and the constables, asserted their birthright and their wartime experience by indulging in ritualistic games of two-up. Until the following day few policemen dared arrest any of the celebrants.

More generally, throughout the period between the wars, the R.S.L. did a great deal to make the values associated with Anzac Day and the 'old digger' dominant in the Australian community. Along with the virtues ascribed to the idealised digger — courage, loyalty, mateship and democratic levelling — went other less admirable characteristics. The stereotyped figure exhibited also tough, sardonic contempt for coloured people and foreigners generally, for minority views, for art, literature, culture and learning; and something not far from contempt — patronage disguised as chivalrous protectiveness — for 'good' women, and brutal disdain for 'bad' ones. He magnified 'male' virtues like decisiveness, directness, physical strength, and despised 'female' ones like thoughtfulness, gentleness, subtlety. The tone of most of the writing in the *Bulletin* or *Smith's Weekly* at this period exactly mirrors the prevailing ethos — levelling values, rough manners and philistine tastes as the outer form; conformity, conservatism and unquestioning Anglo-Australian patriotism as the inner content. The national ethos, in fact, strikingly resembled the constellation of attitudes referred to by women's liberationists of a much later generation as 'male chauvinist piggery'. George Johnson, author of a great novel, *My Brother Jack*, grew up in Melbourne in the 1920s. The book vividly re-creates the authentic texture and atmosphere of Australian life at the time, reminding those old enough to remember of the huge shadow cast by the war, Anzac Day and the digger image — as well as of wowserism, short skirts and other matters.

Finally it must be noted that the R.S.L. which always claimed to be strictly non-political, exercised a very great influence on politics. Indeed for many years it has been the only pressure group in Australia enjoying a *de facto* traditional right of direct access to the federal Cabinet. And yet it was non-political in the sense that it pressed for concessions and took benefits impartially from both major political groupings and rarely directed, or even openly urged, its members to vote for one and not the other. It did, however, concern itself publicly with many aspects of national politics, quite remote from pensions and rehabilitation of ex-servicemen and the like, particularly with defence and foreign policies; and since it was an extremely conservative organisation, its intervention in these fields happened almost invariably to benefit anti-Labor parties whose policies tended to be like its own. Of course many thousands of returned soldiers held radical views. For some years in the 1930s one bemedalled old digger used to break ranks every Anzac Day in Sydney's Martin Place, in front of the Commonwealth Bank building where ex-Prime Minister Hughes received the plaudits of the crowd, in order to shout in his face, 'Hughes, you Rat!'; but it is improbable that he, or comrades who thought like him, troubled to join the R.S.L.

Moreover the League never felt any compunction about intervening openly against dissident left-wing political groups such as the Australian Communist Party, though most of them were, in law, bodies on a par with the Nationalist or Country or Labor parties. Inspired by the vivid, if distant, spectre of bolshevism, the League in 1919 set up an 'Anti-Bolshevik Committee' which organised an 'Army to Fight Bolshevism' of 2000 men. This 'Army' was held in readiness during the 1919 Eight Hour Day Procession in Brisbane to show, said the R.S.L. leaders, that the League could maintain law and order, even if the legitimate government (which was Labor and anti-conscriptionist) could not. The intimidatory effect on left-wing organisations, not to mention peaceful trade unionists on the way to their annual picnic, may be imagined. In later years the R.S.L. resorted less frequently to such openly provocative and forceful tactics, but its powerful influence continued to bear in the same direction.

INDUSTRIAL MILITANCY

Polarisation of society, begun by the war or, more accurately, by the Conscription campaigns, continued throughout the 1920s. Working-class bitterness was exacerbated by what many saw as a continuing deterioration in real living standards. This view received trenchant support from a Royal Commission appointed by Prime Minister Hughes himself, which reported in November 1920 that a just basic wage arrived at by the principles of the Harvester Judgment, would be £5 17s od per week. In fact the basic wage then stood at £4 2s od. In 1919 there were almost as many strikes as there had been at the peak of militant industrial activity two years earlier. In May 1919, for example, the Lumpers' Union struck in Fremantle, Western Australia. Members of the National Workers' Union, formed during a previous strike in 1917 and regarded by the strikers as a bogus 'scab' organisation, tried to unload the tied-up ships. Barricades were thrown up in the streets by the opposing factions: rocks, fists and boots flew, and police armed with bayonets quelled the rioting, killing one genuine unionist in the process. Coming down the Swan River by launch to assess the situation, the Nationalist Premier, Sir Hal Colebatch, was bombarded by rocks and other potentially lethal missiles as his launch passed under the two Fremantle bridges. After five days' rioting the members of the National Workers' Union withdrew from the field. Similar scenes were witnessed all over Australia, the Fremantle strike being unusual only in that it caused actual loss of life: but it was not unique.

The Melbourne Police strike of November 1923 alarmed respectable citizens more than any other at the period. The vast majority of the city's uniformed constables refused duty and, on the night of Saturday the 3rd serious rioting occurred and seventy-eight shop-front windows were smashed and their contents looted. Five thousand special constables, nearly all of them returned soldiers, were sworn in and restored order, one of them losing his life in the process. The Nationalist Premier, H. S. W. Lawson, dismissed 627 of the strikers. By Tuesday the 6th all was quiet and in brilliant sunshine the favourite, *Bitalli*, won the Melbourne Cup, watched by a crowd of 125 000 people.

The Melbourne policemen struck after years of dissatisfaction with their rates of pay and working conditions. In the post-war period militancy was very widespread throughout the trade-union movement and in the Labor Party, shorn of its right-wing by the Conscription split; but most conservative observers, then as always, believed that most of the trouble was caused by a handful of diabolically clever agitators, preferably foreigners. By 1920 these were generally seen as Bolsheviks or Communists. In Australia as everywhere else in the world, the I.W.W. rapidly lost credence and support among radical activists after the Russian Revolution of November 1917. Leninist doctrine roundly condemned the I.W.W. for its 'one-sided' emphasis on industrial action, holding that revolutionaries should be equally active in politics and parliament: and nothing succeeds like success. For the first time in the history of the world the rule of the few, the rich, and the powerful had been replaced by that of the poor, the weak and the many — or so it seemed in the 1920s to millions of idealists and reformers inside and outside Russia. After a great deal of doctrinal bickering between different socialist sects in the major cities and coalfields, a tiny band of Australian Marxists, many of them ex-members of the I.W.W., formed themselves into the Communist Party of Australia in Sydney in June 1922. Most were trade unionists but there was a sprinkling of intellectuals. The Australian Communist Party never achieved any significant degree of popular support. Even at the peak of its influence during the Second World War it polled less than 2 per cent of the Senate vote though, for special local and personal reasons, the Communist Dr Fred Patterson was twice elected to the Queensland Parliament at that time. However, the Party did exercise a considerable influence in the trade-union movement. It did disseminate Marxist theories in a Labor movement notorious for its contempt for intellectual speculation of any kind, and it did for half a century provide an effective bogy to be agitated by conservatives before ashen-faced voters at election after election.

Such was the militancy of the rank-and-file industrial workers that the Labor Party officially adopted at this time a pseudo-revolutionary stance. In the second half of 1920 a severe post-war slump developed and unemployment figures soared. In June 1921 the Federal Executive of the Labor Party convened a conference of trade-union delegates from all over Australia. This Melbourne Conference carried by a large majority a motion 'that the socialisation of industry, production, distribution and exchange be the objective of the Labor Party'. This was seen by right-thinking persons as proof positive that the Labor Party had been taken over by the Communists, but analysis of the voting figures 'suggests that, of the 150 or 160 delegates who were present at any one time' only about twenty-five were Communists.[4]

Four months later the recommendations of the Melbourne Trade Unionists' Conference were submitted to a Commonwealth Conference of the Labor Party convened in Brisbane. By 22 votes to 10 this supreme governing body of the A.L.P. adopted what came to be known as 'the socialisation objective' — detailed above. However, some parliamentarians at the conference, led by E. G. Theodore, Premier of Queensland, ensured that socialisation was a vague, long-term 'objective' — not a part of the 'fighting platform' to be actually urged on the hustings. In addition Maurice Blackburn, a Victorian delegate, moved a resolution which was carried, 'interpreting' the main resolution in such a way as virtually to negate it entirely. The Blackburn resolution stated that the Australian Labor Party 'does not seek to abolish private ownership even of any of the instruments of production where such instrument is utilised by its owner in a socially useful manner and without exploitation'.[5] It will be seen that even at this high-water-mark of militant feeling the A.L.P. simultaneously was and was not in favour of socialism. Nevertheless the 'socialisation objective' of the Brisbane Conference

[4] I. A. H. Turner, *Industrial Labor and Politics*, Canberra, 1965, p.219.

[5] Turner, p.225.

of 1921 continued to be quoted, without the qualifications, by friend and foe for the next fifty years and more.

The implications of the resolution were rendered even more nugatory by the fact that the Commonwealth had no power, under the Constitution, to socialise industry wholesale. In fact it had very little power to regulate in any way the conduct of business corporations. In 1912 and 1915 the Labor Party had sought such powers for the Commonwealth but the referenda were defeated by the people on both occasions. Hughes, ever a centralist though by no means at this period a socialist, had Parliament present two slightly watered-down referendum proposals along the same lines to the voters at the 1919 Commonwealth election, but both were defeated. Yet by an irony of fate the High Court at this time gave to Commonwealth constitutional powers the widest interpretation they had ever received. Sir Edmund Barton died in 1920 and the radical centralists, Isaac Isaacs and Higgins, became more influential members of the Bench. In a series of judgments of which the most significant were the *Engineers Case* and *McArthur's Case*, it was held, for example, that the Commonwealth Arbitration Court's power was so wide that it could hear a dispute between a trade union and a *State-owned* organisation; and that while section 92 of the Constitution, which stipulates absolute freedom of inter-State trade, forbids any interference by a State government in such activities, it does not apply to the Commonwealth Government at all. It is obvious, however, that such a widening of the interpretation set upon Commonwealth powers falls very far short of the power to 'socialise industry, production, distribution and exchange'. The brilliant barrister who fought and won the case for the Amalgamated Society of Engineers was the 25-year-old Robert Gordon Menzies.

HUGHES, BRUCE AND THE EIGHTH PARLIAMENT

In the eighth Parliament, from 1919 to 1922, the Hughes Nationalist Government, owing to the advent of the Country Party, could hardly be said to have a firm majority. The Nationalists had won 37 seats in the House, but Labor had 26 solid supporters and the Country Party ten. The remaining two members of the 75 had stood as Nationalists but had also been 'endorsed' by the farmers' organisations. As time passed they tended to vote more and more often with the Country Party and less and less with the Nationalists. A few Country Party members, especially among the Victorians, could have formed a government in coalition with Labor under certain circumstances: most could never have done such a thing and were determined, on crucial issues, to keep the Nationalists in power.

Add to this the fact that the Country Party members, at first, did not form nearly as cohesive and well-disciplined a group as the Labor, or even the Nationalist members, and that a group of Nationalists was opposed to Hughes's leadership, and his worries may be imagined. His massive majority of 35 out of 36 seats in the Senate did nothing to give him firm control of the Lower House. Then, fate and the troubles of Ireland offered an opportunity for improving the Government's position — one which more scrupulous men might not have taken, but which Hughes embraced eagerly.

Since 1901 the voters in Australia's largest electorate, centring on the Western Australian goldfields at Coolgardie and Kalgoorlie, had returned the same Labor representative to the Commonwealth Parliament. Born in Ireland in 1858, Hugh Mahon became a journalist who was imprisoned for a time by the British Government for his support of the Irish Home Rule movement. He emigrated to Australia in 1882 and started a paper at Coolgardie before being elected to Parliament. In 1920 Britain was still endeavouring to suppress the Irish national movement and feelings ran high among people of Irish descent, in Australia as elsewhere. In a Melbourne park, Mahon, whose two sons had served in the A.I.F., addressed a large crowd on the Irish situation saying, among other things, that 'the sob of the widow on the coffin would one day shake the foundations of this bloody and accursed Empire'. With consummate timing Hughes attacked him in Parliament on 11 November, the second anniversary of the signing of the Armistice by Germany. In a vitriolic speech the Prime Minister moved that by reason of 'seditious and disloyal utterances' Mahon was 'guilty of conduct unfitting him to remain a member of this House'.[6] Only the Labor members voted against the motion and so Mahon became the only member ever to be expelled from the federal Parliament. Sectarian bitterness was so strong at the time that in the by-election the Nationalist candidate won Kalgoorlie, always previously regarded as a safe Labor seat. Thus Hughes's parliamentary position was improved marginally.

November 1920 was a fateful month for Hughes. He expelled Mahon, the Royal Commission he had appointed reported that basic wage-earners were being under-paid by some 30 per cent, and he accepted a cash gift of £25,000 subscribed by anonymous admirers as a tribute to his wartime leadership. No other deed of the Prime Minister so damned him in the eyes of his former comrades in the Labor movement. Twenty-five thousand pounds in 1920 was a very large sum, in purchasing power equal to something well over half a million dollars in 1976. Ever afterwards Labor men held that, in

[6] *C.P.D.*, vol. 94, pp.6382-3.

addition to the other sins he had committed in their eyes, Hughes had accepted a large reward, or bribe, from those who opposed everything Labor stood for. A few months later the left-wing member for Melbourne Ports, Frank Brennan, moved that by accepting this gift Hughes had automatically rendered his parliamentary seat vacant by contravening section 45 of the Constitution, which forbids taking any 'honorarium for services rendered to the Commonwealth'. The debate was inconclusive.

Most of Parliament's time was spent discussing five sets of Government measures, those concerned with first, winding up the war, second the tariff, third arbitration, fourth concessions to Country Party pressures and fifth a further measure of 'state socialism' or Government ownership of industry. In addition to a host of measures for the rehabilitation of returned soldiers, noticed already, there were a number of acts in which Australia formally adhered to peace treaties with former enemy countries and to the Washington Treaty of 1922, by which the United States, the British Empire, Japan, France and Italy agreed to limit the tonnage of their naval capital ships in the ratio of 5, 5, 3, 1.75 and 1.75 respectively. The New Guinea Act of 1920 accepted the former German colony as a C Class Mandate from the League of Nations, and made provision for the Territory's government. Hughes explained that the White Australia Policy was safeguarded and that the trade of the Territory was to be an Australian monopoly. In only one respect did the Act provide safeguards for the welfare of the indigenous people better than the minimum requirements laid down by the League. The Government accepted a Labor amendment to the Bill which forbade the exaction of forced labour in lieu of taxation.

Other legislation repealed the War Precautions Act, but in doing so left some of its provisions effectively embedded in the law — to the detriment of Australian liberty. Thenceforward a new offence of 'sedition' was detailed in the Crimes Act. It became an offence to leave Australia without a passport. A British subject entering Australia might be required to swear an oath of allegiance, and persons advocating the overthrow by force or violence of the 'established government . . . of any . . . civilized country . . . or the abolition of organised government' were defined as prohibited immigrants.[7] The Chanak crisis of September 1922 showed that the two anti-Labor parties — and Australian majority opinion — still remained uncritically and totally loyal to Britain. It seemed that tension between Britain and Turkey might lead precipitately to war. Lloyd George, who had not previously consulted the dominions in

[7] *S.I.*, p.197.

any way about the matter, asked them if they would send troops. Hughes, fully supported by Earle Page, enthusiastically agreed. Labor objected vigorously. No other dominion promised unqualified support and the crisis subsided peacefully.

The Customs Tariff Act of 1921 embodied the first comprehensive revision since 1914 of duties on goods entering the country. It also signalised the complete triumph — despite Country Party misgivings — of protection for Australian industries. Another Act authorised the negotiation of an agreement with New Zealand whereby the sister dominion shared in the preferential tariff rate accorded to British goods. The Nationalist Government also established, as an experiment, a Tariff Board empowered to advise the Minister for Customs on all tariff and bounty questions, including the merit or otherwise of requests from particular industries for some form of protection. The Minister was also given power, with the advice of the Board, to impose extra duties on imported goods which threatened the prosperity of Australian industries.

The Prime Minister personally devised, and set great store by, the Industrial Peace Acts of 1920. These established a complicated system of national and local district councils, consisting of equal numbers of employers' and employees' representatives, and empowered to investigate the facts of disputes and to offer advice and conciliation to the conflicting parties. They also established a series of special district tribunals with power to arbitrate on disputes and hand down enforceable awards. The whole structure was to be under the aegis of the long-established Commonwealth Arbitration Court. The new scheme did not have the great results Hughes seems to have expected, although until 1929 it did perhaps ameliorate slightly the industrial strife endemic in the coal industry.

The new Country Party members, naturally, were most interested in the long and detailed tariff debates. Most of them were still Freetraders at heart, but the same could be said of only two or three men in each of the two major parties. They fought strongly but unavailingly at least to keep down the level of protection in general, and of duties on manufactured goods used on the land in particular. For example, various kinds of fencing wire, agricultural machinery and pesticides, which had formerly been duty-free, were now given substantial protection in the face of the Country Party's frenzied protests. Not long before the 1922 election Country Party pressure did succeed in having some of these duties reduced again, but not abolished except that on wire-netting. At the same time a bounty was paid to Australian wire-netting manufacturers. Forced by experience to recognise that they could never reverse the general trend to higher protection, the primary producers' representatives began instead to demand protection for their constituents too. Thus Country Party pressure produced an embargo on the export of butter, save through a committee of producers which controlled bulk sales to the United Kingdom at a satisfactory price. It also produced low-interest government loans to farmers' co-operative associations engaged in transporting and selling the wheat crop, and the direct payment of bounties on exports of frozen meat. Direct and indirect subsidising of primary industries increased vastly for the next fifty years as the price for continuing Country Party support of the major non-Labor party.

Finally, Hughes still had enough centralist and socialist leanings to get himself into trouble with some of his own supporters but not enough, of course, to soften Labor hostility. The Commonwealth Woollen Mills at Geelong in Victoria had been established by Labor to manufacture uniforms during the war. By 1921 they were making money for the Government in free competition with privately owned mills. This example of successful 'socialism' distressed many conservatives in the Nationalist and Country Party ranks and the mills were sold cheaply to 'private enterprise' against furious Labor protests. At the same time Hughes antagonised many of the same people on his own side of the House by two more ventures into what they saw as 'state socialism'. The Government bought one more than half of the total shares in Commonwealth Oil Refineries, a subsidiary of the Anglo-Persian Oil Company, formed to carry on the business of oil-refining in Australia. A similar (but not identical) arrangement was made between the Commonwealth Government and Amalgamated Wireless Australasia Limited, a company formed in 1913, which then enjoyed a virtual monopoly of wireless communication in Australia.

These deals added to the distrust and hostility with which many non-Labor politicians like Earle Page regarded the Prime Minister. Even under the happiest of circumstances Hughes was not an easy man to work with. Energetic, impulsive, domineering, shrewd, imaginative and unscrupulous, he was distrusted by many of his own party who suspected him, with some justice, of being still at heart an Australian Nationalist, rather than an Imperial patriot, and possibly a dangerous 'socialist' too. During the debate in Parliament on the Chanak incident, for instance, Earle Page had lectured the Prime Minister on his cavalier way of treating important British ministers. Hughes, needless to say, was very well aware of the intrigues against his leadership and took what steps he could to attach party colleagues to his star. At the end of 1921 Sir Joseph Cook resigned as Treasurer to take Andrew Fisher's place as Commonwealth High Commissioner in London. Hughes took the opportunity to replace him with a young, new, but very able Nationalist member whom he fully expected to be grateful for the appointment.

The new Treasurer, Stanley Melbourne Bruce, was a very different kind of man from his patron. In the first place he came from a rich and established family and had been given a conventional rich man's education. Born in Melbourne in 1883, the youngest child of a successful Gold Rush immigrant who had founded the well-known wholesale importing firm of Paterson, Laing and Bruce, he was educated at the fashionable Melbourne Grammar School and Trinity Hall, Cambridge, before reading for the bar at the London Inns of Court. He spent the war as an officer in the British, not the Australian, Army, was wounded with the British troops on Gallipoli and returned to his native country late in 1917. In the following year in a by-election for the Flinders seat, he was elected to the House of Representatives as a Nationalist. Reserved, methodical, well-bred and well-mannered, Bruce's impeccable background and connections must have been reassuring to those who distrusted Hughes. In many ways Bruce was more English than the English themselves: certainly he was very like the popular Australian image of the 'typical Englishman'. He spoke with a carefully modulated Oxford accent, he dressed perfectly in the sober English fashion, he played golf, he drove a Rolls-Royce, he even wore spats occasionally in cold weather — a sure sign of effeminacy or worse in many aggressively male Australian minds.

Frank Anstey's description of him tells us a good deal about the popular stereotype of Australianism and Englishness as well as about Bruce:

> Stanley Bruce, an English gentleman, born in Australia — as other Englishmen are born in China, India or Timbuctoo — moved in the best society, and in the soundest financial and commercial circles of Britain. He was a good looker with . . . a mental alertness hidden by his nonchalance. . . . Nothing was permitted to ruffle the calm of his superiority. No insult could draw from him the slightest protest — only a gaze of curiosity, such as an entomologist might give to a bug.[8]

Anstey wrote with such feeling because he was undoubtedly Parliament's greatest expert at insults, superior even to the Prime Minister, Hughes: but it is instructive to see him quite genuinely dismissing as irrelevant the mere accident of birthplace when thinking of the differences between Australians and Englishmen. Anstey was born to working-class parents in London and ran away to sea at the age of eleven: yet he considered himself an Australian because of his blunt manners and levelling opinions, just as naturally as he considered the Australian-born Bruce an Englishman because of his opposite qualities.

[8] *Anstey Papers*, Australian National Library.

The Woes of a Cartoonist

Herald, 1922-23

In his budget speech of August 1922 the new Treasurer advocated what were standard conservative budgetary policies, except for the heavy emphasis placed on national development. Australia needed, he said, to return to the gold standard, to cut government expenditure, to balance her budgets, a cautious measure of deflation, stable money, no doles and any amount of encouragement of laissez-faire principles in business. The Government should borrow only for reproductive works but, he stressed, Australia was a country of tremendous and largely untapped resources and the Government would be remiss in its duty if it did not borrow heavily 'for the creation of new wealth'.[9] As it turned out, these proved to be the declared aims, if not the actual practices, of the Commonwealth Government until 1929.

BRUCE, MEN, MONEY AND MARKETS

The general election campaign of December 1922 saw a swing to the right in party attitudes. Having moved from the working-class electorate of West Sydney to the more conservative one of Bendigo for the 1917 election, Hughes this time transferred to the blue-ribbon Tory seat of North Sydney. For the Nationalists he stood largely on the Government's record, promised to prune government spending to the bone, but at the same time advocated a vigorous programme, to be worked out in collaboration with the State governments, of assisted immigration of Britons. For good measure he also produced the hoary old election promise, first made by Barton in 1901, of unifying railway gauges. Earle Page for the Country Party agreed, but added that all government enterprises surviving from wartime must be eliminated and, of course, that farmers must be helped by a revision downwards of all tariffs affecting them and in other ways. Matthew Charlton for Labor spent much time criticising Hughes and his Government and vigorously opposed any further immigration as long as there were Australians out of work. In Victoria and South Australia splinter groups of right-wing Nationalists, styling themselves Liberals, and avowedly determined to expel Hughes and other ex-Labor men from positions of power, also stood candidates.

The Nationalists lost nine seats in the Representatives giving a House of 30 Labor members, 28 Nationalist, 14 Country Party, two Liberal and one Independent. The Senate result was 12 Labor, 23 Nationalist and one Country Party member. Obviously the Country Party was in a position almost to dictate its own terms to the

[9] *S.I.*, p.206.

Nationalists in the House. It had only two or three more members than in the previous House but experience had given it much more internal discipline and cohesion. Neither major party could hope to govern without its support and, since Page and most of his comrades stood to the right of the Nationalists on most issues, and far to the right of Hughes, there was never any real possibility of a Labor-Country Party Coalition government. During the campaign Bruce had pledged loyalty to Hughes and promised he too would resign if Hughes were removed from the Government. However, Page and his party refused to work with or serve under Hughes. Eight weeks of backstairs negotiations, threats and promises were summarised thus by Anstey's vitriolic pen:

> [Hughes's] arch enemy was Earle Page, leader of the 'Country Party' — a party whose support of a government depended on the volume of distributed emoluments. Page had denounced Bruce as a "balance sheet fakir", and Bruce described Page as a "paralysed mentality". Bruce would never associate with Page — NEVER. He would never desert Hughes — NEVER. A fortnight later Bruce and Page became partners and Hughes was made to walk the plank.[10]

Bruce claimed that 'Billy forced me to do the thing he never forgave me for'.[11] Having been Prime Minister for seven years, Hughes was to go on sitting in Parliament for another thirty, much of the time as a back-bencher. He never forgave his sometime *protégé*, Bruce — or Page.

These two agreed to form a Coalition Government, which enjoyed three terms in office and in which the Nationalists would have six Cabinet seats to the Country Party's five. They also agreed that any proposal must be agreed to by a majority of at least seven to four, so that at least one Country Party minister would have to be persuaded to agree to a Nationalist initiative and at least two Nationalists to a Country Party one. In February 1923 the new Government was sworn in. Bruce, aged 39, became Prime Minister and Minister for External Affairs, Pearce Minister for Home Affairs and Territories, Littleton Groom Attorney-General and Austin Chapman Minister for Trade, Customs and Health. Earle Page took the Treasury and other Country Party men the Post Office and Works and Railways.

Bruce summarised his policy of the next seven years in the slogan, 'Men, Money and Markets'. The words underline the extent to which Government and people, not just the Country Party and its supporters, were still bemused by the rural myth, the belief that

[10] *Anstey Papers*, Australian National Library.
[11] Cecil Edwards, *Bruce of Melbourne*, London, 1965, p.75.

Australia's manifest destiny lay in the land and what could be produced and exported from it. Of course secondary industry continued to grow and to be cosseted by governments. In fact the value of manufactured goods produced rose by nearly a quarter between 1919 and 1929, from about £320,000,000 to £420,000,000; but nearly all of this was for the home market. When the Prime Minister spoke of 'Men, Money and Markets' people thought of men to go on the land and help populate Australia's 'great empty spaces', of money to be invested in this settlement process and of finding markets for wool, wheat, frozen meat, dried fruits, and other primary export commodities.

We have seen that a great deal of money was spent on settling returned soldiers on the land. At the 1923 Imperial Conference Bruce negotiated a £34,000,000 agreement with the British Government to provide assisted passages for migrants. Migration was a matter for State governments and most of them had in fact begun assisted migration schemes soon after the war. Of these the best known and least successful was the Western Australian Group Settlement scheme. Groups of settlers worked together at clearing land, much of it in the very well-watered and heavily timbered areas of the 'South West' between Perth and Albany. Once the land was cleared each 'groupie' was to be given a personal allotment plus the money he had earned in the clearing gang. Many settlers had no experience of bush work: in fact quite a few were assisted migrants straight from the slums of London, Birmingham and other British cities — men who had scarcely ever set eyes on a pick, a shovel or an axe. Much of the land was unsuitable and there were other troubles. Western Australia did produce more milk, butter and cheese as a result of the scheme, but at the cost of much personal suffering and waste of public money. The Commonwealth's £34,000,000 migration scheme did not seek to replace the State programmes but to encourage them with generous financial backing; but some States at some times did not want encouragement. Up to 1923, for instance, New South Wales had spent only £100,000 of a £6,000,000 Commonwealth grant for migration and 'development'.

A major brake on the rate at which money was spent was the attitude of Labor, which came to power in all States except Victoria during the prosperous middle years of the 1920s. Even in Victoria minority Labor governments held office twice during this period. As Heather Radi observes, 'To win Victoria, whose Country votes had a three to one weighting, Labor needed a miracle'.[12] During the

[12] F. K. Crowley, *A New History of Australia*, Melbourne, 1974, p.401.

1920s the same voters who returned conservative governments to power in the federal sphere often quite happily voted Labor in State elections. The reason seems to be that Labor's wartime and post-war 'image' of extremism, of support for Irish and other revolutionary or anti-British movements, in short of 'disloyalty', was rather irrelevant to the purely domestic concerns of State government. Voters were naturally quite willing to be seduced by promises of improved social services and other welfare-state measures, especially when the promises were carried out.

In New South Wales, for example, the first term in office of Labor Premier J. T. Lang (June 1925 to October 1927) saw the introduction of widows' pensions, compulsory insurance of employees at their employers' expense, a family endowment scheme, better working conditions for rural labourers, a maximum 44-hour working week, the abolition of State secondary school fees, the establishment of a Government Insurance Office to moderate, by competition, the profits of private companies and of adult franchise in local government elections. In Queensland, where Labor governments ruled continuously from 1915 to 1929 a comparable range of welfare state measures was introduced over a longer period. In 1922 E. G. Theodore, then Premier, succeeded in giving effect to what has been a plank of Labor's platform almost ever since there has been a Labor Party. He abolished the nominated Legislative Council. None of the dire consequences, prophesied by conservatives, followed. For fifty years Queensland has been quite as law abiding, and on balance quite as conservative, as the other States — which still retain their Upper Houses.

Though contemporaries spoke of the mid-1920s as prosperous, and even as a boom period, it must be remembered that recorded unemployment never fell below about 6 per cent of the workforce. Generally speaking Labor States signed agreements with the Commonwealth because they needed every bit of money they could get, but then failed to spend much of it because of the long-standing Labor policy of opposition to any immigration while ever Australian citizens were out of work. In the event 261 000 British immigrants, about 80 per cent of them assisted, came to Australia between 1921 and 1930. There were also a few thousand Italians and other Europeans allowed into the country on a quota system, much to the fury of the Labor Party. Despite all the planning and spending, relatively few settled on the land — though the Southern Europeans did enter the sugar-growing industry in North Queensland in large numbers and market-gardening and gold-mining in Western Australia. Most stayed in the cities, like the great majority of all previous waves of newly arrived immigrants before them. There some provided a nucleus of skilled labour in the developing secondary industries, more joined the unskilled workforce or became shopkeepers and petty tradesmen, and some enabled the Labor Party to cry, 'I told you so', by joining the small army of unemployed.

So much for the 'men' in Bruce's slogan. The 'money' came largely from the Commonwealth Government, though not from revenue, buoyant though it was during the period. In accordance with Page's conservative monetary policies, taxation and expenditure were both kept at a minimum while large Government loans were negotiated on the London (and occasionally New York) money market to finance what the Government continued to hope would be 're-productive' developmental works that would 'create new wealth'. Since the Commonwealth had, during the war, entered the income and many other fields of taxation, previously the preserve of the States, the latter were battling with increasing budgetary problems. At the same time the real value of the Commonwealth's twenty-five shillings *per caput* payment to the States had been eroded by inflation to about half what it was when it began in 1910. The States attempted to cope with their difficulties both by borrowing more heavily and, of course, by demanding more from the Commonwealth. In the first of these activities they competed with each other and with the national government so, it was feared, helping to drive up interest rates. These problems were not new: they had plagued State and federal politicians for years, but they were now more pressing than ever. One great positive achievement of the Bruce-Page Government was to arrive at a sensible and workable solution to them.

First, recognising the need for services and living standards to be at least comparable in all States, the Government began the practice of giving extra grants to States with special needs, usually those with large territories and/or small populations. Western Australia received a special grant in 1925 and Tasmania in 1926. Second, by threatening to cease *per caput* payments completely, the Commonwealth Government forced the States to sign the Financial Agreement of December 1927. In this document the Commonwealth took over responsibility for the public debts of all the States and agreed to pay interest on them at the previous rate of *per caput* payments, twenty-five shillings per head of population. In return the States agreed that, for the future, public borrowing commitments of all governments would be decided by the Loan Council, a body in which each State had one vote but the Commonwealth two votes and a casting vote. It will readily be seen that the Commonwealth had only to cajole or coerce two States out of six in order to have its way. The Financial Agreement was ratified at a referendum held in conjunction with the federal election of November 1928. It was approved by nearly 75 per cent of all voters and a majority in all States.

Thus, with remarkably little fuss, was carried through the greatest constitutional change in the history of the Commonwealth. The Agreement tipped the real balance of power decisively in favour of the federal as against the State governments — as was graphically shown when J. T. Lang, the Premier of New South Wales, was dismissed from office four years later.

Another great achievement of the Bruce-Page Government was the effective funding of the Council for Scientific and Industrial Research. The money spent on this was trifling by comparison with that sunk in immigration and other developmental schemes but it is arguable that, at least in the long run, the C.S.I.R. did more for Australian development than all the other schemes of the Bruce-Page Government put together. Wartime shortages had drawn attention to Australia's backwardness in the fields of applied science and technology. With characteristic flamboyance, Hughes in 1916 promised '£50,000 or £500,000 if necessary' to remedy the situation, but actually produced only £10,000 a year to finance an Advisory Council for Scientific Research. In 1920 an Act of the fourth Hughes Government created a Commonwealth Institute of Science and Industries and found a little more money for it, but the organisation was put on a satisfactory footing and given adequate finance only by Bruce's amending Act of 1926. For the next twenty years the C.S.I.R. worked mainly, but not exclusively, on research into problems of primary industry. It too was under the spell of the rural myth. Its work has been of incalculable benefit to Australian farmers and graziers. One example must suffice.

In the last century prickly pears were introduced from America as exotic garden plants. Sometimes they were planted out as hedges in the country. They ran wild and nothing could be done to stop their spread. Infected areas were useless for grazing and agriculture, and the cost of clearing land by the cheapest known method (chemical poisoning) was estimated in 1924 at from £5 to £20 an acre (about half a hectare) — much more than the land was worth. In the same year some 65 000 000 acres (26 000 000 hectares) of good land in central western Queensland and New South Wales were thoroughly choked with the pest. By 1940 prickly pear had been practically eradicated from the continent by an insect imported from South America, *Cactoblastis*. This feat was actually accomplished through the Prickly Pear Board, an organisation set up jointly by the Commonwealth, New South Wales and Queensland governments in

1920, and acting on the advice of the Advisory Council for Scientific Research, the forerunner of the C.S.I.R.; but it provides a spectacular illustration of the kind of work the C.S.I.R. carried on continuously.

In Bruce's programme of 'Men, Money and Markets' the last of the triad provided the most intractable problem. He seems to have hoped that Britain would set up a tariff wall on primary products giving preference to commodities produced in the Empire, but the small preference finally granted on a limited range of products in 1925 had hardly any effect on Australia's export marketing difficulties. These arose essentially from the high and increasing costs of production of flour, dried and canned fruits, frozen and canned meat, butter, tinned milk and other dairy products, which had to be sold on the British (or other overseas) market in competition with similar products from countries which did not have such high production costs. Yet exports had to be maintained — or increased — if the farmers were to be kept on the land and if Australian imports were to be paid for. Under pressure from the Country Party, State and Commonwealth governments spent large sums on railways, country roads and irrigation schemes like those in the Shepparton district of Victoria, in the Murrumbidgee Irrigation Area of New South Wales, and along the Murray banks in both States and in South Australia, but all this did little to bring down the costs of production of rural exports. So the Country Party demanded, and obtained, direct and indirect subsidies for the primary producer. Secondary industries were protected in the home market against cheap foreign competition by the tariff wall. Similarly then, primary industries must be protected, if necessary by direct subsidies from the taxpayer, against cheap foreign competition in foreign markets. The Bruce-Page Government continued the bounty on meat exports, provided loans (later written off) to dried-fruits producers who were in difficulties, paid export bounties on canned fruit and fortified wines and offered farmers a guaranteed minimum price of 3s 8d per bushel for the 1923-24 wheat harvest. It continued the embargo on imported sugar, kept out cheaper New Zealand butter with a high import duty, and subsidised Australian butter exports to Britain by raising the minimum price of butter on the home market high enough to compensate dairy farmers for selling part of their output at a loss in Britain.

BRUCE AND THE TRADE UNIONS

The trouble was that all such subsidies to primary production, like the tariff and other aids to secondary industries, inevitably had the effect, in the overall national context, of further increasing production costs by increasing the price of commodities and hence of the wages (set by arbitration) for the workers who made and consumed them. Subsidies and tariffs also encouraged the establishment or continuance of uneconomic industries, or industries sited in uneconomic areas. In 1928 economists calculated that secondary industries had been subsidised, directly or indirectly, with some £26,000,000 of Government money and primary industries with £22,000,000. They added that prices had risen by about 10 per cent as a result, but that the general standard of living for Australians was also higher than it would have been without tariffs and subsidies. This was undoubtedly true, but again it did nothing to reduce costs in the primary exporting industries.

The Tariff Board put the same problem in another way. It pointed out to the Government again and again the growth of what it saw as a vicious spiral of rising wages, costs, tariffs for the protection of manufacturers and subsidies to aid primary producers. Arbitration tribunals would fix a higher wage in an industry. The employers would immediately apply to the Board for a higher protective tariff to enable them to pay the higher wages while retaining their profit margin. The more expensive finished commodity would increase the costs of the primary producer who then pressed for more subsidies which, in turn, usually enabled Australia barely to keep its share of the overseas market, not to increase it. The vicious circle had to be broken somewhere. As a businessman and a conservative, Bruce naturally decided that it must be done at the expense of the employees by reducing wages. During his long Prime Ministership of nearly seven years he became, like other holders of the office before and since, more and more preoccupied with strikes, lockouts and the system of industrial arbitration.

Industrial trouble began on the wharves late in 1924. Unionists tried to rid the waterfront of the Overseas Shipping Bureau, a strike-breaking organisation formed during the war, which still gave preference to what the unions called 'scab' labour. Seamen and wharf-labourers, in an effort to improve their conditions, continued to strike or cause delays in 1925. Shipping companies and importing firms lost money, and cynics drew attention to the nature of the Prime Minister's family business when the Government rushed two special Bills through Parliament to break the strike. One amended the Immigration Restriction Act to give the Government power to deport immigrants who broke federal arbitration or commercial laws; the second gave the Government power to suspend the Navigation Act which protected Australian coastal shipping from foreign competition. The first Act was avowedly aimed at Tom Walsh and

Jack Johnson, elected officials of the Australian Seamen's Union, who had been born in Ireland and Holland respectively: the second threatened rank-and-file Australian seamen with loss of employment by exposing them to competition from lower-paid British and foreign crews. The trouble with the second scheme was that it threatened equally to cut the profits of Australian ship-owners. Perhaps that is why the strike was settled rather speedily, largely on the men's terms. Walsh and Johnson remained at their posts, the High Court having ruled that they were not immigrants since they had lived in Australia for thirty-two and fifteen years respectively.

At the next triennial federal election of November 1925, the first held under compulsory voting, both the coalition parties fought on a platform of law and order. Bruce promised to curb the activities of 'alien agitators' and of trade-union officials and Page harped even more heavily on the same theme. All over Australia the Nationalists put out a brightly-coloured poster showing Tom Walsh taking a running jump onto an outspread Union Jack, exclaiming as he did so, 'To hell with the British Empire'. Many citizens must have been reminded of Hugh Mahon's expulsion from Parliament. The Nationalists were returned with a considerably increased majority, not quite large enough, however, for them to be able to govern without the Country Party. The Bruce-Page partnership continued — and continued to involve itself more deeply in confrontation with the Labor movement in its effort to reduce export costs. First, in 1926, Bruce amended the Crimes Act to give the Government power to 'proclaim' a serious industrial disturbance. Once this ritual was performed the Government could punish those who took part, or even advocated taking part, in a strike, in the case of immigrants by deportation. Next the Commonwealth Arbitration Act was amended to give the Court greater powers to enforce its awards. Then Bruce passed through Parliament bills authorising two referenda asking for much greater Commonwealth powers over arbitration, working conditions and 'essential services'. Many voters suspected that the Government planned, if the referenda were carried, to restore the 48-hour working week throughout the Commonwealth, since a 44-hour week was being introduced by legislation in some Labor-governed States. In any case the referendum proposals were far too complicated and loosely defined to be understood easily, even by some constitutional lawyers. Voters unsure of the effect of a proposed change naturally tend to vote 'No' to preserve the *status quo*; and so the 1926 referenda were rejected overwhelmingly, as usually happens under such circumstances.

This tenth Commonwealth Parliament at last moved to the new capital city which had been envisaged by the founding fathers of federation. On 9 May 1927 a new session was formally opened in Canberra by the Duke of York, second son of the Monarch who had himself, as second son of Edward VII, presided over the opening of the first Parliament in Melbourne twenty-seven years before. But whether in Melbourne, or in the new Parliament House in the open paddocks by the Molonglo River, Bruce and Page thought more and more about the need to increase exports, which meant to reduce costs, which meant, in their view, to reduce wages or increase the number of hours in the working week. In February 1927 the Commonwealth Arbitration Court granted a 44-hour week to the Amalgamated Engineering Union, thereby setting a precedent for reduction of hours in other Commonwealth awards. The Government reacted by proposing a new Conciliation and Arbitration Bill which was read for the first time in December. It sought to reverse the principle of more than twenty years' standing: the Court in future was to be guided not primarily by the needs of the worker, but by the capacity of industry to pay higher wages and the effect of such on the national economy. At the same time further coercive measures were applied to the trade unions. Penalties for illegal strikes were increased — but could be remitted if the union dismissed militant officials 'responsible' for the illegal action. Lockouts could be legalised in the context of an already existing strike. The Court was given power to inspect a union's books, to disallow its rules and direct that it hold court-supervised secret ballots: all this at the very time when years of endeavour had finally resulted in the creation of the Australian Council of Trade Unions (A.C.T.U.), a kind of federal parliament, or government, of the trade-union movement.

The repressive legislation produced results the opposite of those aimed at. Instead of fewer strikes it produced a menacing wave of industrial anarchy. Large numbers of unionists, feeling themselves persecuted by the new Act, defied the Court's rulings and the law, especially when their jobs were taken by 'free' labourers. Under the new legislation every change in industrial practices involved worse conditions or lower wages. In September 1928, not long before the Bruce-Page Government had to face another general election, Mr Justice Beeby handed down a new waterside workers' Award imposing on the men an obligation to offer for work at the hiring points twice daily — whether they thought work might be available or not. Although the Union had already declared it would not accept this clause, it seemed that its members might. They struck in some ports but not in others. Instead of waiting to see which section was in the majority, Bruce, by now neurotically edgy about waterside troubles, rushed through Parliament yet another coercive Bill aimed specifically at breaking the Waterside Workers' Federation and replacing it with an organisation more acceptable to the employers. The Act as passed actually gave power to the Governor-General, i.e. the Government, to make practically any regulations it liked with respect to the W.W.F., and the stevedoring industry. No such delegation of unconfined powers had ever been made before by a Commonwealth Parliament — except in wartime under the notorious War Precautions Act. Regulations under the Act, requiring the licensing of all waterside workers, were promptly enforced. Unionists called it the 'dog-collar act' and struck immediately. The 'free labourers' had no objection to being licensed, but for months they had to work under police protection. The Government's efforts to enforce industrial peace actually caused violence and intimidation on both sides but, as usual in such affairs, the forces of law and order used terror more effectively, not to say ruthlessly, than their opponents. A unionist demonstrator was shot dead by policemen on 2 November 1928, two weeks and a day before the general election.

Chapter 6

THE GREAT DEPRESSION

c. 1929—1932

Onset of the Depression and the third Bruce-Page Administration — The Scullin Government — J. T. Lang and the Labor 'Splits' — Life in the Depression — Langism and reaction in New South Wales

ONSET OF THE DEPRESSION AND THE THIRD BRUCE-PAGE ADMINISTRATION

With the benefit of hindsight it is possible to date the beginning of the great Depression in Australia from the federal election of 17 November 1928. The candidates and those who voted for them did not think so at the time. People did not begin to talk about 'depression' until 1930. Nevertheless it was in 1927 that the level of unemployment began to rise from a low point of 6 per cent of the workforce to its peak of 30 per cent during the terrible winter of 1932; and it was in 1928 that secondary industrial output began to decline. During the 1920s wool and wheat accounted for nearly a half and nearly a quarter, respectively, of the total value of Australian exports. Wool and wheat prices also began tumbling from a peak in 1928 to little more than a quarter of that figure in 1931, a low point at which they remained virtually stationary for the following two years.

The level of imports began to fall from 1927 onwards, but it was Australia's grossly excessive dependence on world prices for wheat and wool and the drying up of overseas loan funds which did most to ensure that the great Depression lasted longer and caused more misery than in most countries, even if only marginally so — always excepting Germany, which produced Nazism as a result. Unemployment figures are, of course, only one among many ways of measuring the impact of depression, but they are the one which comes nearest to providing some measure of the quantum of human misery and demoralisation caused by economic collapse. The following table compares Australia with six other countries from this point of view:

Bulletin, 5 November 1930

NO TIME TO LOSE.

N.S.W. LABOR VOTER (over his shoulder): "Shake it up, Jack, and stop the cow, like yer promised; the pace is gettin' too flamin' hot."

The Great Depression

Unemployment Rate in Seven Countries[1]

Country	*Peak Year*	*%*	*Five Year Average 1930-34*	*Type of Return*
Germany	1932	43.8	31.8	Trade Union
Australia	1932	28.1	23.4	Trade Union
Canada	1933	26.6	20.7	Trade Union
United States	1933	24.9	19.0	Official Estimates
United Kingdom	1932	22.1	19.2	Trade Union
Poland	1935	16.7	12.3	Employment Exchange
Japan	1932	6.8	5.6	Official Estimates

The Depression made a deeper, and certainly a more lasting, impact on Australians than on most other peoples because of the greater gap between normal conditions and those of the Depression years than existed elsewhere. History shows that it is not the absolute level of poverty or deprivation which causes personal or social misery but rather the extent of the difference between personal and social expectations and what people actually get. As we have seen, in 1928 Australians had enjoyed for about three generations, notwithstanding the depression of the early 1890s, an increasingly high standard of living. On the eve of federation people thought the unfederated Australasian colonies already the most democratic and the most socially advanced countries in the world. After federation the concept of the basic wage, the exclusion of cheap, competitive labour by means of the White Australia Policy, the reduction of working hours and many other advances in social legislation made Australians accustomed to thinking of themselves as the most socially advanced people in the world as indeed, with New Zealanders, they were, if the yardstick be material conditions of life for the masses. In the Great War the diggers received much higher pay and allowances than the soldiers of any other army, including that of the United States; and if living standards for the masses at home declined during the conflict, they picked up again in the early 1920s to surpass, in most respects, all previous levels.

Of course Australia was a thoroughly capitalist society in which poverty and privilege confronted each other starkly enough. As Henry Lawson had written in the *Bulletin* in 1888:

They lie, the men who tell us, for reasons of their own
That want is here a stranger, and that misery's unknown. . . .

C. B. Schedvin, *Australia and the Great Depression*, Sydney, 1970, p.46.

But if the country was in fact very far from being 'the working man's paradise', it was, as we have seen, somewhat nearer to such a state of grace in the years up to the Great War than any other land except, perhaps, New Zealand. Many Australians had long been accustomed to thinking of their nationality in terms of continuing progress towards a greater measure of equality, democracy and material prosperity for all citizens. The war itself, as we have seen, undermined and in some ways negatived this traditional concept. For six years up to 1928 the two Bruce-Page Administrations had seemed increasingly obsessed with the need to cut costs, i.e. wages, thus actually seeking to reverse the long progress towards a better life for all. The third Bruce-Page Administration, faced with falling overseas prices for Australian exports, increasing unemployment and business stagnation, could think of no other policy than more of the same. It attacked living standards so openly as to provoke a massive electoral reaction which swept it out of office in less than a year.

In the 1928 election campaign neither Bruce nor Page made suppression of strikes and 'law and order' their main theme as they had done in 1925. Nor did they pay much attention to the deteriorating economic situation — apart from an undertaking to hasten more slowly with assisted immigration while ever unemployment figures remained high. Bruce advocated a stronger national Air Force and Page devoted much time to explaining and praising his past financial policies. The new Labor leader, J. H. Scullin, accused the Government of responsibility for rising unemployment and industrial unrest and promised, if elected, to raise still further the protective tariff wall for Australian industries. It seems odd that what proved to be the most contentious new intitiative of the Bruce-Page Government, its attempt to dismantle the Commonwealth arbitration system, which the coalition itself had spent so much pains in strengthening, received no mention at all in the election campaign.

The Coalition was returned to power with a reduced majority. The Nationalists won 30 seats in the Representatives, the Country Party 12 and Labor thirty-one. There were two Independents, both rural representatives too radical for the Country Party to accommodate. After the election there were 24 Nationalist, 5 Country Party and 7 Labor senators. Bruce appointed a new ministry, retaining for himself the Prime Ministership and External Affairs and leaving the Treasury to Page as before. The cold, brilliant intellectual, J. G. Latham, a Rationalist who had been the Attorney-General since the previous election, retained his post but was entrusted also with a new portfolio — Industry. The most interesting newcomer to Cabinet was H. S. Gullett, Minister for Trade and Customs.

The third Bruce-Page Administration accomplished little before being overwhelmed by the consequences of its own and its predecessors' reactionary industrial policies. In January 1929, working under the directives of the new Conciliation and Arbitration Act of the previous year, Mr Justice Lukin handed down a new Award for timber-workers. Its provisions were such as to confirm the Labor movement's worst fears about the real purpose of the Government's arbitration policies: wages were cut, the maximum permissible ratio of apprentices to men employed was increased and the 44-hour week, established for the industry by the Court in 1920, was increased to 48 hours. The men immediately went on strike and the recently formed Australian Council of Trade Unions raised a strike-fund of £122,000. The strikers burnt the offending Justice in effigy, singing:

We'll hang Judge Lukin from a sour-apple tree
A sour-apple tree, a sour-apple tree . . .

They used both persuasion and intimidation against 'free labour'. There was a good deal of violence on both sides and from the police, though no one was actually killed. Timber-mills were mysteriously set on fire but, though the strike dragged on for months, in the end the timber-workers found they had simply changed places with 'volunteers' from the increasing army of unemployed.

At the same time, early in 1929, serious trouble erupted on the main coalfield in Australia, the Hunter River area in New South Wales. The mining companies announced that, owing to the declining demand for coal, they would close down the mines unless the men accepted a severe wage-cut. The 12 000 miners on the field refused and were at once locked out by the owners in February. Even under the new Arbitration Act, lockouts, in the absence of a strike situation, were illegal. Would the Government prosecute the employers with the same promptness and stringency with which it had been acting against employees? To the surprise of some cynics, Latham, the Attorney-General, did launch prosecutions against the largest and richest mining concern on the field, John Brown and Co., but then, against Latham's advice, Bruce persuaded Cabinet to withdraw the prosecution and this was announced at an abortive conference on 8 April. The Government stood naked before the electors, having, for class ends, perverted the administration of justice under its own most prized law. Parliament was in recess at the time, but immediately sittings resumed in August a motion of censure was moved by the most capable Labor politician of the day.

Edward Granville Theodore was the child of a Roumanian father and an English mother, both immigrants, and grandson of a Roumanian Orthodox priest. Though a well-educated man with a master-mariner's certificate, his father was working as a wharf labourer in Port Adelaide when Edward Theodore was born on 29 December 1884. Soon after the boy started attending a local state school, the family moved to a small market-garden and orchard property at Aldgate in the Adelaide Hills. The father, an active supporter of the Labor Party, urged his sons to enter politics. Young Ted Theodore had to leave school at 12 and, when only 16, he went off by himself to the Western Australian goldfields. Soon he was digging guano on the Abrolhos Islands with a party of labourers whose rations comprised damper, jam, tea and salt meat. Back in South Australia he carried his swag as a prospector between different mining fields, once being ordered off a station personally by its owner, Sir Sidney Kidman, the wealthiest grazier in the continent. For some years he worked on the ore-face deep underground in mines at Kalgoorlie, and then at Broken Hill where, between shifts, he read omnivorously in the local library. In 1906, hearing of a mining-boom in far North Queensland, Theodore and a mate shouldered their swags and made their way across country about 1600 kilometres to Irvinebank near Chillagoe. In little more than a year he had organised miners, railway workers and others in the district into a very militant union, the Amalgamated Workers' Association, and in 1909 he was sent by the electors as a Labor member to the Queensland Parliament.

Three years later the Queensland Labor Caucus elected him its deputy-leader. Still busy in the industrial sphere, he organised the amalgamation of his Amalgamated Workers' Association and some other rural unions with the giant Australian Workers' Union, becoming President of the combined union in 1913. When Labor came to power in Queensland in 1915, he served in T. J. Ryan's Cabinet as Treasurer and Secretary for Public Works. In October 1919, when Ryan resigned to enter the federal Parliament, Theodore at the age of 34 became Premier of Queensland. Physically he was a tall, dark, strong, handsome man, possessed of a commanding presence and great dignity which set others at a distance from him. He was as tough mentally as he was physically, which is saying a great deal. As a radical union-organiser and miners' leader in the bush, he acquired the nickname of 'Red Ted' and this stuck to him long after he had become a conservative within the spectrum of Labor politics; but whether on the left or the right, in politics or out, he exhibited tremendous energy and capacity for getting things done, ruthlessly if necessary. To this day he is the only Labor leader to have succeeded in implementing the party's policy of abolishing Upper Houses. An anti-Labor Premier of New South Wales, B. S. B. Stevens, said that Theodore possessed 'the coolest, best, and most experienced financial brain in the southern hemisphere'.[2]

In February 1927 Theodore entered the federal Parliament as the Labor member for the Sydney suburban working-class seat of Dalley, at a by-election caused by the sudden resignation of the sitting member, W. G. Mahony. It was common knowledge in Labor circles that Mahony had been induced to resign in Theodore's interest. From his first day in the House of Representatives, the new member for Dalley proved much more troublesome to the Government than any other member of the Opposition, even Anstey. Bruce appointed a Royal Commission to inquire into the allegations of bribery. Theodore admitted subscribing £5 to a testimonial fund for Mahony and giving him a present of £200, but denied any knowledge of bribery. The Royal Commission found that Mahony had been bribed, probably to the extent of £5,000, by persons unknown, to vacate his seat in Theodore's interest. It was generally believed at the time, by those in good positions to know, that John Wren had supplied, or organised the collection of, the money. The incident was characteristic of Theodore's entire career: the tremendous ability, resolution and capacity for leadership which the Labor Party — and the country — needed so badly, were constantly rendered ineffective by imputations of dishonest, or at least, dishonourable dealings.

Soon after the Royal Commission reported, the man whose integrity had been questioned rose in the House of Representatives to move a censure motion on the Bruce-Page Government for administering its own laws in a partial and unjust manner. The handling of the John Brown case demonstrated a deep-seated class prejudice in the Government, Theodore argued, and he pointed to other examples of its partiality towards the rich and its prejudice against the poor. For six years following the Nationalists' accession to power in 1917 they had failed to collect Commonwealth land tax from grazing lease-holders, including the wealthiest among them like Sir Sidney Kidman. Yet they had not scrupled to use dubious evidence from criminal sources in the prosecution of trade-union leaders. They had sold the profitable Commonwealth Woollen Mills at Geelong on extraordinarily generous terms to a rich purchaser, and they had similarly almost given away the Commonwealth Shipping Line to a private and enterprising firm which, in the end, never paid the Government even the small price agreed upon. After

[2] *A.E.*, vol. 8, p.481.

Theodore, Premier of Queensland

Herald, 1922-23

an all-night sitting the censure motion was defeated on party lines, but 'Billy' Hughes and another Nationalist, E. A. Mann, plus the Independent members voted with Labor, thus reducing the Government's majority in the House to five.

By this time the Government was in a state bordering on panic. Since 1923 Bruce had been increasingly obsessed with the need to cut costs and boost exports and his governments had enacted law after law aimed at ending industrial strife and achieving these ends. Yet there were more strikes and lockouts than ever, export prices were falling and factories putting more and more men off work. Bruce was right to feel frustrated and fearful. Though neither he nor others knew it, the great world Depression was beginning. The Government's reaction was to make yet another attempt, its last, to reduce wages and discipline the trade unions. On 23 August 1929 Bruce moved the second reading of the Maritime Industries Bill.

This was a most complex — and deceptively named — measure but its import was clear enough: that the Commonwealth should withdraw completely from the whole field of industrial arbitration, except for that part of it occupied by workers in the interstate and overseas shipping industry. These latter, and federal government employees, were to be placed under a new and much more repressive Commonwealth arbitration system: all other workers were to be handed over to State industrial tribunals. In 1929 Nationalist governments were in power everywhere except in Western Australia. Although Government speakers were coy about saying so in the debate, it was clear that they thought hours must be increased, wages reduced, strikes abolished and worker-productivity increased. The Commonwealth had failed to achieve these goals: perhaps the States would do better. The proposals were so sweeping as to trouble a good many Government members, especially as they had not been consulted by Bruce beforehand. As Theodore said, leading the attack for the Opposition, 'One man is proposing to undo the work of a generation of men'.[3]

Scenting at last the chance of revenge for his deposition by Bruce and Page six years earlier, Hughes engineered the Government's downfall. In one of the most blistering speeches of his career he observed that it was 'characteristic of [Bruce] that he persists with nothing, but proceeds from stunt to stunt', and, referring to the John Brown case, that Bruce could 'no longer pose before this country as a man who is prepared to enforce the law impartially'.[4] In the committee stage he moved that the Bill should be submitted to the

[3] *C.P.D.*, vol. 121, p.340.

[4] *C.P.D.*, vol. 121, p.602.

people for approval, either by way of a referendum or by the calling of an election on the issue. Bruce was provoked into replying that he would have nothing to do with a plebiscite and would treat Hughes's motion as one of confidence. He cut short the debate after only eight speeches, but two Nationalists crossed the floor to vote with Labor and the four Independents, thus defeating the Government by one vote. Bruce advised the Governor-General to dissolve Parliament and call a general election which some wiseacres said he wanted to lose.

He fought the ensuing campaign almost solely on the issue of arbitration and the merits of his Maritime Industries Bill. Earle Page for the Country Party concurred but spent more time in positive attacks on the Labor Party for its 'hypocrisy' in attacking the Government's proposals while condoning strikes. Scullin for Labor reiterated his party's parliamentary arguments — that a decent minimum living standard for all Australians had been built over a generation on the foundation of the Commonwealth arbitration system, and that this must not be abandoned overnight. If the system functioned ineffectively, it must be amended in constructive ways, not scrapped. But Scullin also introduced other issues. He attacked Page's recently introduced profits tax on entertainments because, he said, it would simply be passed on in higher prices for entry tickets to the moving-pictures, the main amusement of the wage-earner. He also promised a much higher tariff to protect (still further!) Australian secondary industries and to nationalise the wireless broadcasting system. The most remarkable feature of the campaign was that politicians, newspapers and people showed no awareness of the dimensions of the world economic crisis which was already beginning to overwhelm them. Speakers referred often enough to economic problems but in a way that assumed things were bound to get better soon, more or less of their own accord. If they had been able to foresee the inevitable miseries of the next few years, it is possible that the political parties would have been competing to lose the election so that their rivals would be the scapegoats for some time thereafter. In every election (except a Tasmanian poll in 1931, heavily influenced by the federal political situation) between 1929 and 1934, the incumbent government was thrown out decisively by electors reduced to the expedient of 'giving the other mob a go — they couldn't be worse'. South Australia elected its last Labor Government for thirty-five years in April 1930 and Queensland its only anti-Labor Government between 1915 and 1957 in May 1929. It should be recognised that, in both cases, massive gerrymandering of electoral boundaries contributed as much to these long periods of one-party rule as did memories of the Depression.

THE SCULLIN GOVERNMENT

Thus the Commonwealth election of 12 October 1929 resulted in a landslide to Labor. Five ministers of the defeated Coalition Government lost their seats, including Bruce himself. He refused the offer of another seat and after the Depression was over he made another career in England, becoming successively a President of the League of Nations Council, Chairman of the United Nations World Food Council and Chairman of the British Finance Corporation for Industry. In 1947 he was raised to the peerage as Lord Bruce of Melbourne. In the House of Representatives Labor won 46 seats to 29 for all other candidates combined — 14 Nationalists, 10 Country Party and 5 Independents. Yet because the previous Parliament had been dissolved less than a year after its inception, there was no election for half the Senate seats where party strengths remained as before — 24 Nationalists, 5 Country Party and 7 Labor. Thus Labor had been returned to office and given responsibility for governing the country but, with an overwhelmingly hostile Senate, hardly the power to do so effectively. Hughes, having engineered the downfall of the Bruce-Page Government, seemed to be hoping for a seat in the Labor Cabinet, but the bitterness surviving in the A.L.P. from the conscription troubles made any reconciliation quite out of the question. Caucus elected the Ministry and Scullin allotted the portfolios as laid down in the A.L.P. rules, retaining for himself External Affairs and Industry as well as the Prime Ministership. The other most important appointments were Theodore as Treasurer, Frank Brennan Attorney-General, J. A. Lyons, an ex-premier of Tasmania, Postmaster-General and Minister for Works and Railways, J. E. Fenton Minister for Trade and Customs, and Frank Anstey Minister for Health and Repatriation.

Son of an Irish railway-worker, the new Prime Minister, James Henry Scullin, was born in a cottage beside the line at Trawalla near Ballarat in 1876. The only formal education he ever had was a few years' attendance at the Trawalla State School, but he read widely and studied at night while working in his first job in Ballarat as a grocer's boy. He also practised debating and public speaking in Ballarat's South Street Society, the Australian Natives' Association and the Catholic Young Men's Society. He became a first-class debater, good enough to impress the imperturbable Bruce who once confessed to a friend, 'When I listen to that little man — and I do that whenever possible — I say to myself "I wish I had your gift of words" '. Scullin joined the Labor Party in 1903 and stood against Deakin for the Ballarat seat in the election of 1906. He became a full-time organiser for the Australian Workers' Union and was elected to the federal Parliament for the Corangamite seat in 1910.

Before and during World War I he edited the Ballarat *Evening Echo*, giving free rein to his fervent belief in Australian Nationalism, Irish liberty and anti-conscriptionism. On 1 September 1917, for example, he wrote that what Australia really needed was:

> a society in which the 'guiding principle would be patriotism in its truest sense . . . love of Australia, and an unswerving determination to advance the interests of Australia' . . . in short . . . 'an Australian Sinn Fein society'.[5]

That Scullin moved the famous 'red' socialisation resolution at the Melbourne A.L.P. conference of 1921 shows, perhaps, how far to the left the consensus of Labor thought was at the time: it certainly does not show that this devout Catholic was then or ever a revolutionary. When Frank Tudor retired from the leadership of the federal Labor Party and from Parliament in 1922, Scullin was elected in his stead for the safe Labor seat of Yarra, which he represented until his retirement in 1949. Caucus chose him as leader when Matthew Charlton retired in 1928. A slightly-built man, he carried himself well and appeared larger than he was. He had considerable charisma and all who knew him at all well were impressed by his integrity and sincerity. He was an intensely patriotic Australian nationalist and racist and, therefore, somewhat anti-Imperialist. He once dismissed as 'legal quibbles' a reasoned statement by J. J. Latham that 'when Great Britain is at war, Australia is also at war'.[6] He was also intensely loyal to his party. With all these qualities he has generally been judged weak-willed, or at any rate lacking in that kind of toughness necessary for political success. Certainly he did not have that overriding, but not over-scrupulous, will to power displayed by Hughes or Theodore but, as his biographer has written, 'it does seem a little strange that a reputation for weakness should cling to the only Australian to have imposed his will on a King [or a Queen] of England'.[7] Perhaps the truth is that Scullin was strong and decisive enough when he knew, as in his confrontation with King George V,[8] that he had the overwhelming consensus of party opinion behind him; but that he became weak and indecisive when his beloved party split into warring factions, as it did almost immediately under the shattering impact of the Depression. Scullin's hair turned white during the first year of his Prime Ministership.

[5] John Robertson, *J. H. Scullin*, Perth, 1974, p.51.

[6] Robertson, p.83.

[7] Robertson, p.399.

[8] See below p.178-80.

The Scullin Government was sworn into office in Canberra on Tuesday 22 October 1929, the very day after the Wall Street share market began to fall drastically. On the following Tuesday 29th the market collapsed in panic and a few of the world's greatest, self-professed, financial wizards suicided, in some cases launching themselves dramatically from skyscraper windows. By mid-November the average value of all stocks listed on the New York exchange had fallen by 40 per cent. These events signalled the beginning of the Depression for the whole capitalist world. No one thought any longer, as most had done only a month before, that things were bound to improve soon. The Government took some immediate steps to meet the situation. Compulsory military training for home defence, enacted by Labor in 1910, was abolished forthwith and other massive cuts were made in defence expenditure. The scheme for assisted migration from Britain was abandoned. These changes were made to save money and help balance the budget, but of course they also fitted happily with the policies or prejudices of most Labor voters. In November Scullin took the first steps in a series of measures which raised the tariff to a record level and in the following year he placed an embargo on certain imports. These measures did result in the establishment of some new factories. Before them most cigarettes, for example, were imported, and after them most were made in Australia; but they had no perceptible effect on the overall decline in manufacturing output, which did not reach pre-depression levels again until 1937.

As Treasurer, Theodore successfully legislated for steep increases in personal taxation on incomes of £450 or more, and in company tax. He also managed to pass through all stages the Commonwealth Bank Act of 1929, which gave the Bank Board power to compel anyone holding gold coin or bullion to exchange it for banknotes, and to prohibit the export of gold. This was a sensible measure designed to strengthen and stabilise the value of Australian currency *vis-à-vis* overseas creditors. It meant of course abandonment of the gold standard, which depends on the free circulation of gold; but such was the mystic veneration in which this sacred financial cow was held, that nearly all concerned — the Board, the Treasurer, the Labor Party and even newspaper and other commentators — took pains to deny that the Act did any such thing.

At the very outset of the Scullin Government's term of office, the debate on this Bill dramatised an insuperable obstacle with which it had to contend to the end. In its original form, Theodore's Bill gave effective power to the Treasurer to control movement of gold. The Nationalist majority in the Senate amended the Bill to give effective power to the Bank Board; and this body, set up by the Bruce-Page

Government in 1924 and consisting almost entirely of conservative businessmen, was responsible to nobody but itself. Sir Robert Gibson, Chairman of the Commonwealth Bank Board, was an arch-conservative and a devout exponent of financial orthodoxy. J. K. Galbraith has shown[9] that the 'conventional wisdom' of the time meant deflationary policies — massive cuts in wages, social services, public works and all other adjustable costs: a package which was anathema to most, though not all, Labor voters and politicians. It was certainly anathema to Theodore who, alone among all politicians, State and federal, seems to have digested J. M. Keynes's early writings and perhaps even to have anticipated the great economist's ideas on mildly inflationary 'pump-priming' policies as the way to combat depression.

Worse, however, than the Bank Board's conventional and distasteful economic dogma was the fact that the Government, responsible to the people for the results of national economic policies, had virtually no control over them. In all probability no government ever formed among men, given the continuance of the world slump and low prices for wool and wheat, could have done much to mitigate the Depression in Australia: certainly the Scullin Government had no hope of doing so, since it had no effective control of national financial policies. The very idea that any government should direct financial policies was then held to be a dangerous, even a bolshevik doctrine. All right-thinking persons, including Nationalist and Country Party politicians, knew that financial policy must be left to private bankers and other expert men of affairs — despite the painful results of this policy being daily manifested.

During the election campaign Theodore had promised that John Brown and Co. would be prosecuted and the lockout on the northern coalfields ended. He and many other leading men in the Government spent much time, quite fruitlessly, in trying to honour this promise. In June 1930 the men were forced back to the pits on the owners' terms. At the same time the Government successfully passed an amending Act which dismantled the Bruce-Page Government's arbitration legislation, stripped the Court of most of its coercive and punitive powers, and abolished the direction to judges that they must consider the general economic effect of their awards. This was one of the few Government achievements but it did nothing to slow down, let alone reverse, the rise in unemployment and the fall in Government and business receipts. Unemployment had increased

[9] J. K. Galbraith, *The Affluent Society*, Cambridge, Massachusetts, 1958, *passim*.

from 12 per cent in September 1929 to 18 per cent in June 1930. The value of the Australian pound, which had for years been at parity with the pound sterling, began to decline sharply. In June Scullin, probably on Theodore's advice, sought 'expert' advice from the Bank of England, which sent out Sir Otto Niemeyer to enquire into Australia's economic position. On 4 July the Nationalist-controlled Senate rejected a Government Bill to set up a compulsory wheat pool with a guaranteed minimum price to the struggling farmers of four shillings a bushel. On the same day the Government received a body-blow which led to the loss of its ablest member.

In May 1929 Queenslanders had elected their only anti-Labor Government for many years. This Nationalist-Country Party Administration, led by A. E. Moore, appointed a Royal Commission to enquire into allegations that Theodore had used his past situation as Premier of Queensland to enrich himself at the expense of the taxpayers. More specifically the charge was that the Government, of which he was the leader, had bought a mine, of which he was part-owner, at an inflated price, and that he had not disclosed his interest in the mine. The Royal Commission reported on 4 July 1930 that as Premier of Queensland Theodore had been guilty of 'fraud and dishonesty' over the sale of the Mungana mine. Theodore resigned his portfolio next day, protesting his innocence and challenging the Queensland Government to prosecute him, which it did — but very tardily. More than a year later, the Mungana allegations were sifted in a civil suit brought against Theodore and others by the Moore Government. The jury's verdict completely vindicated Theodore on all counts, but some of the Royal Commission's mud stuck to his name for the rest of his life. Scullin, assuming wrongly that Theodore would soon be cleared, took over the Treasury portfolio temporarily. Thus the Prime Minister presented the 1930 budget, one which embodied many unpalatable measures thought necessary by Theodore and by orthodox financial opinion. Income and company taxation were raised still higher, postal charges were increased and a sales tax imposed for the first time.

Early in August Scullin persuaded the majority of his Cabinet to renew the appointment of Sir Robert Gibson to the Commonwealth Bank Board for another seven years. Frank Anstey and others on the left wing of Labor thought this step a great blunder, as many more not in that position, have done since. Gibson was implacably opposed to nearly everything Labor stood for. Scullin defended himself by pointing out that the Government, in any case, had not the power to replace Gibson with another Board Chairman. It could only nominate someone else in his stead as a Board member. The Board elected its own Chairman and would be certain to elect another conservative who, however, would not be so well known, and even influential, in overseas financial circles as was Gibson. In truth it seems that Scullin, who did not pretend to any great financial expertise, had come to depend heavily on Gibson for advice and shrank from the prospect of doing without him.

Later in the month the State Premiers conferred in Melbourne where they listened reverently, if glumly, to Sir Otto Niemeyer, who addressed them at Scullin's invitation. His message was simple — and shattering to many beliefs and practices long cherished by most Australians. In many respects he sounded like an echo of the recently defeated Prime Minister, Bruce, in his most pessimistic mood. Australians had long enjoyed an artificially high standard of living, based on reckless overseas borrowing and ever higher protective tariffs. There could be no hope of recovery without drastic reduction of costs, which meant reduction of wages. It behoved governments, in the first place, to set the example by balancing their budgets and by refraining from all 'unreproductive' public works. Equally impressed and depressed, the Premiers and the Prime Minister, in what came to be known as the 'Melbourne Agreement', undertook to balance their budgets in the financial year 1930-31 and to refrain from unreproductive expenditure on public works. Since it was impossible for any of them to raise more loans overseas they all, perforce, kept the second part of the agreement. With the exception of Lionel Hill, newly elected Labor Premier of South Australia, none made any real attempt to achieve a balanced budget, an impossible task under the circumstances of the time.

The Premiers' conference was barely finished when Scullin sailed for London to attend an Imperial Conference. He was absent from Australia for more than four months — from 25 August till 6 January 1931. Many inside and outside the Labor Party criticised him severely for what still seems a very wrong decision. True, it was this conference which gave rise to the Statute of Westminster and a clearer definition of dominion status. It is also true that Scullin was seriously ill when he embarked at Fremantle and badly needed a rest. But he spent six weeks at the Conference and another six weeks on even less vital business in Britain and Europe and, inevitably, nearly another eight weeks at sea. When he left, his party and Government presented a reasonable appearance of unity and strength. When he returned both were a shambles. His one great achievement in Britain was to force a reluctant King-Emperor to appoint, as the first Australian-born Governor-General, none other than the 75-year-old Sir Isaac Isaacs, Chief Justice of Australia and sometime radical Protectionist Attorney-General in the second Deakin Government of 1905-1908. King George's main stated objection to the

Labor Daily, 1931

"According to Plan"

appointment was that Isaacs was an Australian, the very thing which recommended him most to the fervently nationalist Scullin. The point was won and the precedent established that any Australian might aspire to the highest office in his own country; but even Scullin must have asked himself whether the trip had been worthwhile when he found how far the position at home had deteriorated in his absence.

Although the Melbourne Agreement amounted in fact to little more than a solemn declaration of good intentions it, along with the suspicions and divisions created by Theodore's resignation, did much to split the Labor Party into bitterly warring factions whose internecine strife finally brought the Government down. On the right wing of the Parliamentary Party stood a small group led by J. A. Lyons, the Postmaster-General, and J. E. Fenton, Minister for Trade and Customs. With no more knowledge of economics than other members, they passionately believed that Sir Otto Niemeyer and the conventional financial wisdom of the time must be correct. Hence they stood for deflation, wage reductions, pruning governmental spending to the bone, rigid adherence to all existing contracts, and other orthodox financial nostrums put forward by their opponents in the Nationalist and Country Parties. The centre group, led by Scullin and Theodore, agreed that existing commitments must be honoured, that retrenchments must be made and so on; but as the situation worsened its members more and more strongly advocated the expansion of bank credit and controlled inflation to get the unemployed back to work and factories into production again. On the left stood a number of more radical members most prominent among whom were Frank Anstey, Minister for Health, and J. A. Beasley an Honorary Minister without Portfolio. Some of these advocated immediate socialisation of the country, some put forward various schemes of monetary reform, some advocated inflation, some wished to legislate for compulsory reduction of debts or interest rates, and some wanted to suspend or even repudiate payment of overseas debts. The only thing all had in common was that their policies involved, directly or by implication, the variation or abolition of some existing contracts.

Of course these ideological differences were complicated by personal friendships and hostilities. Most notably the right wing disliked and distrusted the brilliant Theodore, while many in the centre and on the left, particularly among those representing New South Wales seats, resented the rapidity of his rise to power and influence, to say nothing of the manner of his entrance to *their* State and to the House of Representatives. However all these divisions, though implicitly present in the Labor Caucus from the beginning, had hardly begun to become obvious when Scullin left for England on the morrow of the Melbourne Conference. In fact the possibility of any split appeared so remote that Scullin asked Fenton and Lyons, the two right-wingers who were to be the first to desert the Government, to act for him while he was away, the former as Prime Minister and the latter as Treasurer.

J. T. LANG AND THE LABOR 'SPLITS'

On 22 October 1930, the first anniversary of the installation of his Government, while Scullin was working at the Imperial Conference in London, his Administration and his own position of authority within it, received another body-blow when the electors of New South Wales, by a huge majority, chose John Thomas Lang to lead his second State Labor Government. Born in Sydney in 1876, the son of a jeweller who lost everything in the depression of the 1890s, Lang had grown up in poverty and had committed himself from boyhood onwards to the Labor movement. He gained experience in local politics in the Sydney suburb of Auburn and was elected to the New South Wales Legislative Assembly in 1913. From 1920 to 1922 he was Treasurer in the Storey and Dooley State Labor Governments and then, as we have seen, became Premier of New South Wales at the head of his own Government from 1925 till 1927 — when a Nationalist-Country Party Government led by T. R. Bavin was set up. Bavin's Government cut public servants' salaries and repealed Lang's Act of 1925 which had established a 44-hour week for all workers in New South Wales. In the State election campaign of 1930 Bavin promised, in consonance with the Melbourne Agreement, to make further economies and retrenchments. For Labor Lang promised to restore civil service salaries and the 44-hour week: but by implication at least he promised much more than that, no less than the reversal, at any rate in New South Wales, of the whole thrust of Commonwealth Labor Government policies and of the Melbourne Agreement.

Though certainly no Communist — he was born and remained all his life a practising Catholic — and in many ways not even any kind of socialist, Lang was the most radical person ever to lead any Australian government. During the 1920s he worked with J. S. 'Jock' Garden and the small Communist faction associated with the New South Wales Trades and Labour Council, and with any number of other individuals and factions in the Labor movement, to build up a loyal personal following and a political 'machine' through which he could influence, 'control' is probably not too strong a word, the whole Labor Party apparatus in the State. In 1930 he was at the height of his power and of his powers. Tall, hefty, and possessed of a jutting jaw and a stentorian voice, he was known to multitudes of admirers as 'the Big Fella'. He could move vast crowds to unbounded enthusiasm, and respectable persons to unbounded fear, with his oratory. He was the greatest demagogue Australia has known, but the evidence suggests that, unlike most demagogues, he believed in much of his own rhetoric. Perhaps this quality of sincerity was the secret of his power over so many. He also believed, no doubt, in the importance of his own possession of power and in the unimportance of the methods by which he achieved it.

His two overriding passions were for a fairer distribution of this world's goods within the framework of the capitalist system and an almost grotesquely parochial Australian nationalism. In his rhetoric it was rarely capitalists or other 'exploiters' who were denounced as such, but nearly always the 'English' or 'overseas' or 'foreign' bond-holders. In his *The Great Bust* Lang recalls how a colleague, Joe Lamaro, had occasion to refer in the State Parliament during Bavin's premiership to a leading British judge as:

> 'a bearded old lady named Lord Bryce'. Bavin indignantly snapped, 'Who — who are you, a foreigner to talk in that way about an English gentleman?' Quietly Lamaro replied: 'I am an Australian, the Premier is not. Only twice have I been out of Australia — first when I went on a short visit to the Premier's native land (New Zealand) and the other time as a member of the A.I.F.'[10]

Lang was purer than that. Just before he died in 1975, aged 98, he was reportedlv still proud of never having left Australian shores at all.

Lang's triumph was also a triumph for the restive left wing of the federal Labor Party, in Parliament and in the country generally. Until polling day on 22 October he had to some extent refrained from direct criticism of federal government policies. Once safely in power again he cast restraint to the winds. From then on the Premier of New South Wales, the Sydney *Labor Daily* and the State branch of the A.L.P. as a whole, loudly proclaimed what left-wing Laborites like Anstey, and a great many other citizens, had long believed, or at any rate wanted to believe: that the Depression had been created purposely by a conspiracy of bankers, capitalists and anti-Labor governments in order to increase profits by forcing reductions in wages and social services, that Niemeyer was the agent of Machiavellian British money-lenders who held Australia in thrall, that debts incurred by Australia's generosity in going to Britain's aid in the Great War were the main cause of financial difficulties, that

[10] J. T. Lang, *The Great Bust*, Sydney, 1962, p.185.

Britain herself had failed to honour her war debt to the United States and hence Australia should suspend or repudiate payments on her public debt to Britain, and that Scullin and the Commonwealth Government must be forced by popular pressure to reverse the thrust of their policies to conform with those of Lang and the New South Wales branch of the A.L.P.

When federal Parliament debated emergency economy measures in November and December all these views were promulgated vigorously in Cabinet and in the Labor Caucus by the left wing. Though he had resigned from the Government, Theodore was still a very active and influential member of Parliament and of Caucus. Though hostile to the wilder schemes of Lang's disciples, he was becoming more and more convinced that a measure of controlled inflation and greater government spending, not the reverse, was needed. He and a majority of Caucus wrangled bitterly with Lyons, Fenton and a majority of Cabinet. Lyons refused to give effect to one Caucus directive (which Theodore had voted against) — an idea of Anstey's to compel Commonwealth bond-holders, in a loan shortly due to mature, to wait another year for their money; but on the whole Caucus had the better of the fight. It agreed to Cabinet proposals for higher taxation but refused to accept further retrenchments.

One of Scullin's first acts on his return in January was to move in Caucus for the reinstatement of Theodore as Treasurer. He was appalled by the difficulties he faced and felt he simply could not do without Theodore's support and financial expertise. Caucus agreed to the Prime Minister's request but by only a narrow majority, and Theodore's return to office had the immediate effect of compounding the hostilities and distractions within the Government's ranks. On the right Lyons and Fenton resigned from Cabinet, partly because they felt it was wrong for Theodore to be restored to office while his name was still under a cloud, but more because of their objections to the policies he represented. On the left many Lang supporters, particularly among New South Wales members, were antagonised by this mark of favour for Lang's greatest enemy — or rival — in the A.L.P. By the reinstatement of Theodore, Scullin alienated both the right and left wing of his own supporters; but worse was to come.

When Parliament reassembled on 6 March 1931 Latham, leader of the Opposition, immediately moved a motion of no confidence. By voting for it Lyons, Fenton and three other right-wing Laborites, joined later by a fourth, formally deserted their party and the Government. Labor right-wingers elsewhere, especially in the three southern State branches, hastened to follow the example of their federal colleagues. Next day an ex-tramway worker, Edward John

Herald, 1931

A Troublesome Member of The Family

In the House of Representatives the Lang group is threatening to create a crisis in opposition to Mr Theodore.— *News Item.*

In New South Wales the Federal Labor Party has offered to forgive and forget if the expelled Langites will reform and return to the fold. *News Item.*

Ward, won a by-election to the Commonwealth Parliament for the blue-ribbon Labor seat of East Sydney. Universally known as Eddy, Ward was a tough fighter and an uncompromising radical. For a generation he remained the Labor Party's *enfant terrible* in the federal Parliament and the whipping-boy of the anti-Labor forces. He had won the by-election on the New South Wales (Lang) Labor Party's platform of inflation and repudiation of overseas debts. In conformity with the policy of the executive committee of the federal A.L.P., Scullin ruled that Ward could not be admitted to Caucus unless he repudiated Langism. Caucus itself concurred, with the result that J. A. Beasley and three other New South Wales left-wingers deserted the federal Labor Party and joined Eddy Ward as a hostile group outside and to the left of Caucus. By the end of the month a special conference of the federal A.L.P. had formally expelled Lang and the entire New South Wales branch of the party which he controlled, and begun to set up a new, purged branch in that State. Langism gained some support in other States, and until 1936 there were two hostile groups both claiming to represent the true and legitimate interests of Labor.

During a single month the Commonwealth Government had been shorn of its right and left wings. The Labor Party, which had begun the twelfth Parliament with 46 seats out of 75 was reduced to a minority position with only 35 members left. Lyons and his right-wing dissidents were already supporting the Opposition on most issues, as were Hughes and the other Independents. The Government could be defeated at any time if the Lang group on its left chose to vote with the Opposition, but Beasley left his erstwhile comrades in place, if hardly in power, till the end of the year.

Meanwhile powerful supporters of the Nationalist Party, for the most part outside Parliament, made informal and unpublicised approaches to Lyons and his right-wing dissidents. It was agreed that Lyons and his followers should join a re-named and re-constructed conservative party, with Lyons as its leader, just as Hughes had done in 1917. The Nationalist Party was formally dissolved and 'replaced' immediately by the United Australia Party (U.A.P.), which included the right-wing ex-Laborites. On 7 May it was announced that Lyons was the leader of the Opposition, Latham having resigned to become his deputy.

Born in 1879 to a struggling farming couple in the Tasmanian bush, Joseph Aloysius Lyons had a difficult childhood, engaging in scrub-cutting and other hard labour to help the family before he was twelve years old. Then he was taken into the home of two aunts in the township of Stanley. They encouraged him to study and he qualified as a Government schoolteacher at the age of seventeen. His own battle for an education made him a doughty champion of greater educational opportunities for others. In 1909, aged 30, he became a Labor member of the Tasmanian Parliament and five years later Treasurer, Minister for Education and Minister for Railways in the State's first Labor Government — disregarding a minority Labor Ministry that had lasted for only a week in 1909. He was instrumental in establishing the first high schools in Tasmania. When the State Labor leader, John Earle, was expelled from the party in 1917 for supporting conscription, Lyons was elected to the leadership. From 1923 to 1928 he governed Tasmania as Premier, Minister for Railways and Minister for Mines, at the head of an Administration which was praised for its caution and economy rather than for any very spectacular advances in social legislation. In 1929, at Scullin's suggestion, he stood successfully for the federal Parliament. A sincere Roman Catholic, Lyons was the first (and at least up to 1976 the last) member of that faith to lead the major non-Labor party. Shrewd and with a great fund of common sense, he was a decent, modest, genial man, blessed with an extremely able wife and eleven children. After her husband's death and after the last of her family had grown up, Dame Enid Lyons had a distinguished federal parliamentary career of her own from 1943 to 1951. Nicknamed 'Honest Joe' by the press and those who supported his policies after 1931, he was denigrated by radicals as just another 'Labor rat' — but hardly hated, even by his bitterest political enemies, as Hughes was after 1916. He was too kindly by nature to bear or inspire lasting grudges. Indeed cartoonists often depicted him as a koala bear, because the benign expression of his features reminded them of the countenance of that amiable marsupial.

For the next three months — until the midwinter of 1931 — the Government strove desperately to implement measures aimed at getting people back to work by boosting the stagnant economy. It was frustrated at every turn by the Opposition majority in the Senate and by the implacable hostility of the Governor of the Commonwealth Bank. From June it was forced, in effect, to implement the policy of its opponents. In March Theodore secured Cabinet backing for a Fiduciary Notes Bill, aimed at putting an extra £18,000,000 into circulation, £12,000,000 to relieve unemployment and £6,000,000 to help wheat farmers. Another Bill suspended the law requiring the note issue to be backed by 25 per cent of its value in gold, and authorised the printing of £60,000,000 worth of bank notes. The amount of currency actually in circulation in 1931 was £50,000,000. Other bills provided for the compulsory lowering of interest rates and the shipment of gold to London to meet loan repayments due on 30

June. The Senate rejected them all. In April Sir Robert Gibson informed the Prime Minister and the six State Premiers that, unless they drastically reduced expenditure as they had agreed to do in Melbourne, he would make no more short-term loans available to them. By May there was nothing left to be tried but the conservative policy of all-round deflation.

The Loan Council appointed a subcommittee of senior public servants and professional economists to advise governments on how to balance their budgets and cut expenditure. The most influential member of the committee was its chairman, Professor D. B. Copland. His report of the Committee's recommendations was accepted, however reluctantly in the case of the Commonwealth and New South Wales, by all governments. The Premiers' Plan, as it came to be known, provided for the reduction by 20 per cent of all public service salaries, pensions and other forms of 'adjustable government expenditure', a reduction of 22.5 per cent in interest rates paid by governments on internal loans, a comparable reduction in bank interest rates, some reduction in private mortgage payments and higher taxation. Virtually all private employers reduced wages and salaries commensurately at the same time. Scullin, Theodore and half of the federal Parliamentary Labor Party voted for this package of 'sound finance': half voted against and two Cabinet Minister resigned. Nationalist and Country Party members of course supported it enthusiastically. Beasley and his four Lang Labor followers voted against, although Lang himself had signed the 'plan' on behalf of New South Wales. He implemented it less than wholeheartedly however.

LIFE IN THE DEPRESSION

The triumph of 'sound finance' had an immediate effect on the confidence of investors in Commonwealth bonds, but none at all on the plight of those who lacked money, work and food. Indeed unemployment rose from approximately 27.8 per cent in midwinter 1931, when the Premiers' Plan was adopted, to 30.0 per cent a year later — from which time, painfully slowly, jobs slowly became less scarce. Though church and other charitable schemes, such as one run by the R.S.L. for its members, helped, basically the unemployed were kept alive by State Government relief schemes. These varied from State to State, and according to whether a Labor or anti-Labor government was in power. Since no government could borrow money, 'the dole' was paid for by a special tax on the wages of those lucky enough to be in work, plus whatever help could be got from the Commonwealth Government. Single men who could prove they were destitute were paid 'susso' — an allowance sufficient to sustain life — amounting in New South Wales in 1931 to five shillings and sixpence per week when the basic wage stood at £3 7s 0d. Allowances to families and for dependent children were proportionately parsimonious. In some States single men were forced to 'travel' — to roam continuously about the country in search of work — in order to qualify for any relief at all.

Thousands more did so voluntarily. Work was hardly more plentiful in the bush than in the city, but food was. Blackberries, and other fruit and vegetables, wild and cultivated, could be picked up in season; corn off the cob from a farmer's paddock; a stray sheep or calf; fish and shellfish along the coast, and everywhere rabbits, 'underground mutton' as they were called, could be obtained by the enterprising. Many 'travellers' and some family groups built themselves semi-permanent camps on old (and some new) goldfields. Others moved into caves and rock-shelters which had been used for thousands of years before the white man's arrival by the first Australians. Irrespective of whether Australia or other countries were on the gold standard or not, the price of gold rose during the Depression while that of nearly all other commodities fell. Production and export of gold rose dramatically. Most of it came from heavily capitalised mining companies, but some from the efforts of workless people, prospecting and 'gouging' the precious metal 'for wages' to eke out the dole.

Generally speaking it was difficult or impossible for married couples with young children to leave the only home they had, and take to the bush. For these, as an alternative to the dole, special 'relief work' was provided from time to time for the breadwinners. Much of it was notably 'un-reproductive' in S. M. Bruce's terminology, and though sometimes paid for at award rates, the quantity of work available to each man was rationed, so as to make it not much more attractive than living on sustenance. For such families their home, whether they owned it, were in the process of paying it off, or merely rented it, was their most prized possession, almost their only one. Yet many families inevitably fell behind in payments to the bank, or building society or landlord. Many financial institutions were quite ruthless, but in some cases the landlord too was in desperate need. Many families were evicted. Under police protection the landlord or his employees forcibly ejected the tenants, dumping their few sticks of furniture and un-pawned belongings in the street before the house. In the big cities the Unemployed Workers' Movement set up committees of local residents to resist evictions. The committees were usually Communist-inspired, but press reports of battles between

'Communists and Police' grossly distorted the truth — which was that most residents in a working-class neighbourhood naturally joined more or less openly in any fight to protect their neighbours from eviction. On 20 June 1931, for instance, the *Sydney Morning Herald* reported 'the most sensational eviction battle Sydney has ever known . . . between 40 policemen and 18 Communists'. All the defenders and 'at least 15 of the police' were injured, but it is clear that a huge crowd 'numbering many thousands' did all it could to help the 'Communists' and hurt the police.

If they were lucky, evicted families simply moved in to share already overcrowded accommodation with relatives or friends; if not, they joined the small army of the dispossessed living in home-made shanty settlements on the outskirts of towns and cities. One of the best-known was 'Happy Valley', situated in the sandhills of La Perouse, an outer suburb of Sydney named after the great French navigator who landed there only a few weeks after the First Fleet arrived in 1788. In such places tens of thousands brought up their children in humpies made of old bags, packing cases, flattened kerosene tins and scraps of driftwood. The dole provided enough to sustain life, but hardly good health. For city children any kind of fruit was an almost unknown luxury. Butter, still exported in quantity and subsidised by the remaining Australian consumers, was in the same category and even jam was too expensive for those out of work. The staple diet for many children was bread and dripping lightly sprinkled with salt and pepper, or bread and treacle (or golden syrup) known since the previous century as 'cocky's joy' — because so many struggling farmers ('cockies') even then had been able to afford little else.

Even so, those who earned their living directly from the land — graziers, farmers, orchardists and so on — at least had enough to eat. Many, who for years past had bought all their provisions in a neighbouring township, learnt again during the Depression to keep a few fowls, pigs, and a cow or two and to grow their own vegetables and perhaps some fruit trees. This did not mean that they were well off. After all, one of the prime causes of the Depression was the catastrophic fall in world prices for primary products. Farmers who had bought tractors sometimes could not afford to buy petrol. They left the tractor to rust in a shed and harnessed their horse-team again for drilling, ploughing and harvesting. In town and country the number of motor-car and motorcycle registrations actually fell while horse-drawn traffic on the roads increased. Oddly enough everyone did not experience a fall in his or her standard of living. The unemployed and practically all self-employed persons did: but those wage and salary-earners, pensioners and others on fixed incomes, who remained fully employed and in receipt of their proper emoluments throughout the Depression, may even have been a little better off than before. This paradox arose because, even allowing for the 20 per cent reduction in all wages and salaries, prices of consumer goods fell on the whole further and faster than wages. Yet very few such people thought themselves as well off as before, and very few were, because of the financial help they felt constrained to give to their unemployed children, relatives, friends or unknown beggars.

Although it was a criminal offence in most States to beg or to offer goods for sale in a public place, beggars and hawkers swarmed in Australian streets, to a degree quite unparalleled before and quite unknown to younger generations since. Shoe-laces, home-made jam or pickles, matches, cotton-reels — anything and everything was offered for sale by desperate people, some of them so desperate that they took their little children with them to appeal more effectively to the reasonably dressed passer-by. Beggars and hawkers knocked every day at every door, but in addition came a small army of salesmen: people with no wage or retainer trying to sell on commission. Their wares ranged from insurance policies, encyclopaedias and often bogus shares in goldmines or pine forests to the new electric gadgets — vacuum cleaners, refrigerators, washing and sewing-machines, which few even of those in work could afford. Electric irons were to be found in many households before the Depression began: not many more were sold during the 1930s. Saddest of all was the plight of young people leaving school. Many had to go on for years living at home on their parents or 'on the susso'. In Australia as a whole 25.7 per cent of the workforce was still unemployed in the winter of 1933, 17.8 per cent in that of 1935 and 10.0 per cent just before war broke out again in 1939.

People had little or no money to spare for recreation. Attendances at picture-shows, including the newly arrived 'talkies' fell steeply, as did the 'gate-money' at prize fights, racecourses, and even the 'Aussie Rules' football matches in Melbourne. In every capital city people still crowded into the live vaudeville theatre when the immortal 'Mo' ('Roy Rene') trod the boards, for he taught them how to laugh at their misery and at the petty pomposities of the powerful, whom they saw as causing it. Born in Adelaide in 1892 of Dutch-Jewish descent, Harry Van der Sluys ('Mo') was incomparably the greatest comedian Australia every produced, deserving to stand with Monash and Isaac Isaacs in the very first rank of Australians. His genius was limited only by its complete dependence on the idiom and folkways of his countrymen. People still visited each other, giving parties and dances; but, except among the minority of the rich and fashionable whose life-style was little affected by the Depression, it became customary for each guest to bring some food, drink, gramophone records or other contribution to the entertainment. They sang and danced in self-mockery to songs like:

I went to a house and I asked for some bread,
But the lady said 'Bum, bum, the baker is dead!'
Hallelujah I'm a bum! Hallelujah bum again!
Hallelujah give us a hand-out to revive us again!

or more often to others, pathetically based on the principle of primitive sympathetic magic, like:

Happy days are here again!
The skies above are clear again!
The country's right, we've got the rain!
Happy days are here again!
All together shout it now!
There's no room left to doubt it now!
Let's tell the world about it now!
Happy days are here again!

Some sports cost little or nothing to practise: surfing and swimming became more popular than ever; football, cricket and tennis hardly less so. Although attendances at sports grounds declined, more people than ever before 'followed' sports on the wireless — a device to which nearly everyone had access by 1930, even in the shanty-towns of dole recipients. In 1932-33 England beat Australia in the Test Cricket matches — unfairly in Antipodean eyes — because the gentlemanly English captain, Jardine, instructed his professional fast bowler, Harold Larwood, to aim his high-velocity balls at the batsman instead of at the traditional target, the wicket. There were many broken bones and angry recriminations. After the third Test Match in Adelaide, Jardine went to the Australian dressing-room not, as might have been innocently supposed, to ask about the state of the injured players, but to complain formally that one of the home team had called his bowler 'a bastard'. The gentlemanly Australian captain, Bill Woodfull, later headmaster of Melbourne High School, was provoked into replying in a traditionally crude Australian way. 'Which one of you bastards', he enquired of his team, 'called this bastard's bowler a bastard?'[11]

[11] Personal communication from the late Stanley Murray, committee member of the South Australian Cricket Association, January 1933.

Many who believed, with the Premier of New South Wales, that the Depression in Australia had been brought about, or at least made worse, by British financiers, had their Anglophobia reinforced by this Test Cricket series. Unlike the Great War, the great Depression produced some first-rate literary work at the time or soon afterwards. In addition to many competent short stories and novels by Ruth Park, Katharine Susannah Prichard, Vance Palmer and others, there were three great books which faithfully reproduced the experience of the time: Christina Stead's *Seven Poor Men of Sydney*, Kylie Tennant's *The Battlers* and Xavier Herbert's *Capricornia*.

LANGISM AND REACTION IN NEW SOUTH WALES

People had only too much leisure time in which to think about the causes of, and possible remedies for, the conditions which forced them and so many others throughout the world to rot in idleness. Communists pointed to the U.S.S.R. as the only socialist country on earth and the only one in which, whatever other horrors might exist, unemployment was unknown. The Australian Communist Party, devoutly Stalinist in complexion, did grow in number from about 300 in 1929 to 3000 in 1935 but it remained a negligible force in parliamentary elections. The 'social credit' theories of a retired English eccentric, Major C. H. Douglas, attracted more support. His followers indulged in anti-Semitic propaganda and taught that poverty could be painlessly abolished, without any interference with existing property relations, if the state legislated so as to equalise the production and consumption of commodities. They polled nearly 5 per cent of the total vote at the 1934 federal elections, more than five times the vote for Communist candidates; but only in one or two Queensland seats did they come within reasonable distance of being elected. Of all left-of-centre prescriptions for curing social ills, that of the Premier of New South Wales, intellectually incoherent as it was, commanded most attention. There were three reasons for this: first, 'the Big Fella's' quite extraordinary charisma; second, some of the proto-Keynesian policies he advocated would in fact have been less painful and more helpful to the nation's condition, had it been possible to implement them, than what was actually done in the name of 'sound finance'; and third, Lang actually carried out more of his glittering promises than was, or is, usual among politicians. We have already looked at Lang's anti-depression rhetoric above, but many remembered that he had introduced child endowment, widows' pensions and an improved workers' compensation scheme in New South Wales during his first premiership.

Early in 1931 he produced his 'Lang Plan', the chief points of which were: repudiation of all governmental interest payments on British loans, until Britain wrote off Australia's war debt as the U.S.A. had written off Britain's; reduction by 3 per cent of all interest payments on government loans within Australia, and abandonment of the gold standard for what Lang termed 'the goods standard'. That Australia had already abandoned the gold standard, in fact though not in rhetoric, over a year earlier is some measure of the vast ignorance of economics harboured by Lang and nearly everyone else inside and outside Parliament. In March Lang began to implement his plan by defaulting on interest payments on New South Wales Government loans due in London. The Commonwealth promptly met the debts and instituted legal proceedings to recover the money from the New South Wales Treasury. On 23 April, two days before the Anzac celebrations, the State Savings Bank of New South Wales was forced by 'a run' of worried depositors to close its doors. Conservatives saw this event as proof of Lang's dangerous lunacy: his supporters believed that the 'run' had been organised by his political enemies. No depositor actually lost a penny though the State Bank was finally taken over by the Commonwealth Savings Bank. As moderate and conservative opinion became more alarmed, hundreds of thousands of radical and working-class people became more convinced of Lang's supposed genius. Those who believed in it implicitly never constituted a majority of the people of their own State, let alone of Australia. By mid-1931 they were a diminishing band, but even a year later when the Premier had been thrown out of office by the English Governor of the State, Sir Phillip Game, he still had the devoted admiration of well over a third of the people of New South Wales. No other Australian politician, before or since, ever had half such a numerous and committed personal following. Hundreds of half-size busts in plaster and bronze, each inscribed with the words 'The People's Champion, J. T. Lang', were distributed through the Labor Electoral Leagues in New South Wales. The slogan 'Lang is Right' was painted on fences or blank walls, from Cape Leeuwin to Cape York, and attempts were made by devout disciples in every State to set up some sort of 'Lang Labor' party machinery.

All this fanaticism produced more than an equal and opposite reaction. In the Imperial Service Club in Sydney, on 18 February 1931, a few months after the election of the Lang Government, some ex-officers of the A.I.F. gathered to plan the formation of a quasi-military, quasi-secret organisation to oppose Langism and uphold what they regarded as national traditions and national honour. Tens of thousands of men, many of them old diggers and most from the 'better' suburbs of Sydney, were recruited to the 'New

Guard' in a few months. Relative to the Australian population, the New Guard was more than ten times as strong as Sir Oswald Mosley's British Union of Fascists. Recruits swore to obey their leaders, chief of whom was Colonel Eric Campbell, a fervent admirer of Mussolini and Hitler, who exchanged the fascist salute with his followers at public meetings. Though the concept of fascism was hardly familiar to most Australians in 1931, the New Guard was a fascist organisation in the sense that it was prepared to use violence to overthrow the democratically elected Government of the State if, in Campbell's words, it made 'any attempt, constitutional or unconstitutional . . . to foist socialization on the people'.[12] In the event the Guardsmen issued a great deal of inflammatory propaganda, labelled as 'communists' all with whom they disagreed politically, and forcefully broke up many public meetings organised by Labor and trade-union bodies. In the process they intimidated many and broke the limbs or heads of some of their opponents with pick-handles, but actually killed none. They were particularly active in disruption of Labor meetings during the federal election campaign of December 1931 — which was brought about by the Premier of New South Wales rather than by anyone in the Commonwealth Parliament.

Since June, as we have seen, the Scullin Government had been reduced to the expedient of implementing the policy of its opponents on the right, while being kept in office only by the votes of the Lang Labor faction on its left. On 25 November, instructed by Lang, J. A. Beasley moved that his principal's greatest rival, Theodore the Federal Treasurer, should be investigated for the third time for alleged corruption. Lang's henchmen in Theodore's Sydney electorate of Dalley, held that the Treasurer had improperly selected, from among unemployed electors, his own supporters as recipients of relief funds. Scullin took the motion as a question of confidence. By crossing the floor of the House with his group of followers to vote with the U.A.P., the Country Party and Independent members, Beasley ensured the Government's defeat and, incidentally, earned a nickname which stuck to him in Labor circles for the rest of his life — 'Stabber Jack': for not even Lang's charisma could for long detach most of its solid traditional support from the A.L.P., no matter what that party's demonstrated weaknesses and betrayals, nor earn forgiveness for schismatics and deserters.

The general election of 19 December 1931 was an unusually complicated affair because of the participation in the propaganda war, if not always in the field of candidates, of the Lang Labor,

[12] K. Amos, *The New Guard Movement* (Litt.B. thesis, University of New England, 1975), p.33 and *passim*.

Douglas Credit and Communist Parties and a plethora of right-wing bodies such as the All for Australia League (created largely by the leading Melbourne sharebroking firm of J. B. Were and Son), the Citizens' League, the Empire Party, the Sane Democracy League, and, in South Australia, the Emergency Committee, besides still-functioning local sections of the dissolved Nationalist Party, which had been unwilling to merge their identity with that of the new-hatched U.A.P. Before, during or not very long after the election, all these latter bodies amalgamated with the U.A.P. or quietly faded away. On 3 December in the middle of the election campaign the banks devalued Australian money, which had long stood at parity with British, so that for the next thirty years the Australian pound was worth only £125 to the British pound's £100. The absence of governmental control over national finance was underscored by the fact that this immensely significant change was hardly even mentioned in the electioneering.

All three leaders for the first time made extensive use of wireless broadcasting in their campaign speeches. Scullin took credit for the retrenchments made under the Premiers' Plan but at the same time promised, if re-elected to power, to legislate for proper governmental control of the financial system in order to introduce a measure of inflationary 'pump-priming' into the economy. He warned that the remaining viable secondary industries might be ruined if tariff levels were reduced. Page for the Country Party promised to do just that. Lyons for the U.A.P. hedged on the issue, promising that there would be no hasty scaling-down of the existing level of protection. He claimed for the Opposition entire credit for forcing the Government to agree to the Premiers' Plan. Both conservative leaders denounced all 'crazy' financial schemes, stressed the need for continued sacrifices and vigorously denounced the Australian Communist movement. There was a massive swing against Labor in every State except Queensland. In the Representatives the U.A.P. won 39 seats — including Eddie Ward's supposedly impregnable Labor stronghold of East Sydney. However the U.A.P. member died almost immediately, of shock some said, and Ward re-won the seat at the by-election. This left the U.A.P. with 38 seats, the Country Party with 16, the A.L.P. with only 13 and Lang Labor with 5 (counting East Sydney). There were 3 Independents. The state of the parties in the new Senate was U.A.P. 21, Country Party 5, A.L.P. 8 and Lang Labor two. Thus the U.A.P. alone had a majority in both Houses, and 'Honest Joe' Lyons became the third (and up to 1976 the last) Labor renegade, in succession to Cook and Hughes, to become Prime Minister of his country at the head of a group whose politics he had opposed for most of his life.

Herald, 1931

Another One On The Slate!

For the sake of Australia's credit, the Federal Government has once more been forced to pay the interest bill for the defaulting State of New South Wales. This time the bill amounts to £950,763.

With federal Labor in such disarray respectable people, if not the unemployed, breathed easily again; but not in New South Wales. Although Theodore had lost his Dalley seat (he never returned to politics), that man Lang still ruled the State from Parliament's 'temporary' headquarters in the old Rum Hospital in Sydney's Macquarie Street, and he showed no sign of abashment at the result of the federal election: rather the reverse. In January 1932 he again repudiated interest payments in London and New York on a loan to his State, but this time the Commonwealth allowed two weeks to pass before footing the bill. The new U.A.P. Government then passed the Financial Agreements Enforcement Act which gave the Commonwealth power to recover from State treasuries moneys owed to it. The validity of the Act was upheld by the High Court and Lang loomed in conservative eyes as a greater ogre than ever, hell-bent on the destruction of private property and public honour. The New Guard continued to drill secretly, to bash reputed Communists, and to conduct public demonstrations of strengh at which Campbell kept hinting at the imminence of some great, but mysterious, coup which would topple, or humble, the Lang Government.

The climax, or rather the anticlimax, came on 18 March 1932 when the Premier opened the Sydney Harbour Bridge, then the mightiest single-arch bridge anywhere in the world. Between the military and police sections of the great procession cavorted a mounted man, dressed in military uniform, who seemed not quite to belong to either. Alert as ever, the Australian guardians of the law and peacetime soldiers failed to question, or apparently even to notice, the lone rider. As Lang stepped forward to cut the ribbon, stretched tautly across the southern end of the bridge roadway, a New Guardsman, Captain Francis de Groot, spurred forward and slashed at the ribbon shouting, 'In the name of the decent and respectable citizens of New South Wales, I now declare this bridge open'. The sword, however, was blunt. De Groot leant downwards to the right out of his saddle in order to hold the ribbon with his left hand while he sawed at it with his right. At that moment Police Superintendent W. J. MacKay lumbered forward, grasped de Groot's left foot and tipped him onto the roadway. The ribbon was re-tied and cut by the Premier. De Groot was taken by the police to be psychiatrically examined. Deemed sane, he was tried and fined £ 5 plus £ 4 costs for 'offensive behaviour on Bradfield Highway'.[13] Thus the brutal melodrama, mounted by the New Guard, ended in low farce. Campbell continued to issue vaguely

[13] K. Amos, *The New Guard Movement 1931-1935*, Melbourne, 1976, pp.76-9.

portentous threats until the fall of the Lang Government two months later, but thereafter his organisation quickly faded from view.

Lang continued to repudiate payment of interest on New South Wales debts and thereby to defy the federal conference of the A.L.P., the Commonwealth Government and finally, the High Court of Australia. The situation came to a head in May 1932 when the Commonwealth moved, under the Financial Agreements Enforcement Act, to recover the monies owed it by the Government of New South Wales. Lang then broke the law of his own State, in addition to that of the Commonwealth, by withdrawing Government funds from banks, and barricading the State treasury building to prevent the entry of Commonwealth officers. On 13 May the State Governor, Sir Philip Game, dismissed the Lang Government from office and commissioned B. S. B. Stevens, the State leader of the U.A.P., to form a Government. The legality of Game's action in dismissing a government, which certainly had the full confidence of the Legislative Assembly, was searchingly questioned at the time and since. Certainly it was without precedent, but so was the situation in which the government of the day was breaking its own laws. On the afternoon of Sunday 5 June Lang addressed an election meeting in Moore Park, adjoining that same Centennial Park which had witnessed the birth of the Commonwealth. An enormous crowd assembled to hear him again denounce British bond-holders and usurers, and to assure him again that he was right: but the majority of their fellow citizens thought him a reckless firebrand. Many held it was the largest gathering of human beings ever assembled in Australia's history. Estimates ranged from 200 000 people (*Sydney Morning Herald*) to 550 000 (*Labor Daily*). There may have been more people present at the dedication of the Melbourne Shrine of Remembrance on Armistice Day, 11 November 1934 — according to the sober *Age* '317 500 people'. However that may be, on 11 June, fortunately for Sir Philip Game, the voters returned a U.A.P.-Country Party coalition to power with an overwhelming majority. Even so it is worth noting that Lang Labor candidates received over 40 per cent of all votes cast. By an irony of fate the Queensland elections, held on the same day, dismissed a conservative government and returned Labor (though not Lang Labor) to power in the northern State.

Chapter 7

CAUTION BEFORE THE STORM

c. 1933—1938

Retrenchment and recovery — Commonwealth-State relations — The arts and ideologies — The Country Party and the U.A.P. — Wowsers and censorship — Foreign policy, fascism and defence

RETRENCHMENT AND RECOVERY

On 9 December 1931, ten days before the election which swept Lyons into power as leader of the United Australia Party, the British Parliament passed the Statute of Westminster. This enactment went practically unnoticed by Australian politicians and people. Nevertheless it had great significance for them. The Statute was the result of the Imperial Conference of 1930 which Scullin had attended. It gave legal force to the declaration of the previous Imperial Conference of 1926, presided over by Lord Balfour, that the self-governing dominions were 'autonomous communities within the British Empire, equal in status, in no way subordinate one to another in any aspect of their domestic or external affairs, though united by a common allegiance to the Crown and freely associated as members of the British Commonwealth of Nations'.[1] It meant in practice that the dominions were completely independent, sovereign states — in every respect save that each owed formal allegiance to the Crown. Other dominions speedily ratified the Statute. Scullin tried, but was overwhelmed by the pressure of other parliamentary business and lost power before he could do so. Then the Lyons Government and its conservative successors made no serious attempt to ratify the Statute for the next ten years. That had to wait for the next Labor Administration in 1942.

There could be no clearer demonstration of the strong imperial loyalty and indifference, amounting in some cases to hostility, towards Australian nationalism and self-reliance, of many conservative politicians. Their anxiety to leave the whole field of foreign policy to Britain is particularly striking when one remembers that this decade of the 1930s was, of course, the period which saw

[1] *A.E.*, vol. 2, p.476.

the rise of the Axis powers, Fascist Germany, Italy and Japan, and their increasingly obvious preparation for the Second World War: a war in which, as many radical Australians foresaw, Britain might be unable or unwilling to defend Australia from a possible Japanese invasion. The first U.A.P. Cabinet was sworn into office on 6 January 1932. Four days earlier the Japanese had proclaimed their puppet-state of Manchukuo and by the end of the month they had occupied Shanghai. Yet conservative Australian opinion was quite unmoved. A new U.A.P. member of the House of Representatives, who subsequently became in turn Minister for External Affairs and Governor-General, R. G. Casey, published a paper in September on 'The International Situation' in which he never even mentioned Japan.

Foreign policy and defence, then, ought to have been a major preoccupation of governments during this period, but in fact were not so until the last two or three years before Hitler marched into Poland. The major preoccupation of federal and State governments was economy, balancing the budget and, within these self-imposed limits, doing what they felt could be done to woo back prosperity.

Since the U.A.P. had an absolute majority in the Lower House, albeit a small one, it was in a position to govern in its own right, without entering into a coalition with the Country Party; and since Page demanded a much greater scaling-down of tariffs than Lyons, the ex-Laborite, was prepared to concede, it did so. Lyons became Prime Minister and Treasurer, Latham Attorney-General, Minister for External Affairs and Industry, Senator Pearce Minister for Defence and H. S. Gullett Minister for Trade and Customs. The most interesting newcomer to Cabinet was C. A. S. Hawker, grandson of a Speaker of the South Australian Legislative Assembly, and a man of immense courage, intelligence and integrity. Severely crippled by a German shell in France, he was elected to the Commonwealth Parliament in 1929. During the 1931 election campaign he promised that, although opposed personally to further drastic reduction of parliamentary salaries, he would vote for the maximum reduction that was proposed. Lyons gave Hawker the portfolios of Markets (Commerce) and Repatriation. In a Cabinet re-shuffle in April he was left with Commerce; but in September he felt obliged to resign from Cabinet, which had proposed a reduction in parliamentary salaries, in order to vote for an amendment moved by a back-bencher, seeking a greater reduction. Hawker was widely regarded as a future prime minister. A past prime minister, Stanley Melbourne Bruce, regained his seat of Flinders at this election, and was given an assistant-ministership in the Treasury. However in September he was sent to London to negotiate a conversion to lower interest rates of Commonwealth loan payments. He succeeded, and saved over £4,000,000 for Australia in the first five years, but then resigned from Parliament to become High Commissioner.

For its first few months of office most of the Government's energies were expended on what seemed to it the vital task of destroying the Government of New South Wales. That accomplished, as outlined in the last chapter, it turned to what it considered the only slightly less important task of cutting living standards still further in order at any cost to balance its budget. By increasing the stringency of the means test and by forcing relatives, who had the means to do so, to support pensioners, the Financial Emergency Act of 1932 and associated measures further reduced the number of people entitled to the maternity allowance, to old-age and to invalid pensions. Wages and salaries of all public servants and of members of parliament were also cut back still further. Less painful was the thorough overhaul of the tariff structure and the negotiation of new overseas trade agreements, some of which changes were necessitated by commitments the Government entered into at the Ottawa Economic Conference of July and August. There the British Government, forced by the Depression to abandon free trade, agreed with other British Empire countries to the principle of Imperial tariff preference and to a wide range of specific preferential agreements on various commodities. The Ottawa agreements did help somewhat to revive Australia's export trade to New Zealand, Canada and other countries as well as to Britain. Producers of frozen meat, wine and dried and canned fruits benefited particularly. The Lyons Government, in accordance with its election promises, courageously lowered the tariff, for the first time since federation, on a whole range of imports. The reductions, made on the advice of the Tariff Board, were judicious, far too cautious and trifling indeed to please most Country Party members; but they did stimulate greater efficiency in Australian secondary industry.

As a result of these measures, of external windfalls like the Hoover moratorium on war debts which saved £4,000,000 and of some luck, Lyons was able to report, to everyone's surprise, that the national government had finished the 1931-32 financial year with a surplus of over £1,000,000; and that Australia's overseas trade balance had been converted from a deficit in 1930-31 of £33,000,000 sterling to a surplus in 1931-32 of £31,000,000 sterling. State governments had not managed so well, though they had, with the exception of New South Wales, made long strides toward budgetary balance. The consolidated deficit for the year of all Australian governments was £18,000,000 instead of the £40,000,000 that had been expected. Except for help to primary producers by the abolition of sales and primage tax on some goods much used by them, Lyons offered virtually no concessions in this budget. However, receipts from customs duties and other sources continued to be more buoyant than expected, so much so that he introduced a supplementary budget in November. In this and the two succeeding budgets of October 1933 and July 1934, the financial screws, which had been clamped upon the whole community, were progressively loosened. Many people outside the House shared the bitterness of Labor members within it at the Government's order of priorities. Reductions in land tax, company tax, income tax, property tax and other measures which favoured the rich, and bounties and subsidies of many kinds to farmers and graziers, always seemed to come faster and give more than measures which favoured the poor, such as the restoration of wage-cuts and pensions to their pre-depression level. So obvious was this bias in the Government's measures that one of its own members, R. G. Casey, failed effectively to refute Opposition charges that the 1933 budget was:

> a rich man's budget, the Government is ladling out a million or so to its wealthy friends, and is offering only a few crumbs to those most needing assistance.[2]

Nevertheless some progress, however slow, was made towards restoration of 1929 living standards. By the end of 1934 increases in soldiers', invalid, age and other pensions and in public service salaries had restored the last mentioned, for instance, to within 15 per cent of their pre-Premiers' Plan level.

J. G. Latham, the Attorney-General, who had held the same portfolio in the Bruce-Page Government in 1926 when it passed its draconian Crimes Act, brought forward another Bill which armed the Government with even more arbitrary power to prosecute persons and organisations it deemed seditious. Aimed primarily at the Australian Communist Party, the Crimes Act of 1932 was thought by many to threaten the civil liberties of all citizens with dissident opinions. It empowered the High Court, on evidence supplied by the Attorney-General, to declare as unlawful associations groups of people advocating sedition or violent revolution. It gave the Attorney-General power to force suspected persons or organisations to produce records and answer questions which might incriminate them, and provided that officers of 'declared' bodies should be disenfranchised in Commonwealth elections for seven years and that

[2] *C.P.D.*, vol. 141, p.3551.

members not born in Australia should be deported. Obviously the Act reversed one of the accepted principles of British Common Law by requiring the defendant to prove his innocence rather than the prosecution to prove guilt. Yet the first prosecution brought under this legislation failed. The publishers of the *Workers Weekly* were charged with soliciting funds for the Communist Party: but five out of the six High Court Judges dismissed the charge because evidence showed that the paper had sought funds for a meeting of a 'United Front' against war and imperialism, and there was no proof that this body had aims identical with those of the Communist Party.

Few people at the time cared, or even noticed, that the area of land under Australian sovereignty nearly doubled under the Lyons Government. In 1933 the Antarctic Territory Acceptance Act took over from Great Britain responsibility for 6 402 000 square kilometres of frozen wastes in the Antarctic continent. All parties accepted it almost as a matter of routine though Norman Makin, Labor member for Port Adelaide and an ex-Methodist clergyman, urged that the whole continent should be handed over to the League of Nations. In the same year Australia took over from Britain the Ashmore and Cartier Islands, four small uninhabited coral atolls about 560 kilometres north-west of the Kimberley District's coastline in Western Australia. The New Guinea Act of 1932 brought the government of the mandated territory of Australian New Guinea into line with that of Papua. That is to say that the Administrator was provided with an advisory Legislative Council, consisting of eight senior officials and seven other members chosen by himself. The Council could make ordinances subject to the Administrator's veto and to that of the Governor-General in Canberra. There was also an Executive Council consisting of the eight officials and one un-official member chosen by the other six. All, of course, were white Australians. No one at the time seems to have even conceived of the possibility of 'Native' representation — any more than they thought of Aboriginal representation on governing bodies at home.

COMMONWEALTH-STATE RELATIONS

In the field of Commonwealth-State relations the Government had two notable achievements: it abolished Commonwealth Entertainments Tax and it established the Commonwealth Grants Commission. Hughes had instituted the Entertainments tax nearly twenty years earlier as a 'temporary' wartime measure. By vacating this tax field to the States, Lyons did something to help them in their constant search for revenue. It will be remembered that in 1925 the

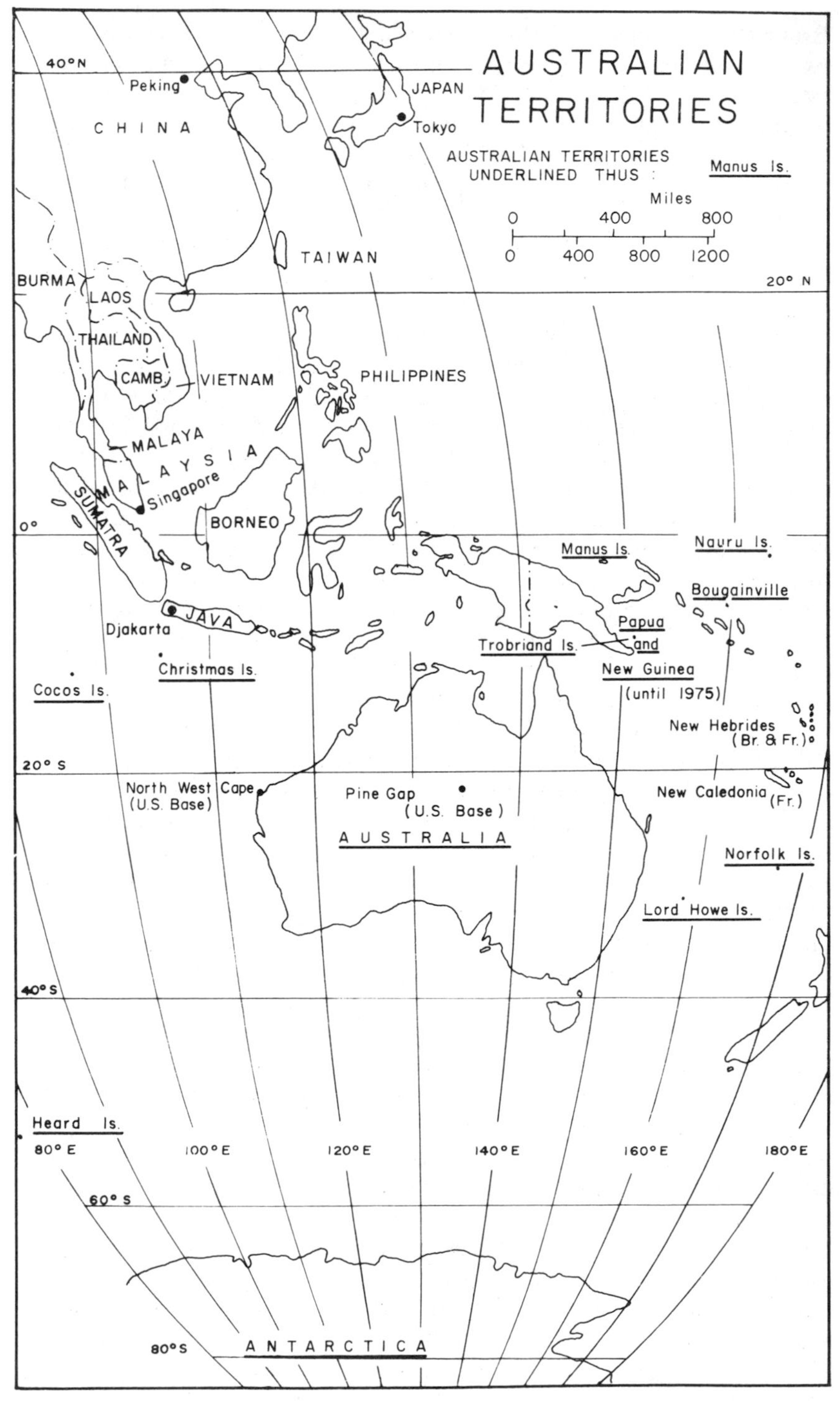

AUSTRALIAN TERRITORIES
AUSTRALIAN TERRITORIES UNDERLINED THUS : Manus Is.
Miles
0 400 800
0 400 800 1200
40° N
Peking
CHINA
JAPAN
Tokyo
TAIWAN
20° N
BURMA
LAOS
THAILAND
CAMB.
VIETNAM
PHILIPPINES
MALAYA
MALAYSIA
Singapore
SUMATRA
BORNEO
0°
Manus Is.
Nauru Is.
Bougainville
Papua and New Guinea (until 1975)
Trobriand Is.
JAVA
Djakarta
Christmas Is.
Cocos Is.
New Hebrides (Br. & Fr.)
20° S
North West Cape (U.S. Base)
Pine Gap (U.S. Base)
New Caledonia (Fr.)
AUSTRALIA
Norfolk Is.
Lord Howe Is.
40° S
Heard Is.
80° E
100° E
120° E
140° E
160° E
180° E
60° S
80° S
ANTARCTICA

Bruce-Page Government had begun the practice of making special or 'extra' grants to the less populous and prosperous States. By establishing the Grants Commission in 1933 Lyons sought a fair and 'objective' method of determining the real financial needs of each claimant State, as opposed to the existing method — that of direct political bargaining, not to say brawling, between Governments. The Act appointed three part-time commissioners with power to take sworn evidence, to consider requests for financial help from the States, and to advise the Commonwealth Government on the merits of such requests.

This federal concern for the special needs of the numerically smaller States was certainly stimulated by the Western Australian secession movement, which in turn was inspired by the Depression. It must be realised that Western Australia joined the Commonwealth in 1901 only at the last minute, and then only because so many 't'other-siders' from the eastern colonies had recently arrived to join the goldrush. Perth is the most isolated capital city in the world, much farther from Sydney or Melbourne than both are from Auckland in New Zealand, or than London is from Moscow. The central Australian desert between the inhabited part of the western State and the rest of the continent was until 1917 a much more formidable barrier than the ocean. Many Western Australians had long believed that they were severely disadvantaged by federal policies, particularly by the settled national policy of protection for secondary industries. With a population of less than 500 000 in 1933 out of a total Australian population of more than 6 600 000, Western Australia had no hope of competing successfully with the established manufacturing industries in the eastern States. Indeed most Western Australians believed that secondary industry in their State had actually fallen back, relative to that of other States, since 1901. Scullin's action in raising the tariff to unheard-of heights seemed the last straw.

In May 1930 the Dominion League of Western Australia began to agitate for secession and setting up the State as an independent dominion like New Zealand within the British Commonwealth. Nearly all Country Party supporters and most Nationalists favoured secession, while probably a majority of Labor voters did not. The Nationalist Premier, Sir James Mitchell, arranged for a plebiscite on the question to be held on the same day as the State election, 8 April 1933. Voting in the plebiscite, though not in the election,[3] was compulsory, and resulted in a majority of approximately two to one

[3] Compulsory voting was introduced in Western Australia at the next State elections in 1936.

in favour of secession. On the same day a Labor Government led by Phillip Collier was elected to replace the Mitchell Government. Collier, nevertheless, felt in duty bound to arrange for a deputation to petition the British Parliament for an amendment to its Act of 1900 which had constituted the six colonies as 'one indissoluble Federal Commonwealth under the Crown of the United Kingdom'. After a long delay a British Parliamentary Committee in May 1935 agreed with the best legal opinion in Australia — including Perth — that the petition could not properly be received.

By 1935 there were signs of returning prosperity, nowhere greater than on the Western Australian goldfields, and the secession movement collapsed. Indeed the gold-mining revival helped greatly to pull Australia out of the Depression, since the price of gold rose dramatically while wool and wheat prices remained abysmally low. Between 1929 and 1939 the annual value of gold produced in Australia rose from about £2,000,000 to £16,000,000 and the great bulk of it was dug in Western Australia. Not surprisingly, the goldfields had been the only part of the State to show a majority vote against secession. They were also the only part of Australia to produce riots, serious enough to involve murder, as a result of the Depression. Because of its prosperity, competition for jobs was keener in Kalgoorlie than elsewhere. In January 1931 an Australian was killed in a fist-fight with an Italian barman at the *Home from Home Hotel*. A great deal of property was destroyed and two Yugoslavs murdered by a rioting mob before Kalgoorlie settled down again to its normally easy-going life.

The hard times did not inspire any other State to attempt secession from the Commonwealth, but they did resuscitate movements of some importance within two States, New South Wales and Queensland, for the separation and establishment of certain regions as new States of the federation. In the last century North Queensland sugar-planters and others had constantly agitated for the separation of North and/or Central Queensland from the distant and urbanised south of the State centred on Brisbane. The separation movement has never quite died, and it is surprising that it was really less active during the Depression than at other periods before and since. The same cannot be said of two separation movements in New South Wales. Almost from the time when Victoria was separated from New South Wales in 1850 some of the leading inhabitants of the border district, known as the Riverina, had agitated sporadically for the creation of a new colony or, after 1901, a new State in the area. The same was true of the New England and North Coast region to the north of Newcastle and the Hunter River. In both districts well-to-do graziers and town businessmen tended to be the strongest supporters of the 'New State' movement, because they particularly resented the domination of political affairs by the mass of the population living in or near distant Sydney. Naturally they believed wholeheartedly in the myth of superior rural virtue, which, as we have seen, has had such a strong influence in Australian history; and inevitably they felt that separation from New South Wales became doubly and trebly urgent when the Lang Labor Government was ruling them from Sydney. During the worst years of the Depression the separation movements undoubtedly enjoyed majority support in both areas.

In February 1931 Charles Hardy, a leading Wagga Wagga businessman, addressed a crowd of 10 000 widly enthusiastic 'New Staters' on the banks of the Murrumbidgee. Meetings in New England were smaller but more frequent. So much feeling was roused that the Stevens-Bruxner U.A.P.-Country Party Coalition Government, which had succeeded Lang, felt constrained to appoint H. S. Nicholas, K.C. as a Royal Commissioner to inquire into the whole question of 'New States' in New South Wales. In 1935 he recommended division of the State into three, if a plebiscite first approved the change in each proposed area — New England and the North Coast; Sydney, the Blue Mountains and the South Coast; and the remainder of the State. Federal and State Governments took no action but the agitation was not entirely fruitless. At the federal election of 1931 Charles Hardy became a Country Party senator, just as Earle Page before him had founded his political career on the aspirations of 'New Staters' in the North Coast and New England districts. Like a great many other Country Party politicians, State and federal, they appeared to become less interested in the separation movements after their translation to the existing seats of power.

Though understandably cool towards the proposed subdivision of its territory into three parts, the Stevens-Bruxner Government made one important change in the Constitution of the mother-State. From the inception of responsible government New South Wales and Queensland had been provided with Legislative Councils consisting of members nominated for life by the State Governor-in-Council. As Premier of Queensland, Theodore had abolished the northern State's Upper House in 1922, but that of New South Wales had been a thorn in the side of the Lang Government. Nevertheless it was reconstituted by that Government's conservative successor. From the conservative viewpoint the trouble with a nominated Upper House, no matter how sagacious and senescent its members, is that in a crisis it may be 'packed' by the Government of the day. The Stevens-Bruxner Government proposed, therefore, that the old nominated Council should be replaced by one chosen by the members of the

Legislative Assembly and of the Legislative Council itself, voting together as an electoral college. Obviously such an arrangement ensured that the Council would remain strongly conservative in complexion for quite a few years, though not necessarily forever. The change was approved by the electors of New South Wales in a plebiscite in 1933.

THE ARTS AND IDEOLOGIES

Nothing done by the first Lyons ministry has earned such acclaim from posterity as its establishment in 1932 of the Australian Broadcasting Commission: yet the Bill had been drafted by the Scullin Government and was introduced by Fenton, an ex-Labor minister. It sprang not from any bold and far-seeing initiative by either Government, so much as from the necessity for regulating a technological service which had grown, almost overnight, from nothing to a huge and continually expanding sector of the entertainment industry. The Bill was vigorously debated, though not along strict party lines, many amendments being carried and more discussed. In its final form it set up a statutory Commission, to be sponsored by Government funds but independent of Government direction, to take whatever measures it wished to develop 'suitable broadcasting programmes . . . to . . . establish . . . groups of musicians for the rendition of orchestral, choral and band music of high quality', to gather news and information and to publish journals.[4] To the increasing gratitude of posterity, the Act specifically forbade the A.B.C. to engage in any form of advertising or to carry any kind of 'sponsored' programme. That field was left to the numerous commercial broadcasting stations.

From its inception the A.B.C. has been tremendously effective in raising the level of culture, education and information in Australia, especially in the field of musical appreciation. By 1937 the Commission employed over 300 full-time, professional musicians, including those working in large A.B.C. orchestras in each capital city. It sponsored 'live' tours of Australia by some of the finest musicians in the world, and 'live performances' by its own musicians in cities and country towns. Government sponsorship of the arts, on such a generous scale, was most unusual anywhere in the world in the 1930s, but music was only one of the fields in which the A.B.C. exercised its benignly stimulating influence. As time went on it provided expert talks and book reviews on literary, artistic, scientific, historical and other subjects, with some degree of special emphasis

[4] *A.E.*, vol. 2, p.138.

Herald, 1931

In His Element

The Government's new policy of nationalising broadcasting provides another opportunity for political interference.

on Australian achievements in these fields. It raised the level of political awareness and understanding by broadcasting sessions of the Commonwealth Parliament, a great deal of local and overseas political news and, more importantly, views on the news given by expert commentators of differing political complexions. It broadcast dramatic performances ranging all the way from Shakespeare and Sophocles to popular contemporary radio plays, and paid at reasonable rates local authors who wrote some of the latter. It broadcast special educational features for schools and young people, and perhaps reduced attendance at church services by bringing them and other religious programmes into people's homes. It provided more objective and authoritative daily news bulletins and information services than the commercial stations, or the metropolitan daily newspapers which often owned them, could sometimes match; and it broadcast 'live' accounts of cricket, football and tennis matches, horseraces and other sporting events, which so many Australians continued to consider much more important than the other matters with which the A.B.C. was concerned. All these good works did not save the A.B.C. from constant charges of political 'bias', levelled usually but not always by conservatives.

Broadcasting and musical appreciation aside, cultural developments in the 1930s were important as indications of better things to follow, rather than for themselves. Australian painters were very slow to be touched by the post-war modernist influences, partly perhaps as Geoffrey Serle has pointed out, because of 'the chance that [Max] Meldrum and Norman Lindsay — the two leading rebels against the orthodox Establishment — were reactionary in their theories on art'.[5] One of the first events to disturb the torpid scene was an exhibition of colour reproductions of modern paintings arranged in 1932 by the Melbourne newspaper magnate, Keith Murdoch, who was knighted in the following year. Private owners lent originals by Matisse, Utrillo, Modigliani, Picasso and Dufy. Other such exhibitions followed. George Bell in Melbourne and Rah Fizelle and Grace Crowley in Sydney painted and taught in the new manner and formed the Contemporary Group in 1932. Traditionalists became alarmed and in 1937 launched a movement to obtain a royal charter for an Australian Academy of Art. They were led by none other than the Attorney-General of the Commonwealth, Robert Gordon Menzies, who delighted equally his admirers and critics by producing many of the urbane, pompous and crassly philistine statements about art which both groups expected of him. A later Attorney-General, Dr H. V. Evatt, whose wife was a

[5] Geoffrey Serle, *From Deserts the Prophets Come*, Melbourne, 1973, p.161.

student of Bell's, supported the modernists who managed to agree to form the Contemporary Art Society in 1938. The proposed Academy did not obtain its royal charter, but held a few exhibitions before it expired during World War II.

In the last chapter we noticed some of the prose writings produced by the Depression years. Two major poets, Kenneth Slessor and Robert D. FitzGerald, had already published some of their best work by 1939 but they were prophets with very little honour in their own country. One of the effects of the Great War, as already noted, was to accentuate the always strong Anglophile tendencies of Australian conservatives; and love of England very often involved denigration of all things Australian — political, spiritual, cultural and material — just because they were Australian. Perhaps the most astonishing illustration of this all-pervading 'colonial cringe' was provided by the Adelaide Club, the oldest, most conservative and most exclusive institution in South Australia. Most of the wine produced in the continent is made within eighty kilometres of Adelaide and some of the finest of it by Club members and their fathers before them: yet not a drop of Australian wine was ever served on Club premises until stocks of French and other overseas vintages became uncomfortably low at the end of the Second World War in 1945. In the same way Australian poetry tended to be patronised, deplored or ignored by the literary establishment. Universities usually taught no Australian literature. Apart from the 'Red Page' of the Sydney *Bulletin*, literary critical journals hardly existed, and the Saturday morning 'cultural pages' of the better metropolitan daily newspapers noticed mainly English or other overseas books, from writers who had already been certified as great and good by overseas critics. As Serle writes:

> The extreme imperialists constantly talked and dreamed of 'home', decried everything Australian, kept alive the tradition of exile, were babus. Before 1915 they believed Australian soldiers would never be disciplined enough to be useful as infantry, they debunked all Australian manufactures, they imported English bishops, headmasters and professors and under-rated local candidates.[6]

It was partly in reaction to this sort of thing that an aggressively Australian literary movement, which developed some fascist overtones, sprang up in the 1930s.

Born in 1901, P. R. Stephensen was educated at Maryborough Grammar School, where the great Australian pre-historian Vere Gordon Childe taught him Latin, and at the University of

[6] Serle, p.137.

Queensland. He was prominent in student politics and claimed in later life to have joined the infant Australian Communist Party in 1921. He won the Rhodes Scholarship for Queensland in 1924 and was active as a Communist propagandist at Oxford, being also the first translator into English (from French) of Lenin's *Imperialism*. With another Australian expatriate, Jack Lindsay, son of the brilliant Norman, he published the *London Aphrodite* and founded the Fanfrolico Press. When he returned to Australia in 1932 he had become bitterly anti-Communist, though he still delighted in scandalising respectable persons. In 1936 Stephensen published a short book which had a tremendous impact on young writers of that generation. *The Foundations of Culture in Australia* passionately denounced what A. A. Phillips was in 1950 to define brilliantly as the 'Cultural Cringe'. In a frankly exaggerated and partisan way, it called upon Australian writers and artists to emancipate themselves from the national inferiority complex, which so many shared, by basing themselves firmly in Australian intellectual and cultural traditions. 'Art and literature are at first nationally created, but become internationally appreciated.'[7] Australians, and above all Australian writers and artists, must stop looking over their shoulders, whether consciously or unconsciously, for British approval, and create their own nationality. They must learn to put Australia first, if necessary, at the expense of Britain.

Stephensen's most influential disciple was Rex Ingamells, an Adelaide poet. Born in 1913 to a Methodist parson and his wife and educated at Prince Alfred College, Ingamells published much competent verse and a long poem of epic proportions, *The Great South Land*. In 1938 he published *Conditional Culture* and founded the Jindyworobak movement which stressed, far more heavily than Stephensen had done, the importance for Australian artists of soaking themselves in the natural environment and even in the culture of its first denizens, the dispersed and despised Aboriginals. Jindyworobak, indeed, was said to be an Aboriginal word meaning 'to annex' or 'to join'. Thoughtful writers like Vance and Nettie Palmer had been preoccupied for two generations past with this problem of making Australian literature something positive and *sui generis* rather than an anaemic copy of its English exemplar; but the Jindyworobaks brought a new urgency, not to say fanaticism, to the problem. For them at their worst, British cultural influences were positively poisonous. Ian Mudie, another Adelaide poet, summed up the Jindyworobak attitude thus:

[7] P. R. Stephensen, *The Foundations of Culture in Australia*, Sydney, 1936, p.16.

Caution Before the Storm

Deep flows the river,
deep as our roots reach for it;
feeding us, angry and striving
against the blindness
ship-fed seas bring us
from colder waters.

'Inky' Stephensen, as he was popularly known, and the 'Jindies' produced little or no major literature, but their ideas did influence more or less strongly the work of most major writers of the following generation. In particular, Ingamells's stress on the Aboriginal heritage encouraged later writers to give more thought to the subject.

They may also be seen as symptomatic of a very important change that occurred in the cultural field in the 1930s. Of course there were many notable exceptions but before that time most Australian intellectuals — academics, teachers, writers, artists, journalists and so on — had felt themselves to be part of respectable, established society, or at least they usually shared its values and attitudes. After the 1930s, again with many exceptions, this was no longer so. The experience of the Depression, the wowserish and politically illiberal censorship of federal and State governments, and the provincial philistinism supported so strongly by Menzies, for example, in the controversy over modernism in art — all these things, in Serle's words, opened up 'a deep gulf . . . between governments and the intelligentsia'.[8] Before the Depression most Australian intellectuals seem to have voted conservative: after it most voted Labor.

THE COUNTRY PARTY AND THE U.A.P.

The general election campaign for the fourteenth Commonwealth Parliament took place during August and the first half of September 1934. Lyons for the U.A.P. stood on his Government's record and made few promises except increased aid to the States for relief of unemployment and increased subsidies to farmers. He expended most energy on frightening the electors with visions of the Labor and Douglas Credit candidates' 'wild' monetary schemes and of Lang, red in tooth and claw, lurking behind the mild-mannered Scullin. The latter promised, if Labor were returned, to set up a full-scale inquiry into Australia's banking and financial system, and to make the general policies of the private banks subject to direction by a central bank, controlled by a single Governor responsible for policy (though not for his tenure of office) to Parliament. He again advocated higher tariffs to protect secondary industries and

[8] Serle, p.154.

immediate full restoration of the wage and salary cuts made under the Premier's Plan. Beasley, for the New South Wales (Lang) Labor Party, concurred with Scullin but placed emphasis on inflationary procedures as a means of restoring prosperity. Since the Country Party had been excluded from government in the last Parliament, there was a good deal more open hostility between it and the U.A.P. than in most previous election campaigns. Dr Earle Page felt free to demand a general reduction of tariff levels, total abolition of customs duties on capital goods, abolition of the land tax and many other measures of sectional advantage to the man on the land. Surprisingly, while attacking Labor's financial proposals, he agreed that there should be a thorough-going inquiry into the banking and financial system.

To no one's surprise the non-Labor Parties were re-elected to power, though Labor made enough gains to deprive the U.A.P. of its absolute majority. In the Lower House there were 32 U.A.P., 15 Country Party, 18 A.L.P. (19 with the non-voting member for the Northern Territory), 9 N.S.W. Labor Party and no Independent members. Thus Lyons had to seek an accommodation with Page to establish a U.A.P.-Country Party Coalition Government. As no ministers had been defeated, an exclusively U.A.P. Administration held office for four weeks while the negotiations were going on. The Coalition partners made a clean sweep of all the Senate seats contested, the state of the parties in that house being 26 U.A.P., 7 Country Party and 3 A.L.P. In the bargaining over portfolios Lyons proved tougher than Bruce had been in 1923 and Page had to be content with fewer ministries for his party. Lyons remained as Prime Minister and Treasurer until October 1935 when he gave R. G. Casey the Treasury. Page became Minister for Commerce and in fact, though not formally so named, Deputy Prime Minister. The Country Party had only one other ministry, that of the Interior while, in addition to Lyons, there were six full Cabinet members from the U.A.P. 'Billy' Hughes was brought from the back benches to become Vice-President of the Executive Council and Minister for Health and Repatriation and the other ex-Labor man, Senator Pearce, was given External Affairs and Territories. T. W. White remained at Trade and Customs and two run-of-the-mill party hacks, A. Parkhill and Senator A. J. A. McLachlan, received Defence and the Postmaster-Generalship respectively. That left the Attorney-Generalship, which had apparently been the object of some interesting back-room bargaining.

J. G. Latham, the previous Attorney-General, had, it will be remembered, stepped down from the leadership of the Nationalists in order to make room for Lyons, when the conservative forces were reorganising themselves as the U.A.P. in 1931. At the dissolution of the thirteenth Parliament Latham retired from the Attorney-Generalship — and from politics — to make way for another newcomer, being rewarded in due course by a knighthood and elevation to the position of Chief Justice of the High Court of Australia. The new Attorney-General was Robert Gordon Menzies, destined to become incomparably the most capable, conservative and long-tenured Prime Minister in Australian history.

Menzies was born in 1894, the third son and fourth child of a struggling storekeeper in Jeparit, a 'one-pub township' as bush people said, in the bare Victorian Mallee district. Politics was a family avocation. His maternal grandfather, John Sampson, was a working miner and a militant trade-unionist, who helped W. G. Spence form the first miners' union in Victoria and who later became first President of the Miners' Federation. His father, James Menzies, represented the Mallee electorate of Lowan in the Victorian Parliament from 1909, when the family went to live in Melbourne, until 1919. From his tenderest years young Bob was a voracious reader and a brilliant student, winning scholarships to take him from the one-roomed Jeparit State School to a better state school in Ballarat, to a private secondary school in that city, Grenville College, to Wesley College in Melbourne and finally to the University there. He began his Law course in 1913, serving in the Melbourne University Rifles in which he reached the rank of Captain by the time his period of compulsory military service ended. The Great War broke out towards the end of the second term of his second year at the University. Bob was not the youngest son: by this time there was a fifth child, ten-year-old Syd who sold papers after school at the Melbourne suburban Camberwell Railway Station. The two elder brothers joined the A.I.F.; Bob did not. At nearly 20 he was no longer a child and the decision was his, though it was made after a family conference in which it seems most of the participants, especially his mother, urged him to stay at home. He wrote much earnestly patriotic verse about the heroism of the diggers, observing however, in one sonnet, that his own life was too valuable to be used for cannon-fodder. The phrase may have been meant ironically, but naturally was not so understood by most readers.

The incident exemplifies the impression of enormous arrogance, ambition and considerable pomposity which he made upon most people throughout his life and which, despite his great gifts, prevented most from feeling for him any personal warmth. He graduated with first-class honours at the end of 1916 and was articled to Owen Dixon, perhaps the most brilliant legal mind Australia ever produced and later Chief Justice of the High Court.

Menzies's own legal calibre was such that, less than four years after his graduation, he made history by winning the *Engineers Case* before that same High Court.[9] He married in the same year, 1920. Before he was fairly into his thirties, he was acknowledged as the leading constitutional lawyer in Victoria though observers noted that he often lost cases involving juries because of the patronising way in which he 'talked down' to them. In 1928 he was elected to the Victorian Legislative Council and was made, within a few months, Minister without Portfolio in the McPherson Nationalist Government. The Nationalists were in opposition for two years. When they returned, as a U.A.P.-Country Party Coalition in May 1932, Menzies was Deputy Premier, Minister for Railways, Attorney-General, Solicitor-General and Vice-President of the Board of Land and Works. In July 1934 he resigned, as we have seen, to take over by arrangement from J. G. Latham, the blue-ribbon U.A.P. federal seat of Kooyong and the Commonwealth's Attorney-Generalship.

During this fourteenth Parliament the Country Party more than compensated for its paucity of Cabinet posts by securing for its supporters a vastly disproportionate share of what Americans would call the contents of the pork-barrel. A very large number of Acts handed out subsidies, bounties, or other forms of help to almost every kind of farmer, grazier or orchardist: and in most cases there was no equivalent of the means test applied to pension-recipients. Farmers received manna from the taxpayer whether they needed it, as they most often did, or not. A tax on wool financed an Australian Wool Board, dominated by pastoralists, to advertise, seek markets for, and conduct research into, all aspects of the wool industry. Several Acts provided for bounties to wheat-growers, financed by a flour tax, and for grants to the States to assist in the writing off of wheat farmers' debts. New or increased subsidies were also provided for the producers of apples and pears, oranges, other citrus fruits, prunes, meat and eggs. All farmers were subsidised for the use of artificial fertilisers. Existing subsidies to sugar-growers, dairy-farmers and other primary producers were continued.

As always rural interests pressed for reduction of tariffs protecting secondary industries. In May 1936, however, the Government announced a new 'trade diversion' policy, the whole thrust of which was to reverse its cautious lowering of the tariff wall. Higher duties, bounties and import licensing were to reduce imports of Japanese textiles and American motor cars in order to favour British textile and motor car manufacturers, whether their plants were operating in

[9] See above, p. 145.

Britain or Australia. The aim of the policy was two-fold: first to further the traditional conservative policy of all possible aid to Britain, and second to encourage the manufacture of motor cars in Australia, partly for defence reasons. The results were disastrous. Three years later the two greatest powers in the Pacific had been antagonised. The volume of imports from each remained about the same as before, while Australian exports to each had fallen away seriously. Still the Government negotiated bi-lateral trade agreements with France, Belgium, Czechoslovakia, South Africa and, despite the trade-diversion policy, Japan. Consequential tariff reductions, and others made during the fourteenth Parliament, had the effect of lowering British preferential duties by about 30 per cent from the peak reached under the Scullin Government.

Most of these rural subsidies were handed out soon after the re-election of the Lyons Government. Deeming the plight of pensioners to be less desperate, or perhaps merely less politically significant, the Government made them wait longer for relief — until, in fact, the pre-election budget of August 1937. By then overseas prices for wool and wheat had improved, the latter so much as to remove the necessity for a subsidy. The budgets of all seven Australian governments taken together showed a surplus for the first time since the onset of the Depression. Unemployment at about 10 per cent was not markedly worse than it had been during much of the 1920s. At last R. G. Casey, the new Treasurer, restored pension levels to their pre-depression maximum figure of £1 a week. Other useful measures were the building of a standard-gauge rail link between Port Pirie and Port Augusta in South Australia, which reduced the break-of-gauge trans-shipment points between Brisbane and Perth from four to three, and to give the M.P. for the Northern Territory a vote on matters directly affecting his electorate.

Useless, as might have been expected, was yet another attempt to change the Constitution by referendum to gain more powers for the Commonwealth. By March 1937, when two referenda were held, it should have been obvious that the proposals, no matter who sensible and desirable in themselves, would be defeated by the usual combination of State, party and local jealousies with the massive ignorance or, more often, deliberately created confusion, in the minds of most voters. One Act asked the people for Commonwealth power over marketing laws for the disposal of Australian commodities overseas and the other for control over airways and aircraft. With or without Commonwealth help, air transport was firmly established during the 1930s. In fact the first regular passenger service, unsubsidised by government money, opened between Sydney and Brisbane on 1 January 1930 and ten years later all State capitals and many large country towns were connected with each other and with Canberra by air. In December 1934 Qantas and the British company, Imperial Airways, jointly began a regular mail and passenger service between Australia and England. By the end of the decade the journey took little more than a week, or about a quarter of the time taken by the fastest ships. By 1939 air transport was used often by politicians or businessmen in a hurry, or others travelling on an expense account; but most people still thought of flying only in cases of sudden illness or other emergencies.

WOWSERS AND CENSORSHIP

During the life of this Parliament many things happened to widen the gulf, noticed above, between Australian artists and intellectuals and Australian governments. Hardly had Parliament met in October 1934 when what became known as the Kisch case brought great discredit on the Commonwealth Government and in particular on Menzies, the Attorney-General and T. Paterson, a Country Party hack, who was Minister for the Interior. By this time the larrikin methods, violent rhetoric and revisionist aims of the fascist powers were worrying democrats everywhere. Japan was consolidating her grip on key points in China and had announced her withdrawal from the League of Nations. Hitler had grasped supreme power in Germany and taken his country too out of the League. Three days after the re-election of the Lyons Government on 15 September 1934, the Union of Soviet Socialist Republics was admitted to the League, where it zealously pursued its 'collective security' policy of building a 'united front' with the western democracies to scotch, or at least contain, Nazism. Australian Communists and other left-wing activists arranged an Australian Congress against War and Fascism to be held in Melbourne in November 1934. Among others invited to attend were Gerald Griffin, a New Zealand Communist, and Egon Kisch, a learned Czech writer and journalist, whom the Government believed to have been a member of the Czech Communist Party. To Lyons, Menzies, Page, and most of their parliamentary colleagues, no matter what fears they might have had about Germany, Japan and Italy, the very idea of reaching any kind of accord with Communist Russia was unthinkable. They therefore forbade the landing in Australia of the two speakers.

The Immigration Restriction Act was used in a way never envisaged by those who had framed it. Griffin was given a dictation test in Dutch, failed and declared a prohibited immigrant. Worried by Kisch's reputation as a gifted linguist, the immigration officials gave him a test in Scottish Gaelic, the almost extinct language of a few

Bulletin, 1934

ANOTHER ALIEN

"C-c-couldn't we give him a t-t-test in Gaelic?"

thousand Highlanders. He too failed, but both men literally jumped from their ships onto the wharf. Kisch broke his leg and was taken to hospital under police guard. He then challenged the order for his deportation in the High Court, and was upheld, their Honours determining that Scottish Gaelic was not a European language within the meaning of the Act. Griffin eluded the constables and spent several weeks in Australian cities, addressing crowds many times larger than those he would have attracted had he been allowed into the country legally. Indeed the anti-fascist campaign associated with the dramatic appearances of Griffin and Kisch sometimes crowded off the front pages of the newspapers His Royal Highness the Duke of Gloucester, least gifted member of the reigning family, who had been invited to preside over the Victorian State centenary celebrations and the opening of the Commonwealth Parliament. It has been said that 'all the world loves a lord', but in Australia most people do not love policemen. Kisch and Griffin achieved such widespread support, even from many who disagreed with their views, partly because their behaviour continually embarrassed and ridiculed the police — and the repressive Commonwealth Government. It was believed by newspaper men and women that the mysterious John Wren, with his influential underworld connections, helped Griffin to defy the law for so long.

The Government was derided for its bungling, and in radical and intellectual circles for its repressive aims; but it seems clear that most citizens supported its intention of denying freedom of speech to 'foreigners' with 'seditious' views. The same could not be said about its next misuse of the 'dictation test' two years later. An Englishwoman, Mrs M. M. Freer, was given the test and refused entry by the egregious Minister for the Interior, without any reason being given. A liberal-minded Government back-bencher, Bill McCall, refused to let the matter drop. Pressure in Parliament and press finally showed that Paterson had acted alone on the strength of an uncorroborated statement, in a letter from an interested party, to the effect that, if admitted, Mrs Freer would be likely to break up 'a perfectly good Australian marriage'. Further, when people began to demand the facts Menzies and the rest of Cabinet, in the Prime Minister's absence, agreed to back their blundering colleague and 'cover up'. It was too much, even for a portion of the feared 'wowser vote'. Public opinion forced the Government to back down and Mrs Freer was permitted to breathe the pure air of Australia in July 1937.

Nevertheless, to judge by the state of censorship, the wowser vote was more influential during the dull Lyons regime than at any other time. Ever since the first settlement by Europeans, the vast majority of all books read in Australia had been imported from abroad and

Grundy at the Customs
The Customs Department has prohibited the importation of Boccaccio's Decameron
IF YOU MUST 'AVE LITERCHOOR GO TO THE PITCHERS!
CAN'T I HAVE SOMETHING CLEVER TO READ?
AUSTRALIA
MILKSOPS FABLES
MA GRUNDY MINISTRESS OF CUSTOMS
BOCCACCIO'S DECAMERON
WELLS

Herald, 1934

not published or printed in the country. Hence, perhaps, arose the administratively convenient, but intellectually monstrous, practice of censorship by imperfectly literate Customs clerks under section 52 of the Commonwealth Customs Act. A few locally published books which troubled the prejudices of the conventional could be, and were, dealt with by police prosecution for obscenity. Before the Depression, curiously enough, there seems to have been little attempt to censor incoming books. On the theory, cynics said, that only the poor were capable of being corrupted by bawdy books, cheap editions of classics by lascivious foreign writers like Rabelais, Balzac and Boccaccio were kept out by Customs. Expensive editions were imported without trouble. Under the prime ministerships of the devout Catholics, Scullin and Lyons, the Customs officers became more vigilant in protecting Australians from what they conceived to be impure or dangerous thoughts. By 1936 approximately 5000 titles had been excluded. Among them were great works of literature, ancient and modern, such as some books by Defoe, D. H. Lawrence, Aldous Huxley, George Orwell, Ernest Hemingway and James Joyce.

This sexual or 'moral' censorship was bad enough and made Australia the laughing-stock of the civilised world; but much worse was the political censorship which grew up under T. W. White, Lyons's Minister for Trade and Customs. In the middle 1930s all writings by Marx, Engels, Lenin and Stalin and almost all other Communist, or near-Communist, works were prohibited imports. In 1936 F. A. Chaffey, the Colonial Secretary of the U.A.P.-Country Party Government of New South Wales, sent police to stop a performance of Clifford Odets' anti-Nazi play, *Till the Day I Die*, on the stated ground that it was 'unfitting for the preservation of good manners and decorum'.[10] In 1934 a Book Censorship Abolition League, strongly supported by academics, authors, publishers and other cultural workers, was formed. With kindred organisations it soon combined to form the Australian Council for Civil Liberties, whose most inspired and indefatigable leader for a generation thereafter was the distinguished historian, Brian Fitzpatrick. By the end of the Depression decade, the worst excesses of censorship had been mitigated by the sustained attack of Australian intellectuals, led by Fitzpatrick. However, occasional prosecutions and furtive bannings continued into the 1960s, but ceased almost entirely from 1970 when Mr Don Chipp became the Liberal Government's Minister for Customs.

Another measure of the deplorable state of cultural life in Australia

[10] *M.A.D.* I, p.562.

between the wars was the run-down condition of public libraries. In the half-century or so before World War I many city suburbs and nearly all country towns had had their Mechanics' Institute or School of Arts, which provided free or subsidised library service; but by the time of the Great War these had decayed almost completely. As Ken Slessor wrote of *Country Towns* in the 1930s:

At the School of Arts, a broadsheet lies
Sprayed with the sarcasm of flies:
"The Great Golightly Family
Of Entertainers here Tonight"
Dated a year and a half ago,
But left there, less from carelessness
Than from a wish to seem polite.

In 1935 two American experts, R. Munn and E. R. Pitt, in a report sponsored by the Carnegie Corporation, forcefully drew attention to the fact that public libraries scarcely existed, apart from one in each State capital. Municipal, State and national cultural facilities did improve from this time onwards. They could hardly have done otherwise, but there was no great change until after World War II. There had been one under-staffed and poverty-stricken university in each State capital for many years and this position continued also until after the war — with two slight modifications. In 1929 the Canberra University College was set up as an annexe of the University of Melbourne, and in 1938 the University of New England was established in Armidale, N.S.W., as an offshoot of the University of Sydney.

FOREIGN POLICY, FASCISM AND DEFENCE

We have seen how little interest there was in foreign affairs up till 1934, when the Lyons Government was re-elected, but even the most isolationist of Australians could not remain unmoved by the implications of Italy's invasion of Abyssinia in October 1935 and the outbreak of the Spanish Civil War in July 1936. It is paradoxical that, although politicians and some electors began to argue about Australian foreign policy as though the outcome of the debate would affect the country's fate, in fact there was virtually no staff in the Department of External Affairs (*two* in 1934), and Australia was in effect bound to support the policies of the British Foreign Office — which took little or no notice of Australian views. It must be added that most conservative Australians thought this a very proper situation.

Since the British Government went through the charade of supporting the League of Nations' application of (ineffective) sanctions against Italian trade, the Lyons Government followed suit. Similarly it followed the official British policy of non-intervention in the Spanish Civil War. In the parliamentary debates on these subjects, and on the recommendation of the 1937 Imperial Conference, most U.A.P. and Country Party speakers naturally followed the line of wholehearted support for British policies; but not the Minister for Health and Repatriation. Advancing years had not tamed the irrepressible 'Billy' Hughes. He published a book on the Abyssinian Crisis, *Australia and War Today: the Price of Peace*, which severely criticised Government policies. Lyons naturally demanded his resignation from Cabinet in November 1935 but he was restored, if not forgiven, by the following February.

The Opposition spoke in these debates with many voices. In 1935 John Curtin succeeded the ailing Scullin as Labor leader and the New South Wales (Lang) branch of the Party was formally received back into the fold; but Labor was still rent by faction fighting in that State and in South Australia. Moreover the issues at stake in Spain and Abyssinia were such as to divide Labor opinion. Traditionalists, including many older members who had been prominent in the anti-conscription campaigns, usually agreed with 'Eddie' Ward and J. T. Lang that no overseas quarrel was worth the sacrifice of one Australian life. These people opposed sanctions and urged strict neutrality in the Spanish war. In August 1935 an international meeting of Communists urged their comrades in democratic countries to support their governments against Fascism. Labor left-wingers like Maurice Blackburn, influenced by the resulting 'popular front' propaganda, vehemently supported sanctions and, of course, the anti-Fascist Government side in the Spanish Civil War. Catholic Labor men, on the other hand, knowing that the U.S.S.R. supported the Spanish Government, that Catholic Italy (and Nazi Germany) were helping the rebel General Franco, and that he was strongly favoured by the Spanish Catholic hierarchy, were at best luke-warm about sanctions against Italy and strongly pro-Franco. Indeed the Spanish War was the catalyst which gave rise to a militantly conservative, anti-Communist, political movement among Australian Catholics, known usually as Catholic Action. The first issue of its monthly journal, the *Catholic Worker*, came out in January 1936, edited by a brilliant young law student at the University of Melbourne, Bartholomew Santamaria, son of an Italian immigrant. Twenty years later his movement was to bring about another Labor split, and to detach a considerable section of Catholic voters from their traditional support of the A.L.P.

Curtin's function was to compose the disastrous divisions in his party, not to accentuate them by siding with any one faction. He did so by saying remarkably little about Spain or Abyssinia and concentrating attention instead on Australian defence. The Government was spending most on renovation of the Navy. Curtin, prophetically, urged the development of a defensive air arm, underlining one of the points in Hughes's book, that the Royal Australian Air Force should be built up to at least parity with the total Japanese carrier-borne striking force. He also predicted that Singapore, the supposedly impregnable British bastion on which all Imperial (and Australian) defence plans depended, was likely to prove what a later generation would have called a 'paper tiger'.

Prophetic or not, Curtin and his party were again defeated at the Commonwealth general election of 23 October 1937. Germany had flouted the Treaty of Versailles by occupying the Rhineland. The Rome-Berlin Axis had been proclaimed and both powers had intervened openly in Spain, sending troops, aircraft and warships to support the rebels. Madrid was under siege. Nearer home the Japanese had seized Pekin and Tientsin. For the first time since the Great War defence was a major issue, indeed the major issue, on the hustings; and the voters were far too conservative and far too devoted to the traditional conservative policy of unquestioning dependence on Britain, to set much store by Curtin's warnings. Besides, Lyons and Page spoke with one voice on defence, while Labor, as we have seen, had three conflicting policies. On the domestic front the Coalition promised, if returned, to establish a national insurance scheme financed partly from taxation but partly from employer and employee contributions. Lyons also deplored the fall in the birthrate and promised increased maternity payments and a renewal of assisted migration from Britain. Curtin countered by promising a non-contributory scheme of insurance against unemployment and considerably more generous pensions. Both leaders promised some action on the recommendations of the Royal Commission on Banking and Monetary Reform which had reported not long before. J. B. Chifley, an ex-Labor M.H.R., urged nationalization of banking in a minority report. The majority, while opposing nationalization, urged federal government control over monetary policy: but nothing was done.

The election results made hardly any difference to the state of the parties in the Lower House. Labor had two more members than in the preceding Parliament, 29 instead of 27, and the Coalition strength dropped correspondingly from 47 to 45, including two newly-elected Independents, P. C. Spender and A. Wilson who usually supported the U.A.P. and the Country Party respectively. In the Senate, however, Labor won all the contested seats except the three in South Australia, giving an Upper House of 20 Government and 16 A.L.P. members. In the next three years Labor took three more seats in the Representatives from the U.A.P. and retained one of its own at by-elections. The Country Party obtained greater strength in Cabinet by the appointment of V.C. Thorby to the Defence portfolio, left vacant by the defeat of Senator Pearce in Western Australia. Hughes became Minister for External Affairs, Minister for Territories and Vice-President of the Executive Council. Otherwise there were few initial Cabinet changes and no important ones.

During this Parliament the Coalition Government was plagued by accidental misfortunes and almost wrecked by personal jealousy, intrigue and faction fighting among its leading members. The major single cause of dissension was the determination of the able but unloved Menzies to become Prime Minister as soon as possible, no matter how many colleagues, including the much loved Lyons, had to be shouldered aside in the process. God, or fate, seemed to be on Menzies' side. Charles Hawker, the gifted South Australian who might have been a threat, was killed in an aircraft crash in October 1938.

Meanwhile the last major piece of legislation, not directly relating to defence, was debated in both Houses with whatever energy the members had to spare from their off-stage manoeuvrings for place. Many U.A.P. members, including Menzies, were very keen on the two National Health and Pensions Bills, both for their obvious merits and because their enactment would force the poor to contribute something to the cost of national pension and welfare schemes, thus reducing the contribution of the richer taxpayers. Country Party members were luke-warm because they shrank from compelling rural employers to contribute at a time when world prices for primary products were generally declining. Labor of course objected to compulsory contributions to pensions and maternity allowances but not, necessarily, to health and unemployment benefits. Many amendments, including some from the Labor side of the House, were accepted in committee and the Bills were finally enacted. The scheme was never put into operation, however, mainly because of the stubborn and self-regarding resistance of most doctors banded together in the British (later Australian) Medical Association, easily the most influential trade union or professional association in the country.

While the Health and Pension Bills were being debated, fascism continued to gain ground in Europe and China. In Spain the Republican forces were being steadily crushed by Franco with

"Don't take any notice of that old optimist! Listen to Billy and me, and we'll freeze your blood!"

German and Italian help. At the end of September 1938 Neville Chamberlain, the British Prime Minister, returned from Munich, brandishing in addition to his furled umbrella, a piece of paper bearing his own and Hitler's signature which, he assured a sceptical world, guaranteed 'peace in our time'. True to Australian conservative policy of following Britain's lead in all things, the U.A.P.-Country Party Government supported the Munich sell-out. Menzies, then and for long afterwards, was the arch-appeaser in the Commonwealth Parliament, but Curtin too endorsed Munich. There was, however, a considerable and growing body of Australian opinion, inside and outside Parliament, which opposed appeasement and advocated a collective security agreement between the democracies and the Soviet Union to stop fascism in Europe and perhaps also in China and the Pacific. This, of course, was Stalin's policy and that of the four thousand odd members of the Australian Communist Party, but as in other countries, it was endorsed also by large numbers of non-Communist intellectuals, liberals, radicals and trade unionists, not to mention some patriotic conservatives like Winston Churchill in Britain and 'Billy' Hughes, then Minister for External Affairs, in Australia. Many of these groups tried to organise boycotts of Japanese goods or to find other ways of hampering Japanese aggression.

In the summer of 1938-39, in the steel and coal town of Port Kembla ninety kilometres south of Sydney, members of the Waterside Workers' Federation refused to load pig-iron for Japan on the *Dalfram* and other ships. The strikers made no claim for better pay or working conditions. They simply held that the pig-iron would be used by Japan to manufacture armaments for its war on China and, perhaps at no distant date, on Australia; and they were strongly supported by public opinion in Port Kembla and throughout the country. As Attorney-General, Menzies tried to coerce the men under the provisions of what they called the 'Dog-Collar Act'. He had the courage to meet the Union leaders at Port Kembla, but suffered the humiliation of having to be protected by them from furiously hostile crowds. In the end a compromise was reached, by which the men loaded 23 000 tons of pig-iron but not the 300 000 tons or more which had been contracted for. This incident did more than anything else before or afterwards to give Menzies the reputation of being pro-Fascist. During his long public career it was inevitable that such a dominating figure would acquire many nicknames. He was known at this period among close associates as 'Buck' Menzies, in allusion to his taste for good wine, good food and stimulating female company. Some called him 'Ming the Merciless' in allusion to the Scottish way of pronouncing his name, 'Ming-is'. Later he became the 'Knight of the Thistle' or the 'Pig and Whistle', but from 1939 onwards his most popular sobriquet — which he hated — was 'Pig Iron Bob'. Sir Isaac Isaacs, who had retired from the Governor-Generalship in 1936, wrote at the time:

> I believe that Port Kembla with its studied, but peaceful and altogether disinterested attitude of the men concerned, will find a place in our history besides the Eureka Stockade . . . as a noble stand against executive dictatorship and against an attack on Australian democracy.[11]

A few days after the Munich crisis, and before the eruption at Port Kembla, Menzies addressed the Constitutional Association in Sydney on the need for firm and inspiring leadership in the face of the troubled international situation. Though he modestly refrained from direct praise of himself or criticism of his leader, 'Honest Joe' Lyons, since he was deputy-leader of the U.A.P., his speech was taken as a bid for the leadership of the party and the nation. Lyons's supporters regarded it as a stab in the back.

By the new year it was becoming obvious that the Health Insurance scheme never would be implemented. Suddenly on 14 March 1939, the very day that the Nazi troops seized what was left of Czechoslovakia, Menzies resigned from the Ministry and as deputy-leader of the U.A.P., declaring that he did so as a protest against the shelving of the liberal national health and insurance scheme. Most people, including Lyons, interpreted his resignation differently. They believed he had resigned to embarrass the Government as much as possible and to make a renewed bid for the leadership by demonstrating how weak Cabinet would appear without him. He wished also, it was thought, to test the strength of the group supporting him — generally the most conservative, business-backed section of the U.A.P. — as against the more liberal party men, including Hughes, who favoured the ex-Labor man, Lyons. Within a month, on Good Friday 7 April, Lyons died of a heart attack, his end having been hastened, in the view of his friends, by Menzies' tactics. Thus the U.A.P. was left without a leader or a deputy-leader, and the country without a Prime Minister. There followed two weeks of the most complicated manoeuvring for power within the Coalition parties.

Under the circumstances the Governor-General, Lord Gowrie, commissioned Earle Page, as Deputy Prime Minister, to form a Government. Page did so on the understanding that he would serve

[11] Kevin Perkins, *Menzies, Last of the Queen's Men*, Adelaide, 1968, p.61.

only until the majority party, the U.A.P., had selected a new leader, and that if the new leader were Menzies, whom he hated, he (Page) would not be prepared to serve under him in a reconstructed Cabinet. Hughes had succeeded to the Attorney-General's portfolio on Menzies' resignation. Page made no changes in the membership of his caretaker ministry. Fearing that Menzies had the numbers in the U.A.P. caucus, Page and Casey cabled S. M. Bruce, Australian High Commissioner in London, begging him to return to the leadership of the conservative party and the nation. Page hated Menzies so much that he offered to resign from his safe seat so that Bruce could succeed to it in a by-election. Bruce, however, would agree only if he was to lead a National government representative of all parties, and to this Curtin was inflexibly opposed. The Country Party caucus met and declared publicly it would support no government led by Menzies. On 18 April the U.A.P. caucus chose him as its leader, reportedly by 23 votes to 19 for 'Billy' Hughes, after Casey and T. W. White had been eliminated in earlier ballots.

Page was still determined to prevent Menzies from becoming Prime Minister. To this end he launched an unprecedented personal attack on him in the House of Representatives on 20 April. He traversed many of Menzies' past deeds and then came to the heart of the matter which had divided the nation so deeply for the past twenty-five years — whether one had been a 'digger' or not. He said:

> Some twenty four years ago the right honourable member for Kooyong was a member of the Australian Military Forces and held the King's Commission. In 1915, after having been in the military forces for some years, he resigned his commission and did not go overseas.[12]

'That is dirt', interjected the Labor ex-coalminer, Rowley James, member for Hunter, succintly stating the reaction of almost the whole House.[12] Usually a consummately crafty politician, Page on this occasion utterly miscalculated the public's reaction. His malicious attack destroyed not Menzies but himself. On 26 April Menzies was sworn in as Prime Minister at the head of an all U.A.P. minority Government, dependent on 'discriminating' Country Party support, and five months later Page was forced out of the leadership of the Party he had largely created, and had led for twenty years.

In his first Government Menzies was Treasurer as well as Prime Minister. The other most important Cabinet members were W. M. Hughes, Attorney-General and Industry; R. G. Casey, Supply and Development, a new portfolio to cover many aspects of war

[12] *C.P.D.*, vol. 159, p.16.

preparations; G. A. Street, Defence; Sir Henry Gullett, External Affairs; J. N. Lawson, Trade and Customs; Sir Frederick Stewart, Health and Social Services; and J. V. Fairbairn, Civil Aviation and Vice-President of the Executive Council. The new Government carried through a scheme, decided on before Lyons's death, to provide once again assisted passages for British migrants. There had been virtually no immigration, assisted or otherwise, since the onset of the Depression ten years earlier. Since about 9 per cent of job-seekers could still find no work, Labor men opposed the scheme bitterly. They need not have worried. Only about 3000 Britons came to Australia in 1939 out of a total number of some 14 000 migrants. Most of the rest were refugees from Nazism. Although they were promptly dubbed 'reffos', and discriminated against by many Australians, most of them assimilated successfully and fairly rapidly into the community.

Most of the Government's energies inevitably were taken up in preparations for the coming war. Defence spending reached a higher level than ever before in Australia's peacetime history, and contingency plans were made to gear the national economy to war production. Fortunately for Australia, manufacturing had expanded more than other areas of production during the decade. In Adelaide E. W. Holden, heir to a saddlery business, moved into the building of motor-car bodies in 1921, and in 1931 amalgamated with the Australian branch of the American firm, General Motors, to form General Motors Holden's Limited. The rival American organisation, Ford, set up a plant at Geelong in Victoria, and by 1939 practically all motor bodies and chassis used in Australia, though not engines, were locally produced. A partnership between Government and private investors, the Commonwealth Aircraft Corporation, was producing at Fishermen's Bend near Melbourne, a training aeroplane for fighter-pilots, the Wirraway. Other munitions were being made locally and the Broken Hill Proprietary Company, having achieved a monopoly of the Australian iron industry, was producing steel as efficiently and cheaply as any foreign firm anywhere. It supplied all Australian requirements and was beginning to build up a small export trade. Factory workers were more numerous, more skilful and more productive than ever before: but for all that the country still depended mainly on primary production. Certainly, if all overseas supplies were to be cut off, Australian industry alone had no hope of fully sustaining fighting forces on land, at sea or in the air.

Despite the threat of imminent war, most Australians continued to think more about sport. In February 1938 the Empire Games were held for the first time in Australia. To no one's surprise the hosts, more especially the hostesses, carried off most of the honours at Sydney winning 24 first places compared with 15 for England, the next country on the list. At Bondi Beach on 6 February 1938, a hot Sunday, a succession of three freak waves swept thousands of surfers out to sea and within seconds hundreds were in distress. Nearly seventy volunteer life-savers were on the beach at the time. Five people were drowned but over 200 were saved. In the following summer, in the second week of January 1939, the most terrible bushfires since white settlement devastated wide areas. In Victoria alone seventy-one people were burnt to death and on the worst day, 'Black Friday' the thirteenth, it seemed in the words of Judge L. E. B. Stretton, the Royal Commissioner appointed to inquire into the disaster, 'that the whole State was alight'.[13] The destruction in 1939 led to improved fire-fighting methods thereafter.

There was a curious air of unreality about Menzies' preparations for war, perhaps because he remained a convinced advocate of appeasement. Soon after his succession to the Prime Ministership, the sober *Sydney Morning Herald* was moved editorially to deny that he had 'a Fascist mentality'. In the few months before war broke out he continued to speak well of Germany and Japan and to denounce Churchill as an unstable character lacking in judgment. At the time of the Munich agreement a few months earlier, the fiery Hughes, then aged 74, when asked his opinion had answered,

> I'm not allowed to talk. I'm only the Foreign Minister. But if the road from here to Broken Hill was paved with Bibles, and that man Hitler swore on oath on every one of them, I wouldn't believe a damned word he said. Otherwise, I've got nothing to say.[14]

Menzies removed Hughes from the External Affairs Portfolio. On 9 July Churchill urged that Britain should conclude a military alliance with the U.S.S.R., but Chamberlain and his Cabinet were not impressed. Convinced that the leaders of the democracies would never give up hope of turning Hitler's legions against Russia by appeasing him in the west, Stalin decided to reverse the process and to deflect the Nazi attack towards the west by appeasing Hitler in the east. The U.S.S.R.-German Non-Aggression Pact was announced on 23 August and ratified on the 31st. The next day Germany invaded Poland and on 3 September Britain and France declared war on Germany.

No living Australian was more British in outlook than Menzies. For him there were no sordid questions of what were Australia's best

[13] *A.E.*, vol. 2, p.207.

[14] *A.E.*, vol. 5, p.27.

interests, nor nice constitutional questions of whether the King of England can be at war while the King of Australia remains at peace. Commitment was automatic. Within minutes of Neville Chamberlain's announcement he spoke to the nation on the radio. In carefully considered words he said,

> It is my melancholy duty to inform you officially that, in consequence of a persistence by Germany in her invasion of Poland, Great Britain has declared war upon her and that, as a result, Australia is also at war.[15]

[15] Paul Hasluck, *The Government and the People 1939-1941*, Canberra, 1952, p.152.

Chapter 8

AUSTRALIA IN THE SECOND WORLD WAR
c. 1939—1944

The 'phoney war' and political fighting — Labor leads against the Japanese thrust — The Home Front and limited conscription — Blamey, MacArthur and victory in the Pacific

THE 'PHONEY WAR' AND POLITICAL FIGHTING

As the Nazi troops marched into Poland, the Australian attitude to the trial ahead contrasted dramatically with that of August 1914. There was no wild enthusiasm and little of the harrying of enemy aliens which had characterised the beginning of the 'war to end wars' almost exactly twenty-five years earlier: and there was no false optimism. No one believed that the war might be 'over by Christmas'. Although the Russo-German Pact had apparently undermined the Anti-Comintern Pact between Germany, Italy and Japan, Nippon's southward thrust in China continued and German-Japanese relations remained good. People knew that a long and bitter struggle lay before them, and one in which Australia itself might be involved.

Despite this, the nation was at first less united behind the war effort than it had been in the earlier conflict. In 1914-18, as we have seen, support for the war and national unity decreased as time went on: in 1939-45 the opposite was true. In Australia, as in Britain, Communists and a large section of trade-union, Labor and intellectual opinion initially had grave reservations about the war, not at all because any of these elements were pro-Fascist, but because they feared that their own Government might be covertly so. The Prime Ministers of both countries had been strong advocates of appeasement and rapprochement with Germany almost up to the last moment of peace. After 3 September it was clear that Britain and Germany were waging war on each other at sea, but by no means clear on land or in the air. For the first eight months, while Germany and Russia divided eastern Europe between them, Britain and France refrained from any aggressive ground action in the West and the Royal Air Force rained little more lethal than propaganda leaflets on Germany. During the northern winter of 1939-40 Finland's

Bulletin, 1939

HANDING IT ON.

heroic resistance to Russian aggression occupied more space in the newspapers than news of hostilities between Germany and the western Allies. There was talk of giving aid to the Finns and so 'switching' the war, possibly in alliance with the Nazis, against the U.S.S.R.

In the Allied countries those to the left of centre, who hated fascism and all it stood for more than they hated Communism, felt less than wholly committed to support for a war whose aims seemed so uncertain. This mistrust of the leadership of Chamberlain in Britain and Menzies in Australia spread far beyond the left. The great majority of people, who scarcely troubled to think about politics whether of the right or left, felt uneasily that something was wrong and their misgivings were reflected in the popular expression, 'the phoney war', which gained currency at this time.

Many of the first measures taken to put the country on a war footing closely followed 1914 precedents. Indeed the same man was responsible for drafting the legislation on both occasions. As Attorney-General from 1939 to 1941, W. M. Hughes passed through Parliament two National Security Acts which, like the War Precautions Acts of the Great War, clothed the Government with very wide-ranging emergency powers to make regulations having the force of law. These Acts specifically forbade conscription for overseas service. However compulsory military training for home defence was immediately re-introduced under the existing Defence Act and a new Act, little noticed at the time but having great importance for the future, extended the application of the Defence Act to Commonwealth territories, i.e., in the first instance, to Australian New Guinea and Papua. Trading with the Enemy Acts also revived special wartime laws. In the first few months of war the Government also took over responsibility for the marketing of the wheat crop and the wool-clip along lines made familiar a generation earlier. Another measure provided benefits, similar to those for servicemen, for merchant seamen injured or killed by enemy action. Less traditionally sanctioned were three Supply and Development Acts which established a Department to promote and direct the acquisition and manufacture of war supplies. In 1940 a Department of Munitions began work under Essington Lewis, managing director of the Broken Hill Proprietary Limited steel monopoly, and son and grandson of South Australian pioneers. Only his enormous drive and ability muted criticisms based on the possible clash of interests between those of the nation and of the B.H.P.

As a matter of course the Royal Australian Navy was placed, as before, under the overall direction of the British Admiralty. Also as a matter of course the Government began recruiting a second volunteer 'Australian Imperial Force'. Cynics claimed that with unemployment at 10.2 per cent in the third quarter of 1939 many of the early enlistments were 'economic conscripts'. No doubt some were, but there is equally no doubt that most were inspired by deeply patriotic motives. Many of them felt, however, that precedent was being followed too slavishly when the Prime Minister disingenuously announced that the basic rate of pay for a private soldier would be the same as in the Great War — five shillings a day. The most simple-minded recruit knew that inflation had reduced the purchasing power of money by at least half since 1914. Still, no one, even among the unemployed, joined up to grow rich. Later Labor Governments raised services pay somewhat, but throughout World War II Australian servicemen remained very much poorer than their American counterparts, not richer as they had been in World War I.

Even the destination of the Second A.I.F. seemed to be determined largely by precedent. Despite some misgivings about future Japanese action, it was decided that the diggers should be sent in the first instance to the Middle East, where so many of their fathers had trained and fought. Ever since the opening of the Suez Canal in 1869, the umbilical cord of trade, tradition and sentiment binding Australia to the 'old country' had passed through it. The decision to send the first two divisions of diggers, the Sixth and Seventh, to the Eastern Mediterranean where three continents meet, seemed natural, almost inevitable, to most people. It seemed fitting too that they should be sent to base camps in the British mandated territory of Palestine, which their fathers had done so much to win from the Turks. When war broke out the Royal Australian Air Force (R.A.A.F.) consisted of 164 combat aircraft, most of them obsolete, and there seemed to be little chance of getting any more in the foreseeable future. There was, however, no shortage of men wishing to enlist. On 22 September the Australian Government's High Commissioner in London, S. M. Bruce, on his own initiative proposed to the British Government what came to be known as the Empire Air Training Scheme. Partially trained air-crews were despatched from Australia (and other parts of the Empire) to Canada for further training, and thence to Britain where they were assigned to combat air squadrons. It was fortunate for the Allies that the 'phoney war' lasted as long as it did, for there were not then enough war planes in existence to accommodate the men who wanted to fly them or to defend the British Islands.

In Australia there was little sense of urgency. The politicians continued to wrangle — but about power and place more than about how best to further the war effort. The Government parties had not recovered from Earle Page's vicious attack on Menzies. Page and at least half of the U.A.P. caucus continued to intrigue against the Prime Minister and his leadership, some because they did not trust him, some because they honestly believed other leaders would be better, and many because they resented his inability to suffer fools with apparent happiness. In April 1940 the A.L.P., carefully nursed back to unity by Curtin and others, split again. In New South Wales most, though not all, of the previous followers of Lang, formed themselves into the self-styled 'Non-Communist Australian Labor Party'. A small splinter group of left-wingers, including some who were actually Communists, marched under the name of the 'New South Wales Labor Party'. The majority, led in the State by W. J. McKell, remained in the official A.L.P. under Curtin's leadership. Business carried on as usual. Crowds at the races, the picture-shows, the football matches and the surfing beaches were as great as ever. Perhaps to persuade themselves that the war was real, people sang:

> *We'll hang out our washing on the Siegfried Line . . .*
> *If the Siegfried line's still there,*

and

> *Roll out the barrel ! Let's have a barrel of fun !*
> *Roll out the barrel ! We've got their troops on the run !*

Then the 'phoney war' came to an end quite suddenly.

In the northern spring on 9 April 1940 the Nazis invaded Denmark and Norway and the name of the leading Norwegian Fascist, Major Vidkun Quisling, became a synonym for traitor in most European languages. A month later, on 10 May, Neville Chamberlain the appeaser, left the House of Commons with Cromwell's charge to the Long Parliament ringing in his ears: 'You have sat here too long for any good you have been doing . . . In the name of God, go!'[1] Churchill formed a National Government with Clement Attlee, Ernest Bevin and other leading Laborites in his Cabinet. On the same day the Nazis invaded Holland, Belgium and Luxembourg. At the end of the month the remnants of the British Expeditionary Force were evacuated from Dunkirk. On 10 June when it was quite obvious that Paris was about to fall, Mussolini declared war on France and Britain. In July and August the Royal Air Force began bombing Germany and the Luftwaffe rained bombs on England. At the height of the Battle of Britain, Australian airmen helped to shoot down 180 German planes in one day (15 August). The war against Fascism had really begun, but in Australia one of

[1] Alfred F. Havighurst, *Twentieth Century Britain*, New York, 1966, p.292.

Menzies' first reactions was to issue a National Security regulation making the Communist Party an illegal organisation, something Churchill saw no necessity for in beleaguered Britain. Before Australian servicemen joined in the fighting on a large scale, the 1940 federal general election was fixed for 21 September: and before the campaign got fairly under way the U.A.P. suffered a crippling blow with the death of three senior ministers, Fairbairn, Gullett and Street, in an air crash at Canberra.

Menzies for the U.A.P. promised all possible aid to Britain and stressed that his Government had already armed 230 000 men — 180 000 of them in the Second A.I.F. and the R.A.A.F. having volunteered for service anywhere. Page's successor as Country Party leader, 'Archie' Cameron, was a singular phenomenon in two respects: though a devout Catholic he often wore kilts to emphasize his Scots descent, and he belonged to one of the major non-Labor parties. He emphasized unity with the U.A.P. because in fact it was under considerable strain, and even offered to resign his party leadership if it would help to make an all-party National Government possible. Curtin for Labor also promised total support for the war effort, but placed more emphasis on the defence of Australia. He also urged immediate increases in pensions and servicemen's pay and greater attention to planning for a more egalitarian society after the war.

Polling showed further loss of support for the Government parties — or for Menzies' leadership. The voters sent to the Representatives 23 U.A.P., 13 Country Party, 32 Labor, 4 Lang Labor and 2 Independent members. Thus the Coalition parties could muster 36 votes to 36 for Labor and Lang Labor combined. However one of the Independents, A. W. Coles, a chain store magnate, usually voted with the U.A.P. and the other A. Wilson, with the Country Party. In the Senate the Coalition parties had 19 seats to the A.L.P.'s seventeen. Before another Government could be formed, separate caucus meetings took place for the assessment of the position. That of the Country Party was particularly stormy. This small group had never settled down since the disturbance caused by Earle Page's outburst against Menzies' record in World War I, and his subsequent replacement in the leadership by Cameron. The latter was now deposed, partly because of prejudice against his religion. The victors could not agree, however, on whether to have Page back again or the rugged and able Victorian, John McEwen. As a compromise the deputy leader of the party, Arthur Fadden, became 'temporary leader'. Within six months he was confirmed in the job and within a year he became 'for forty days and forty nights', as he was fond of saying, Prime Minister.

Born in Ingham, North Queensland, in 1895, Fadden had only a primary education at a state school in the Mackay district. At 15 he went to work as 'billy boy' in a cane-cutters' gang, but being 'smart at figures', he soon became an office-boy in a sugar-mill, then assistant to the Town Clerk and finally Town Clerk of Mackay. He studied at night to become a chartered accountant and became well known from Townsville to Rockhampton as a footballer, cricketer and boxer. Elected to the Queensland Parliament in 1932, he was defeated at the next election but sent to the Commonwealth Parliament by the electors of Darling Downs in 1936. Having achieved the leadership of his party almost accidentally only five years later, he retained it until his retirement from politics in 1958. He was as well liked as Menzies was not. He was an admirer and personal friend of the Labor leader, John Curtin, though they abused each other in public freely enough. Indeed Fadden's political success was built on his personal qualities. Journalists, colleagues, voters and even many of his political opponents liked him, perhaps because his virtues and his vices might have stood for those of the archetypal Australian male. Tough, enduring, earthy; shrewd but not subtle or cultivated or over-scrupulous; he loved yarning and drinking with friends and liked to call a spade a bloody shovel. Above all, he possessed, without being in the least aware of it, a trait noted by an English visitor in 1826 as being the leading characteristic of native-born Australians. He 'seemed to consider himself just on a level with' everyone he met, no matter what their position or status.[2] He acquired the nickname of 'Call me Artie', because of his own reiterated invitation to all he met. Despite, or because of his upbringing, he was quite as conservative as most other Country Party politicians — except that he had no feeling of deference towards upper class Englishmen or of exaggerated 'loyalty' to Britain.

With the party meetings over the new Menzies Government was sworn in on 28 October. The other leading ministers were Fadden (Treasury), Hughes (Attorney-General and Navy), McEwen (Air), Senator H. S. Foll (Interior) and an extremely able newcomer to the U.A.P., though he had been an Independent member since the general election of 1937, Percy Spender (Army). These six comprised the inner War Cabinet. Having shaken Menzies' hand in an arranged meeting which must have been painful to both parties, Page was also given a portfolio as Minister for Commerce. At the same time, a very useful body called the Advisory War Council was established. By the Coalition parties it was seen as some sort of substitute for the all-party National Government on the British

[2] Alexander Harris in, C. M. H. Clark (ed.), *Settlers and Convicts*, Melbourne, 1964, p.5.

model, to which Curtin remained implacably opposed. The War Council's first members were Menzies, Fadden, Hughes, and Spender from the Government, Curtin, Forde and Makin from Labor and Beasley from the small Lang Labor group. The Council had no power to make decisions. As its name implied, it was a secret forum in which the Government could brief Opposition leaders on what were often confidential developments in the war situation, while the latter could give their advice to the Government, both sides being free of the necessity to adopt the critically hostile poses almost inseparable from public parliamentary debate.

R. G. Casey was conspicuously not made a member of the Advisory War Council. Instead Menzies made him in January 1941 Australia's first Minister to a foreign country — the U.S.A. Undoubtedly it was a wise and necessary appointment. Undoubtedly too, though Casey does not seem to have realised it at the time, he was being 'kicked upstairs' as a possible threat to Menzies' leadership of the U.A.P. Before the year was out Sir John Latham had been sent as Australian Envoy to Japan and Sir Frederick Eggleston to China.

During the election campaign and the political manoeuvring that followed it, Italian forces reached Sidi Barrani on the Egyptian coast and, more ominously for Australia, Japan on 28 September 1940 signed a ten-year economic and military pact with Italy and Germany. The Royal Australian Navy had already seen action. In July H.M.A.S. *Sydney*, named after the ship which drew first blood in the Great War, had sunk the Italian cruiser *Bartolomeo Colleoni* in the eastern Mediterranean, and in the following March the destroyer H.M.A.S. *Stuart* was part of the British fleet which routed a superior Italian force at the Battle of Cape Matapan. Meanwhile men of the second A.I.F. figured prominently in the British General Wavell's attack on the Italians who were driven back out of Egypt and Cyrenaica. By the time the Australians captured Benghazi in February 1941, ten Italian divisions, about one-sixth of the entire combat strength of the Italian army, had been destroyed and about 125 000 soldiers taken prisoner for minimal British losses. Hitler then sent General Rommel to the rescue of his Italian allies and a German counter-offensive opened on 31 March. At the same time 60 000 men, including many Australian and New Zealand units, were detached from the African front and sent to Greece and Crete to help resist an Italo-German invasion there. They had little chance against the greatly superior German forces on the ground and in the air, but gave a good account of themselves before being ordered to withdraw. About three-quarters of the entire force lived to fight another day.

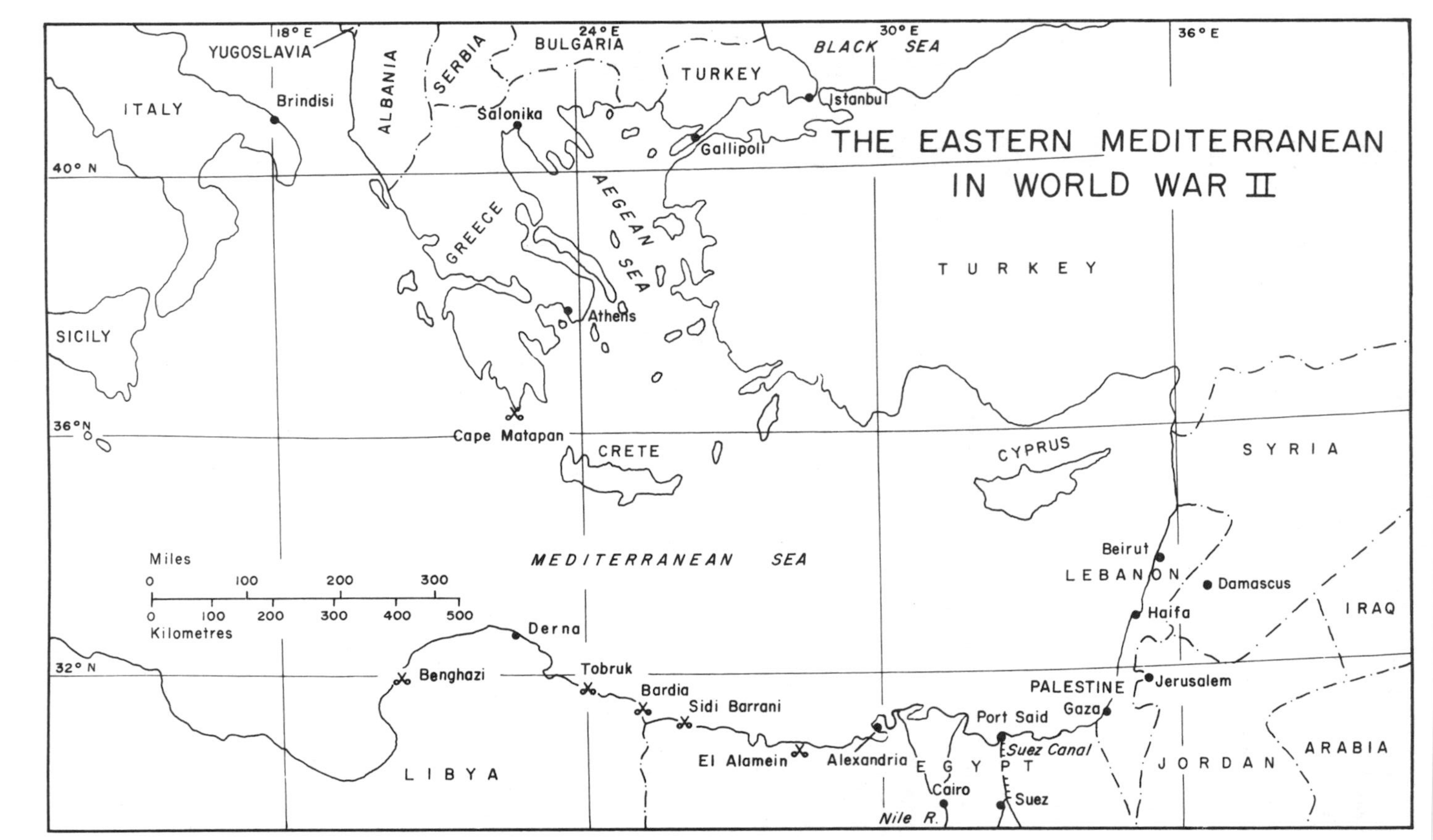
THE EASTERN MEDITERRANEAN
IN WORLD WAR II
18° E
24° E
30° E
36° E
40° N
36° N
32° N
YUGOSLAVIA
ALBANIA
SERBIA
BULGARIA
TURKEY
BLACK SEA
Istanbul
Gallipoli
ITALY
Brindisi
Salonika
GREECE
AEGEAN SEA
Athens
SICILY
Cape Matapan
CRETE
T U R K E Y
CYPRUS
S Y R I A
MEDITERRANEAN SEA
Miles
0
100
200
300
0
100
200
300
400
500
Kilometres
Derna
Benghazi
Tobruk
Bardia
Sidi Barrani
El Alamein
Alexandria
L I B Y A
E G Y P T
Cairo
Nile R.
Port Said
Suez Canal
Suez
Gaza
PALESTINE
Jerusalem
Haifa
Beirut
LEBANON
Damascus
IRAQ
J O R D A N
ARABIA

Meanwhile the German counter-offensive in North Africa reached the Egyptian border and Nazi troops recaptured Bardia on 13 April. On the same day Stalin signed a neutrality pact with Japan, an event which made it difficult for any but the self-deluded to doubt the direction the Japanese thrust would take when it came. The Australian Eighth Division was committed to the defence of Singapore. The German advance by-passed Tobruk, isolating about 30 000 Allied troops, most of them Australians, who successfully beat off repeated German attacks until they were relieved in October. During the northern summer other Australian forces played a major part in denying the use of Syrian bases to Hitler's Vichy-French allies, but all these events were overshadowed by Hitler's invasion of Russia on mid-summer's day, 22 June 1941. Encouraged by initial German successes the Japanese began to move south, landing troops in Indo-China from the end of July.

The deteriorating war situation abroad intensified wrangling within the Coalition and criticism of Menzies' leadership at home. Few doubted his ability but many of his own party colleagues believed, rightly, that his sobriquet of 'Pig-Iron Bob' reflected the electorate's belief that his past support of appeasement rendered him, like Chamberlain in Britain, unfit to lead the nation in a life-and-death struggle against the Fascist powers. A young and fearless back-bencher, Bill McCall, did most of the lobbying against his leadership within the Coalition parties. Attacked on all sides, the Prime Minister again appealed for a National Government, declaring his willingness to serve under whosoever was chosen to lead it. When Curtin refused the bait, Menzies resigned and the Coalition parties elected Fadden as joint leader in his stead.

On 29 August the new Government was announced, but the only substantial change was that Fadden added the Prime Ministership to his Treasury portfolio. Menzies retained his responsibility as Minister for Defence Co-ordination. Otherwise the Cabinet remained exactly as it had been. Fadden successfully demanded that the Australians in Tobruk should be relieved by other troops, but of course the public knew nothing at all of this. The Australian people had lost confidence in the Government, not merely in its leader. During Fadden's brief period as Prime Minister a trivial incident showed just how unpopular the Government had become, particularly among reporters and others who tend to lead public opinion. On a warm September night the Australian Journalists' Association was conducting its annual 'ladies night' party in its Sydney premises. From the nearby Commonwealth Offices in Martin Place an aide rang the A.J.A. President and asked if the Prime Minister could come to the party. When he arrived at about midnight, Fadden stood on a table while the President, both hands raised, begged for silence; but the Prime Minister of Australia could scarcely make himself heard above the booing and catcalls. Once, those who were trying to listen, heard Fadden appeal to 'my old friend John Fisher over there', Fisher being a Communist journalist and a son of Andrew Fisher, the Prime Minister at the beginning of the Great War: but the appeal was vain.[3] The hostile demonstration was not aimed at Fadden who, as we have seen, was personally popular, especially with journalists, but at the Government he was briefly leading. Finally the Government was discredited by the 'leaking' of confidential information. It was disclosed that with Fadden's permission, W. M. Hughes, as Attorney-General, was dispensing a secret fund of about £ 5,000 of taxpayers' money to publish apparently disinterested propaganda against strikes and to bribe trade-union leaders. A subsequent Royal Commission found that the President of the Miners' Federation, 'Charlie' Nelson, had accepted £ 300.

LABOR LEADS AGAINST THE JAPANESE THRUST

On 1 October during the annual budget debate Curtin moved what amounted to a motion of no-confidence in the Government. Specifically Labor opposed Fadden's proposal for compulsory loans — a form of income tax beginning at a lower income level than had previously been subject to taxation; but everyone knew that the motion was really an A.L.P. bid for power. Wilson, the Independent, radically inclined member from the Wimmera district of the Victorian wheat-belt, had decided that the country wanted a Labor Government and that Curtin would make a better war leader than the Coalition parties could provide. The other Independent member, Coles, was a strong Menzies supporter. However he had become disillusioned and disgusted by the incessant quarrelling and intrigues in the U.A.P. and, apparently, convinced that Menzies had been worn out by them. During the debate he decided also that the A.L.P. offered a better chance of stable and energetic direction of the national war effort and that the electorate wanted the change. In their assessment of public feeling outside the House both Independent members were certainly right, as the next general election was to show. On 3 October Coles and Wilson crossed the floor to vote with Labor and Fadden gladly relinquished the burden he had not been very keen to take up. It was reported that members of the Labor Caucus sang to celebrate their victory a parody of the popular song, *There'll always be an England*. Written by a gifted young poet and

[3] The writer was among the witnesses of this scene.

musician, James McAuley, at that time a leading member of the radical Sydney New Theatre League, whose performance of an anti-Nazi play had been banned before the war, the verses were the theme-song of an anti-Government review, *I'd Rather Be Left*. They began:

There'll always be a Menzies while there's a B.H.P.
And all the proper people talk upon the A.B.C.:
But we might lose our Menzies: wherever would we be —
If Menzies means as much to you as Menzies means to me?

The Curtin Government was sworn in on 7 October.

John Curtin was born in 1885 at Creswick near Ballarat, the son of a police sergeant, and left school at the age of only 13 to obtain clerical work in Melbourne. He read widely, played football and cricket rather well on weekends and joined the Labor Party, in which he was strongly influenced by the radical Frank Anstey. During the Great War he became secretary of the Victorian Anti-Conscription League, was sentenced to three months' gaol for having failed to enlist in accordance with a proclamation issued under the War Precautions Act, but released four days later when the proclamation was revoked. Late in 1916 he went to Perth as editor of the *Westralian Worker* and was fined for sedition in connection with his anti-conscriptionist views. In 1917 he married Elsie Needham and settled down in the West. They had one son and one daughter. He won the Fremantle seat in the federal Parliament in 1928 and, except for the period of the first Lyons Administration from 1932 to 1934, held it until he died.

As a young man in Victoria Curtin had abandoned the Catholic faith of his Irish forbears and become a rationalist and a utopian socialist, believing in the improvement and greater happiness of men and women in this world. Embittered by Labor's long period in the political wilderness after 1917, and frustrated by its brief tenure of place without power during the Depression, he seemed at times to be in danger of becoming a drunkard. By the time he became federal leader of the Parliamentary A.L.P. in 1935, he had won that battle and was practically a teetotaller for the rest of his life. A man of complete integrity, tall, dignified and somewhat aloof in manner, Curtin was a great orator who sometimes mauled Menzies in debate; but the salient difference between them lay in their conceptions of patriotism. For Menzies Britain, or the British Empire with Australia in its proper subordinate place in the Empire, came first: for Curtin, as for his party generally, Australia came first all the time. Perhaps that was the fundamental reason why the electorate turned to Labor as ominous portents of a southward Japanese drive multiplied.

Another great Australian nationalist was Curtin's most prominent lieutenant, the Attorney-General and Minister for External Affairs, Herbert Vere Evatt. Born in the same year as R. G. Menzies, at East Maitland, New South Wales, Evatt was the third of six brothers brought up by their mother who was widowed when 'Bert' was only six. Educated at the local state school and then at Fort Street High School and the University of Sydney, he was probably the most brilliant student ever to graduate there. Between 1912 and 1918 he obtained first-class honours in English, Mathematics and Philosophy in his Arts degree and first-class honours with the University Medal in Law. He became a brilliant barrister, a lecturer in Law at the University, a Doctor of Laws, a King's Counsel in 1929, and in 1930 at the age of 36 the youngest judge ever appointed to the High Court Bench. In the following ten years he wrote four scholarly and substantial books on aspects of Australian history. Then in 1940 he resigned his judgeship to contest the Sydney suburban seat of Barton at the federal general elections in September. His countrymen were very impressed. Ever since 1903 they had been quite accustomed to the spectacle of leading politicians retiring from the uncertain, nerve-racking hurly-burly of politics to the secure dignity of the High Court Bench. The precedent had been established by the first Prime Minister, Edmund Barton, after whom Evatt's electorate had been named. Here was the almost inconceivable reverse process taking place: for no other apparent reason than Evatt's desire — or ambition — to serve his country in the wartime crisis. He won the seat easily and his candidature probably helped the A.L.P. to make substantial gains throughout the country.

Evatt was a hard man to understand. The private secretary and friend, who served him for twenty years, wrote a biography entitled *Evatt the Enigma*; but certain aspects of the man's character, often apparently mutually contradictory, stand out. Like Curtin, he had no religious belief but an unshakeable faith in humanity and its capacity for moral and material improvement. He believed passionately in the importance of civil liberties at home and the rule of law abroad. His mind was a quite extraordinarily powerful, acute and supple instrument: yet towards the end of his life it became, imperceptibly at first, more unreliable, erratic and confused; and even in his younger days, despite his great gifts, he was capable of making gross errors of judgment in practical matters which would have presented no problems to people with half his ability. His consideration for people's feelings inspired the devoted loyalty of many of his associates: yet he was quite insensitive, even thoughtlessly brutal, in his behaviour to others. He was almost childishly vain, needing admiration and frequently seeking it openly from those around him.

He was, in many ways, a prophet vastly more honoured abroad than he ever was in his own country; for he rarely failed to do what he thought right, however politically unpopular, even predictably disastrous, it might be.

The other members of Curtin's inner or War Cabinet were F. M. Forde, Deputy Prime Minister and Minister for the Army, an uninspired party hack; J. B. Chifley, Treasurer and, as it happened, the next Prime Minister; J. A. Beasley, Supply and Development; Norman Makin, Navy and Munitions; and A. S. Drakeford, Air and Civil Aviation. The most able ministers apart from most of these were 'Eddie' Ward, Labour and National Service, and J. J. Dedman, War Organization and Industry. Dedman, a Scottish migrant, had been in Parliament only since winning the by-election for Corio, made necessary by Casey's departure to Washington in January, but he was co-opted to the War Cabinet two months later.

The new Government had hardly been sworn in when it was called upon to lead the nation through the greatest crisis in its history. In November 1941 the cruiser H.M.A.S. *Sydney* was sunk in the Indian Ocean, only a few hundred kilometres north-west of Fremantle, by the German raider *Kormoran*, disguised as a Dutch merchantman. The whole crew of 645 officers and men went down with the ship. Then on 7 December without prior declaration of war, the Japanese made their devastating attack on Pearl Harbour in Hawaii, the major American naval base in the Pacific. Thereby American might was enlisted on the side of the Allies, but no one could tell how long it would take to replace the ships sunk in the sneak attack, or how far south Japanese forces might strike meanwhile. It is worth noting that, in keeping with Labor's nationalist stance, the Government did not wait to follow Britain's lead but actually declared war on Japan before the British Government did so. Later in the following year when the war situation was improving, it underlined the point by having Parliament ratify the Statute of Westminster.

Three days after Pearl Harbour the only British capital ships in the Indian and Pacific Oceans, H.M.S. *Prince of Wales* and *Repulse*, were sunk off the coast of Malaya by Japanese shore-based aircraft. For the first time most Australians began to wonder whether Singapore was, after all, such an impregnable bastion. They were not left long in doubt. In the next two months Japanese forces occupied Guam, Wake Island, Hong Kong, British North Borneo, Rabaul in New Britain, the Celebes and Moluccas in the Netherlands East Indies, Burma and the entire Malay peninsula. The Australian Eighth Division, with Indian and British troops, was driven rapidly back to Singapore Island. The fortress surrendered on 15 February

1942 and its defenders were made prisoners of war. Of the 15 384 Australians 4783 were murdered or died of illness or wounds while in Japanese hands. Major-General Gordon Bennett, commander of the Eighth Division, and two aides escaped to Australia minutes after the surrender and were much criticised for doing so. Four days later Japanese aircraft made their first devastating air raid on Darwin. Two weeks later another Australian cruiser, H.M.A.S. *Perth*, was lost in the Battle of the Java Sea. Nothing seemed to impede Japan's southward thrust or to stand between her victorious forces and an attack on the Australian mainland. The day, so often foretold in fantasy by nationalists and racists, when white Australia would have to stand alone against a 'coloured' Asiatic invasion, seemed to be at hand.

It is impossible to overestimate the effect of these events on Australian attitudes. For 150 years most people had, like R. G. Menzies, taken British protection for granted. Even fervent Australian nationalists like Curtin or Evatt had hardly envisaged the suddenness and the extent of British disasters. Three hundred thousand Australians had travelled to the other side of the earth to defend Britain only twenty-five years earlier. Now, when Australia's peril seemed to be even greater, Britain was not able, or willing, to spare three thousand men to defend her. It was against this background that Curtin made his historic appeal for American help, in the last days of 1941 while the Eighth Division was still fighting in Malaya. In a New Year's message to the Australian people he said:

> Without any inhibitions of any kind, I make it quite clear that Australia looks to America, free of any pangs as to our traditional links or kinship with the United Kingdom . . . We know . . . that Australia can go and Britain can still hold on. We are, therefore, determined that Australia shall not go, and we shall exert all our energies towards the shaping of a plan, with the United States as its keystone, which will give to our country some confidence of being able to hold out until the tide of battle swings against the enemy.[4]

The speech was overwhelmingly endorsed by public opinion, but not by many conservative Austral-Britons. Menzies, Hughes and Spender were among the leading Opposition members who denounced it as 'false', 'dangerous' and a 'great' or 'egregious blunder'.[5]

Naturally the Americans were glad to occupy Australia as a base from which they could organise and mount a counter-attack on the

[4] *S.M.H.*, 29 December 1941.
[5] *S.M.H.*, 29, 30 December 1941.

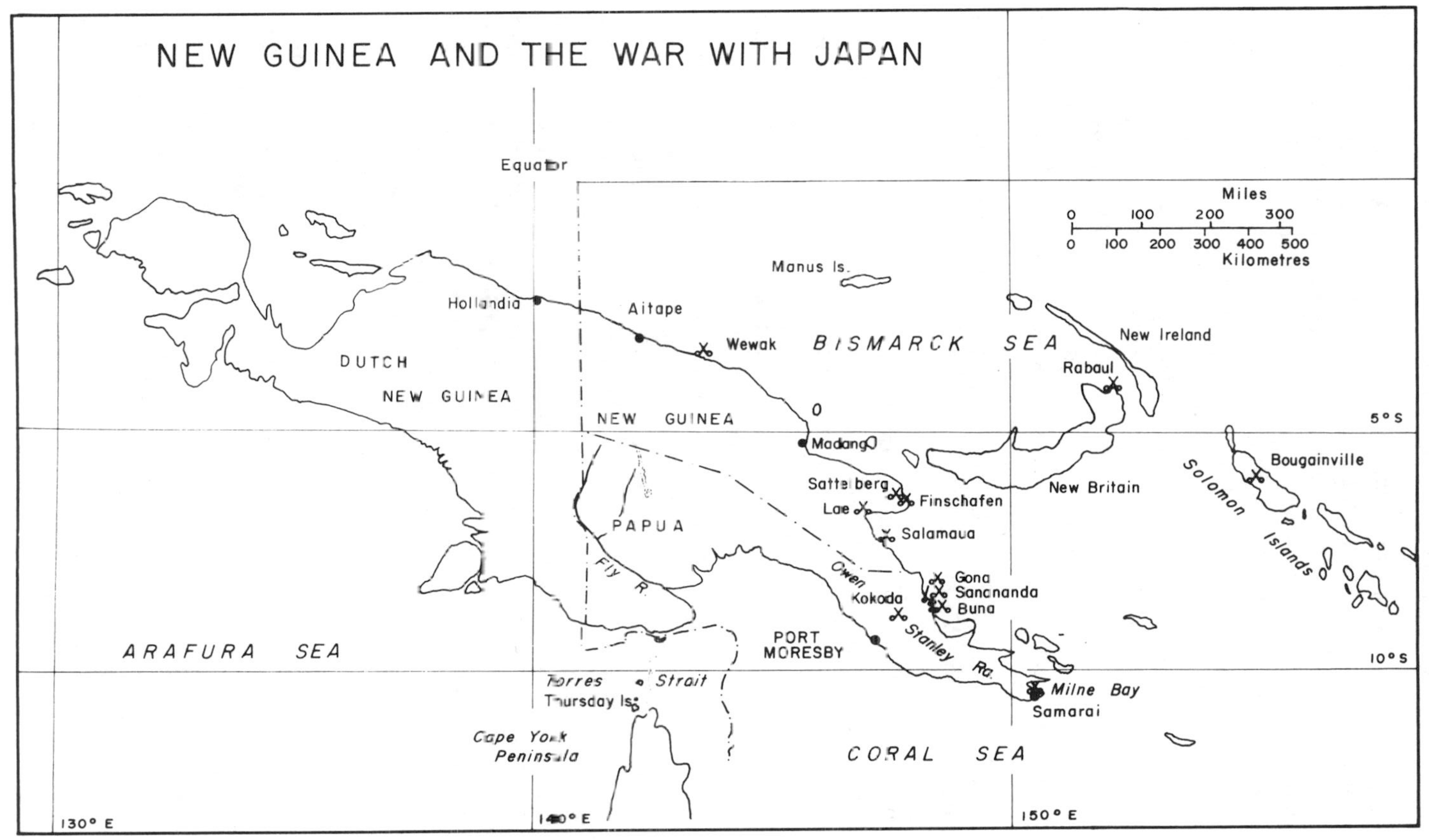
NEW GUINEA AND THE WAR WITH JAPAN
Equator
Miles
0 100 200 300
0 100 200 300 400 500
Kilometres
Manus Is.
Hollandia
Aitape
Wewak
BISMARCK SEA
New Ireland
Rabaul
DUTCH
NEW GUINEA
NEW GUINEA
5° S
Madang
Bougainville
Satteberg
Finschafen
New Britain
Solomon Islands
Lae
Salamaua
PAPUA
Owen
Gona
Sananda
Fly R.
Kokoda
Buna
Stanley
PORT MORESBY
Ra.
ARAFURA SEA
10° S
Torres Strait
Thursday Is.
Milne Bay
Samarai
Cape York Peninsula
CORAL SEA
130° E
140° E
150° E

Japanese; and Australians were more than glad to welcome the first American servicemen to their shores. In March General Douglas MacArthur, U.S. commander in the Philippines, flew to Australia on President Roosevelt's orders and in April set up his headquarters in Melbourne. The Australian and other Allied Governments accepted him as supreme commander in the South West Pacific Area. Under him were two other Americans commanding air and sea operations, but the Australian General Thomas Blamey was to command all land forces. However, large numbers of American troops and planes could not be despatched to Australia as quickly as MacArthur and his staff. Japanese forces landed on the north coast of New Guinea in March and began their advance over the Owen Stanley Range to Port Moresby. By that time, thanks to the change of government, 46 000 A.I.F. veterans of the Sixth and Seventh Divisions had been brought back from the Middle East to meet them.

At the beginning of 1942 the only land forces available to defend Australia were some 200 000 militia men only partly trained and totally inexperienced in warfare, about 50 000 A.I.F. men better trained but equally inexperienced, and the three veteran divisions in the Middle East. On the day that Singapore capitulated the chief of the Australian General Staff, General Sturdee, recommended to the War Cabinet that the Ninth Division should be brought home to defend Australia at an early date and that the Sixth and Seventh should be brought home at once. Cabinet agreed unanimously and cabled Churchill accordingly. The British Prime Minister, however, considered that the Seventh A.I.F. Division should be sent to Burma to bolster its defences and, true to their traditionally deferential posture towards Britain, the U.A.P. and Country Party members of the Advisory War Council — Fadden, Hughes, Menzies, Spender and McEwen — supported him. Sir Earle Page, still the Australian Government's representative in London, went so far as to disobey, or perhaps only to misunderstand, his instructions. He failed to oppose Churchill's wishes as requested to do in a series of cables from Curtin.[6] Churchill insisted and even had Roosevelt also bring pressure to bear on the Australian Government, but the Labor Cabinet, fortunately for all concerned except the Japanese, stood firm. The official British and Australian War Historians agree that the last minute arrival of one or two Australian divisions in Burma could not have affected the situation there — but they did affect the situation in New Guinea in the third quarter of the year, probably decisively. Churchill never recognised his mistake and never forgave

[6] John J. Dedman, 'The Return of the A.I.F. from the Middle East', *Australian Outlook*, August 1967, vol. 21, no. 2, pp.151-64.

the Australian Government, or Australia, for having thwarted him. His view was that, if Australia fell to the Japanese, it could be liberated at the end of hostilities.

After the first air raid on Darwin (19 February 1942), Japanese planes bombed Broome, Wyndham and other points on the mainland from time to time. On the night of 31 May-1 June three midget submarines were released from five large Japanese submarines off the New South Wales coast. The midgets entered Sydney Harbour and, before they were destroyed, one of them torpedoed a naval depot-ship killing nineteen sleeping seamen. A week later at night the Japanese submarines shelled Newcastle and Sydney but did no appreciable damage. During the whole war twenty-six Allied merchantmen were sunk in Australian waters, some of them within sight of the coast. The tide began to turn early in May with the Battle of the Coral Sea, in which a combined American-Australian fleet turned back a strong Japanese task-force escorting troops to invade Port Moresby, the Australian base on the southern coast of New Guinea. Actually American losses were heavier than those of the Japanese, but the enemy's invasion plans were scotched by the action. Three months later the heavy cruiser H.M.A.S. *Canberra* was lost by enemy action in the same general area. Meanwhile, however, the final outcome of the war in the Pacific was decided at the Battle of Midway — though not everyone realised it at the time. Between 3 and 6 June 1942, in what was incontestably the greatest naval battle of World War II, the Americans crushingly defeated the Japanese, who never thereafter regained the initiative in the war at sea. It was another four months before the previously invincible army of Nippon suffered its first defeats.

During that time the enemy had been occupying other points in the Pacific, consolidating his grip on the Dutch East Indies and the northern coast of New Guinea, and advancing south over the Owen Stanley Range towards Port Moresby. By mid-September the Australian troops, including some Middle-East veterans who had been thrown into the fighting a month earlier, had been forced back to Imita Ridge only about fifty kilometres from Port Moresby. Meanwhile a small number of Australian and American troops had been building an airfield at Milne Bay on the eastern tip of the New Guinea mainland. On the night of 26 August they were attacked by a strong sea-borne enemy force. In a week of murderous fighting, most of it by night in jungle and swamp, the Japanese were smashed and the survivors taken prisoner or driven back to their base. In terms of the numbers of men involved it was not a battle of great importance, but it did much for Australian, and indeed American, morale; for it was Japan's first defeat on land during the whole Pacific war. It also did much to improve relations between the two great sections of the Australian army, the A.I.F. and the Militia. The latter, conscripted for home defence only, were often sneered at as 'chocolate soldiers' or 'koalas' — because they were 'protected' by legislation like the native-bear — but militiamen and the A.I.F. both fought heroically at Milne Bay. At the same time, in the last few days of September, Australian troops began their counter-offensive outside Port Moresby. By 2 November the Japanese had been driven back over the range and Kokoda, the key point in the pass, had been re-occupied. From this time onwards, though years of hard fighting lay ahead, the Japanese were strategically on the defensive throughout the Pacific.

On the same day that Kokoda was re-occupied by A.I.F. troops of the Seventh Division's 25th Brigade, their comrades on the other side of the world were playing a vital part in a larger but equally decisive battle. At El Alamein the Australian Ninth Division formed part of General Montgomery's Eighth Army which smashed Rommel's Afrika Corps and began the long pursuit which cleared the Nazis out of Africa by May 1943. Before the month was over, the Russian armies at bay had won the decisive battle of the whole war at Stalingrad. When Curtin made his New Year broadcast at the end of 1941 the Allies had suffered defeat after defeat and it was hard for the greatest optimist to see any immediate hope anywhere. Ultimate victory could only be a matter of faith, defined as belief in something despite overwhelming evidence to the contrary. At the end of 1942 it was tolerably clear that, however long and hard the road, the war could end only in victory for the Allies. And Australians felt that they had repelled the threat of imminent invasion by the Japanese.

THE HOME FRONT AND LIMITED CONSCRIPTION

This turning of the tide was not achieved without a considerable degree of sacrifice on the home front. Although civilian hardships were not to be compared with those suffered by the belligerent peoples in Europe — or Asia — by the winter of 1942 Australians were more severely rationed, regimented and censored than they had ever been since the early convict days. Since every drop of oil had to be imported, petrol was available only to the armed services and their auxiliaries, public transport systems and taxi-cabs. Most private car-owners jacked their vehicles up on blocks for the duration of the war. Price and rent-controls were introduced. These reduced but did not abolish a rising rate of inflation. Clothing, butter, tea, sugar and meat were strictly rationed — and this in a country where meat had always been more plentiful and cheap than perhaps anywhere else in the world. Tobacco was strictly rationed and many other luxuries, such as imported wine and spirits, simply disappeared from hotels and stores. Even beer became so scarce that many citizens began, illegally, to brew their own in the family copper. Butchers, bakers and other tradesmen generally stopped delivering their goods to the harassed housewife. Coal was saved for war purposes by the imposition of a nation-wide 'brown-out'. Public air-raid shelters were built and most people dug slit trenches in their own gardens or backyards. 'Manpower' became a familiar word, as a department was set up to control the allocation of men to the most necessary tasks. Every able-bodied male of military age was conscripted to the armed services, except those allotted by 'manpower' to other essential services. In 1942 Curtin brought Theodore back to public life, making him Director-General of Allied Works. In this honorary position his great abilities were harnessed to the task of controlling tens of thousands of civilian workers engaged in building airfields, roads and other works necessary to back up the war effort. The Commonwealth Government also took over, under its wartime defence powers, the collection of *all* income tax, thereby making the incidence of this form of taxation uniform throughout Australia, but also depriving the State governments of a major source of revenue and making them more dependent than ever on Commonwealth disbursements or 'charity'. After the war it proved to be practically, though not constitutionally, very hard to go back to the old system.

Of course there was plenty of grumbling, but the vast majority of people accepted these manifold restrictions as necessary. Hundreds of millions of pounds were raised in internal war loans, much of the money being subscribed by relatively poor people who had never invested before, and were never to do so again, in anything but savings bank accounts, insurance policies or horseraces. Figures provide some idea of the scope of the national effort. By the end of the war there were, or had been, very nearly a million men and women serving in the Army, Navy and Air Force or in auxiliary services such as the Women's Australian Air Force (W.A.A.F.). The remaining six million, including children, invalids, the sick and aged, had to provide food, clothing, equipment and some weapons and ammunition for the service personnel — and food and facilities for nearly half as many American servicemen serving in the South West Pacific area. Throughout the war the United States provided over £ 300,000,000 worth of goods and services to Australia under 'lend-lease' arrangements, but Australia supplied the United States with even more goods and services in return, being the only Allied country to achieve a favourable balance under the agreement. It is remarkable that all this was accomplished with so little discontent.

At least from the time Russia entered the war in June 1941, the only hint of dissent came from a few hundred sympathisers with the self-styled 'Australia First' movement, led by the writer and publicist, P. R. 'Inky' Stephensen. Most of these like the South Australian poet, Rex Ingamells, were simply extreme Australian nationalists whose fanaticism led them to be incautiously critical of Britain and America and the current Australian Government: but Stephensen himself may have been more dangerous. For some years as editor of an obscure journal, the *Publicist*, he had denounced the British connection, praised Nazi Germany and, especially, Japan, and filled his columns with the most rabid anti-Semitism. He continued to air these views at public meetings in Sydney after Japan entered the war until the night after the first bombing of Darwin — when his meeting was broken up and taken over by a band of wharf-labourers. On the recommendation of military intelligence reports, Stephensen and twenty others were arrested in March 1942. Some were released after a few days and some interned for varying periods.

One of the greatest achievements on the home front during World War II was the great advance made in the fields of manufacturing and technology. It is hardly too much to say that secondary industry reached what economists have called 'the take-off point'. Under the goad of necessity, Australian factories began producing a whole range of sophisticated commodities which previously had had to be imported. The basic steel and chemical industries, which had already begun to expand in the 1930s when most others remained depressed, reached an unheard-of level and diversity of output. The B.H.P. Company's shipment port for iron-ore in Spencer's Gulf, Whyalla, became and remained a substantial ship-building centre. At Newcastle, Sydney, Port Kembla, Melbourne and elsewhere factories produced most of the munitions required by the armed forces: rifles, bayonets, machine and submachine guns — including the Australian-invented Owen gun, anti-aircraft and anti-tank guns and shells, armoured cars, torpedoes and, most impressive of all, some internal combustion engines for locally-made motor vehicles and aircraft. The key to industrial expansion, technologically speaking, is the capacity to produce machine-tools — machines to make other machines. Before the war nearly all such had to be imported. 'For the three firms that were manufacturing these tools in 1939, in 1943 there were more than a hundred, producing all kinds of lathes, drills, milling machines, precision grinders, presses and so forth.'[7] Optical, radio and telegraphic precision intruments were also made in Australia, many for the first time.

[7] A. G. L. Shaw, *Economic Development of Australia*, Melbourne, 1966, p.177.

To finance the war effort a whole range of new and old taxes was imposed in addition to the Commonwealth's 'uniform' income taxation noted above. The Menzies, and then the Curtin, Governments legislated for taxation of wartime company profits, of gifts made by companies or individuals, and in 1942 the Curtin Government re-introduced Hughes's emergency measure of World War I — a Commonwealth Entertainments tax. Quite new was a Pay Roll Tax, introduced by Fadden and continued by Chifley, the Labor Treasurer. This taxed all employers, including governments, in respect of the wages paid to their employees. Not all of the increased revenue went into the war effort. In 1941, to forestall an impending rise in the basic wage, the Menzies Government passed a Child Endowment Act giving a small weekly payment to each citizen (but not, save in exceptional cases, to Aboriginals) who supported more than one child under 16 years of age, the sum being increased according to the number of children supported. There was no means test. To this the Curtin Government added a pension for widows maintaining one or more children, and for widows over fifty years old not caring for dependants; but these pensions were subject to a means test and again did not cover Aboriginals except in 'special' cases. Curtin held that, far from being an extravagance in wartime, such minimal social service payments were among the measures necessary to ensure maximum efficiency in the prosecution of the war.

Nineteen-forty-three opened with the enemy strategically on the defensive everywhere, including the South-West Pacific area. This fact, however satisfactory in every other respect, created one great problem for the Australian Government: it inevitably raised again the question of conscription for overseas service, the rock on which the Labor Party had been shattered during the Great War and which, many feared or hoped, would now shatter it again. While ever Australian forces had been on the defensive, the vast majority of troops were in any case needed in Australia or Australian territories — Papua and Australian New Guinea, where the actual and potential fighting was to be done. However, with the Japanese retreating it seemed increasingly ludicrous that militia troops might help to turn the enemy back over the Owen Stanley Range, rout him out of jungle strong-points on the north coast, but not pursue him over an imaginary line on the map constituting the border of Dutch New Guinea, or into some islands under British or Dutch rather than Australian sovereignty.

The situation was doubly embarrassing because all the American troops, fighting side by side with the Australians, were conscripts, and they were a great deal farther away from home than the militiamen. Yet, as we have seen, the question of one's attitude to compulsory overseas service in wartime had for a generation been the most divisive one in the Australian community. For many old Labor men and women, particularly in the trade-union movement, 'no conscription for overseas service' had become a shibboleth, something to be cherished at all costs and beyond the reach of reasoning or argument. As a leading anti-conscriptionist himself twenty-five years earlier, none knew the strength of such feelings better than the Prime Minister. He gradually persuaded the majority of his own party organisation outside Parliament to agree to the change, before introducing the necessary amendments to the Defence and National Security Acts early in 1943. The legislation enabled militiamen to serve in a defined area between longitude 110° and 159° E and northwards as far as the equator. Conservatives denounced it as not going far enough and some diehard Labor men objected that it went much too far, but it was endorsed by public opinion generally and certainly by majority opinion in the Labor movement. Acceptance of 'limited conscription' by the unions and the radical left wing of the movement was made much easier by the Australian Communist Party's vigorous support for the move. Never more influential than during World War II from June 1941 onwards, when the U.S.S.R. was doing much to bleed the common enemy, the Communists' influence was used to minimise strikes and to promote the war effort in every way. In December 1942 the Curtin Government lifted the ban Menzies had placed on the party.

Parliament's three-year term ran out in the third quarter of 1943 and the date of the general election was set down for 21 August. For some months there had been bitter party strife, in and out of Parliament, over 'Eddie' Ward's 'Brisbane Line' allegations. The radical Minister for Labour claimed to have evidence that the previous U.A.P.-Country Party Government in 1941 had approved a plan, in the event of a Japanese landing, to defend only the south-eastern corner of the continent on a line running roughly from Brisbane to Adelaide, while abandoning the rest of Australia to enemy occupation. It is probable that any responsible government would have considered such a plan as a last-ditch contingency, to be provided for if the worst came to the worst. Indeed Curtin conceded that his Government had considered such a possibility in the early days of the Japanese thrust southwards; but the previous Government ministers vigorously denied the allegations and succeeded in having a Royal Commissioner appointed to sift them. He found that no such document as Ward had alleged existed, did exist; but he could say nothing more final than that, because Ward stood on his parliamentary privilege and refused to answer questions.

HANGING OUT THE WASHING ON THE BRISBANE LINE

Tribune, 1943

Probably some of Ward's mud stuck with the electors, especially in Western Australia and Queensland, but all the signs suggest that the Labor Government would have been elected with a large majority even if the mud had never been thrown. Although the people knew nothing of the U.A.P.-Country Party leaders' support for Churchill's attempt to divert the homeward bound A.I.F. Seventh Division to Burma, they understood intuitively that the Labor Government was fighting more vigorously to place Australian interests first within the alliance than the other parties would have been likely to do, and they knew that the Ninth Division too had been brought home in February 1942 after El Alamein.

Curtin led a united party into the campaign, Lang Labor and the left-wing 'New South Wales A.L.P.' having been reduced to the veriest splinters. His policy speech, broadcast from Canberra, stressed the Government's record in organising the nation's resistance to Japan and promised to plan for full employment, greatly expanded social services and a generous and comprehensive scheme of re-training and rehabilitation for ex-servicemen and women after the war. During the campaign he specifically promised not to socialise any industry while the war lasted. The Opposition was hopelessly divided against itself. Formally Fadden was leader of the Country Party and of the combined Coalition team, while Hughes led the U.A.P.: but in fact many members of that party continued to regard as their leader Menzies, who had never ceased to intrigue for his return to the leadership of the anti-Labor forces. Fadden promised that, if elected, the Coalition would introduce conscription for service anywhere and establish a single Australian army. He also proposed to refund one-third of future wartime income tax revenue to the taxpayer after the war was over. Like Hughes, Menzies and other leading Coalition speakers, he made the usual attacks on Communism and its influence on the trade unions and the Labor Party. Speaking to his Kooyong electors, Menzies disagreed with Fadden's proposals for the post-war return to taxpayers of a proportion of income tax payments. Fadden immediately told reporters that Menzies had stabbed him in the back in 'another betrayal in the series for which Mr Menzies has become notorious'.[8] This public brawling destroyed whatever chances of re-election the anti-Labor parties might have had. Even the staidly conservative *Sydney Morning Herald*, for the first time in its existence, urged its readers to vote Labor. People were not to know what most journalists in Sydney believed: that this *volte-face* sprang largely from the dislike of Menzies felt by the *Herald's* proprietor for purely personal, not political reasons.

[8] *S.M.H.*, 26 July 1943.

In terms of the percentage of votes cast for the major parties, the 1943 general election was as great a triumph for the A.L.P. as the 1932 election had been for the U.A.P.-Country Party coalition. Evatt, for instance, won Barton, by no means a solid Labor seat, with over 51 000 first preference votes, the highest number ever recorded for any candidate in any seat since federation. Labor won all the Senate seats being contested with 55 per cent of all valid votes cast giving, after 1 July 1944, an Upper House of 22 A.L.P., 12 U.A.P. and 2 Country Party senators. This was the first time Labor had achieved a majority in the Senate since the general election of 1914. In the House of Representatives the A.L.P. gained 49 seats, the U.A.P. 14, the Country Party 9 and the Independents (Coles and Wilson) two. Since all ministers had been re-elected, the Cabinet carried on as before with only minor reshufflings from time to time. The most important of these were as follows: A. A. Calwell, newly elected as member for Melbourne in 1940, entered Cabinet as Minister for Information. Since December 1942 Chifley had been responsible for a new Department of Post-War Reconstruction as well as the Treasury. In February 1945 Dedman's Department of War Organisation of Industry was subsumed in Post-War Reconstruction, which he took over from Chifley. Both were among Curtin's ablest ministers and the change emphasised the attention and detailed planning given by the Government, long before hostilities ended, to the difficult transition back from war to peace. After the election much more energy was devoted to this task, but of course winning the war remained the first priority. Although final Allied victory, as we have seen, became increasingly obvious from the end of 1942, there were many sacrifices and difficulties before it was achieved.

BLAMEY, MACARTHUR AND VICTORY IN THE PACIFIC

Some of the difficulties sprang from personal and national friction in the alliance, between MacArthur and Blamey and between Australian and American troops. Both men were extremely ambitious, strong-willed, capable soldiers, but they had little else in common. MacArthur was a tall, handsome patrician with an unequalled gift for 'public relations', for presenting himself and his policies in a favourable, even a theatrically glowing light. Blamey was a coarse-grained, stocky plebeian, forceful and dominating but quite unable, indeed unwilling, to conciliate the feelings of others. Born at Lake Albert near Wagga Wagga in 1884, seventh child of a battling farmer and drover, Thomas Albert Blamey was taught in the infants' class at the Wagga state school by Mary Cameron, better known in later years as Dame Mary Gilmore, poet, nationalist and radical. Always ambitious, he worked hard and became a student-teacher at Lake Albert. Also living in his parents' house at this time, as a boarder and friend, was Louis Stone, future author of *Jonah*. Though a tough fist-fighter, horseman and practical bushman, young Blamey also knew much of 'Banjo' Paterson and some of Kipling by heart. With this background it is not surprising that he grew up with, and retained all his life, an intensely Australian nationalist outlook. He it was who prompted Fadden, during the latter's brief Prime Ministership, to have the garrison of 'Tobruk rats' relieved. The son of good Methodist parents, he grew up also as a teetotaller and lay-preacher. Considering that the New South Wales Department of Public Instruction was too slow to recognise his abilities, he resigned in 1903 and took ship to the West to teach for three more years in the Fremantle Boys state school. In 1906 he won by competitive examination a lieutenant's commission in the Cadet Instructional Staff of the Australian Military Forces, then being established by Deakin's second Government. His military career had begun.

In Melbourne he married, continued to work furiously at his profession and, at the end of 1911, won the solitary place available annually to an Australian officer at the Quetta Staff College in India. There the bush-bred Methodist boy learnt that gentlemen, particularly military gentlemen, should drink alcohol, smoke tobacco and perhaps indulge in other dissipations frowned on by the Church. Blamey enjoyed them and learnt to excel his brother officers in these areas also. From Quetta he was ordered to England for further experience, worked in the War Office for a time, but joined the First Division of the First A.I.F. in Egypt in December 1914. He served with distinction in Gallipoli and in France, becoming by the end of the war a brigadier-general and Monash's right-hand man as Chief of the General Staff to the Australian Army Corps.

In peace, as head of the police force in the State of Victoria, he became involved in scandals which besmirched his reputation ever afterwards. First, he habitually broke the law it was his duty to enforce by drinking openly with friends in fashionable hotels long after the six o'clock closing time. Second, he — or a man in possession of his police-badge number 80 — was found in a brothel during a raid by three of his own constables. Blamey swore that the badge was missing from his possession for two days but one of his senior officers was equally adamant that he had seen it on Blamey's desk during an interview a few hours before the raid. The three constables, whose prospects depended on Blamey's goodwill, swore the man in the brothel was not he. Notwithstanding the scandals, he was knighted in 1935, but then forced to resign in 1936 for having lied in the witness box before a Royal Commission. Most people thought his career was finished, but such was his military reputation that he was appointed by Casey, who had served under him in France, and by Menzies, to command the Sixth Division of the Second A.I.F. when war broke out. Appointments to command of the entire Australian expeditionary force, and then of all Allied land forces in the South West Pacific Area, followed in due course. Curtin, who came to trust and support Blamey against all criticism for his soldierly abilities, once conceded that he was 'a good hater'. He was hated by many in return and was generally unpopular with the troops he led, but he was given grudging respect and obeyed implicitly. The record shows that the confidence of those who appointed him was not misplaced.

Tough as he was, Blamey had to obey the orders of his commanding officer, the 'Supremo', as MacArthur was often called; while the latter did not, in some respects, obey the orders of his commanding officer on the other side of the Pacific. When the South-West Pacific Area command was established General Marshall, in the United States, ordered MacArthur to establish an 'integrated' command structure with Australian and American officers working in a single team at his headquarters. Blamey tried to co-operate but MacArthur ignored his instructions, surrounding himself entirely with American officers whose first loyalty was to him personally. Until the last year or so of the war Australian land forces in the area greatly outnumbered American ones and Blamey was supposedly in charge of all Allied troops. For the first few months, when there were virtually no front-line American troops in the area and Australian soldiers stopped and turned back the Japanese offensive in Papua and New Guinea, he was; but as soon as American troops began to arrive in significant numbers, Blamey was their commander only in military legal fiction. MacArthur smoothly explained that they constituted a special task force responsible directly to him, and there was nothing that Blamey or the Australian Govenment could do about it. Not only that, but as supreme commander MacArthur alone decided where the Australian troops under Blamey and the American troops under his own orders should be deployed. He enforced a kind of military *apartheid* under which the Australians were given the unspectacular, but often gruelling and bloody, tasks of liquidating innumerable Japanese pockets of resistance in New Guinea and the East Indies while the Americans, generally speaking, were given the more glorious and spectacular assignment of pushing forward the 'front' by making the first landings on Japanese-held islands far to the north. It is hardly surprising that tension existed between the American and Australian commanders throughout the war: it is perhaps surprising, given Blamey's temperament, that relations remained correct enough not to destroy the co-operation necessary for victory.

The same may be said of relations between American service personnel generally and Australians, whether in the services or not. Nearly everyone was unfeignedly glad of American material and moral help. Thousands of enduring friendships — and hundreds of marriages — were made, and yet there was increasing friction, especially evident between American and Australian servicemen on leave, over rates of pay, female favours, and what seemed to many the privileged position of the Americans. The worst-paid U.S. private soldier was, in terms of real purchasing power, about twice as well off as his Australian counterpart. His uniform was smart and well cut, quite unlike the drab, baggy jungle-greens of the Australian soldier. His rations were vastly more palatable and his luxuries more available. For instance, ten shillings Australian would buy a carton of 200 good cigarettes in an American services canteen — to which Australians, naturally, had no access. In their own canteens a single packet of twenty cigarettes of inferior quality cost two shillings and sixpence. Taxi-drivers in search of lavish tips understandably refused to pick up their own countrymen, or women, if an American was in sight. The same could be said of many Australian 'good-time girls'. Ill-natured rumours and jokes began to circulate, such as: 'There's only three things wrong with the Yanks — they're over-paid, over-sexed and over here'.

By November 1942 widely hated American Military Policemen were breaking up about twenty fights a night in Brisbane. On 26th of that month occurred the biggest, though by no means the first or the last, brawl between troops in base areas. In what became known as 'the Battle of Brisbane' a mob of three or four thousand Australians, mostly soldiers on leave, attacked and besieged an American 'PX Store', or Army canteen, and its occupants. One Australian soldier was shot dead and about twenty were more or less seriously injured on each side, all the American casualties being Military Policemen. Censorship naturally suppressed any reporting of the affair, but rumour spread exaggerated accounts of this deplorable 'battle' throughout both armies and the nation.

Meanwhile the real battle continued in New Guinea and the islands to its east, north and west, very little affected by the petty jealousies and brawling between the Allied armies in base areas. Fighting in the Pacific War was peculiarly savage and bloody, because of the cruelty and fanatical capacity for self-sacrifice of the Japanese troops. In every war propaganda accuses the enemy of cruelty to prisoners-of-war and other atrocities and there are always, on both sides, some examples of such conduct which can be magnified and multiplied to give plausibility. In this war, particularly in its early stages, the Japanese forces did habitually ill-treat and murder prisoners. For example, on 20 January 1942 Rabaul in New Britain was attacked by 120 Zero fighter-planes. The entire defending force of eight obsolete Wirraways was shot down in as many minutes. Three days later the Japanese landed in overwhelming force and drove back the defending garrison of some 700 Australians. One group of 150 formally surrendered to a Japanese naval landing party. They were bound hand and foot and cold-bloodedly butchered by Japanese marines who used them for 'bayonet practice'. Three survived to reach home with the evidence. After the fall of Singapore, twenty-one fugitive Australian nurses were murdered in the same way on Banka Island: and so on, and on. Knowledge of such practices encouraged Allied troops to fight to the death, rather than surrender, even when all hope was gone. Perhaps partly because they expected Allied soldiers to do as they had been done by, enemy troops usually fought to the death too.

Disease, climate and terrain were enemies almost as formidable as the Japanese. Most of the fighting took place in stifling, humid, jungle country, criss-crossed by precipitous mountains, the ground usually a quagmire from torrential tropical rain. Roads of any kind were virtually non-existent. Almost perpetually wet, men had to claw and hack their individual paths through the tangle of vegetation. They fell ill in thousands and tens of thousands with malaria, dengue fever, dysentery, tropical ulcers and a hundred other painful diseases. Often the nearest hospital or medical aid post was several weeks' journey distant. Corporal John Metson, a Victorian who was shot through the ankle in a skirmish, refused his mates' offers to carry him and crawled along with them for three weeks through the muddy jungle, till they reached a native village. When the rescue party arrived, it found that a Japanese patrol had been there first and murdered the helpless man. Throughout the whole campaign in New Guinea many more men were incapacitated by illness than by enemy action, but the long push back continued. A series of outlandish place-names — Melanesian, German, Dutch, French and Malay — stretching along the northern coast of New Guinea and into the East Indies, became familiar household words in Australia: Buna, Gona, Sananada, Lae, Salamaua, Finschafen, Sattelberg, Moratai, Bougainville, Wewak, Tarakan and Balikpapan. During 1944 American industrial might provided the Allies with overwhelming superiority at sea and in the air, and to that extent the going became easier.

It became easier still, at least psychologically speaking, with the end of the war in Europe, when the Third Reich capitulated to Eisenhower in the West and to Zhukov in Berlin itself on 8 May 1945. All major Australian army units had been brought back to fight the war with Japan by 1943, but thousands of individual soldiers and some small units remained in the Middle East or Europe, attached to formations of British troops. In the same way, although nearly all Australian naval craft had long been serving in the South West Pacific area, about 500 officers and men were attached to British ships in other waters. Relative to the total strength of each of the three services, there were throughout the war far more Australian airmen and aircraft fighting in the European and Middle-East theatres of war than there were soldiers or sailors. R.A.A.F. men took part in the Battle of Britain, the bombing raids on Germany, the bombing of submarines in the ocean approaches to Britain, covering the Normandy landings on D-day and in the final assault on the Third Reich. In the war against Germany and Italy 5116 R.A.A.F. personnel were killed in action or died as prisoners-of-war as against 1331 in the war against Japan. So there was direct personal cause for joy in thousands of Australian homes when the fighting ended in Europe, and in many thousands more whose inmates could look forward to the return of prisoners captured by the enemy years before in Greece, Crete, Libya or Syria. Best of all was the universal anticipation that, with Germany crushed, victory over Japan could not be far away.

It came three months later, but the Prime Minister of Australia who had done something to bring it about, did not live to see it. Throughout his term in office he had slept little, agonising over the responsibilities he carried and over the validity of every decision he had to make. Those who knew him best said the strain was greatest after his fight with Churchill, while the Sixth and Seventh A.I.F. Divisions were at sea on their way home. In June when it was obvious that he was gravely ill, his friend James Scullin, still a devout Catholic, came to see him and said: 'I know you don't believe much in God, Jack, but don't you think it's time you made peace with your Maker?' 'I've seen it through like this so far', replied Curtin, 'and I'm not going to change now'.[9] The person who saw most of him in his last days was a personal friend who happened to be a Presbyterian minister. Curtin died on 5 July, the day the British people went to the polls to vote into power the Attlee Labour Government. His body was taken back to Western Australia for burial in the Karrakatta cemetery near his Cottesloe home.

[9] Kevin Perkins, *Menzies, Last of the Queen's Men*, Adelaide, 1968, p.147.

On 6 and 9 August President Truman authorised the dropping of atomic bombs on Hiroshima and Nagasaki, a step inspired more by what he saw as the need to impress his Soviet ally, than to defeat his Japanese enemy. Threatened with more atomic devastation, Japan capitulated on 14th and formally signed the surrender documents at a ceremony on board U.S.S. *Missouri*, anchored in Tokyo Bay, on 2 September 1945. The war, which had made racism a dirty word, was over. Blamey signed on behalf of Australia, but one morning a week later conducted a purely Australian-Japanese ceremony on the island of Morotai in the Moluccas where he received the surrender of Lieutenant-General Teshima, commander of the Second Japanese Army which had been operating in Australia's near north. Accompanied by six Japanese officers, Teshima was led to a table surrounded by ranks of Australian troops seven deep. Blamey arrived at eleven o'clock and both men signed the document. Then, while the Japanese stood to attention, the Wagga drover's son, whom Curtin had described as 'a good hater', said:

> In receiving your surrender I do not recognise you as an honourable and gallant foe, but you will be treated with due but severe courtesy in all matters. I recall the treacherous attack on our ally, China . . . I recall the treacherous attack made upon the British Empire and upon the United States of America in December 1941, at a time when your authorities were making the pretence of negotiating peace. I recall the atrocities inflicted upon the persons of our nationals as prisoners of war and internees, designed to reduce them by punishment and starvation to slavery.
>
> In the light of these evils, I will enforce most rigorously all orders issued to you, so let there be no delay or hestitation in their fulfilment at your peril.[10]

Many Australians winced at the vindictiveness of the speech, but more applauded it. The war against Japan had been a deeply traumatic national experience. Nevertheless, as the future was to show, it had much more positive effects than the Australian experience of World War I. First, as with other western countries in the grand alliance, though not with the U.S.S.R., the destruction of the nation's most promising young men was not nearly so great. In all three services fewer than 30 000 men were killed in action as against the 60 000 deaths in the Great War. Relative to total population in each case, this meant that Australian casualties were little more than a quarter as heavy. Second, the rehabilitation of servicemen and women into the civilian community was very much

[10] John Hetherington, *Blamey, Controversial Soldier*, Canberra, 1973, p.375.

more intelligently planned and successfully carried out. Third, the victory celebrations ushered in an era of nearly thirty years of full employment, economic expansion and prosperity, which contrasted graphically with the troubled 1920s and the depressed 1930s. Finally, Britain's inability to help in 1942 fractured the materially, morally and politically dependent role which the nation had so long adopted. Events challenged Australians to think more realistically about their relationship with the rest of the world, and particularly with their Asian neighbours. They responded by assuming a greater degree of national self-awareness and responsibility for their own destinies. Those to the left of centre sought to build, within the American alliance Labor had negotiated, more self-confident, independent, home and foreign policies: many, but not all, of those on the right, after recovering from the trauma of severance from their unconditional dependence on the maternal breast of Great Britain, tended simply to substitute for it the avuncular bosom of the United States.

Chapter 9

RECONSTRUCTION AND REFORM

c. 1945—1949

Chifley and post-war reconstruction — The 1946 election and the new immigration policy — Evatt and foreign policy — Boom and expansion — Banking, Communists, 'Groupers' and the return of the Liberals

CHIFLEY AND POST-WAR RECONSTRUCTION

When John Curtin died on the eve of victory, most people thought that 'the Doc', as he was called by his friends, would be chosen by the A.L.P. parliamentary Caucus as his successor. Evatt was far better known, both in Australia and abroad, than any other possible candidate, but his party colleagues had other ideas. Some resented him as a newcomer to the political battleground where they had fought for so long, and some distrusted him as a middle-class intellectual aspiring to the leadership of what they considered a working-class party; but all were in a position to know, far better than the general public, the strengths and weaknesses of all candidates. After the event, most observers agreed that they were right when, on 13 July 1945, they chose as leader of their party, and so of the nation, the man who had been Treasurer since the Labor Government had come to power in 1941.

Joseph Benedict Chifley, son of an Irish-Australian blacksmith, was born at Bathurst, New South Wales in 1885. Educated first in a small bush state school and then for two years with the Patrician Brothers at Bathurst, he took a job as a cashier's assistant at 15 and as a Government Railways shop-boy two years later. Tall, tough and rangy as a young man, he played Rugby Union football well enough almost to be selected as a member of the Australian team which toured Britain in 1908. He also studied monetary and economic theories deeply enough to make his knowledge of such matters a source of wonder to permanent officers of the Commonwealth Treasury when he became their minister. From his youth onwards he was an active member of the A.L.P. and of the trade-union movement. We have already noted his victimisation in the great railway strike of 1917. Throughout his life he was invariably loyal to the official Labor Party and against the schismatics, whether of the right or the left, who did so much to weaken it. He did more than any other individual, including Curtin, to restore party unity in New South Wales in 1936 after the Lang 'split', and to have 'the Big Fella' himself expelled from the A.L.P. in 1939. Dignified, yet approachable and homely in manner, 'Chif' was probably better loved than any other Australian Prime Minister. Apart from Jack Lang, even his political enemies usually held him in considerable personal affection. Despite his easy-going attitude to others, he displayed an iron will in pursuit of his party's policies and an even-tempered mastery of himself — and the situation — in the face of no matter what hysteria or provocation from opponents. He was an extremely effective platform speaker, despite a 1935 campaign against Lang in his own bailiwick of Auburn, which left Chifley's vocal chords, in a medical specialist's opinion, in 'the hopeless condition of worn-out leather'. Utterly unaffected, direct, almost self-deprecating in manner, with a harsh, but oddly pleasing gravel-voice, he impressed by his sincerity and by the use of extraordinarily apt but home-spun imagery as when, for example, he observed that for the Dutch to try to re-impose their rule on the 70 000 000 Indonesians by force would be 'like poking a stick into water'.

The Chifley Government's most urgent task was dismantling the war-machine and finding congenial jobs in the peacetime economy for the hundreds of thousands of service personnel. That it was done so well was largely due to the forward planning carried out by the previous Curtin Government from the very moment when the tide of war had turned decisively in favour of the Allies, in December 1942. It will be remembered that in that month Chifley himself had been made first ministerial head of the new Department of Post-War Reconstruction. Nevertheless, there were many difficulties to be overcome or circumvented. Chief of these was the old bugbear of all federal governments — the severe constitutional limitation of their powers. While the war lasted the Commonwealth could do almost whatever it thought necessary under the Defence power, but reorganising the country on a peacetime basis would take years, during which the federal Government would be able to exercise only its normal, restricted peacetime functions.

In a demonstration of the triumph of hope over experience Evatt, as Attorney-General, in February 1944 brought forward a Bill to seek by referendum fourteen additional Commonwealth powers. They were power over rehabilitation of servicemen and women, employment and unemployment, companies, monopolies, marketing, prices and profiteering, distribution of goods, air transport, uniform railway gauges, overseas borrowing, exchange and investment, national works, Aborigines, family allowances and national health. During debate on the Bill, Evatt added three more proposals: that freedom of speech and of religion should be expressly guaranteed in the Constitution and that any regulations made under the new powers could be disallowed by resolution of *either* House of the Commonwealth Parliament. Finally the powers were sought for five years only from the end of the war. Few electors thought they understood the implications of all the powers asked for and fewer still felt certain that they wanted to grant *all* of them, but the ballot paper did not allow a choice: it demanded yes or no to the whole package. With the honourable exception of P. C. Spender, nearly all Opposition politicians, State and federal, opposed the granting of powers because they feared that a post-war Labor Government would use them to 'socialise' the country. Whatever chance the electors had of understanding the issues was considerably lessened by the quite extraordinary degree of obfuscation and downright lying engaged in by Opposition spokesmen. The referendum was defeated by a decisive majority when put to the people in August 1944.

The seventeenth Commonwealth Parliament passed many other measures concerned with post-war reconstruction rather than with the war itself, some before the end of hostilities and some soon afterwards. From 1944 Commonwealth payments were made to unemployed people and to anyone prevented by sickness from working. In the same year the Government took the first step towards the establishment of a free national health scheme such as that set up in 1946 by the Attlee Government in Britain. Certain medicines prescribed by doctors and dispensed by chemists were to be provided free of charge to all, the Government footing the bill; but even this modest step towards a national health service was bitterly opposed by most doctors. Some of them in Victoria arranged to have the legislation challenged in the High Court where it was duly disallowed in November 1945. The Hospital Benefits Act of 1945 met a happier fate. It subsidised from Commonwealth revenue State public hospitals on condition that they provided certain services gratis.

At war's end the Government set out to rationalise — and nationalise — interstate air transport. Setting aside privately owned motor cars, it was obvious that air travel was rapidly replacing sea and rail transport as the major means of moving passengers about the continent and many people thought that the airways should be a government-owned utility as railways had been for nearly a century. The National Airlines Act of 1945 established Trans-Australia Airlines, a corporation wholly owned by the Commonwealth Government, to conduct interstate air services. The same Act set up an Airlines Commission to service aerodromes and control civil aviation generally, and it provided for the closure of privately owned interstate airline companies. These naturally challenged the legislation in the High Court, which disallowed the last-mentioned provision of the Act under section 92 of the Commonwealth Constitution providing for absolute freedom of interstate trade and commerce. Two years later in 1947 the Government nationalised Australian overseas air-services by simply buying up all shares in Qantas. In 1949 an Australian Shipping Board was authorised to re-establish a Government shipping line.

The structure of the coal-mining industry was also changed. In 1945 the great bulk of Australia's coal was dug in New South Wales in three areas known as the Northern (Hunter River Valley), Western (Lithgow) and South Coast (Port Kembla region) fields. Since the coal had first been hewn by convicts in the 1830s, industrial relations in the industry had been appallingly bad. 'Trouble' on the coal fields, as we have seen, played a considerable part in bringing down the Bruce-Page, the Scullin, and the Fadden Governments; and, despite the efforts of Communist and some other left-wing union leaders to step up production for the war-effort, strikes and other troubles continued to plague the industry. The accident that Labor Governments held office in New South Wales from 1941 to 1965 made it possible for federal Labor to influence the situation. Between 1944 and 1946 the Commonwealth and State Governments co-operated in setting up a Joint Coal Board and in carrying out other changes which gave to the industry (as far as New South Wales was concerned) much of the substance, though not the legal form, of nationalisation.

The new Prime Minister, it will be remembered, had written a minority report as a member of the 1935 Royal Commission on Banking. Like most of his followers he had never forgotten what he regarded as the most important lesson of the great Depression — that the national Government, and not a number of private bankers, however enterprising, should be in control of the nation's economy. Accordingly he lost no time, once the war was over, in passing laws to give the government of the day control over the Commonwealth Bank and banking policy generally. In 1945 two Acts established the Commonwealth Bank as the nation's Central Bank which, however, was also to carry on all kinds of general banking business on a competitive basis. The Commonwealth Bank Board, which had so plagued Scullin and Theodore, was abolished. Instead the Bank was placed under a single Governor, assisted by an *advisory* board of Government and Bank officials, and responsible to the Treasurer of the day for carrying out general Government policy. 'Private' banks were compelled by law to deposit a proportion of their reserves with the Central Bank and to charge rates of interest determined by it. Finally all Commonwealth, State and local governments, and their instrumentalities, were compelled to bank with the Commonwealth or State Government banks. This last provision was immediately challenged by the Melbourne City Council and, nearly two years later, found invalid by the High Court. Nevertheless, what was left of the legislation did place control of national financial policies, for the first time, firmly in the hands of the elected government.

The other 'lesson' of the Depression years, burnt into the minds of Labor voters and indeed of most Australians, was the tragedy of unemployment, underlined by the paradox of poverty in the midst of plenty. Chifley and his supporters were preoccupied, not just with getting the soldiers, sailors, airmen and women in the auxiliary services back to work, but with ensuring that there was, as far as possible, congenial and productive work for all. As it happened, this was no problem in the post-war period. Concentration of national energies on the war-effort had necessarily brought about shortages in civilian goods and services of all kinds: so much so that rationing of petrol and some other essential commodities continued even for some years after Japan's surrender. It is true, for example, that scarcely a single dwelling-house, block of flats, shop, or any other building except those directly geared to war purposes, had been built in the whole of Australia for over four years; and existing buildings were sadly in need of paint and repairs. Yet with demobilization came scores of thousands of marriages, postponed till 'after the war', and a corresponding demand for homes. Many young couples bought a block of land, pitched a tent on it and set out gradually to build some sort of dwelling for themselves and their children. Others, in desperation, 'squatted' in empty, disused or derelict buildings, while looking round for something better. Most crowded into temporary accommodation shared with relatives or friends.

At first there were equally severe shortages in many other areas — in civilian clothing, luxury goods like alcoholic drinks, and consumer durable goods like refrigerators, washing machines and motor cars, for example. The problem of government was not to find jobs for men and women but to find enough people for the jobs crying out to be done. For the first time since the depression of the 1890s in eastern Australia, there was a state of really full employment; or, as some employers sourly thought, of 'over employment'. Prices and wages rose, accelerating the inflationary spiral which had been gaining momentum through the war years despite government efforts to control it. It was obvious that the sooner people could be got back into the workforce the sooner would shortages be alleviated and, perhaps, inflation checked by increasing production of commodities.

So, sighing with relief at the thought of being their own people again, men and women poured out of the services faster than after the Great War, but not as haphazardly. Every serviceman and woman was interviewed by a vocational guidance officer and given the choice of a wide range of occupations, for all of which free or subsidised training or re-training, was provided. Almost as an incidental part of the rehabilitation programme the Commonwealth Government entered the field of education for the first time. A Commonwealth Office of Education and a Universities Commission, responsible for supervising free tertiary educational courses for ex-service men and women, were established. They were responsible also for disbursing Commonwealth funds for universities to the States and the universities themselves and for supervising the new Commonwealth Scholarship scheme, under which many thousands of bright children, previously disqualified from a university education by the poverty of their parents, were given free tuition and reasonable living allowances while they obtained their degrees. By an Act of 1946 the Government also established at Canberra the Australian National University, with special responsibilities and generous endowments for post-graduate study and research. In a rare demonstration of inter-party co-operation, this massive Commonwealth move to improve tertiary education in Australia was supported by most Opposition members in Canberra. During the last years of the war Menzies had re-established his leadership of the conservative forces, giving to them in the process another new (or revived) name and a new 'image', if not really a new policy. The U.A.P. was dissolved and reconstituted as the Liberal Party. Its leader's greatest claim to liberality with a small 'l' was probably the warm support he gave on this occasion, and continued to give when he returned to power, to the growth of Australian universities.

One of Menzies' great political assets was the ability to keep on learning from his mistakes. Two controversies rocked the world of art and letters at this time but, cooled by his unfortunate sally into the battle over an Australian academy of art some years earlier, the leader of the Opposition kept out of them. When he died in 1919, J. F. Archibald, founder and editor for many years of the Sydney *Bulletin*, had bequeathed two notable gifts to his countrymen. One, in Sydney's Hyde Park, was the magnificent Archibald Fountain, symbolising the friendship in World War I between France and Australia: the other was the prestigious Archibald Prize for the best portrait painted in Australia each year. Entries usually close on the last day of the year and the best pictures are exhibited in the following months. Early in 1944 the prize was awarded to William Dobell for his portrait of a fellow artist, Joshua Smith. Modernists thought it a magnificent painting: many traditionalists thought it a disgraceful daub. Some of the latter felt so keenly about the matter that they took legal action to prevent the award being made, on the ground that Archibald's will specified a portrait but that Dobell's picture was, at best, a cartoon. Surprisingly, perhaps, Mr Justice Roper of the New South Wales Supreme Court decided that the work was a portrait; but the furore created a great deal more interest in art than had been usual in the Australian past, and this newly awakened public concern with art did not die away with the controversy.

At the same time the Australian literary world was stimulated to roars of laughter, but also to more critical and creative activities, by what came to be known as the 'Ern Malley hoax'. A young South Australian publicist and poet, Max Harris, and a Melbourne patron of the arts, John Reed, published from Adelaide an *avant-garde* cultural periodical called *Angry Penguins*. In 1944 a special issue was devoted to the posthumous poetry of one Ern Malley, an unknown motor-mechanic and insurance peddler who had died in Sydney in the previous July of 'Graves' disease'. The verse showed, wrote Harris, that the dead man had been 'a poet of tremendous power, working through a disciplined and restrained kind of statement into the deepest wells of human experience'.[1] It was then revealed that 'Ern Malley' had never existed and that his verse was nonsense, 'consciously and deliberately concocted' by two young poets in the army, to test whether some of those who championed *avant garde* verse could tell the difference between genuine poetry and 'Ern Malley's' certified rubbish. One of the hoaxers was James McAuley, the radical song-writer of the early war period. After the war, he was converted to Catholicism and became Professor of English in the University of Tasmania. While remaining a distinguished poet, he became a pillar of the traditionalist Catholic right, as conservative in politics as he had been radical in his youth.

These controversies, which made headline news throughout the country, reflected the exuberance of the arts at this time, so different from the corresponding period after World War I. In both prose and poetry ex-servicemen produced a good deal of first-rate work, springing directly from their wartime experiences. Eric Lambert's *Twenty Thousand Thieves* gave a moving soldier's eye-view of the war in the North African desert, while his second novel, *The Veterans*, like 'David Forrest's' *The Last Blue Sea*, did the same for New Guinea. Most of these 'war books' were not published until the early 1950s. Tom Hungerford, Eleanor Dark and Katharine

[1] *Angry Penguins*, Autumn 1944, p.2.

Susannah Prichard were other distinguished novelists of the period. In addition to McAuley and A. D. Hope, Judith Wright, R. D. Fitzgerald, Kenneth Slessor, Douglas Stewart, John Manifold and David Martin all achieved national, and some of them international, fame in poetry. Like the great painters of the time, Russell Drysdale, Sidney Nolan, Arthur Boyd and Dobell himself, to go no further, they were inspired largely, though not exclusively, by the great myths of the Australian landscape and the Australian past.

Two journals of cultural criticism, which also carried much original creative work, *Southerly* and *Meanjin*, had been first published in 1939 and 1940 respectively. In the past scores, even hundreds, of such journals had been published for a few months or years and then been seen no more: but these two survived newsprint rationing and other extraordinary difficulties of the war years. By the end of the decade it was clear that they had come to stay. Despite this cultural renaissance, 'wowserism' and censorship continued to flourish — more vigorously than anywhere else in the English-speaking world, except perhaps for the Republic of Eire. The only important Australian play of the 1940s, Sumner Locke-Elliott's *Rusty Bugles*, was temporarily banned in 1948 because the soldier characters used on the stage 'the great Australian adjective', bloody. At one performance of this play an incident highlighted the unaffected simplicity still common in most areas of Australian life — and in Chifley's character. Ten minutes before the curtain went up, the theatre managers discovered the Prime Minister quite unattended, shuffling along in the queue to buy his ticket.

However great the post-war educational and cultural growth, it occurred inevitably, in a field which absorbed the energies of only a minority of ex-service personnel. Most men and women took up trades or professions ranging all the way from brick-laying or crane-driving to medicine or becoming air-hostesses. No matter what work a returned soldier wanted to take up there was, providing he was capable of benefiting from it, free training available to him under the rehabilitation scheme. The obsessive belief which had bemused all past generations of Australians, faith in the virtue and importance of 'going on the land', at last lost some of its force. Relative to the numbers involved in World War I, very many fewer men wished to become farmers, graziers, or orchardists, and the federal and State governments were less willing to spend big sums in financing large-scale land settlement schemes. Those who did take up rural work were better selected, better trained, more generously assisted in the initial stages and, on the whole, vastly more successful than had been the soldier settlers after World War I.

The question of preference in employment opportunities for ex-service people, versus preference for trade unionists, proved much less divisive than it had done twenty-five years earlier. The Commonwealth Government passed laws which gave preference to servicemen for a seven-year period while at the same time safeguarding the jobs of only partially trained tradesmen, who had been accepted by the unions under pressure of the war emergency, or who were ex-servicemen given short 'crash-courses' in the trade concerned. Yet much of this legislation was unnecessary. It generated less political heat than of yore simply because there was no unemployment but rather a labour shortage. Preference in employment became somewhat irrelevant when there were more jobs than men to fill them. The Government also established a nationwide Commonwealth Employment Service to help in placing men in the most suitable jobs. Another Act authorised the payment of a generous gratuity, proportionate to the length of service, to all discharged men and women to aid them in re-establishing themselves in civil life.

The desperate housing shortage was also alleviated by government action, though not fast enough for those sharing a house 'temporarily' with a father- or mother-in-law. The Commonwealth and State Housing Agreement Act of 1945 provided massive Commonwealth funds to State governments, which in turn established Housing Commissions to build houses for rental, or sale at low interest rates, to ex-servicemen and to other classes of persons in urgent need of homes. In the debate on the Bill the Liberal and Country Parties predictably argued that a larger proportion of the houses, than that proposed by the Government, should be sold rather than rented. J. J. Dedman, the extremely capable Minister for Post-War Reconstruction, was provoked into saying that the Government was 'concerned to provide adequate and good housing for the workers . . . not . . . with making the workers into little capitalists'.[2] Since most workers wanted nothing more than to be made into 'little capitalists', at least in so far as home ownership was concerned, the Opposition seized on the remark with delight. Some conservatives were still quoting it thirty years later in a 1975 debate on housing, as evidence of the sinister socialist intentions of all Labor governments.

THE 1946 ELECTION AND THE NEW IMMIGRATION POLICY

A few months before the election the Government introduced three Constitution Alterations Bills to the Parliament. The first asked the

[2] *C.P.D.*, vol. 185, p.6265.

electors for Commonwealth power to organise marketing of primary products, notwithstanding any implications of section 92 of the Constitution. The second sought power to regulate 'terms, and conditions of employment'. The High Court decision of November 1945 having placed in doubt the legality of all Commonwealth pension and social service schemes, the third Bill sought specific power over pensions and social services of all kinds including medical, dental and hospital benefits. The Liberals opposed the first Bill while the Country Party, though dubiously, supported it. All Opposition members opposed the second and, with only two or three exceptions, supported the third. At the referenda, held concurrently with the election, the first two proposals were very narrowly defeated. The majority of the people voted 'Yes', but there was a 'No' majority in three of the smaller States — Queensland, South Australia and Tasmania. The 'social services' proposal, not surprisingly, was carried by large majorities everywhere.

Chifley's policy speech broadcast from Canberra on 2 September might have been mistaken for that of a conservative leader. He made few glittering promises, appealing rather to the wartime record of the Labor Governments and the successful initiation of the change-over to a peacetime economy of the year just past. He made no offer of tax concessions but promised, if the 'social services' referendum was carried, to increase pension payments and extend social services as revenue became available, beginning with the creation of a national health service including the provision of free medicines which had been disallowed by a judgment of the High Court. The conservative parties, as so often when they are in Opposition, promised an array of beguiling and 'progressive' reforms, many of the kind usually associated with Labor electioneering. Menzies for the Liberals attacked the Government for its failure to abolish strikes and industrial unrest and promised, like S. M. Bruce before him, to make strikes and lockouts illegal, to punish vigorously those who broke the law, to have all trade-union officials elected by Arbitration Court-controlled secret ballots and so on: but he also promised a 20 per cent reduction in income, company and some other forms of taxation, to pay child endowment for the first child in a family instead of only the second and subsequent children as under Labor, and to begin a contributory social service system in which there would be no means test. His profound conservatism appeared more clearly in his remarks on foreign policy. Labor's vigorous initiatives in this field were wrong, he said, because Australia should follow Britain's lead rather than develop an independent foreign policy of her own as Dr Evatt was doing. For the Country Party Fadden made what were, in Chifley's view, even more irresponsible promises. He advocated an

Mr. Chiffley and the 1946 Election

Argus, 27 September 1946

immediate cut in income tax of 28 per cent, and the immediate distribution to wheat growers of £7,000,000 held in a 'pool' to offset possible future slumps in world prices. He also demanded outright banning of the Australian Communist Party.

Surprisingly, perhaps, the electorate responded positively to Chifley's low-key campaign. The A.L.P. was returned to power in both Houses, this being up to 1974 the only occasion on which it won two federal elections in succession. In the Representatives Labor had 43 seats, the Liberals 17, and the Country Party twelve. The two remaining seats were won by Independent Labor members, one by J. T. Lang who hated Chifley personally and one by Mrs Maurice Blackburn, widow of a former Labor left-winger who had been expelled from the party in 1943. For the last time the Senate was elected under the preferential voting system, which habitually gave all the seats in a State to the major party or grouping which polled slightly better than its opponent. In 1946 the A.L.P. won 52.06 per cent of all votes cast for the Senate in Australia and a majority in every State except Queensland, where there was a swing against the Government and the Labor vote was only 42.62 per cent. Thus the Senate chamber from 1946 to 1949 contained 33 Government and only 3 Opposition members.

This being the case it was a wise and self-abnegating act for the Chifley Government to change the system of Senate voting, although the new procedures tended to produce a House in which deadlocks or very small majorities were the norm instead of the massive majorities of the past. Since 1901 the population of Australia, and the average population of each federal electorate, had doubled; but each member of parliament had still to attend to the troubles of all his constituents. In 1948 acts were passed increasing, as from the next general election, the number of 'full' members of the House of Representatives from 74 to 121. At the same time, because of the fixed constitutional provision that the Senate must contain, as nearly as is practicable, half the number of members who sit in the Representatives, the number of senators was increased from thirty-six to sixty, or ten from each State, with the old provision that half should be elected every three years, for six-year terms. As noted above, senators in future were to be elected by a very complicated proportional representation system, which gave some chance of representation to minority parties that could muster more than some 6 or 7 per cent of the total Senate votes cast in a State. In the following year the vote was given to Aboriginals who were already enfranchised in their own States or who had served in the defence forces, and the Australian Capital Territory was given an M.P. who, like the Northern Territory member, could speak on any subject but cast a vote only on ordinances affecting the Territory.

The new Cabinet was sworn in by the most inane of Australia's Governor-Generals, His Royal Highness the Duke of Gloucester, who had been nominated for the post by Curtin. He was replaced in March 1947 by the new-minted knight, Sir William McKell, a boiler-maker by trade, a lawyer by profession, a friend of Chifley and until the eve of his appointment, State A.L.P. leader and Premier of New South Wales. The Opposition parties were outraged: but McKell in office proved completely and properly impartial, and the Liberals followed the precedent some twenty years later by appointing conservative Australian politicians to the position. It is perhaps an indication of the stability and self-confidence of the federal A.L.P. at this time that the second Chifley Government was the only one in the history of Australia to last throughout a three-year parliamentary term without a Cabinet re-shuffle or a single change in the Ministry. Forde, Minister for the Army, and briefly Prime Minister, lost his seat in the election. Makin (Navy) and Beasley (Defence) retired to become, respectively, Minister to the United States and High Commissioner to the United Kingdom. The leading men in the new Cabinet were Chifley, Prime Minister and Treasurer; Evatt, Attorney-General and Minister for External Affairs; E. J. Holloway, Labour and National Defence; J. J. Dedman, Defence, Post-War Reconstruction and in charge of C.S.I.R.O.; E. J. Ward, Transport and External Territories; A. S. Drakeford, Air; and A. A. Calwell, Information and Immigration. The last-named, a future leader of the A.L.P. presided over what can best be understood as a very important change of direction in Australian immigration and racial policies.

Born in Melbourne in 1896 to Irish-Australian parents, Arthur Augustus Calwell was educated at the North Melbourne Christian Brothers' College and went to work at the age of 17 as a public servant, first in the Victorian Department of Agriculture and from 1923 onwards in the Treasury. He married and had one daughter. He joined the Labor Party as a youth and by 1931 had become President of the Victorian branch. As we have seen, he was elected from the seat of Melbourne to the federal Parliament in 1940 and attained Cabinet rank after the 'landslide' election of 1943. In many ways Calwell was absolutely typical of many A.L.P. activists of his generation. Lower middle rather than working class, a white rather than a blue-collar worker, a clerk in a secure position in government service, a good Irish Catholic though not one to follow the hierarchy if it wished to lead him out of the Labor Party, intensely loyal to reformist ideals but never a revolutionary, a good mixer at a smoke-social with a glass of beer in his hand but intensely respectable, even puritanical, in other ways, rather formal and old-fashioned in manner even as a young man, he was a lifelong opponent of any and every form of conscription for overseas military service. Tall and dignified, he spoke persuasively to friendly or polite audiences, but was easily rattled by hostile interjections, a weakness his political opponents were quick to exploit. On such occasions his voice was apt to break as he compulsively repeated a word or a phrase, in a vain effort to silence his tormentors. It may have been this habit, or the shape of his rather prominent nose, or both, that earned him the nickname of 'Cocky' Calwell. Like nearly all Australians of his generation, he believed in the White Australia Policy hardly less passionately than in his religion, yet he did more than any other single person to weaken Australian xenophobia — except perhaps for Adolf Hitler.

By their systematic murder of many millions of men, women and children not lucky enough to have been born into 'the master race', the Nazis demonstrated to the whole world the logical and actual consequence of the racist delusions which Australians, in common with most people of European descent, had entertained for so long — albeit in a less 'extreme' form. Allied propagandists were quick to make use of the Nazis' and, to a lesser extent, of the Japanese racist precepts and practices. In World War I as in previous wars generally, propaganda on each side proclaimed the enemy low and wicked because of his supposed 'racial' or genetic inferiority. Thus, to the Allies, the Germans were 'boches', 'Huns', 'square-heads' and so on. Throughout World War II Allied propaganda had an enormous effect because, for once in a while, it was absolutely true. The Nazis were said to be wicked, *not* because they were in any way inherently inferior to Englishmen, Frenchmen, Russians or Negroes, but because they preached and practised the scientifically false and morally monstrous doctrine of racism.

All over the world millions of whites, who had long actively or tacitly believed in the innate inferiority of 'coloured' peoples, began to question their assumptions. The results may be seen in the post-war liberation of Asia and Africa from white colonial rule and in the 'black revolution' for complete equality and integration in the U.S.A., Australia and other 'racially' mixed societies. Australians were also influenced, much more than in the Great War, by actual contact with foreigners. To begin with, most of the fighting was against the Japanese. However hateful and frightening they might be, it was hardly possible to consider them innately inferior in physical or mental prowess. During the war many thousands of Australian service personnel met and worked with Melanesians, Malays, Filipinos, Indians, Chinese, Indonesians, and the Dutch colonial masters of the latter people. Relations were generally very good, as they were between the civilian population at home and the thousands of war-refugees — torpedoed seamen, escapees from the Netherlands East Indies and the like — living in Australia for the duration.

Fear and hatred of foreigners then, while still widespread enough in all conscience, was unquestionably much less so than it had been in 1939. Moreover the war had frightened many people into wanting immigration on a much more massive scale than in the past. Ever since federation radicals, nationalists and a good many conservatives, had been fond of echoing 'Billy' Hughes's slogan: 'Populate or Perish'. These warnings, discounted by most easy-going citizens in the past, had just come unpleasantly close to being realised. At war's end most people needed little convincing that the greatest single need for the future defence of Australia was more Australians. It was also the greatest need, as it always had been, for national development and greater national wealth. The question was how and where to get them, and the trouble was that the A.L.P. now in power federally and in all States except South Australia, had always been implacably opposed to 'assisted' migration schemes while ever men and women in Australia lacked paid work. The trouble was too that almost everyone, but especially people in the Labor movement, had always taken it for granted that only British migrants could, or should, be helped, or even allowed to settle in Australia. No one knew the depth and extent of these traditionally held attitudes better than the Minister for Immigration, Arthur Calwell. Of course there were no unemployed for the first time in living memory: nevertheless it took great courage for a Labor minister to initiate the reversal of his party's long-held policy. Calwell grasped the nettle with both hands.

In 1946 he made an arrangement with the British Government under which ex-servicemen and their families, who wished to migrate, received free passages, and other Britons paid a trifling sum towards their fares — far less than it would have cost one member of the family to stay in a cheap boarding house for the three or four weeks during which all were on shipboard. In the following year the Australian Government arranged to pay the fares of hundreds of thousands of refugees, displaced by the war. In return these immigrants were required to work for two years, at proper award wages, not wherever they wished to, but wherever they were directed by the Government according to the needs of the national economy. The boom continued, as it happened, for over twenty years, and partly because of the continually increasing demand for goods and services stimulated by the continual flow of migrants. When the demand for passages from war refugees slackened, Calwell and his successors in following Liberal-Country Party governments made similar agreements with the governments of Holland, Italy, Greece,

Yugoslavia and other European countries. By the time the long boom period began to show signs of faltering about 1970, more than 2 500 000 immigrants had settled in Australia, over two-thirds of them from continental Europe.

Not the least of Calwell's achievements was his initiation of an intelligent and effective propaganda campaign designed to break down prejudice and secure for the newcomers, if not a universal welcome, a 'fair go' and equality of opportunity and social treatment. Those who remembered the strength of Australian xenophobia and provincialism before the war were amazed at the high degree of acceptance accorded the newcomers. Old, insulting, slang terms such as 'dago' (Italian or Southern European) and 'reffo' (refugee) went out of general use to be replaced by the blanket term 'New Australian'. Good Neighbour Councils, special A.B.C. broadcasts and English language classes were established to help their assimilation. Contemporaries lavished praise on the programme. Later generations thought far too little had been done. However, if the migrants themselves sometimes did not relate completely to their new country, their children usually did so despite continuing educational deprivations.

They contributed their share to a material prosperity greater than Australia had ever known before, but they contributed much more to cultural advance and diversification. New Australians soon joined the leading figures in business, science and technology, but also in painting, sculpture and even poetry, so much more difficult an art for people not born to a language. David Martin, a Hungarian by birth, was soon writing not only novels and criticism in supple, natural English, but poetry in the native Australian idiom. The New Australians changed the nature of society for the better. After their arrival Australia was a much more cultured, sophisticated, tolerant and varied place than it had been for so long before. The revolution in eating and drinking habits highlights the change. The ancient menu, uniform in home, restaurant and hotel, of steak or chops-and-eggs, or roast meat and vegetables, was not replaced but supplemented by most of the dishes known in Europe and Asia. People discovered that Australia produced some of the best — and cheapest — wine in the world, and they began to drink it instead of beer with meals. Wowsers, decreasing in influence, still drank water.

A high proportion of the New Australians were Catholic, or, like many Italian males, at least nominally Catholic in religion. The long-term result of the migrant inflow was to increase somewhat the Catholic percentage of the total Australian population from 20.7 per cent in 1947 to 27 per cent in 1971, and at the same time to weaken slightly in the Australian Church the century-old dominance of rigid

Irish puritanism. The Church too became less provincial and more sophisticated. Another result, certainly not foreseen by Calwell, was to strengthen for many years the electoral appeal of the Liberal and Country Parties at the expense of his cherished A.L.P. Many post-war European migrants were refugees from Communism rather than from Fascism — which lay in ruins. In their strange new country they tended to vote for the parties which made most noise about being anti-Communist. Moreover 'screening officers', attached to Australian embassies in Europe, tended to discourage the emigration of left-wingers and be more tolerant of right-wing people. Inevitably, perhaps, quite a few ex-Nazis and wartime collaborators slipped through the screening process.

General acceptance of white foreigners showed that the tide of racist passion in Australia had begun to ebb at this time — not far enough, however, to enable general acceptance of black or brown or yellow people. Calwell himself, the architect of the new, liberal immigration policy, remained to his dying day an unrepentant proponent of the White Australia Policy and, while he was the responsible minister, one who inflexibly enforced its provisions. In so far as he could he ensured that every one of the 5473 non-European wartime refugees was repatriated, forcibly if necessary. One person to remain was an Indonesian widow and mother of eight children, who married an Australian named O'Keefe. Calwell was determined to deport her, but the High Court allowed her to stay owing to a technical deficiency in the law. Probably most Australians agreed with Calwell, if not with his inflexibility in every individual case: but equally probably most young people under 25 or so did not. Colour-prejudice in Australia waned quite rapidly from this time onward, faster it seems than most professional politicians were able to recognise. Many people were disgusted rather than amused by Calwell's notorious quip, made at this time, 'Two Wongs do not make a White'.[3]

EVATT AND FOREIGN POLICY

The more sophisticated and mature immigration policy was matched by a more vigorous and sophisticated foreign policy. Indeed it is broadly true to say that, apart from the two or three years under 'Billy' Hughes at the end of World War I, Australia had never before had a foreign policy of its own as distinct from its self-appointed role of following Britain's lead in all such matters. We have seen how the Labor Government, to the scandalised 'tut-tutting' of the Opposition, made the great change in 1941-42 of

[3] *C.P.D.*, vol. 195, p.2948.

substituting for Britain the United States as our great and powerful friend and protector; but while the Government remained in power, this was not the only change. As Minister for External Affairs, Evatt pursued, within the basic framework of the American alliance, a far more positive, independent and enterprising foreign policy than had been seen before, or was to be seen again, until the re-election of Labor to power in 1972.

During the war years most of Evatt's energies were spent in working for the diversion of a greater share of Allied resources to the war in the Pacific, and for a greater Australian voice in the decision-making at war's end. By 1942 Churchill and President Roosevelt had already agreed on the strategy of beating Hitler first and nothing Evatt, MacArthur or anyone else could do, could reverse that decision; but within that over-all constraint, Evatt had some success with both aims. Before the crucial year was over he had persuaded Britain and the United States to establish in Washington, under Roosevelt's chairmanship, a Pacific War Council in which Britain and Australia spoke with equal weight. He led Australian missions to London and Washington in the same year and again in 1943. In 1944, to the anger of conservatives who held that any Australian treaty must be made through or with Britain, he entered into an agreement with New Zealand in which both powers claimed the right to be heard in any discussion of arrangements for the South-West Pacific after Japan's defeat and agreed to collaborate for the future in regional defence and to devise a common trusteeship policy for the guidance toward self-government of Pacific Island peoples. To this end the two governments established the South Pacific Commission in 1947.

It was also agreed that wartime occupation of island bases must not constitute any claim to sovereignty. This related in particular to Manus Island in the Admiralty Group to the north-east of New Guinea, of which mandated territory it formed a part. The Americans had made it into a major base which they wished to go on using after the war but Evatt would not agree because the United States refused to grant Australia reciprocal rights in some captured Japanese islands farther to the north. The party which had made the alliance with America wanted to keep it as the basis of Australian foreign policy and it did so, but it did not want a subservient, one-sided relationship of complete dependence. Evatt pursued the same line in the early years of the United Nations Organisation — that of the candid friend, basically loyal to the United States but frequently critical of specific aspects of American policy.

At the San Francisco conference, called in April 1945 to establish the United Nations Organisation, Evatt became a world-figure while poor Frank Forde, Deputy Prime Minister and the official leader of the Australian delegation, remained the same drab, ineffective politician he had always been at home. The draft charter, prepared mainly by U.S. diplomats, gave a great deal more power than Evatt (and most nations' representatives) thought proper to the great powers with permanent seats on the Security Council — the United States, Russia, Great Britain, France and China. Evatt moved 38 amendments of which 26 were adopted, in whole or in part, by the conference. He failed to remove from the charter the 'big five's' power of veto on final decisions, but succeeded in removing their proposed power to veto discussion of an issue in the General Assembly. By the time the conference was over Evatt — and Australia — had been hailed by the world's press as the champion of the small powers and of just, democratic procedures in international affairs. Most Australians were delighted to see their country presenting such an independent and progressive image on the world stage, but the Opposition, and some of those who voted for it, were appalled that Australia should presume to have any differences with the United States or Great Britain.

Opinion was similarly, though less strongly, divided about the Government's hard line towards defeated Japan. Determined that Australia's voice should be heard — and heeded, Evatt engineered the establishment of an Allied Control Council to guide MacArthur, Supreme Commander of the Allied Occupation forces. Moreover he obtained British agreement to the appointment of W. Macmahon Ball, Professor of Political Science at the University of Melbourne, as the representative on the Council of the whole British Commonwealth. Nevertheless, MacArthur the autocrat ruled Japan as he thought best, paying very little heed to the Control Council, or indeed to his own Government in the United States, just as he had gone his own way as Supreme Commander during the war. After the event it was clear that he had succeeded admirably in implementing the United States' twin objectives for the defeated enemy: to strengthen the democratic forces in Japan and to strengthen its shattered economy so as to make the country a strong bastion against Communism in the U.S.S.R. and China. At the time, Evatt and most of his countrymen agreed with the first objective but not with the second: indeed the second seemed, in a measure, to contradict the first. Memories of Japanese atrocities were too near in time and space to let most Australians take the more detached long-term view of their American friends. Evatt did succeed in having a leading Australian judge, Sir William Webb, appointed president of the international tribunal which tried and sentenced some of the more senior Japanese war criminals.

PARIS RODEO

Argus, 20 August 1946

As chairman of the United Nations Commission on Palestine, Evatt again incurred the displeasure of Australian conservatives: this time for opposing Britain, who was reluctant to give up her mandate. Evatt sought to stop the fighting but also to forward the creation of a Jewish national state. Probably Australian majority opinion agreed with his stand on this issue also. Israel was proclaimed on 14 May 1948. A few months later in September when the United Nations met for the first time in its permanent quarters in New York City, Evatt was elected President of the General Assembly. With the General Secretary, Trygve Lie of Norway, he was instrumental in easing the mounting tension which built up as a result of Russian bad faith during the crisis over the Berlin blockade. As President of the United Nations, he also protested vigorously at the Hungarian Communist Government's arranged 'trial' and imprisonment of Cardinal Mindszenty, the Roman Catholic Primate of the country. This action naturally earned him the bitter enmity of Vyshinsky, the Soviet U.N. delegate, but did nothing to mollify the malice of conservative politicians at home who continued to denounce him as a crypto-Communist or friend of Communism.

Evatt roused such passion among his opponents because in fact at this time he was so much abler, and above all more far-seeing, than they. Like Attlee and the British Labour Government of the day, Evatt and the Australian Government realised that the time when white men could go on ruling black, brown and yellow men, for what the former considered to be the latter's good, had ended. They believed that colonies like India and the Dutch East Indies should be free to govern, or mis-govern, themselves; but they also knew that, in the not very long run, it would be impossible, with no matter what application of military force, to prevent them from doing so. British and Australian conservatives had no such views. 'I have not become the King's First Minister', said Churchill in a famous phrase, 'in order to preside over the liquidation of the British Empire'. Fortunately for Britain its people did not call on him to do so. With unforced goodwill the Attlee Government organised the transfer of power to Nehru and his Indian Congress Party. Australia's good offices at this time were so much appreciated in the Indian subcontinent that the newly independent states of Pakistan and India agreed in 1949 to appoint, as arbiter of their dispute over Kashmir, Australia's most distinguished High Court judge, Sir Owen Dixon. In the same way it was fortunate for Australia that Labor was in power at this time. Her freely given friendship and encouragement to liberation movements in the emerging ex-colonial nations of southern Asia earned considerable goodwill and even dissipated some of the resentment felt at her continued adherence to the White

Australia Policy. This was shown most clearly by the Government's handling of the Dutch-Indonesian dispute, easily the most important of Australian foreign policy initiatives, both at the time and in its future consequences.

Three days after the Japanese surrender, on 17 August 1945, the Indonesian nationalists declared their independence but the Dutch Government formally refused to recognise the new republic. Having ruled the Malay archipelago since 1601 and drawn untold wealth therefrom, the Dutch stood pat on their legal right to return to their wealthy colony. Australia ineluctably was deeply involved since many thousands of diggers were stationed in the islands, and most of the Dutch colonial administrators and thousands of Indonesian seamen and other refugees were living in Australia, waiting to return. In 1942 the Government had in effect promised to help the Dutch re-establish their rule in the islands when the war ended, but doubts came with the heady air of victory. The Labor Party had traditionally supported national independence movements, like that of the Irish for example; and many Australians, probably the majority, felt that the Indonesian people were just as entitled as others to independence and self-government, especially at the end of a war fought supposedly to ensure such basic human rights. Many too, believing that the 70 000 000 Indonesians were bound to win in the end, thought it would be to Australia's interest to support their struggle and so earn the goodwill of her nearest neighbour.

While Evatt and the Government temporised, the trade-union movement acted, especially the maritime unions which had already concerned themselves with foreign policy before the war. The trade unions, many of them led by elected Communist officials like 'Big Jim' Healy of the Waterside Workers' Union, who had been wounded in France during World War I, imposed boycotts and black bans on the movement of Dutch persons or supplies in or out of Australia, while they did all they could to help the Indonesian independence movement, many of whose leading figures were among the refugees. Boycotts lasted for five years on and off and were very effective. Nearly forty Dutch ships, loaded with supplies, arms and Netherlands East Indies Government files, were completely immobilised. The Government did nothing to discourage the union boycott — much to the fury of Menzies and the conservative press, who wished to see Dutch rule restored if possible, and who sometimes tended to see the issue as primarily a matter of 'race'. On 25 September 1945 in Parliament Menzies affirmed that the Indonesian Government was simply a puppet of the Japanese led by 'the Quisling of Java', and that the Chifley Government, by not breaking the union action, was deliberately insulting a wartime ally.

'Eddie' Ward replied that the moral principle behind the union boycott was just as valid as when they had refused to load pig-iron for Japan in 1938, a *riposte* to which 'Pig Iron' Bob had no effective reply. As the dispute dragged on the Government moved more and more towards positive support of the Indonesian nationalists, who nominated Australia to sit on a U.N. conciliation committee in 1947. Fighting broke out nonetheless. As President of the United Nations Evatt did all that was possible to stop the bloodshed and bring the two sides to the negotiating table, persisting despite the most rabid Opposition attacks. In 1949 the Dutch finally recognised the full sovereignty of the Indonesian Republic. Both sides thanked Evatt for his efforts and both countries have remained generally friendly with Australia since.

Evatt also deserves credit for initiating long overdue reforms in Papua and the trusteeship Territory of New Guinea. While the war was still being fought he denounced the basic premise of all past Australian governments: that dependent territories must be made to pay for their own development — a policy which meant that, after twenty years of Australian rule, very little had been accomplished towards preparing Papua and New Guinea for self-government. Most of the inhabitants were still illiterate, some had acquired a rudimentary primary education, a few had had some secondary education, and there was not one university graduate. Too little too late it may have been, but the Labor Government did begin increasingly large subsidisation of New Guinea development. In 1939 Papua had been voted £ 45,000. In 1946-47 the corresponding figure for Papua-New Guinea was over £ 2,000,000. As Minister for External Territories, 'Eddie' Ward, devoutly hated by most white planters, authorised an ordinance fixing a maximum 44-hour week for indigenous labour and a number of other reforms. In 1949 he carred through Parliament the first legislation giving at least some semblance of representative government to the territory. Papua and Australian New Guinea were made one and placed under an Administrator assisted by an Executive Council and a Legislative Council. The latter consisted of the Administrator, 16 ex-officio public servants, 9 other nominated members, 3 from Christian missions, 3 other non-official white persons and 3 non-official indigenes, and finally 3 non-official elected members. The Administrator retained the right to veto any ordinance as did the Governor-General in Australia. The Act also established a Supreme Court and a School of Pacific Administration (in Australia) to train officers for the Papua-New Guinea Government.

As Minister for External Affairs Evatt did more for Australia's prestige and security than any other holder of that office before or since. When he was appointed in 1941 there seemed to be nothing to prevent a Japanese occupation of Australia. When he left office eight years later, firm and lasting bonds had been created with the United States. In 1941 a Department of External Affairs could hardly have been said to exist: in 1949 a large and efficient, permanent diplomatic corps had been brought into being, and a method of recruitment established which ensured that some of the country's ablest young people would be its diplomats of the future. On 1 October 1949 the People's Republic of China was proclaimed. Evatt and Chifley planned to recognize China and exchange diplomats after the federal election of 10 December — which, however, returned a Liberal-Country Party Government. But not even the resulting paranoid foreign policy of the next twenty-two years, and the lamentable folly of Australian military participation with America in the undeclared war in Vietnam, could quite cancel the goodwill built up in South East Asia.

Evatt also deserves much of the credit, or blame, for the establishment in Australia of a secret police force later known as the Australian Security Intelligence Organisation — A.S.I.O. He and Chifley were persuaded that a secret counter-espionage service was necessary and a liberal man of great integrity, Mr Justice Reed of South Australia, was appointed as Director-General of Security early in 1949. He was replaced a year later by a conservative ex-military officer, Brigadier Charles Spry, when the Liberal-Country Party Coalition had returned to power. From then onwards the organisation was better known for its efforts to hamper any kind of critical or radical thought, than for the number of spies it caught, and it helped to shatter Evatt's own career.

BOOM AND EXPANSION

At home the immediate post-war years were a time of prosperity, unparalleled in Australia's past. Despite the great expansion and diversification of secondary industry during the war, the state of the economy still depended mainly on that of the primary exporting industries, especially wheat and wool. Both commodities were in great demand because of war-caused devastation and shortages in so many other countries. In 1947 the world market price of wheat rose to fifteen shillings a bushel, more than six times what it had been in 1939, and it never dropped below that figure subsequently. Acreage sown to wheat and crop-yield increased accordingly and in 1948 the Commonwealth Government, in co-operation with the States, passed the Wheat Industry Stabilisation Act — which did just that. After so many wartime expedients and abortive attempts, a permanent wheat 'pool' was established under a Wheat Board, with power to buy wheat and sell it in another State or overseas. The Board guaranteed a minimum price to farmers. Surplus profits from good years were used — with a government subsidy if necessary — to make up the minimum payments per bushel in bad years.

Wool-growers also enjoyed unheard of prosperity in the immediate post-war years. After the long slump of the 1930s graziers thought an average price of two shillings a pound in the 1946-47 season very good, but this climbed rapidly to twelve shillings in 1950 — with choice lots realising more than £1 a pound. Such a great increase in the money supply as this caused was not without its negative aspects. Free spending by newly-rich graziers combined with the returned soldiers' and New Australians' huge demand for goods and services, helped to cause the worst bout of inflation Australia had known to that time. Throughout most of the war Chifley had managed to keep prices almost stationary, but with the loss of the second referendum seeking power to control them, prices and wages began to spiral upwards. From 1947 onwards the inflation rate reached nearly 10 per cent a year. The continuing shortage of, and the banked-up demand for, consumer goods also had an inflationary effect. Motor cars — as opposed to motor-bodies — refrigerators, washing machines, inner-spring mattresses and a host of other consumer goods were being made in Australia for the first time. So long were the waiting lists of customers wanting new Holden cars that little-used, second-hand models actually sold for more than new ones.

Only the mining industry was in the doldrums, though many miners and many New Australians found work in the much-praised Snowy River scheme. For generations many Australians had dreamed dreams, and even written books, about irrigating the dry western plains of eastern Australia by diverting the headwaters of rivers draining into the Pacific, back over the Great Dividing Range into the often dry beds of streams, draining westwards into the Murray-Darling river system or Lake Eyre. P. F. Adams, Surveyor-General of New South Wales in 1884, Ion L. Idriess, a popular novelist of the outback, J. J. C. Bradfield, the engineer who designed the Sydney Harbour Bridge and the Story Bridge across the Brisbane River, and Sir Earle Page, father of the Australian Country Party, were among those who wrote and spoke of such a plan. The Chifley Government actually began work on the Snowy River scheme in 1949. In agreement with the governments of New South Wales, South Australia, and Victoria, an Act established the Snowy Mountains Hydro-Electric Authority which set about its task at once. The headwaters of the Snowy River were to be held back in artificial lakes by a series of dams, and diverted through tunnels in the Dividing Range to the Tumut River and thence to the Murrumbidgee and Murray. Thus millions of gallons of water which ran to waste in the Pacific every year, were to be used for irrigating crops of rice, fruit, wine-grapes and so on, in the dry interior. In its fall through the tunnels the water was also to generate cheap electric power. Successive governments carried on with the scheme as planned. When finished in 1974 it delivered nearly four million kilowatts of electric power into the 'grid' connecting Melbourne, Canberra, Sydney and many country towns, increasing the total amount of power available by about 12 per cent. It also increased by about one-third the amount of water available to farmers in the Murrumbidgee irrigation area.

Chifley's policy-speech promise, to establish a scheme for the distribution of free medicines, was again frustrated by the opposition of the extremely conservative British Medical Association (Australian Branch) and by yet another adverse judgment of the High Court. National Health Acts giving the Government extensive powers to establish the scheme were passed in 1948 and 1949. Then a Pharmaceutical Benefits Act, substantially identical with the ones which had been disallowed by the earlier Court judgment, was passed. However, its validity was again challenged in the High Court which found, despite the new power over social services specifically granted to the Commonwealth by the 1946 referendum, that the proposed legislation was unlawful. The Act itself contained a clause expressly forbidding any form of military or civil conscription, and a majority of the Bench held, rather puzzlingly to the lay mind, that to compel doctors to use Commonwealth forms for prescription of free medicines was a form of 'civil conscription'.

BANKING, COMMUNISTS, 'GROUPERS' AND THE RETURN OF THE LIBERALS

Another adverse High Court decision triggered one of the greatest political wrangles in the history of Australia, the fight over Chifley's attempt to nationalise the banking system. On 13 August 1947 the Court ruled that section 48 of the 1945 Banking Act, compelling State governments and their instrumentalities to conduct their business with the Commonwealth (or a State) Bank, was invalid. This judgment really left quite unimpaired Commonwealth control, under the Act, of national financial policies: but the Prime Minister and the whole Labor movement, with their bitter memories of the great Depression, over-reacted. Chifley believed that the judgment would encourage the private banks to challenge other and more vital sections of the legislation, and he had little difficulty in persuading Cabinet that the only sure way to keep control of financial policy in government hands was to nationalise the private banks — that is, incorporate them all in the Commonwealth Bank, of course with proper protection for their share-holders, depositors, borrowers and staff. Cabinet unanimously endorsed the plan on 16 August and, without any kind of prior explanation or qualification, Chifley boldly announced the Government's intentions on the same day. Even the minority of citizens who favoured bank nationalisation shared in what had been Cabinet's initial reaction, 'complete stunned shock'.[4]

As people realised that the incredible was happening, that an Australian Labor Government was actually taking a large step towards the implementation of its professed socialist policy, the numbness gave way to jubilation in the minds of some citizens and to hysteria in the minds of others. A public opinion poll taken a year earlier had shown 32 per cent in favour of bank nationalisation, 50 per cent against and 18 per cent undecided. Needless to say practically all proprietors of newspapers, broadcasting stations and banks were among the majority. They spent lavishly on the most intense anti-government propaganda campaign ever mounted in Australia, with the possible exception of those against Lang during the Depression and against Whitlam years later in 1975. Regiments of bank clerks, most of them volunteers but some pressed men, were marshalled to attend protest meetings. The Labor movement conducted counter-demonstrations and meetings. Many swinging voters were effectively frightened into believing that Chifley, Evatt and the whole Federal Government were dupes or allies of Communism. The Government pressed on, apparently unmoved by the clamour, and the Banking Act was signed into law by Sir William McKell, the Governor-General, on 27 November 1947.

The private banks and the States of Victoria, South Australia and Western Australia immediately took steps to challenge the Act on various grounds in the High Court. Judgment was delivered on 11 August 1948, almost a year after the Cabinet meeting that had started the fight. Four of the six judges on the bench found the Act invalid, chiefly because in their view it infringed section 92 of the Commonwealth Constitution — the rock on which so much federal legislation, whether sponsored by Labor or anti-Labor parties, has been shipwrecked. Since the private banks all carried on interstate business, prohibition of private banking, their Honours held, contravened section 92's guarantee of absolute freedom of interstate

[4] L. F. Crisp, *Ben Chifley*, Melbourne, 1960, p.327.

trade. In a minority judgment Chief Justice Latham, an arch-conservative in politics before his elevation to the Bench, and Mr Justice McTiernan, an appointee of the Scullin Government, dissented. In their view a few incidental amendments would have validated the entire Act. The Government appealed to the judicial committee of the Privy Council in London. Seven law Lords began the hearing which lasted for two and a half months — a record. Evatt, whose judgment was becoming much more erratic, lectured their Lordships for twenty-two days while Barwick, for the private banks, charmed them for only nine. Two Lords died during the marathon hearing. After another two months the survivors, on 26 July 1949, upheld the High Court's decision, and then deliberated for another three months before giving the reasons for their decision — only about seven weeks before the looming federal general election.

The battle for the banks was over, but not forgotten. Most of the individuals and organisations, actively engaged in opposing the Banking Act, remained active continuously until the defeat of the Government at the polls on 10 December 1949. By the end of 1948, for instance, the associated banks had made detailed plans for the election campaign a year ahead. Twenty-five bank officials were to be freed from normal duties, in the Sydney metropolitan area alone, to spend their full time on anti-Labor propaganda work. From the time of the banking crisis onwards vast sums of money were spent in portraying the Government as a collection of ruthless socialist bureaucrats, hell-bent on the destruction of Australian liberties and the creation of a regimented society which would differ only in degree, and not at all in kind, from that of Soviet Russia. Overseas events made it easier to work on people's fears. During 1947 and 1948 Soviet pressure snuffed out tentative steps towards a degree of national independence and freedom of thought in Poland, Hungary, Czechoslovakia and most of the rest of Eastern Europe. In China the Red armies appeared irresistible, and it then seemed axiomatic to almost everybody that all Communists everywhere constituted an indivisible, menacing revolutionary force. Since Churchill's famous speech at Fulton Missouri, on 5 March 1946, sympathy for a great wartime ally had been replaced by growing fear and repugnance for the whole Soviet system. The Cold War, in short, was growing steadily colder — or hotter. Every kind of reactionary and illiberal policy was justified in the name of anti-Communism, nowhere more than in Australia except, of course, in the United States of America. And yet despite the electorate's hatred of bank nationalisation, despite inflation, and despite the continuing campaign to smear the Chifley Government with the Communist brush, public opinion polls showed that the Government regained majority support during the first half of 1949, after the banking legislation had been disallowed by the High Court. Conservatives felt that the campaign had to be stepped up: their fear of Communism was real enough. Early in 1947, Sir Raymond Connelly, Lord Mayor of Melbourne and prominent businessman, organised a proto-fascist society of ex-servicemen under the leadership of the retired General Blamey. Known simply as the Association, or the White Army, it may have had as many as 100 000 members, many of them armed, and it conducted its affairs with such secrecy that most Australians never heard of its existence, either at the time or afterwards when it disbanded, following the election of a conservative federal government. New members were told that the Association's sole aim was to be ready at all times to frustrate any Communist attempt at a *coup d'etat*.[5] But how much fire was there in this intolerable deal of smoke? What was the real strength and influence of the Australian Communist Party and its relationship with the A.L.P.?

It should first be said that there never was the remotest possibility of any Communist *coup* in Australia, or even of any being attempted, except in the fevered imaginings of some conservative citizens. True, the Australian Communist Party just after the war was stronger numerically than ever before or since. Its leaders claimed a membership of 25 000 an estimate which most certainly did not err on the side of modesty. Many of them were women and none were armed with anything more lethal than their tools of trade, perhaps a wharf-labourer's cargo-hook, a coalminer's pick or a schoolteacher's fountain pen. Most of them believed in revolution as Christians believe in eternal life, something inevitable but certainly not to be prematurely and officiously sought after for oneself. Further, in terms of popular electoral support the party's influence was negligible, and its members, like everyone else, knew it. Communist candidates never achieved more than about 3 per cent of the total vote in any general election, State or federal, and usually very much less.

Even so, the party's influence was by no means negligible in the Labor movement as a whole. Known Communists were rigidly excluded from membership of the A.L.P. but in the trade unions Communists and militant Labor men often stood together for election to positions of leadership on 'unity tickets'. In the aggregate scores of thousands of trade-union members, who had little time for Communism as a political creed, voted men and women they knew

[5] John Hetherington, *Blamey*, Canberra, 1973, pp.389-92.

to be Communists into leading union positions simply because the Communist candidates were so often dedicated and capable fighters for better pay and conditions. In this way during the early post-war period, Communists achieved leadership of several important unions — the Coal Miners, Seamen, Wharf-Labourers and Ironworkers for example, and less important ones such as the Sheet-Metal workers and the New South Wales Teachers' Federation. It is misleading to think, as alarmed conservatives did, that Communists 'controlled' these bodies. A union's officials could usually lead their members into a strike or other action seen, or believed to be, directly conducive to better working conditions, but could usually not lead them into overtly political, as opposed to industrial, strikes. It is certain that neither leaders nor led ever seriously entertained the idea of initiating a political *coup*, if only because it would have been flagrantly un-Marxist to do so in the absence of anything that looked like a revolutionary situation in Australia. For the Australian Communist Party placed much emphasis on the study of politics. Weak though it was in many ways, it tirelessly disseminated Marxist theory and radical propaganda to anyone who would listen. In the Australia of the 1940s hardly anyone interested in politics, who considered himself in any way 'progressive', could entirely escape its influence.

An ideological force working in the opposite direction was Bartholomew Santamaria's Catholic Social Studies Movement, a group of Melbourne Catholic intellectual laymen who, as young people at the University ten years before, had been stimulated by the Spanish Civil War into dedicating their considerable talents to opposing Communism at home and abroad. 'The Movement' set out to weaken Communist influence in the trade unions by what it conceived to be the methods of Communism — secrecy, total commitment and a faith that the end justifies the means. After the war 'the Movement' organised the establishment of what it called 'industrial groups', within the trade unions and within the Labor Party. Generally but not necessarily Catholic unionists, the 'Groupers' set out to expose Communist chicanery where it existed, to counteract Communist propaganda everywhere and to take over, wherever possible, the leadership of trade unions, or even of A.L.P. Branches, from Communists or from those whom they deemed to be Communist-sympathisers — often in practice anyone standing to the left of the Groupers' own position on the far right of Labor politics. By the time of the 1949 election the industrial Groupers had had a good deal of success, enough in fact to make some moderate Labor men begin to wonder whether the Grouper cure might not prove worse than the Communist disease. Most notably, leadership of the powerful Federated Ironworkers' Union had been wrested from a tough English Communist migrant, Ernie Thornton, and placed in safely non-Communist, or at least non-Stalinist, hands. Though they claimed much credit for it, this victory was by no means entirely due to the industrial groups. The Communists in this union had in fact been rigging ballots, packing mass meetings with non-union members and so on, practices not unknown in some right-wing unions for years past, but nonetheless heinous for that. It was more difficult to dislodge left-wingers from leading positions in other unions which conducted their affairs honestly. However, the major achievement of the groups was not the winning of leadership in this union or that, but their substantial contribution to the conservative campaign to discredit the federal government. Their every move helped to identify Labor with Communism in the public mind — precisely the aim of the private banks and a host of right-wing propaganda agencies that proliferated as the election approached.

The real Communists, who certainly did not want to see a Liberal-Country Party victory, nevertheless probably did more than the Groupers to bring it about by precipitating the last and most troublesome strike of the decade. On 16 June 1949 the leaders of the Miners' Federation called a stop-work meeting which accepted their recommendation for a general strike, to protest at what the militants regarded as the dilatoriness of the Coal Tribunal in considering a Federation claim for a 35-hour working week. The 40-hour week had recently been introduced by legislation in New South Wales by the Labor Government of that State, and was becoming general throughout industry. Because of accumulated wartime shortages there was virtually no reserve of hewn coal 'at grass', and heavy industry in most States still depended mainly on New South Wales black coal. Factories closed down progressively as their supplies of coal ran out and more than half a million people were made jobless in July and August. Drastic electricity rationing reminded people unpleasantly of the wartime 'brown-out'. Railway services were reduced almost to vanishing-point and domestic gas supplies for cooking were rationed to one hour a day in Melbourne and Sydney. The popular idea that the Government was unwilling or unable to deal effectively with Communism was strengthened, despite the fact that Chifley dealt with the strike more firmly than any non-Labor Government would have dared to do. Evatt rushed through Parliament a National Emergency (Coal Strike) Act freezing the Miners' funds and making illegal payment and receipt of funds to aid the strike. Several Communist and other union leaders were gaoled and finally Chifley, the striking engine-driver of 1917, took the ultimate step of sending in troops to work open-cut mines for coal to maintain essential services in hospitals and power-stations. When the strike collapsed on 15 August, Communist influence in the community had been considerably weakened but so, however unreasonably, had the popularity of the Government.

Some of those who heard Chifley speak in the election campaign during November and early December, felt that he had become just a little smug and over-confident. Certainly he made no effort to beguile the voters with 'glittering promises'. Essentially the Government stood on its record and asked the electorate to trust it to go on safeguarding peace, prosperity, progress, full employment and maximum development of the national resources. The need to conserve dollar exchange, Chifley said, made the continuation of petrol rationing necessary.

In contrast the Liberals produced a programme which, had it been enunciated by Labor, would have been denounced by the entire daily press as an irresponsible attempt to bribe the electors. In his hunger for power Menzies promised to abolish petrol rationing, to make substantial reductions in taxation, to introduce a contributory national insurance scheme, to ban the Communist Party and Communists, to extend child endowment to cover the first child in every family, and above all to halt inflation — to 'put value back in the pound'. Included among this array of good things were two other promises perhaps not calculated to win votes. He would re-introduce compulsory military training and restore the Commonwealth Bank Board. Though no financial genius, Menzies must have known it was impossible to carry out even half his other promises and at the same time to halt or even reduce the rate of inflation. The parties of Imperial patriotism were quite uninhibited, in their grasp for power, by their own professed principles. Chifley had retained petrol rationing and a number of other such restrictions at Britain's request, primarily to help the mother country in its post-war fight for solvency *vis-à-vis* the United States. These measures were represented by the Opposition as evidence of repression for its own sake and of a sinister plan for the destruction of liberty and the establishment of a Communist-type dictatorship. The sometime off-sider to a gang of Queensland cane-cutters, 'Artie' Fadden, leader of the Country Party, summed up the theme of the Opposition's campaign in a characteristically reckless speech:

> If you choose the Labor Party, then your ballot paper will truly be your last will and testament, disposing in your own lifetime of your liberties and your property and condemning your children and your children's children to the living death of socialist regimentation.[6]

[6] Crisp, *Ben Chifley*, pp. 371-2.

"GOING MY WAY — ON A FULL PETROL TANK?"

Bulletin, 1949

Fadden spent much time embroidering a favourite image in the Opposition's armoury, that of 'Snow White and the Seven Dwarfs': Chifley might be Snow White but he was manipulated by seven evil dwarfs, engaged in planning the final triumph of bureaucratic regimentation. It happened that seven leading Commonwealth Government servants were all physically small men, the smallest of all being Dr H. C. 'Nugget' Coombs, Director-General of Post-War Reconstruction. Cast by Fadden in the role of chief and most sinister of the dwarfs, he was in fact probably the ablest and most democratic public servant in Australia. Like the others, he was prevented by public service rules from defending his reputation. The tenth of December 1949 was a hot Saturday in most parts of Australia. People made their way to the polling booths while doing the weekend shopping in the morning, or on their way to the surf or sportsfield or pub in the afternoon, or to the pictures or to friends' houses to listen to the election results on the wireless in the evening. Well before midnight it was clear that the Liberal and Country Parties had won easily and, in the richer suburbs of the great cities, many normally well-behaved citizens turned up the volume control on their radio sets to blare their triumph through the quiet tree-lined streets. It shows something about the cynicism of Australian politics, as well as about 'Artie' Fadden, that he rang Coombs in the morning to say: 'That you Nugget? Don't take any notice of all that bullshit I was talking during the election. We'll be needing you, you know'. The new Government in fact immediately made Coombs Governor of the Commonwealth Bank. [7]

[7] Personal communications from Sir A. Fadden and Dr H. C. Coombs to author, 1973.

Chapter 10

THE MENZIES HEGEMONY

c. 1950—1960

Menzies and the Communist Party Dissolution Bill — The Petrov Case and the Labor 'Split' — Foreign policies and racist feelings — Increasing affluence — Culture and censorship

MENZIES AND THE COMMUNIST PARTY DISSOLUTION BILL

The triumphant Coalition Government was sworn in on 19 December 1949, with Fadden as Treasurer and John McEwen as Minister for Commerce and Agriculture holding the major Country Party portfolios. Sir Earle Page was relegated to the relatively minor position of Minister for Health. The most important Liberal Party portfolios went to Harold Holt, a young *protégé* of Menzies, Labour, National Service and Immigration; P. C. Spender, External Affairs and Territories; and R. G. Casey who held, though not concurrently, no fewer than six portfolios, including the two vacated by Spender from the date of his retirement in April 1951, just prior to the next election, when Menzies made him Australian Ambassador to Washington. Holt, of course, was a future prime minister, though not thought of as such in 1950 as Casey was. Altogether there were 14 Liberal and 5 Country Party ministers. There were 55 Liberal, 19 Country Party and 47 Labor members in the Representatives, but the Government parties were in a minority in the Senate, 26 to 34 A.L.P.

The Coalition parties were luckier than they, or anyone else, knew at the time, just as Labor had been extremely unlucky twenty years earlier. In 1929 the A.L.P. was elected to power at the very onset of the Depression, just in time to be blamed by the electors for all the hardship and misery of the following decade. In 1949 the Liberal-Country Party Coalition was sent to the Treasury benches near the beginning of what proved to be a period of economic expansion, diversification and prosperity greater than Australia had ever known before. In both cases governmental policies and actions were only to a modest degree responsible for the prevailing economic climate, but naturally, in both cases, governments received much of the credit for what happened. The Menzies-

Fadden Governments indeed deserved considerable credit for managing the booming economy intelligently and maintaining full employment, but little for the establishment of the machinery which enabled them to do so. This, in essence, was the Treasurer's power to control national financial policy through the Commonwealth Bank — which had been established by Chifley's initial banking legislation in 1945. As we have seen, the Opposition members at the time, particularly the new Treasurer, Fadden, balefully denounced Chifley's banking measures and promised in their 1949 election propaganda to amend them. In due course they did so, but not in such a way as to limit seriously the Commonwealth Government's effective control of financial policy.

As we have also seen, the new Treasurer lost little time in making the man he had denounced as a sinister, socialist bureaucrat, head of the Commonwealth Bank; but not even 'Nugget' Coombs's mastery of monetary matters could at first do anything effective towards implementing the Government's promise to 'put value back in the pound'. Instead wool and sheep prices rose to undreamt of heights, partly as a result of demands created by the Korean War which broke out in June 1950, and inflation proceeded at a faster rate than ever. Many Liberals wished to appreciate the value of the Australian pound against sterling: this would have had at least some beneficial effect on the inflationary spiral, but since it would also have hurt the pockets of primary producers, it was bitterly opposed by the Country Party and nothing came of the proposal. In the 1950 budget Fadden produced one novel measure which probably had a slightly deflationary effect and which was bitterly resented by many of his own Country Party voters. A proportion of every pastoralist's inflated wool-cheque was compulsorily set aside to meet future income-tax liabilities.

Some of the Government's other election promises were honoured promptly. Petrol rationing was abolished almost at once, without most of the dire results Chifley had prophesied. Again luck was with the Government: during 1950 the British Government persuaded U.S. oil companies to supply oil and refining plant in exchange for British *commodities* — instead of dollars. Endowment for the first child was also enacted without opposition from Labor. The other two major measures approved by the electors, restoration of the Commonwealth Bank Board and banning of the Communist Party were held up in the Labor-controlled Senate. We must examine each in turn.

Fadden's 1950 Bank Bill provided for the restoration of the Bank Board, but five of the Board's ten members were to be Treasury and Bank officials and its first Chairman was to be

Chifley's *protégé*, Dr H. C. Coombs. Moreover the Board was still to be responsible to the Government of the day for general policy and the Bank was to be provided with more capital. Many intellectual backwoodsmen among Government supporters damned the Bill for not going far enough — for leaving the Commonwealth Bank, and hence national financial policies, effectively in the hands of the Government. Many Labor supporters, for the same reasons, felt there was no need to oppose it. Chifley, however, was not among them. Almost neurotically obsessive about banking, he believed that the Bill was only a first, moderate-seeming step towards the re-establishment of the situation which, he believed, had brought about so much misery twenty years earlier: that of a supposedly national bank controlled by a Board of businessmen responsible to no one but themselves. He persuaded both the Federal Executive of the A.L.P. and the Labor Caucus in Canberra that Fadden's Bank Bill must be fought to the death. He personally felt the same about what came to be seen as the Government's major election promise — the banning of the Australian Communist Party.

This was the political question which overshadowed all others in 1950 and 1951. True to his campaign promise, Menzies brought forward the Communist Party Dissolution Bill at the end of April, 1950. Its provisions destroyed forever whatever claims he might have had to be a liberal with a small 'l'. The Communist Party was to be outlawed and its assets forfeited to the Commonwealth. The Government could 'declare' as similarly unlawful, any organisation it deemed to be controlled by or affiliated with the Communist Party, and any individual who was, or had been in May 1948, a member of the party or of any 'declared' organisation. 'Declared' persons were then barred from holding any government position or any office in important trade unions. Finally, in a reversal of one of the basic principles of British common law, 'declared' organisations and persons had to prove their innocence: the Crown had no obligation to prove guilt. Simple 'declaration', on evidence supplied usually by anonymous informers or secret policemen who could not be cross-examined, was to be sufficient. The reliability of such evidence was immediately, if unwittingly brought in question by the Prime Minister himself. During the Bill's second reading debate, he announced to Parliament a list of fifty-three avowed and alleged Communist trade-union leaders. A few days later he had to admit that five of these named people were not Communists and one was not even a trade unionist.

The Bill might have been designed, among other things, to cause the maximum amount of dissension within the Labor Party,

COFFEE FOR ONE?

Sydney Morning Herald, 1950

perhaps even to bring about another Labor 'split'. Chifley, Evatt and perhaps the majority of rank-and-file M.P.s hated every clause but a large and growing minority of Groupers, both in and outside Parliament, was more anti-Communist than 'Pig Iron Bob' himself and would have favoured even more drastic legislation. Between these two opposed factions was a shifting band of waverers, many of whom simply feared for their parliamentary seats and salaries — a Gallup poll taken in May showed that approximately 80 per cent of the electors favoured the ban. Some genuinely liberal members of the Liberal Party also opposed the Bill, but their dissent from their own colleagues' view was not nearly as passionate and vociferous as that of some Catholic zealots in the Labor Party, to whom the Catholic Chifley was wont to refer among friends, as 'all those mad buggers'. Chifley and Evatt had a duty to preserve the unity of their party as well as to oppose the Bill they thought wholly obnoxious. They persuaded Caucus to agree, though by no means unanimously, to the following position.

Since the Government had a clear mandate from the people to ban the Communist Party, Labor would not oppose this part of the Bill; but it would move major amendments to the sections concerned with the 'declaration' of individuals and organisations and to the provisions for placing the onus of proof, or rather of disproof, on the accused. With its Senate majority Labor was in a position to enforce acceptable amendments or to bring about an appeal to the electors. So the Bill passed back and forth between the Chambers for some months, until the A.L.P. Federal Executive met on 16 October. Swayed by the growing strength of the Groupers, and fearing the loss of Catholic votes in an election, the Executive by 8 votes to 4 instructed the federal Parliamentary Party to drop its Senate amendments and pass the Bill. Chifley, Evatt and some others were appalled but could do nothing but obey.

However the law's validity was immediately challenged in the High Court by the Communist Party and ten militant trade unions, one of which, the Waterside Workers' Federation, briefed Dr Evatt to appear for it. Democrats and liberals throughout the nation were delighted that such a distinguished advocate should again take up the cudgels for civil liberty. Reactionaries like Menzies were delighted for a different reason: they could smear Evatt and the whole Labor Party with accusations of pro-Communism. Right-wing Labor supporters, especially Catholic zealots in Santamaria's movement, were appalled; for however much Chifley and Evatt himself stressed that he was acting solely in his private and

[1] Crisp, *Ben Chifley*, p. 394.

professional capacity as a lawyer, his court appearances inevitably created the impression in many minds that the A.L.P., in the person of its Deputy-Leader, was 'pro-Communist'. What 'Billy' Hughes, who had virtually created the Waterside Workers' Federation just half a century earlier, thought of its action is not recorded. He died a year later.

While the case was proceeding Chifley was struck down by a coronary occlusion and confined to his bed in the Bathurst Hospital from the end of November. Though warned by his doctors that another, possibly fatal, heart attack was likely if he did not rest, he was up and working again at his usual killing pace a month later. On 9 March 1951 the full Bench of the High Court by a majority of six to one, ruled that the Communist Party Dissolution Bill was wholly unconstitutional. With the Chief Justice, Sir John Latham, sometime leader of the United Australia Party, dissenting, the Court held that, notwithstanding the fighting in Korea, Australia was not at war and consequently the Commonwealth could not use its defence powers to justify invasion of the property and civil rights fields, which belonged to the States. Quite undismayed, the Prime Minister immediately set the stage for a double dissolution of Parliament. At the time a National Service Bill for compulsory training for home defence was being debated. No doubt in the belief that this would not be such a popular election issue as others, Menzies brought forward the Bank Bill and an Arbitration Bill providing for secret ballots for trade-union elections. Chifley accepted the challenge. The Labor-controlled Senate for the third time failed to pass the Bank Bill and the Governor-General, Sir William McKell, granted a double dissolution only ten days after the delivery of the High Court verdict.

Formally of course the main issue in the election campaign should have been banking and the proposed arbitration legislation, but Menzies made it plain from the outset that he would fight on the matter of banning Communism. Only a month earlier, returning from a conference of British Commonwealth Prime Ministers in London, he had announced as an established fact that war would break out again within three years at most. Communists, busily sponsoring peace conferences everywhere, were actually the devilishly cunning agents of the enemy in Australia and elsewhere. Hence the major plank of the Liberal-Country Party election campaign was a promise, if returned, to ask the people in a referendum for the power, denied by the High Court, to proscribe the Communist Party, its affiliates and 'fellow-travellers'. The Government stressed also its intention to build up Australian defences against the same 'menace' outside Australia and to proceed with its arbitration legislation.

Privately Chifley and Evatt simply did not believe in an early war. The Russian Government, they thought, would be preoccupied for at least a generation with domestic reconstruction after the Soviet peoples' fearful wartime sufferings — the best estimates were that they had lost about 20 000 000 dead. Labor tried to make inflation, and the Government's total failure to cope with it, *the* election issue. The Government had promised to reduce the number of public servants and to cut expenditure to 'put value back in the pound', but in all three areas the position was actually much worse than before. Labor Party machine men also ensured that Chifley's policy speech, unlike those at the previous two elections, contained a reasonable number of 'glittering promises', but disunity in Labor ranks ensured a Coalition victory. Menzies' strategy of subordinating everything else to the 'menace of communism' had already divided his opponents. During the campaign, the Grouper-dominated Victorian Branch of the A.L.P. passed a motion 'censuring' Evatt for appearing for the Communist trade-union leaders.

On 28 April the people endorsed Menzies' policies. The Coalition gained control of the Senate with thirty-two seats to Labor's twenty-eight. Labor won five seats from Government candidates in the House but the Government still had a substantial majority of sixty-nine seats to fifty-two. There were two new faces in the reconstructed Cabinet, William McMahon, Navy, a future Prime Minister; and P. M. C. Hasluck, Territories, a future Governer-General. Members reassembled on 12 June, but the main business of the week was the celebration of the Jubilee of the Commonwealth Parliament. Despite Labor's second successive defeat at the polls, Caucus had re-elected Chifley, unopposed, as Leader of the A.L.P. On the following night members, their friends, and distinguished guests attended a State Ball in Parliament House. Chifley took some papers to the Hotel Kurrajong to work over during the evening. He had another heart attack and died in the Canberra Hospital before midnight. The State Ball was abandoned. On 17 June he was buried in his native Bathurst with the full rites of the Catholic Church which, despite his regular attendance, had denied him its sacraments since his marriage in a Presbyterian Church thirty-seven years before.

A deeply divided Caucus elected Evatt to the leadership of the federal Parliamentary A.L.P. He, and the nation, was at once confronted with another political campaign on Communism, the issue which continued to overshadow all others in the press and Parliament. The 22nd September 1951 was fixed as the date for the referendum at which the people would be asked to amend the Constitution so as to give the Commonwealth Government power to suppress Communism and Communists. Probably no other referendum, except the two World War I conscription plebiscites, ever roused such passionate debate. Voluntary organisations, political parties, even families were often divided against themselves. Many right-wing Labor men and women were even more anxious for a 'Yes' vote than the Prime Minister himself, though the majority of Labor supporters followed Evatt in his brilliant leadership of the 'No' campaign. On the other hand many habitual Liberal Party supporters, and some members, strongly advocated a vote for 'No'. Almost everyone, whatever his hopes or fears, believed that the referendum was virtually certain to be carried easily. Ranged on the 'Yes' side were practically all the newspapers and radio commentators in the country, the powerful resources of the Government of the day and the persuasive oratory and unmatched political skill of its leader. Public opinion was overwhelmingly anti-Communist and it seemed that the 'No' case was too subtle to be appreciated by many voters. In essence that case was that existing laws gave ample power for the punishment of criminal and seditious acts, but the Government wanted the power, already wielded so viciously by Communist and other totalitarian regimes, to punish a person for harbouring unconventional, dissident or 'dangerous' thoughts. As Chifley had put it during his last days in Parliament, in a fruitless endeavour to influence some of his co-religionists on the back benches: 'The multitude can make grave mistakes. It was the multitude, by its vote, that sent Christ to be crucified.[2]

As the campaign warmed up, hundreds, even thousands, of artists, writers, teachers and other thoughtful citizens who usually took no part in politics, spoke out clearly in defence of what they saw as freedom of thought and speech. From his retirement in Perth old Walter Murdoch, a nationally respected essayist and newspaper columnist, wrote:

> The government is asking for . . . the power to punish a man for his beliefs — or for what some spy alleges him to believe. It will be a sad day for Australia if she allows this spiritual poison to get into her system.

On the same day the Prime Minister assured his countrymen that

> Nobody other than a communist can under any conceivable circumstances, be affected.[3]

[2] Crisp, *Ben Chifley*, p. 389.

[3] Brian Fitzpatrick, *The Australian Commonwealth*, Melbourne, 1956, p. 254.

It is a striking tribute to the occasional political maturity of the Australian people, the courage of their intellectuals, and above all to the heroic endeavours of Dr Evatt, that the referendum was defeated, though by only the narrowest of margins. 'No' votes comprised 50.48 per cent of all valid ballot papers.

THE PETROV CASE AND THE LABOR 'SPLIT'

Nevertheless the Government continued to derive political advantage from the exercise known in the vernacular as 'kicking the Communist can'. S. M. Keon, a Catholic zealot representing the safe Labor seat of Yarra once held by Scullin, and W. C. Wentworth, a Protestant great-grandson of the pioneer statesman, representing the safe Liberal seat of Mackellar, attacked, under parliamentary privilege, the reputations of such nationally respected figures as Vance and Nettie Palmer and universities and intellectuals generally. On 28 August 1952, for instance, Keon told the Prime Minister that he was insufficiently zealous at fighting Communism and that

> the Australian National University has become deliberately, according to a planned scheme, a nest of Communists who are busy building up their own organizations to subvert the institutions of this country.[4]

Yet despite its best efforts the Government was losing electoral appeal. In a general election for half the Senate seats and two casual vacancies, held on 5 September 1953, the A.L.P. polled 50.61 per cent of all valid votes cast compared with 44.43 per cent for the combined Liberal and Country Parties. Seventeen Labor and fifteen Coalition senators were returned. With a general election for the House of Representatives due by mid-1954 at the latest, the auguries looked black for the Government. On 6 April the conservative *Sydney Morning Herald* wrote:

> The Liberal Party is hoping that the Prime Minister, Mr. Menzies, will pull a couple of rabbits out of the top hat which he wore with such assurance during the Royal tour. It looks as if he will have to do so if his Government is to survive the election in May.

A week later the most sensational 'red scare' in Australian history fell, or was placed, in Menzies' hands.

On 13 April in the dying hours of the nineteenth Parliament, at the peak radio listening time of eight o'clock in the evening, the

[4] *C.P.D.*, vol. 218, p. 719.

Prime Minister made a dramatic announcement to the House. A third secretary of the Soviet Embassy in Canberra and self-confessed M.V.D. spy, Vladimir Petrov, had contacted the Australian Security Intelligence Organisation and had been granted political asylum. Petrov had brought with him a mass of documents relating to a Soviet 'spy ring' in which some Australian citizens appeared to be involved. Evatt, Leader of the Opposition, was away in Sydney and in any case there was no time for Parliament to debate the matter as members were dispersing next day for the election campaign.

In Britain, the United States and other countries, the defection of foreign spies is usually kept as quiet as possible, if only to avoid giving warning to the defector's fellow agents. Menzies, by contrast, announced the appointment of a Royal Commission to sit in public and give maximum publicity to the whole affair. There was some delay while Menzies found three judges, both willing to act and deemed suitable by him, but the Commission opened in the Albert Hall, Canberra, on 17 May just twelve days before the general election. Inspired 'leaks' and newspaper speculation had already done incalculable damage to Labor's poll prospects, although the fact that Australian security officers had paid Petrov a cash bribe of £5,000 as an inducement to defect, was not made public until after the election. The spy scare was sufficient to arrest the swing of popular opinion against the Government. On 29 April it regained some of the ground lost at the recent Senate election, polling 47.07 per cent of the vote as against 50.03 per cent for the A.L.P. Owing to the inequity of the Commonwealth electoral system, this gave a House of 47 Liberals, 17 Country Party and 57 Labor members.

In an atmosphere more akin to that of a 'show-trial' in Moscow than to judicial procedures in a democratic country, the Commission proceeded for nearly a year — until 31 March 1955. Its final report appeared only in the following August. It examined 119 witnesses and besmirched, more or less, the reputations of most of them, although its own final report held that not one had committed any treasonable or other act punishable by law. The report also solemnly asserted what every educated person already knew: that the U.S.S.R. (like every other great power) conducted espionage in Australia through some of its accredited diplomats who doubled as spies. Best of all, from the point of view of political advantage for the Government, among those haled before the Commission were many Labor Party supporters and members, including three of Evatt's personal staff. Once again, though he was now leader, not deputy-leader, of the A.L.P. Evatt unhesitatingly stepped in to argue the case of those he regarded as victims of a political plot. In his three weeks before the tribunal, he virtually took over its direction from the more slow-witted judges. Yet he also exhibited alarming signs of the mental instability and paranoia which was to destroy him. Even more obviously than in the Banking Case in London, he seemed unable to stop talking or to come clearly to the point of an argument. He charged, in effect, that the Commission had been brought into existence for a political purpose and that it amounted to a conspiracy to damage his clients, himself and, by association, the A.L.P. Despite his verbosity he seemed to be well on the way to proving his case when their Honours expelled him from their presence.[5]

Whether or not damaging the Labor Party was the purpose of those who set up the Royal Commission on Espionage, it was certainly its major result. In the minds of many citizens the Australian Labor Party and its leader were ever afterwards guilty, by association, of Communist sympathies and even of disloyalty to Australia. Even more gratifying, from the Liberal-Country Party point of view, was the fact that the Commission did more than anything else to precipitate the final 'split' in the A.L.P. Right-wingers, the industrial groups and Bartholomew Santamaria orchestrating them all, were outraged by Evatt's appearance before the Commission. To them it was final proof that he was, if not a secret Communist, a 'friend of Communists' who had to be removed from the leadership of the party if its credibility was to be maintained. On the other hand to Labor left-wingers and moderates, including good Catholics like 'Eddie' Ward, Arthur Calwell, Evatt's deputy-leader, and N. McKenna, A.L.P. Leader in the Senate, it was those to whom Chifley had referred as 'all those mad buggers' who had to be purged or silenced.

In October 1954, after his expulsion from the 'Petrov Commission' but long before its hearings ended, Evatt issued a press statement denouncing a small group of Labor Party members for working against party ideals under the direction of an outside organisation. Santamaria, Keon and their fellows had no doubt about what was meant. Soon afterwards the A.L.P. Federal Executive called a special conference of the party in Victoria, the Groupers' stronghold, to elect a new anti-Grouper State Executive. At the party's federal conference, held in Hobart in March, 1955, this new Victorian delegation was admitted while the old 'pro-Grouper' delegation was locked out. The Conference, dominated by left and centre elements, then proceeded to pass motions opposing the use of Australian troops in Malaya, advocating

5 Nicholas Whitlam and John Stubbs, *Nest of Traitors*, Brisbane, 1974 *passim*.

recognition of Communist China and — most divisive of all — directing State branches of the Party to withdraw their support from the industrial groups. The new Victorian State Executive set to work with a will, expelling hundreds of A.L.P. members who remained loyal to the old right-wing Executive. In April these Ishmaels formed themselves into the Anti-Communist Labor Party which, naturally, bitterly opposed A.L.P. candidates at the State elections in June. Naturally too the Victorian Labor Government of John Cain was crushingly defeated and conservative governments were continuously re-elected in that State thereafter.

In New South Wales Cardinal Gilroy encouraged Catholic Labor men and women to stay in the A.L.P. instead of urging them to follow Santamaria's lead, as Archbishop Mannix did in Victoria. Nevertheless a relatively small band of Groupers in 1956 formed themselves into the Democratic Labor Party in that State. In Queensland the split was delayed for another year and, when it came, was based more on the endemic tension in the Labor movement between trade-union and parliamentary members. In April 1957 the Premier, Vincent Gair, and most of his ministers were expelled from the party. With a number of back-benchers in support, they styled themselves the Queensland Labor Party, and were promptly defeated in the House. In the following election the conservative Coalition parties won and were subsequently re-elected again and again as in Victoria. In 1957 the Anti-Communist Labor Party and the Democratic Labor Party merged under the latter name. The Queensland Labor Party retained a separate identity until the mid-1960s, but it early became identified in people's minds as, in effect, the Queensland branch of the D.L.P. Inspired by the able and indefatigible Santamaria and his Victorian cohorts, the D.L.P. quickly established branches and stood candidates for election in South Australia, Western Australia and Tasmania also. Everywhere and always D.L.P. candidates religiously gave their second preference vote to Liberal or Country Party candidates.

The D.L.P. remained a minority party with no chance, even in Victoria, of having a candidate elected to a Lower House[6]; but its preferences were sufficient to keep conservative governments in power in that State, in Queensland and in the Commonwealth Parliament, and were sometimes decisive in elections in other States also. Owing to the system of proportional representation for

[6] Except by accident. At a N.S.W. election in 1974 in the safest conservative seat in the State, the Liberal candidate forgot to nominate. The electors of Gordon voted for the D.L.P. rather than the A.L.P. candidate.

Sydney Morning Herald, 1957

"Disgustingly Advanced for 4½ Months, Isn't He?"

the Senate, introduced by the Chifley Government in 1949, a handful of D.L.P. candidates became senators who, in the twenty years after the Labor 'split' sometimes held the balance of power in that chamber. For fifteen years and more from 1955, the D.L.P. polled a minimum of about 5 per cent of all the votes cast in national elections, rising to a maximum of nearly 10 per cent in 1961. In Victoria the D.L.P. percentage ranged between about 10 per cent and 18 per cent while it was correspondingly lower than the national average in some other States such as South Australia.

Of course not all D.L.P. members and supporters were zealous Catholics. The party attracted some Protestants and unbelievers who held extremely conservative views and others who innocently supposed that, as its name implied, it was a moderate party between the Liberals and Country Party on the right and the A.L.P. on the left. Equally obviously, the majority of Catholic Australians continued to vote for the A.L.P., or some other party of their choice — except in Victoria. There B. A. Santamaria, Archbishop Daniel Mannix and the church hierarchy generally placed tremendous pressure on good Catholics to support the D.L.P. and probably most did so. One of the large minority who did not was Arthur Calwell, deputy-leader of the federal parliamentary A.L.P. from 1951 to 1960 and leader from 1960 to 1967. In 1957 the Vatican decreed that Santamaria's Movement must not remain in direct relationship with the Catholic hierarchy. In due course it was re-named the National Civic Council and continued its work with less open and direct support from sections of the episcopate. Calwell, incidentally, was made a papal knight in 1967.

As though all this were not enough to cheer and comfort members of the Commonwealth Government, the Leader of the Opposition himself presented them with a political bludgeon. On the night of 19 October 1955 Evatt was addressing a packed House of Representatives on the final report of the 'Petrov Commission' which had recently been tabled. In the course of an otherwise masterly speech, he gratuitously announced that he had written to the Soviet Foreign Minister, V. M. Molotov, who had replied that the Petrov documents were forgeries. After a moment of stunned silence, bedlam broke loose and the rest of Evatt's speech was practically inaudible. He had added this sentence at the last minute, unknown to any of his advisers. To his judicial mind it was necessary to allow the accused, in this case the Soviet Government, to enter a defence. He had always been prone to misjudge ordinary people's reactions in the realm of practical affairs, but the Molotov blunder was more than that: it was the first unmistakeable sign of the degeneration of his formidable mental and physical powers.

Menzies was delighted. In his reply a week later, he represented Evatt as a man who preferred the word of the Soviet Foreign Minister to that of three Australian judges who were all returned soldiers to boot. He hastened to ask the Governor-General for an early election, ostensibly to bring House and Senate elections back to the same day, but actually to take advantage of the total disarray in Labor ranks and of the Anti-Communist Labor Party's help. The result of the December 10th election was a foregone conclusion. For the Senate, Liberal, Country Party and D.L.P. candidates together polled 54.77 per cent of the votes to 40.6 per cent for Labor. Interestingly, the Communist Senate vote reached its highest point ever in this election — 3.64 per cent. The new House of Representatives seated 57 Liberals, 18 Country Party and 47 Labor members. As the D.L.P. improved its organisation the Government's position became more secure. At the next triennial election on 22 November 1958, 58 Liberal, 19 Country Party and 45 Labor members were returned to the House. Early in 1960, more obviously ill than ever, Evatt resigned as leader of the Opposition to become Chief Justice of the Supreme Court of New South Wales. Rapidly failing health forced his retirement from that position. He died on Tuesday 2 November 1962, while most of his countrymen were thinking about the runnning of the Melbourne Cup.

In July 1956, while Labor was still engaged in tearing itself asunder, Menzies encouraged the process by having the Commonwealth Government pay interest on loans raised by church schools for new buildings in the A.C.T. Seen, correctly, as the thin end of the wedge of general restoration of Government aid for church schools, and wealthy Commonwealth Government aid at that, the move was enthusiastically welcomed by Catholic spokesmen and, naturally, by many Catholic parents. At the end of the 1950s serious political analysts thought it likely that the A.L.P. would not gain federal power in the foreseeable future, because of the D.L.P.'s policies. The three major planks in the D.L.P. platform were restoration of government financial aid to church schools, which had been discontinued in all the Australian colonies some eighty years earlier; harrying of Communist, radical and 'permissive' persons and ideas at home; and fanatical opposition to anything savouring of Communism abroad. We have seen that the party had already achieved much in each of these areas and was in a strong position to get more from the not unsympathetic Liberals. It is time to look at changes in Australia's relations with other countries during the decade and in particular her relations with those in the Asian Pacific region.

FOREIGN POLICIES AND RACIST FEELINGS

The great change had already occurred during and immediately after the war when Evatt, through the professional diplomatic service he virtually created, had initiated direct relations with a growing number of countries of which the United States was the most important, more so in fact than Britain itself. Although the greatest of all Australian Anglophiles, R. G. Menzies, talked and sometimes acted as though nothing had changed, indeed as though the pre-war dependent relationship with the United Kingdom had been restored, in fact he and his governments carried on with Evatt's policies, but with different emphases. As time went on they placed relatively less importance on cultivating direct, friendly relations with Asian and other countries and relatively more on conciliating their great and powerful ally at almost any cost: so much so, that by the end of the 1950s Australia adopted a dependent, neo-colonial position *vis-à-vis* the United States, very like its former relationship with the mother country. Certainly no Australian diplomat or minister could know what his country's policy was on a given issue until he had ascertained the American view. Then, almost invariably, it was a case of 'we too only more so'.

On the positive side of fostering good relations with Asian neighbours, Evatt's successor as Minister for External Affairs, P. C. Spender, deserves most of the credit for initiating the Colombo Plan — a truly liberal, anti-Communist scheme which did great good and no harm to those participating in it. In January 1950, soon after being sworn in to office, Spender attended a meeting in Colombo of Foreign Ministers from British Commonwealth countries. In the belief that poverty, ignorance and disease provide fertile breeding-grounds for Communism, they resolved to make a joint effort to promote industrialisation, health and education in 'backward' Asian countries. Spender suggested the outlines of the scheme which was adopted, initially by the representatives of Australia, Canada, Ceylon, India, Pakistan, New Zealand and the United Kingdom. By the end of 1954 practically every country in South East Asia had joined: Malaya, Singapore, North Borneo, Sarawak, Brunei, Burma, Indonesia, Thailand, Laos, Cambodia, Vietnam and the Philippines — not to mention Japan and the United States.

The essence of the plan was that the richer and more industrialised countries, like Australia or Japan, should provide financial, technical and professional help to the less developed countries like Thailand and Indonesia. The help might be given free or on easy terms of repayment, but was always to be supplementary to the efforts at self-help being made by the recipient countries. The givers decided how much, or how little, they would contribute. To the great credit of the first post-war Menzies Government, it decided to give much more per head of population than any other country involved, beginning with £ 31,250,000 for the first six years. Another £ 3,500,000 was to be spent initially on scholarships to give Asian students professional and technical skills at Australian universities, teachers' training colleges and technical schools. The graduate students were then to return to their own countries to teach others and assist in development schemes.

The results perhaps verified the gospel adage that it is more blessed to give than to receive. The populations of the developing countries were so immense that, with the best will in the world on everyone's part, the Colombo Plan made only a marginal impact on their problems: but the Colombo Plan student made a significant impact on Australia. They and other students from Asia, Africa and the Pacific Islands came in quite large numbers to study, to play and to live with Australian students. At times 'coloured' people comprised up to 10 per cent of a university's student population. Because of the continuing boom and full employment, and also because they were avowedly learning skills to take home to their own countries after a few years' study, they were not seen, as Chinese coolies for instance had once been, as potential competitors for scarce jobs. For the first time in the history of Australia, tertiary students, who tend to become opinion-leaders in every country, had the opportunity of getting to know large numbers of non-white foreigners. Indeed they could hardly help doing so. The visiting students were received in a way that troubled some old-fashioned parents and deeply shocked some surviving grand-parents. Cross-cultural friendships, love affairs and marriages became more and more frequent and raised fewer and fewer eyebrows, even among the older generation.

The Colombo Plan benefited Australia by helping significantly to break down the racist sentiment which still sustained the White Australia Policy. Even the Minister for Immigration, A. R. Downer, probably more conservative than the Prime Minister himself, was affected, however slightly, by changing attitudes. In 1958 he introduced to Parliament legislation which abolished the notorious dictation test. Instead 'undesirable' aliens were to be kept out simply by denying them, on the recommendation of the Minister, an entry permit. In practice this gave a little more flexibility to what actually happened under the fixed immigration policy.

The extent of the change became known in 1960 when a group of men and women at the University of Melbourne published a pamphlet, *Control or Colour Bar?* This Immigration Reform Group conducted research and put out propaganda in favour of substituting, for the White Australia Policy of total exclusion, one of controlled, selective immigration from Asian and African countries. Chairman of the Reform Group was a lecturer in Economics at the University of Melbourne, Kenneth Rivett, a son of Sir David Rivett, pioneer leader of the Council for Scientific and Industrial Research, and a grandson of Alfred Deakin who had fathered the Immigration Restriction Act in 1901. During the 1950s the Group conducted a series of public opinion polls. Those interviewed were told that people of certain nationalities were prohibited absolutely from settling in Australia. They were then asked if they would favour admitting at least fifty migrants a year from each of these countries. Between 1954 and 1959 the answers changed as follows:

Year	*Keep Out*	*Let In*	*No Opinion*
1954	61%	31%	8%
1956	51%	42%	7%
1957	55%	36%	9%
1958	45%	44%	11%
1959	34%	55%	11%

Unfortunately for Australia the author of the Colombo Plan, as we have seen, was hurried off to Washington before the scheme was fairly under way. His colleague, the Minister for Territories, also concerned with aspects of Australian race relations, remained in Cabinet until 1969 when he became Governor-General. Born in Fremantle in 1905, Paul Hasluck became a lecturer in History in the University of Western Australia and then a diplomat in the Department of External Affairs during Evatt's period as Minister. Like Evatt, he was a distinguished historian in his own right, as was his wife Alexandra. Like Evatt too, he became Minister for External Affairs — in 1964 after serving for thirteen years in Territories. He was one of the ablest ministers in the long succession of Menzies governments, perhaps the most capable of all; but he lacked the forcefulness, and possibly a degree of personal charisma, which might have ensured his early translation to another sphere. Menzies did not fear him but, privately, despised him. Astute, cautious and rather rigidly conservative in most ways, he was nevertheless liberal, with a small 'l', in the field of race relations and genuinely concerned, though in a completely paternalistic way, for the welfare and advancement of the indigenous peoples of Australian territories.

That his caution generally outweighed his concern is shown by the very modest extent of the reforms he achieved in the Northern Territory. All Aboriginals, *including* people of mixed blood known popularly and insultingly as 'yeller-fellers', were subject to the Aboriginals Ordinance which effectively deprived them of all citizen rights and made them wards of the Commonwealth Government. In 1953 people of mixed blood were exempted from the provisions of the ordinance — *except* for those living with and in the manner of Aboriginals and those under 18 years of age already under the authority of the Director of Native Affairs. It is a measure of how strongly racist Australian society still was, as well as of Hasluck's conservatism, that this measure at the time was considered a wonderful forward step by almost everybody, including those mixed-blood people who benefited from it. Those who did not, and the full-blood Aboriginals, were considered to have no opinion.

Hasluck and the Government, also came under increasing pressure in the United Nations Organisation. As the emerging African and Asian countries acquired more influence on its deliberations, the United Nations displayed more interest in the pace of the progress of Papua and New Guinea towards self-government than Australian Governments had ever done in the past. Hasluck took his responsibilities very seriously, travelling frequently and extensively through the Northern Territory as well as Papua and New Guinea. During his term Government spending on schools and public works increased rapidly, most of the more remote areas were brought under control, and the whole administrative apparatus was tied much more closely to the growing departmental bureaucracy in Canberra. More indigenous people were drawn out of the traditional subsistence-farming life of the villages into the slowly growing cash economy. Coffee for the first time joined copra as an export crop of some significance, but it was nearly all grown on Australian-owned plantations. Most important of all was the rapid growth of local government with the indigenous people taking a limited part in it. Yet despite Hasluck's best efforts, self-government and independence seemed almost as far away as ever when he gave up the portfolio in 1963.

When Spender retired to Washington in April 1951 the Ministry of External Affairs was taken over, and retained for the rest of the decade, by Richard Gardiner Casey. Born into an old pastoral family in 1890 in Brisbane, he was educated, like Stanley Melbourne Bruce before him, at Melbourne Grammar School and

"Deplorable! Something must be done—when we can decide who's to pay for it."

the University of Cambridge. Like Bruce, too, he epitomised the traditionalist Anglo-Australian, moving freely between two worlds as he pursued his career. He graduated from Cambridge with honours in Mechanical Science, retaining a life-long interest in the subject and being throughout the 1950s responsible for the Commonwealth Scientific and Industrial Research Organisation as well as External Affairs. Tall, handsome and dignified, he was respected by political friends and foes alike for his integrity. He lacked, perhaps, the driving ambition and capacity for intrigue which might have made him Prime Minister. When Menzies had been manoeuvring for the leadership in 1938 and 1939, Lyons knew that some of his ministers were plotting his downfall but rightly dismissed the possibility of Casey's being involved with the remark that he was a gentleman. Sent to Washington as Australian Minister by Menzies in 1940, he was co-opted by Churchill as a member of the British War Cabinet and U.K. Minister of State to the Middle East in 1942 and 1943. For the next three years he served as Governor of the troubled Indian province of Bengal, where his taste for tiger-hunting sorted well with his pre-war pastime of shooting wedge-tailed eagles from his private aeroplane. When he re-entered Australian politics in 1949 as Liberal member for the Victorian seat of Latrobe, Menzies had consolidated his leadership of the party so that Casey did not have to be sent on his travels again.

At the end of World War II security against the possibility of renewed Japanese aggression dominated all other considerations in Australian foreign policy. In 1947 Evatt called a British Commonwealth Conference in Canberra which drew up a series of proposals for a very 'tough' peace treaty. However the Cold War and the victory of the Chinese-Communists over Chiang-Kai-Shek in 1949, brought about rapid changes in American policy. On 6 April 1950 the greatest Cold-War warrior of them all, John Foster Dulles, was appointed Foreign Policy Adviser to the U.S. Secretary of State. He already saw Japan, not as a possible aggressor, but as an ally against Communist China and Russia. Japan must therefore, he thought, be strengthened and, if possible, re-armed.

The Korean War, which conveniently broke out on 25 June 1950, played into his hands. Formerly a Japanese colony, Korea, on Japan's surrender, had been divided at the 38th parallel of latitude between Russian occupying forces in the north and American in the south. Naturally the governments approved by the two occupying powers each claimed to be the legitimate authority with popular support throughout the country. When the fighting began, the U.N. Security Council met immediately and, in the absence of Russia which was boycotting the Council in protest at its refusal to accept Communist China, labelled North Korea as the aggressor and called on U.N. members to restore peace in the area. Two days later American forces went to the assistance of South Korea, and within a week of the outbreak Menzies announced that Australian sea and air forces had been committed to help the Americans. A volunteer expeditionary force of diggers followed in due course. In July Menzies visited Washington and received a hero's welcome in the U.S. Congress.

After a year's large-scale fighting, and two more years of trench warfare while negotiations proceeded, an armistice was signed at Panmunjon in July 1953. Two hundred and eighty-one Australians and scores of thousands of Americans, Chinese and Koreans had been killed, but the political division of Korea remained exactly as it had been when the war began. Not so, however, the relationship between the United States and Australia: this was warmer and closer than at any time since the Japanese thrust in 1942. Australia's support in the Korean War was part of the price paid for the ANZUS (Australia, New Zealand and United States) Pact, signed in July 1951 soon after Casey had taken over the External Affairs portfolio. The other part of the price was Australia's acceptance, however reluctantly, of the very generous 'soft' peace treaty with Japan which America wanted. Under the terms of ANZUS the United States guaranteed to help Australia and New Zealand if either were attacked by another power. At the time most Australians feared a resurgent Japan, but by the end of the decade most had probably come round to the American view and feared more a Chinese, or unspecified 'Communist' attack.

There was and still is, however, considerable argument about the worth of the ANZUS treaty. The vital clause, Article IV(i) reads as follows:

> Each party recognises that an armed attack in the Pacific area on any of the Parties would be dangerous to its own peace and safety and declares that it would act to meet the common danger in accordance with its constitutional processes.[7]

Most, though not all, Australian conservatives read this as a firm commitment to send all possible military, naval and air aid immediately to the signatory under attack. Most, though not all Australian liberals and radicals believe it amounts to no more than a promise to consult and send messages of sympathy. 'Eddie' Ward,

[7] Alan Watt, *The Evolution of Australian Foreign Policy 1938-1965*, Cambridge, 1967, p.125.

for instance, denounced it during the ratification debate in Parliament as a 'meaningless document'. In fact neither view is correct. In the event of an attack on Australia the words of the treaty would be interpreted by the U.S. Government in the light of what it conceived its best national interest to be at the time — as the words of all treaties have been interpreted by governments since time began. The words are vague enough to allow of any desired construction being placed upon them. If national interest dictated all possible military aid, this would doubtless be despatched at once, as it was after Pearl Harbour in the absence of any treaty whatever: if not, not.

With the ANZUS Pact signed, the Government adhered, without too many misgivings and only two months later to the Peace Treaty with Japan. Casey, the new Minister for External Affairs, expressed the national sentiment temperately but accurately when he told Parliament:

> In speaking to the Press in Japan I made it clear that it would be misleading for the Japanese to expect Australia quickly to forget the past. At the same time I expressed the view that if Japan by her actions demonstrated in the future that she had, in fact, cast off for all time the ambitions and objectives of Japanese Imperialism, then Australians would be prepared to meet the Japanese people half way.[8]

Conclusion of the Japanese Peace Treaty by no means put an end to diplomatic activity in the Pacific area. Successive French Governments had not matched the wisdom of the British in voluntarily handing over power to the indigenous people in their colonies. In Indo-China the French continued to support what they saw as democratic elements in a bitter war against Communist insurgents led by Ho-Chi-Minh. Most of the inhabitants of Vietnam, Laos and Cambodia, on the other hand, saw the war as one of national liberation from French Imperialism and its puppet regimes. With John Foster Dulles' appointment as Secretary of State under President Eisenhower in 1953, American policy became even more obsessively concerned with 'containment' of Communism, and Australian policy with the desirability of embroiling the United States in South-East Asian affairs. From 1951 onwards Casey made frequent visits to the countries of South-East Asia, Australia's 'near North', as some were beginning to call it. He opened diplomatic posts throughout the area and became convinced that Australia should work for the creation of a new military defence pact, much wider in scope that ANZUS. The

[8] Watt, pp.212-13.

Americans too wanted such a pact as at least a step towards active intervention to help the French in Indo-China.

In the first months of 1954 it seemed that all of Vietnam was about to fall to the Communists — or, according to the point of view, the National Liberation Forces. Dulles wishes to intervene with U.S. air power at Dien-Bien-Phu, where a French army was surrounded, and even meditated the use of atomic weapons. Britain and, for Australia, Casey, opposed the plan because they thought such action would be ineffective, would be opposed by world opinion and might lead to general war and atomic annihilation. A conference at Geneva, which ended on 21 July 1954, agreed to what proved a temporary truce in Vietnam with the country divided by the seventeenth parallel of latitude, but seven weeks later, on 8 September, a new anti-Communist agreement, which was later used to justify American intervention in Vietnam, was concluded in Manila. The South-East Asia Collective Defence Treaty embraced the United States, the United Kingdom, France, Australia, New Zealand, Pakistan, the Philippines and Thailand: an odd collection of new and old states, merely to list which immediately raises the question of why so many more South-East Asian nations were *not* signatories. The three (or four!) states of Indo-China and Malaya, Indonesia, Burma and India all denounced the treaty as unnecessarily divisive, not to say inflammatory, because it brought great colonial or neo-colonial powers into Asia. The parties to the Manila Pact, usually known as SEATO (South-East Asia Treaty Organisation) agreed in substantially the same words as those of the ANZUS Pact to 'act to meet the common danger in accordance with [their] constitutional processes' in the event of aggression against any one of them. They also agreed to co-operate with each other, in a totally unspecified way, in the economic and technological fields.

All this did not in fact mean very much. When, for instance, Pakistan and India went to war in 1965 none of the signatories to SEATO even seriously considered going to war with India. The sting of the SEATO arrangement was in the tail. First, the document enabled members not only to help each other in a war, but also to fight in the defence, with its consent, of any other state or territory, not a party to the treaty but 'designated' unanimously by all the SEATO members. A protocol 'designated' Cambodia and Laos and the southern, French-occupied, part of Vietnam. Finally American obligations under the treaty, unlike those of other members, were specifically limited to cases of 'Communist' aggression. These three points made it tolerably clear that SEATO was not meant in reality to be just a friendly regional arrangement for mutual co-operation and defence, but a link in the Cold-War 'front' against Communism. The bitter fruit of Australian intervention in Vietnam, allegedly under the SEATO umbrella, was not tasted until more than ten years later when Casey had become Governor-General.

Two months after the conclusion of the SEATO agreement in November 1954, few noticed Casey's announcement to Parliament that, in the gradual process of her withdrawal from the Indian Ocean, Britain had handed over to Australia responsibility for the Cocos Islands about half way between Fremantle and Colombo.

Meanwhile the Menzies Government entered into yet another defence commitment with Malaya, since before World War II the pivot, from Australia's point of view, of South-East Asian defence. In 1949 the Labor Governments of Britain, Australia and New Zealand had agreed to co-ordinate defence plans in what came to be known as the ANZAM (Australia, New Zealand and Malayan) region. Succeeding conservative governments in all three countries carried on with and extended the arrangement, which remained just that. ANZAM understandings were never set down in a formal treaty. However on 1 April 1955 the Prime Minister announced that Australian (and New Zealand) troops would in future be stationed in Malaya, for training, to strengthen the defences of that country standing on the eve of independence, and for use against Communist rural guerillas who were threatening its stability. Never before had Australian soldiers been stationed abroad during peacetime. The Labor Party protested vigorously but majority opinion endorsed, or at least tacitly accepted, the Government move.

This revolutionary break with past traditions was probably acceptable because all those sent to Malaya were volunteers or permanent, professional military personnel. Menzies' 1949 election promise to restore compulsory peacetime military training was implemented after the double dissolution of Parliament and his return to power in May 1951. All young men had to register at the age of 18 and, if fit, had to serve in the Army, Navy or Air Force for a period of from five to six months. Six years later in 1957, and four years after the date (1953) for Armageddon announced in 1950 by the Prime Minister, the Government decided that world war was less likely. If it came it was likely to be a thermo-nuclear holocaust in which the existence of a large number of partially-trained troops would be irrelevant. Australia needed, it was said, a small, highly mobile and efficient, professional striking-force to combat Communist guerilla activity and engage in 'brush-fire' wars in South-East Asia. So in 1957 the annual intake of National Service trainees was reduced from 33 000 to 12 000 and in 1959 the compulsory training scheme was abolished — much to the fury of spokesmen for the Returned Soldiers' League.

Less acceptable to public opinion was the Prime Minister's personal intervention in foreign relations, notably in the Suez Crisis in the last months of 1956 and in a United Nations Assembly debate four years later. Both incidents highlighted two things: Menzies' almost absolute domination of his own party and his successive Cabinets, and the blind, unquestioning loyalty he always felt for the British monarchy and British institutions, a sentiment so strongly held as to set him somewhat apart from his colleagues even in what a conservative scholar has called 'the party of ex-colonial loyalists'.

On 26 July 1956 President Nasser of Egypt seized the Suez Canal, under a decree nationalising the waterway which Britain and Australia had for the previous eighty-seven years regarded as vital to Imperial security. Nevertheless Egypt was a sovereign state whose right to nationalise an undertaking on her own territory was endorsed by virtually every country in the world — including the United States — except Britain, France and a few other interested parties. It was generally recognised that the time when great powers could enforce their will on smaller ones by the despatch of a gunboat had gone by: but not by Menzies. He backed Sir Anthony Eden's Conservative British Government policy on Suez without the slightest qualification, overruling Casey, his own responsible Minister for External Affairs, and imposing his will on Cabinet. He attended the London Conference of Canal-users in August and agreed to represent its views personally to President Nasser who, he records in his autobiography, had an irritating habit of rolling his eyes upward and smirking while he (Menzies) was talking to him. Finally on 29 October Israel attacked Egypt. Two days later Britain and France joined in, botched the business, and in effect capitulated to Nasser after three days. Both at the time and ever afterwards Menzies publicly justified the use of force outside the provisions of the U.N. Charter, and maintained that his policy and actions had been wholly right and proper. No other single action of his did so much to undermine the goodwill of the 'Third World' governments towards Australia, which had been built up by Evatt and Chifley, and to re-establish the image of the country as an arch-conservative, racist, neo-colonial power ever ready to support imperialist policies in the Third World.

The Prime Minister's attachment to the United Kingdom, and on this occasion also to his country's 'great and powerful friend' the United States, plus his own vanity, placed both Australia and himself in a humiliating position again in 1960, when he was acting also as Minister for External Affairs just after Casey's retirement. At a meeting of the U.N. General Assembly in October, attempting to please Britain and the United States, he moved an amendment to a motion sponsored by India's Pandit Nehru and the delegates of four other Third World countries. The substantive motion urged Khrushchev and Eisenhower to renew their contacts notwithstanding the breakdown of the proposed 'summit meeting' in Paris in the previous May. The amendment was overwhelmingly defeated after an excoriating speech by Nehru denouncing Menzies' proposal as 'negative, untenable and verging on absurdity'. One Australian journalist concluded that 'Sir Robert's reputation as a world statesman was left in tatters on the floor of the Assembly'.[9]

INCREASING AFFLUENCE

And yet Menzies was not far out of touch with public opinion. Though at least half of the British electorate roundly condemned Eden's Suez adventure, it seems that most Australians, on this issue at least, agreed with their Prime Minister. Throughout the 1950s Britain remained, as it always had been, more important as a trading partner than any other two or three nations put together: although the trend was downwards. In 1949 the United Kingdom supplied 50.5 per cent of Australian imports and took 42.4 per cent of her exports. In 1960 these figures had fallen to 35.7 per cent and 25.6 per cent respectively. By comparison imports from and exports to the United States, the next most important country, had risen from 10.3 per cent and 3.9 per cent in 1949 to 18.2 per cent and 8.2 per cent in 1960. In 1949 trade with Japan, the ex-enemy, was almost non-existent, but by 1960 she had moved into third place, supplying 4.5 per cent of Australia's imports and taking 14.5 per cent of her exports. Within fifteen years Japan was to become incomparably Australia's major trading-partner, displacing both Britain and the United States, but this was by no means obvious in 1960. The turning point in Japanese-Australian relations came only in 1957 when Menzies and John McEwen, the extremely capable and forceful Minister for Trade and Leader of the Country Party, both visited Japan, and Nobusuke Kishi, the Japanese Prime Minister, made a return visit to Australia. A Trade Agreement giving very much freer and fairer access to each other's markets was signed, and this was revised and renewed in 1963.

In any country prosperity depends on the level of internal trade

[9] Kevin Perkins, *Menzies: Last of the Queen's Men*, Adelaide, 1968, p. 249.

even more than on external trade. In this area too the boom continued. Many older citizens who had been adults during the Depression could not believe that a major slump was not bound to occur before long. The rising generation on the other hand took full employment and increasing affluence for granted, almost as though they were part of the natural environment like sun, wind and rain. Prosperity was built partly on the steadily rising level of investment in both the public and private sectors of the economy. Most of the overseas money still came from Britain in the 1950s but, as with imports and exports, the United States was beginning to overhaul Britain's lead. Much more of the capital was Australian however — more than ever before and more than came from abroad.

The manufacturing industry was particularly prosperous. For the first time in history the great majority of *all* manufactured goods, from plastic ball-point pens and carpenters' tools to motor cars and railway locomotives, were made in Australia instead of being imported. By the end of the decade people had become accustomed to this state of affairs, so much so that most of them no longer believed that all things Australian, especially manufactured goods, were necessarily inferior to imported articles. Gross figures give some idea of the expansion that was taking place, though they are misleading unless seen in the perspective of continuous inflation, the rate of which slowed down considerably in the middle and later part of the period. Between 1949 and 1959 the real value of an Australian pound dropped by about half to something like ten or eleven shillings. In the same period however the total value of factory production rose from £489,000,000 to £1,843,000,000. At the same time the population grew rapidly, owing both to the massive migration programme and to what was sometimes called the post-war baby boom. Even so the total value of factory production rose in the period from £64 to £185 *per caput*.

The rapid economic growth meant a real and visible, if not quite so rapid, rise in the Australian standard of living. People dressed better and ate more nutritive food than their ancestors had done. Popular magazines pointed out that fresh fruit, salads and green vegetables were much better for children and adults than pudding, cakes and potatoes, and most readers, for the first time, were able to buy quantities of fruit without having to ration it to themselves and their children. By the end of the decade, the housing shortage had been overcome. Tall blocks of flats replaced many acres of terrace-houses in the inner city areas, but most Australians still preferred to live in separate cottages, each on its own block of land, in endless miles of suburban streets. It cannot be said that most of the less expensive houses, many built by State Housing

Commissions, were in all respects an improvement on earlier buildings of the same type. The most pleasant and useful feature of nineteenth-century Australian houses had been their verandahs, sheltering three or even four sides from sun and rain. As time went on verandahs were cut down in length and breadth, partly to save money but partly to follow an idiotic fashion. By the 1930s they had been reduced to a narrow gesture across less than half the house-front, to remind the beholder of what had been. In the 1950s the verandah disappeared altogether from most houses. What was left, too often, was a brick, timber or 'fibro' box with lower ceilings than of yore and nothing to keep the summer heat off its walls. Nevertheless the average suburban house was bigger and set on a bigger block of land than its predecessors had been.

Greater emphasis on secondary industry meant, of course, acceleration of the rush to the cities. Australia had always been one of the most, perhaps the most, heavily urbanised countries in the world. By 1960 more than two thirds of the population lived in the six capital cities and the 'urban sprawl' attaching to each. In New South Wales close settlement, if not quite suburbia, extended continuously for about 300 kilometres along a coastal strip from Port Kembla through Sydney to Newcastle. Air pollution and movement of people and goods within the cities were becoming increasingly intransigent problems, especially in Sydney and Melbourne.

Despite the crowding, those who lived in the new suburbs enjoyed a great deal more leisure from domestic work as well as a little more time away from the business of earning their livings than had their ancestors. Affluence was most apparent in the proliferation of labour-saving devices and gadgetry. Television, for instance, was introduced in Sydney and Melbourne in the last months of 1956 and by 1960 was available in all capital cities, except Hobart, and in some country towns. Prophets of woe feared that it would debase public taste and distract children from their homework, just as others had feared the worst when broadcasting was introduced thirty years earlier. In fact, despite many trashy programmes, T.V. probably raised the level of taste, education and political understanding in the community. By 1960 T.V. sets were well on the way to becoming standard equipment in every home. There were approximately 1 120 000 viewers' licences taken out, almost half the number of broadcast listeners' licences. By that year too most, if not all, homes were equipped with a whole range of appliances which, even as recently as the end of World War II, had been rather scarce middle-class luxuries or almost unknown. Cake-mixers, pressure-cookers, vacuum cleaners, electric steam-irons, washing machines and refrigerators made housework much easier, while motor-lawnmowers and power hand-tools, such as circular-saws, lightened work in the garden and the backyard shed. The greatest single symbol of affluence was, and is, the private motor car, still a somewhat unusual luxury in middle-class families in the 1940s. By 1960 possession of a 'family car' was usual, though of course not universal, among all classes. In 1948 there were 143 registered motor vehicles (commercial and private and including the relatively few motorcycles) on the road per 1000 of the population. In 1960 there were 276 per 1000, or about one motor vehicle (excluding motorcycles) to every four people including children.

The family car served a multitude of purposes in addition to that of carrying people to and from their workplaces. Home delivery of groceries, meat, bread, fruit and vegetables, suspended during the war to save manpower, was for the most part never re-established. Supermarkets with adjacent parking space began to replace many small family businesses and corner stores. The car was taken on shopping expeditions and driven home laden with provisions. On weekends or after working hours it carried people on visits to friends, relatives or entertainments, or on picnics into the country. More than ever before teenagers — and older people — used the car as a necessity for personal transport and as a mobile love-nest.

It also served to carry more people than ever before to watch or participate in games. Surfing, an increasingly popular sport since the beginning of the century, became something of a cult among young males. Its devotees bleached their hair white and drove hundreds of miles searching for the perfect wave to ride. They referred disparagingly to their female companions as 'grunters'. Sometimes bloody affrays took place between 'Surfies' and members of another cult, the 'Rockers', who generally came from poorer suburbs, dressed in leather, moved on motorcycles rather than in cars, and sang more often than others the immensely popular tune 'Rock Around the Clock'. Water skiing also became tremendously popular in the last years of the 1950s. Many practitioners towed their motor-boats to the water on a trailer hitched to the family car. In 1956 for the first time in history Australia acted as host country for the Olympic Games. They were relayed 'live' from Melbourne on the newly installed television service and watched by millions. In the 'unofficial' competition between nations the two Cold War giants, the U.S.S.R. and the United States, gained thirty-seven and thirty-two gold medals respectively. To most Australians it seemed strange that their country, with only about one-twentieth the population of either, should have trailed so far behind as to come third with only thirteen gold medals.

CULTURE AND CENSORSHIP

Within a few weeks of the ending of the Olympic Games on 30 January 1957 newspapers published details of the winning design for Sydney's new opera house. The competition, promoted by Joseph Cahill's State Labor Government, showed, among other things, how much art and culture mattered — at last — in the Australia of the 1950s. Conceived by the Danish architectural genius, Joern Utzon, the building was to be situated in the heart of Sydney on Bennelong Point, the last camping place of one of the very first Aboriginals to be dispossessed and debased by the European invaders. It was to soar over the harbour like a great yacht. It was also to cost £ 3,500,000 and so was sardonically dubbed by some the 'Cahill Mahal'. In the end it cost upwards of £ 100,000,000, but the breath-taking beauty of the design stifled all but the most philistine criticism. By the time of the official opening in 1973 most people felt that cost was irrelevant. If there were seven architectural wonders of the modern world, as there were of the ancient, the Sydney Opera House would certainly rank among the greatest of them. The old rivalry between Sydney and Melbourne ensured that planning of an Arts Centre in the latter city began soon afterwards. The first stage, opened in 1968, should have been considered a splendid building in its own right. In 1954 that great public servant, H. C. Coombs, Chairman of the Commonwealth Bank Board, took the lead in establishing the Elizabethan Theatre Trust to foster Australian drama, opera and ballet. Starved of funds by Commonwealth and State Governments, the Trust had not accomplished very much by 1960, though it did help with the launching that year of the biennial Adelaide Festival of the Arts.

Modelled on the magnificent Edinburgh Festival, the Adelaide gatherings were at first disfigured by the kind of censorship to be expected in the capital of wowserdom, for in the 1950s puritanical philistinism was still strong everywhere. Although thousands of suburban picture theatres closed after the advent of television, all films were heavily censored as a matter of course and Customs clerks, policemen and State politicians banned books continually. Censorship on political grounds was much less severe than in the 1930s, in fact almost non-existent; but censorship on 'moral' grounds still flourished. Creative artists and intellectuals

Bulletin, 1966

considered it a great advance towards sanity when in April 1958 the Minister for Customs and Excise, Senator Henty, released a list of 178 banned books including *Ten Tales* from Boccaccio's *Decameron*, and J. P. Donleavy's *The Ginger Man*. The list covered only works considered by the censors to have literary merit. Photographs of naked or semi-naked men and women, magazines and 'pulp' type books about sex were banned out of hand.

One healthy reaction to continuing puritanism was the growth at this time of the Sydney Libertarian Society and its offshoot, the 'Push', groups of men and women inspired largely by the ideas of Professor John Anderson of Sydney University. Philosophical free-thinkers and hedonists, they made a virtue of flouting conventional moral maxims, especially in the sexual sphere. Few artists or intellectuals entirely escaped their influence during the 1950s and 1960s. One of the first indications that the 'wowser vote' was weakening came in New South Wales. On 13 November 1954, while the Petrov Case was proceeding, the Cahill State Government conducted a plebiscite on hotel closing-time, asking people to vote either for the retention of six-o'clock closing or the extension of trading hours till ten at night. Ten o'clock won the day but only by about 10 000 votes in almost 2 000 000; and so what people had long been wont to call the 'six o'clock swill' came to an end in the most populous state after nearly forty years. In Victoria the 'swill' continued till 1965. Another reform in social law was carried through the Commonwealth Parliament in May 1959 by the Liberal Attorney-General, Sir Garfield Barwick. For years Australian divorce law had been a lawyer's dream and a petitioner's nightmare. The law was quite different in each State, but slow and highly restrictive in all. Barwick's Act introduced one law for the whole of Australia; reduced possible grounds for divorce from 30 or more to 14 — including one quite new ground which roused frantic wowser opposition: divorce, with certain safeguards, by consent.

Despite the continuance of philistinism in many high places, the post-war cultural and artistic renaissance continued and expanded during the 1950s. Writers, teachers, journalists and academics spent more time than ever before exploring the Australian past. Ballads, folksongs, popular yarns and bush music were collected and published, giving rise in the following decade to the growth of a new sector of the entertainment industry. Sidney Nolan, Albert Tucker, John Passmore, Ian Fairweather, Arthur Boyd and Charles Blackman joined Drysdale and Dobell in the very first rank of painters. Australian poetry flourished — and was published far more widely than ever before because of the proliferation of Australian publishing houses, and of serious literary periodicals like *Overland, Quadrant, Australian Letters, Prospect* and *Westerly*, to say nothing of the two major journals already established, *Meanjin* and *Southerly*.

Merely to list some of the leading prose-writers who came into prominence at this period would be a formidable task. For the first time, a large number of professional writers for a popular market, such as Jon Cleary, Morris West, Arthur Upfield, and D'Arcy Niland were able to make a reasonable living from their work. More serious writers still generally had to have some source of income other than their writing, although Vance and Nettie Palmer did not. Among other leading prose writers of the 1950s were Alan Marshall whose masterpiece, *I Can Jump Puddles*, sold over 2 000 000 copies, and Hal Porter, Dal Stivens, John Morrison, Martin Boyd and Randolph Stow. Frank Hardy's *Power Without Glory* (1950) was a thinly disguised history of the seamy side of Victorian and Commonwealth politics, which provoked the ageing John Wren to launch, through his wife, an unsuccessful action for libel. Pre-eminent among the novelists was Patrick White, who had published *Happy Valley* in 1939, but was not much noticed until he returned to live in Sydney after the war. *The Tree of Man* (1955) and *Voss* (1957), though savagely attacked by some Australian critics, with others immediately established their author as one of the greatest living novelists writing in English, perhaps the greatest. In 1973 he was to become the first Australian writer awarded a Nobel Prize.

There were no discordant critical voices, however, when Ray Lawler's *Summer of the Seventeenth Doll* was first performed at the University of Melbourne's Union Theatre on 28 November 1955. Twenty years later it still seemed that this 'play will always be considered as the beginning of the Australian national theatre'.[10] In the characters of a tough cane-cutter and his friends, Lawler dramatically held up to Australians a mirror of all that was best and worst in themselves — or in the traditionally sanctioned view of themselves. For reasons which remain somewhat obscure, Australian playwrights had never previously matched the achievements of poets, novelists, short-story writers, painters or even musicians. *The Doll*, as it quickly came to be known, changed all that. Lawler's success inspired other plays of which the best was Seymour's *The One Day of the Year*, a dramatic questioning of the national myth associated with Anzac Day. The coming of television

[10] Geoffrey Serle, *From Deserts the Prophets Come*, Melbourne, 1973, p. 197.

also stimulated live theatre both directly by providing a new market for playwrights and actors, and indirectly, by taking most of the audience out of suburban picture-shows. The 1950s saw a proliferation of little theatres, both amateur and professional, as well as of playwrights. The dramatic explosion was not a flash in the pan. If anything the movement accelerated in the following decades. If anything, too, T.V. seemed to stimulate the voracious taste for reading which had long distinguished Australians. As Geoffrey Serle puts it:

> About 1960, despite all the homes with or without one single bookshelf, Australia still spent more per head on books than any other English-speaking people, bought more than a quarter of British book-exports and had relatively twice as many book-shops as Britain and four or five times as many as the United States; and almost half the residents in local government areas which had libraries were enrolled as borrowers.[11]

In the 1950s universities expanded less rapidly than they had in the immediate post-war period or than they were to do in the following decades when the children of the post-war 'baby boom' had reached the age for tertiary education. Only one really new university was founded — Monash in Melbourne, happily named after the great scholarly soldier of World War I. However the University of New England, founded as a small college of Sydney University in 1938, became autonomous in 1954. The New South Wales University of Technology, founded by the State Government in the wave of post-war expansion, became the fully-fledged University of New South Wales in 1958; and in 1951 this institution set up the dependent Newcastle University College. Universities were lively places compared with what they had been before the war. Governments provided money much more generously. More frequent appointment of Australian graduates to lectureships and chairs reflected increased confidence and maturity: and yet the Cold War, Menzies' anti-Communist crusade and the smearing and harrying of liberals and radicals during this time when Joseph McCarthy rode high in the United States, had its effect. In 1961 the University of New South Wales was forced by one of its ex-professors to admit that it had habitually sought the views of secret policemen on the suitability of applicants for academic posts, and to promise reform for the future. In all universities it was a common complaint that students, generally speaking, were far more cautious, conformist and conservative than their ageing teachers. They worked to obtain their professional

[11] Serle, p. 189.

qualifications, but most shrank from inquiry into anything savouring of 'politics' and from the trouble into which, their parents warned, it was likely to lead. Except for growing hostility to any form of racism, including the White Australia Policy, student radicalism seemed to be dead.

Chapter 11

THE HEIGHT OF THE BOOM
c. 1961—1968

Menzies scrapes home — Relations with South-East Asia, Britain and the United States — Commonwealth and State developments — Embroilment with Vietnam and Indonesia — Holt succeeds Menzies — Unparalleled prosperity

MENZIES SCRAPES HOME

In 1960, after ten years of uninterrupted conservative rule in Canberra, the position of the Liberal-Country Party Coalition, and of Menzies within it, seemed to be more firmly assured than ever. The Prime Minister had been made a Queen's Counsel, a Privy Councillor, and a Companion of Honour and had graciously accepted eleven honorary degrees from universities all over the world. In the next decade he was loaded with seventeen more degrees, made a knight of the exclusive Order of the Thistle in 1963 by the Queen and, acme of any Anglophile's ambition, in 1965 became Lord Warden of the Cinque Ports in succession to Winston Churchill. He also acquired another, unofficial, overseas title when the Afrikaner press, in recognition of his support at Imperial Conferences and elsewhere for South African policies fondly dubbed him 'Oom Robert' — 'Uncle Bob'. In 1973, long after he had retired to private life, the Imperial Japanese Government conferred on him the Order of the Rising Sun (First Class). All this was matter for sardonic jest among Labor voters and for something approaching awe among those who favoured the Coalition governments. To the former Menzies was an unscrupulous and arrogant reactionary, to the latter an urbane, far-seeing, world statesman; but not even those who hated him most could deny his tremendous ability. After 1949 he came near to political defeat only once, in the general election of 9 December 1961. On that occasion he and his party were almost beaten not, fundamentally, by the Opposition so much as by the overwhelming pride and self-confidence which always clouded his great gifts.

Throughout the long post-war boom, the major problem of government was not to maintain full employment by maintaining prosperity but, on the contrary, to control inflationary pressures by applying financial brakes to the national economy from time to time. In 1960, chiefly owing to the tremendous inflow of private and public investment funds from abroad, an incipient balance of payments crisis developed. At the same time wages and prices were spiralling upwards. There was a labour shortage in some key industries and heavy speculation in land and buildings. With the advice of his departmental experts, Harold Holt, the Treasurer, introduced a complex series of budgetary measures aimed at curbing the inflationary spiral and at improving the balance of payments position. By 1961 these inevitably unpopular measures had succeeded, to a degree, in both their aims, but at the cost of creating a higher level of unemployment than any known in Australia since the early days of World War II. It is true that in 1939 nine per cent unemployment had been thought reasonable, even good, compared with the horrors of the Depression, but there had been a revolution in people's expectations. In 1961 anything over 2 per cent seemed well-nigh intolerable, not just to those without work and their friends, but also to many businessmen who usually supported the Liberal Party, but who hated to see their profits declining as demand for their products fell away. It was obvious that there was a great deal of dissatisfaction with the Government's performance. Some conservative newspapers criticised the 'credit squeeze' and 'stop-go' economic policies, but as the election approached Menzies seemed as confident as ever, and not disposed to exert himself unduly over it.

With Dr Evatt's retirement from politics, Labor's chances seemed to be enhanced. Evatt was already a palpably sick man when he went to the Bench of the New South Wales Supreme Court, and Calwell was enjoying his 'honeymoon' period as Labor leader. There was even talk, though it came to nothing, of a rapprochement now that Evatt was gone, between Labor and the D.L.P. Calwell promised that, if Labor were elected to power, it would introduce a supplementary budget, if necessary, to restore full employment. He also promised to double child endowment payments, to make increases in a wide range of pensions, to make cheap housing loans available to young couples, to reduce from twenty to ten years the period of residence required for migrants to qualify for pensions, to recognise Communist China and to bring home the Australian troops stationed in Malaya.

Menzies matched Calwell's offer to migrants but otherwise made virtually no specific promises, being content, despite warnings from some in his own party, to stand pat on the Government's record. Not only that, but out of pique he deliberately prevented Liberal Party candidates from making use of free television time to put forward their case. This was the first general election in which at least the metropolitan area in all states, including Tasmania, was covered by T.V. The A.B.C. announced that it would give a brief few minutes each to all candidates for seats in the viewing areas, to expound their policies. The Prime Minister objected that this scheme would give minor party candidates, including Communists, as much time to put forward their views as Government candidates had, and he ordered Liberal candidates to boycott the programme — which of course they all did. It says much for the integrity and independence of the A.B.C. that it resisted formidable pressure from the Prime Minister and went ahead with the programme as planned, though without any Liberal spokesmen. In addition the A.L.P. bought much more advertising time on commercial T.V. and used it more imaginatively than the Liberals, such was the hubris of the latter and especially of their leader. The campaign was also remarkable for effective anti-White Australia Policy lobbying by university students especially in Victoria. Politicians in all the major parties were closely questioned on their attitude to the policy and usually embarrassed as a result.

The election was the most evenly contested in the history of the Commonwealth. For more than a week it looked as though there would be a deadlocked House of Representatives with 61 Coalition and 61 A.L.P. members. Finally however D. J. Killen, a Liberal, was elected for the Queensland seat of Moreton by only 110 votes after the distribution of preferences. In fact he owed his seat largely to the lucky chance that his name was high up on the ballot paper. This gave a House of 45 Liberal, 17 Country Party and 60 A.L.P. members. The Government also lost seats in the Senate so that the balance of power in that chamber was held by two Tasmanians — one D.L.P. member and one ex-Labor Independent. The veteran Country Party member, Sir Earle Page, was also defeated, but died in hospital before the declaration of the poll in his native Grafton.

If Menzies was shaken by the result of the election he did not show it. With his customary aplomb he consulted McEwen, the Country Party Leader, about new appointments to the Cabinet made necessary by the defeat of three ministers at the polls. Two of the newcomers were exceptionally able men, Allen Fairhall, Minister for Supply, and Leslie Bury, Minister for Air and Assistant Treasurer. However Bury was forced to resign seven months later for publicly contradicting McEwen and Menzies over Britain's proposed entry into the European Common Market. Bury thought, correctly as it turned out, that British entry would do negligible harm to Australian trade. He was soon reinstated in another Cabinet post. When Parliament met, despite his minute majority,

Menzies immediately re-established his authority over the Chamber.

After its narrow escape the Coalition Government's first priority was to get the economy moving again. The 'credit squeeze' had successfully halted inflation. In the first half of 1962 prices remained steady and even fell slightly at times, but unemployment figures in January rose to about 132 000, a new post-war record. The Government was sufficiently impressed to begin thinking about setting up a committee to advise on the structuring of the national economy. However this very expert committee of leading businessmen and academic economists, under the chairmanship of Dr James Vernon, managing director of the Colonial Sugar Refining Company, was not finally appointed till February 1963. As Treasurer, Holt had the primary responsibility for introducing a series of mildly inflationary measures — special grants to the States for public works to provide jobs for the unemployed, an increase in payments to those out of work, a 5 per cent income tax cut and so on. No doubt partly as a result of these measures the employment position improved slowly but steadily. By the second half of 1963 the country was again so prosperous that the Prime Minister hastened to call another election.

RELATIONS WITH SOUTH-EAST ASIA, BRITAIN AND THE UNITED STATES

Yet, though national economic health remained the first preoccupation, both Government and governed during the 1960s became increasingly embroiled with foreign, or at any rate overseas, affairs. Except for the actual years of the two World Wars, and perhaps the year prior to the World War II, this had never happened before. Most Australian electors had always been notoriously indifferent to events outside their own country. The first problem to obtrude itself on their attention was that of Dutch New Guinea or, as the Indonesians called it, West Irian.

The area was inhabited by Melanesian tribes akin to those of the Australian part of the island, but having little more in common, ethnically, culturally, historically or in any other way with the Indonesians than they had with their Dutch rulers or, for that matter, with Australians. The Dutch had remained in control when they handed sovereignty of the rest of their East Indian empire to the mainly Malay Indonesians in the last days of 1949. From that time Indonesia had claimed that West Irian was rightfully part of her territory. However the issue remained dormant until March 1960 when President Sukarno, a colourful, popular, radical,

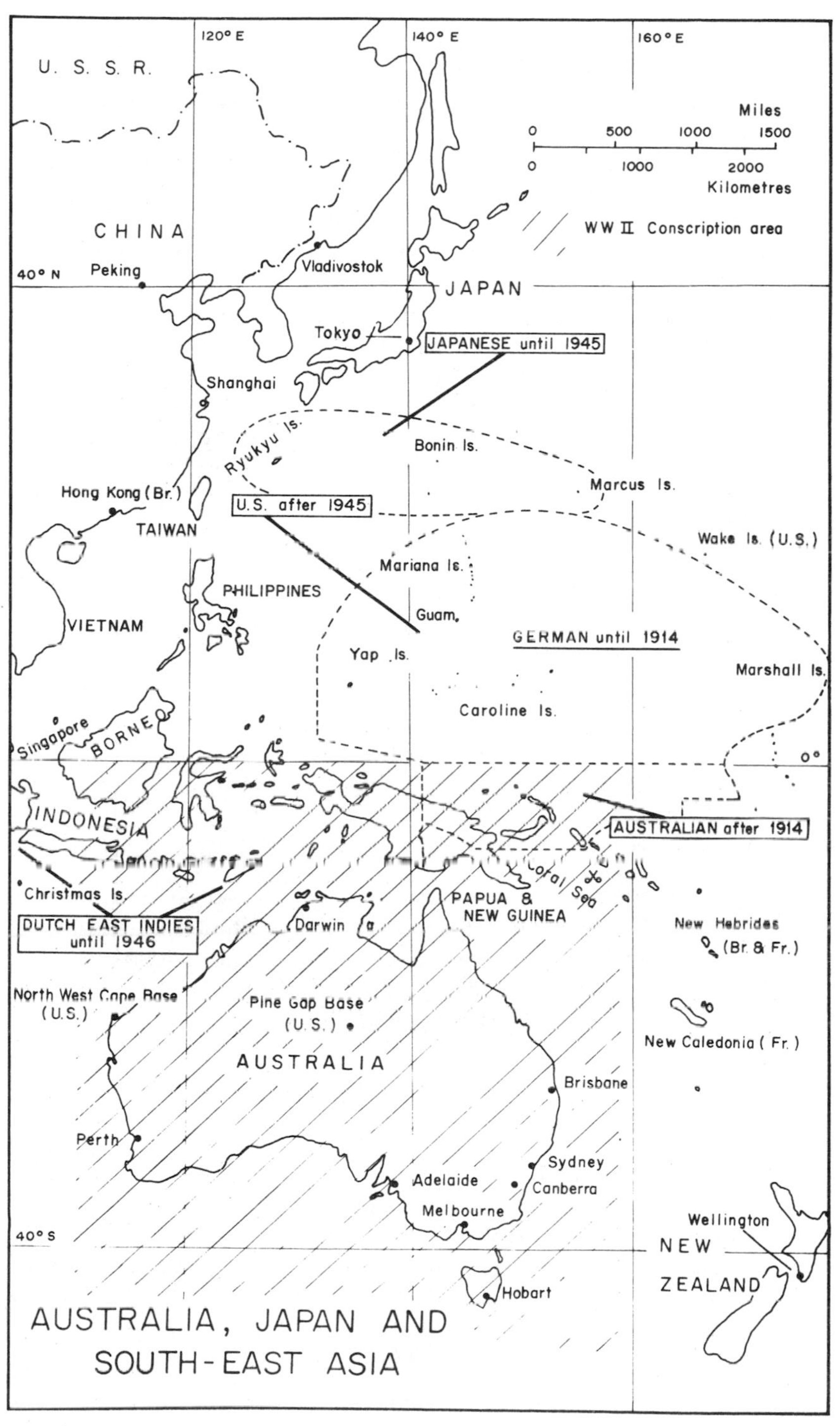

AUSTRALIA, JAPAN AND SOUTH-EAST ASIA

nationalist demagogue, who ruled the archipelago by means of what he liked to call 'guided democracy', began a campaign for the cession of West Irian to Indonesia. Australia was immediately and anxiously involved.

Since the foundation of the Republic, relations with Indonesia had been good and virtually all Australians wished to keep them so. At the same time few or none were anxious to acquire a long and virtually indefensible land frontier with an Asian power, however friendly it might be for the present. Moreover, as the campaign progressed, the Soviet Government supplied to Indonesia on easy terms more and more light and heavy arms including warships. It had long been known that most of Sukarno's support within the country came from the Indonesian Communist Party and other left-wing groups. Thus Australia was in a quandary. Conservatives, particularly, would have liked best to keep the Dutch in West Irian — for the rest of time if possible. If not, then the indigenous people should be allowed to rule themselves, probably after a period of tutelage under the United Nations. At the very least, outright war between the Netherlands and Indonesia must be prevented; for who could tell where it would stop? So, usurping rather, as he was wont to do, the function of Sir Garfield Barwick, the Minister for External Affairs, in April 1961 Mr Menzies told an envoy of Sukarno Australia's position. There must under no circumstances be any resort to armed force. Negotiations between the Netherlands and Indonesia must be freely carried out without duress on either side. Any agreement so reached would be fully respected by Australia.

In a U.N. debate at the end of the year Australia reiterated that the essence of her position was that the people of West Irian must, under any settlement, be allowed the right of self-determination. Meanwhile, Sukarno stepped up his policy of 'total confrontation' so that negotiations did in fact take place under constant threat of war. During 1962 the Dutch capitulated to Indonesia pressure and Australia to pressure from her ally, the United States. America wished above all to avoid war and to placate Sukarno, lest opposition should strengthen the Communist forces in Indonesia. Australian fears and the right of self-determination for the indigenous people counted for little in Washington: and so, despite ANZUS, SEATO and twelve years' faithful conciliation of U.S. wishes, the Australian Government was forced to acquiesce in Sukarno's annexation of West Irian. In August it was agreed that Indonesia should take over the territory after a few months of formal U.N. administration and that she would provide for an 'act of self-determination' by the inhabitants by the end of 1969. Few believed that this last provision would be meaningful.

In the early 1960s people and politicians were even more concerned about their ancient relationship with distant Britain than about their new relationship with their nearest neighbour. Late in 1961 the British Government began talking seriously about entering the European Economic Community, or Common Market, as it was usually called. The implications of such a step seemed shattering to most Australians, particularly to older people and conservatives. In fact the United Kingdom, as Australia's chief trading partner, was being very rapidly replaced just at this time by the United States and an economically resurgent Japan, but most people were scarcely aware of this. They did know that the United Kingdom had taken the great bulk of wool, wheat, and other Australian exports from the earliest pioneering days and during their own lifetimes. It was feared that British entry into the Common Market was bound to mean abolition, or at least scaling down, of preferential tariff arrangements for Australian goods. No one, naturally, was more alarmed than the Country Party and its leader Mr John McEwen, Minister for Trade and (after 18 December, 1963) Trade and Industry.

Born in 1900 at Chiltern in northern Victoria, not far from the Murray River where it flows out of the southern Alps at Albury, McEwen served with the First A.I.F. while still hardly more than a boy. After the war he became a battling wheat-farmer in the Victorian Mallee district. He joined the Country Party and, from 1934 until his retirement in 1971, successively represented the voters in three different country federal electorates in his native State. In 1949 he attained cabinet rank as Minister for Commerce and Agriculture. Then in 1958 he succeeded 'Artie' Fadden as leader of the Country Party and Deputy Prime Minister. It was immediately apparent that here was a new force to be reckoned with. McEwen was a self-made man whose face looked as though it had been hewn out of granite. Tall, saturnine and tough, he was an Australian nationalist and a realist, with none of the inbuilt deference towards Britain which marked the Prime Minister and most of his colleagues. In this last respect at least, he had more in common with Labor men that with most of those in the Liberal and Country Parties.

From 1958 onwards 'Black Jack' McEwen built up the strength of the bureaucrats in the Department of Trade until it rivalled the Treasury and Prime Minister's Departments in the moulding of Government policies. He was the only person in the Menzies governments with the strength to fight against the Prime Minister, very often effectively, for his own point of view. Menzies respected him accordingly and privately considered him the ablest man, after himself, in either Coalition party. Naturally he dominated the Country Party quite as firmly as Menzies dominated the Liberals. The two leaders had no quarrel, however, over British entry into the Common Market. Most Liberal and Labor parliamentarians shared, more or less strongly, the hostile attitude of McEwen and his Country Party cohorts. Bury, a British migrant member of Cabinet, was one of the minority who was forced, as noted above, to resign his portfolio over the issue. In March and April 1962 McEwen toured North America, Britain and Europe, forcefully putting the Australian viewpoint and bargaining for special treatment when Britain joined Europe. Menzies followed two months later. How effective their intervention was can never be known because, in the event, British entry into Europe was virtually vetoed by President de Gaulle of France in January 1963.

Yet another aspect of foreign relations was not at first debated as it should have been. On 17 May 1962 the Prime Minister made a guarded, not to say cryptic, announcement that the United States was proposing to establish a 'radio communications centre' at North West Cape in Western Australia. For the rest of the year, despite questioning from Labor members, he had no more to say on the subject. Then on 9 May 1963 the Government signed a treaty with the United States, and the question was debated in Parliament. The 'communications centre' proved to be in fact an integral part of the United States' world-wide nuclear deterrent system, its prime function being to communicate with Polaris submarines from which inter-continental ballistic missiles might be launched. Australia might be 'consulted' about the station, but was to have no control whatever over it or the uses to which it might be put.

Australian opinion was deeply divided. The Government parties, and most of their supporters, thought it a realistic and praiseworthy arrangement for committing U.S. power to Australia's defence. On the other hand most radicals and many nationalists denounced it as something which would ensure that Australia was an early target for nuclear missiles in a war between the great powers, even though her own interests and safety might not otherwise be threatened. Moreover existence of the base made nonsense of Labor's policy of banning nuclear weapons and of working for a nuclear-free zone in the Southern Hemisphere. First mooted in 1955, this policy was strengthened in 1958 by the agreement in May of that year between all the powers interested in the Antarctic Continent to ban therefrom all (not just nuclear) weapons and military installations. After a period of agonising reappraisal the A.L.P. decided to welcome the establishment of the base at North West Cape but, on its return to power, to re-negotiate the agreement with the United

States so as to give Australia a somewhat greater measure of control. Illogically the party went on denouncing all nuclear testing and advocating a nuclear-free 'zone of peace' in the Southern Hemisphere or, sometimes, in the Indian Ocean.

In the same fateful month of May 1962, again with minimal discussion or explanation, the Menzies Government took the first step into the quagmire of Vietnam. Exactly a week after the Prime Minister's statement about North-West Cape, the Minister for Defence, Athol Townley, announced that thirty Army instructors would be sent to help train South Vietnamese troops. He stressed that Australia was obliged to do this under the SEATO Pact and that the men would not be engaged in combat duties. Both statements were false. The relevant article of the SEATO Pact 'obliged' Australia to do nothing more than 'consult' her allies, and the thirty instructors did join in the fighting almost immediately, many of them earning South Vietnamese decorations for bravery under fire. In fact the troops were sent for political, not military, reasons at the request of the United States Government, which wished thus to demonstrate to hostile world opinion that the United States was not alone in its war on Vietnamese Communism — or nationalism.[1] Considering that this was the beginning of what was to be, for the next ten years, the greatest and most divisive political issue before the nation, the matter slipped by with very little opposition or even comment. One reason for this was that people's attention was already preoccupied with President Sukarno's takeover of West Irian.

No sooner was this accomplished than the Indonesian Government began to threaten further aggression. As early as May 1961 the Prime Minister of Malaya, the Tunku Abdul Rahman, had suggested that all ex-British colonies in the Malay archipelago might join with Malaya to form a new federated state of Malaysia. British North Borneo, Sarawak, the island sultanate of Brunei and Singapore were the areas concerned, the former two having a land frontier with Indonesia which embraces the major portion of the great island of Borneo. The 'advanced' inhabitants were Malay-speaking people as, of course, were those of the Indonesian part of the island, and the undeveloped mountain and jungle regions in both parts were inhabited by Dyak and other tribes-people.

A few weeks after the final settlement of the West Irian dispute in September 1962, Singapore and North Borneo decided to join the proposed Malaysian Federation. Sukarno immediately stepped

[1] R. G. Neale, *Australia's Military Commitment to Vietnam*, Canberra, 1975, pp. 1, 2.

up his campaign of 'confrontation', that is, of making bombastic threats and carrying on subversion and intermittent guerilla warfare against the states of the proposed federation. As with the West Irian dispute, Australian interest and honour alike demanded she preserve peace and protect the Malaysian states without antagonising Indonesia: or at any rate without antagonising her more than was absolutely unavoidable. External Affairs Minister, Sir Garfield Barwick, and senior diplomats in his department worked busily during the first half of 1963 to bring interested parties together. In June a conference of foreign ministers at Manila announced complete agreement on how to solve problems arising from the creation of Malaysia. The Australian press congratulated Barwick on the success of his efforts — prematurely as it turned out.

On 9 July agreement was reached in London between the sometime Malay colonies that Malaysia would be inaugurated on 31 August. Sukarno immediately resumed confrontation. A U.N. mission to Sabah (British North Borneo) and Sarawak reported that the majority of the inhabitants favoured joining Malaysia and the new state was proclaimed on 16 September. Next day, watched by complaisant policemen, Indonesian rioters sacked the British Embassy in Djakarta. Press and public opinion in Australia clamoured for action, or at least for a clear statement of Government intentions. As we have seen, Australian troops and airmen had been stationed in Malaya for some years under the ANZAM arrangement, but this did not amount to a treaty involving any clear and specific obligations. The Labor Opposition in Canberra took the opportunity to demand that it should. The Government refused, but on 25 September the Prime Minister told the House of Representatives that Australia's position had been made clear to the Governments of Malaysia, the United Kingdom, New Zealand and others concerned. Any armed invasion of Malaysia, or subversive activity inspired from outside that country, would meet military resistance from Australia as well as from British and Malaysian forces.

However these brave words were not followed by deeds. In October and November Indonesian troops, variously described as 'insurgents', 'terrorists' or 'guerillas' began sporadic fighting with British and Malaysian forces in the jungles of North Borneo but, despite hints from London, the Australian forces remained in Malaya itself — at any rate until long after the general election of November, 1963. The Government apparently believed that, so long as the fighting was not very serious, it could do more to help Malaysia by intensifying its diplomatic activities behind the scenes.

"Anyway. MY daddy's bigger'n YOUR daddy!!!"

The Government also had much to worry about in Papua and New Guinea. In July 1962 the U.N. Trusteeship Council, after a close study of the Territory, reported that progress towards self-government was too slow, though Australian efforts had been praiseworthy in some respects. In particular the report condemned 'stubborn adherence to a policy of gradualism', thereby singling out the very principle to which the Minister for Territories, Paul Hasluck, was most attached. It condemned racial discrimination in the liquor laws and recommended that, by 1964, a parliament of 100 members, elected by universal adult franchise, and a university should be established. These proposals really shocked conservatives like Hasluck, once described by a political opponent as 'a stuffy little man'. Nevertheless under the pressure of critical world opinion the Government acted quickly, if not as quickly as the report demanded. By the end of the year the liquor laws had been amended to abolish all distinction between whites and blacks and a committee of inquiry into tertiary education for the Territory had been established. In mid-1963 Parliament passed a Bill which provided for an enlarged Legislative Council to advise the Administrator and a new House of Assembly. The latter was to consist of forty-four members elected by universal adult suffrage, ten non-indigenous elected members, and ten official members.

Although the U.N. report had been concerned only with Papua and New Guinea, it is possible that its concern for the rights of indigenous people directed public and ministerial opinion to the rights, so long ignored, of Aboriginal Australians. At any rate, under legislation passed in 1962, Aboriginals were enabled, but not compelled as white citizens were, to enrol for and vote in Commonwealth elections. Voting, for those who did enrol, was compulsory. They cast their first votes sooner than most people could have expected when the Bill was passed.

COMMONWEALTH AND STATE DEVELOPMENTS

By the winter of 1963 the economy was again prosperous and unemployment figures continued to fall steadily. In August Holt's budget provided for a moderate rise in expenditure. Most pensioners and recipients of social service payments received up to ten shillings a week more money and there were the customary *douceurs* to rural interests — a bounty on superphosphates and additional taxation concessions for farmers. In October a decimal currency Bill was introduced to Parliament and carried fairly expeditiously. Nearly everyone agreed that decimal currency was desirable, but there was surprisingly passionate public argument, before the Bill was introduced, about the name of the new currency unit. The newly ennobled Sir Robert Menzies wished to symbolise Australia's link with Britain by calling it a 'royal' or perhaps a 'crown'. Most people felt this was both pretentious and unacceptably Anglophile, and preferred to talk of dollars and cents, already familiar as part of the rapidly increasing American influence. So the Bill was passed and, after 14 February three years later when the scheme actually came into operation, the Australian dollar had to be distinguished from the Straits dollar, the American dollar and others.

On 14 October statistics showed that the number of unemployed had fallen to about 59 000, the lowest figure since December 1960 when the recession was beginning. Sir Robert Menzies immediately advised the Governor-General to dissolve the House of Representatives, and on the following night announced that the election would be held on 30 November 1963, a year earlier than was legally necessary. The real reason was that he thought returning prosperity favoured the Government's chances but to announce this would hardly have pleased 'swinging' voters. He therefore argued that an early election was necessary to produce a Government with greater authority in foreign affairs than that possessed by the existing administration with its hair's breadth majority of one. Australian support for the North West Cape agreement and for Malaysia must be placed beyond doubt, he said.

Arthur Calwell, the Labor leader, immediately challenged this attempt to make foreign policy the major election issue. The real question, he declared, was whether the voters could afford to re-elect a government which three years before had brought about by its 'credit squeeze', a wholly unnecessary recession. In his policy speech a few weeks later he held, truly enough, that Labor and the Liberals did not really disagree about Malaysia. He then went on to offer a wide range of benefits from the Commonwealth Treasury — greatly increased child endowment, more money for home-building, the armed services, for public works in the States and so on; but the most beguiling promise was to set up a Commonwealth Ministry of Education which would manage a scheme of greatly increased scholarships for tertiary and secondary students, tenable equally in both state and church schools. Thus Labor began belatedly to compete with the Liberals for 'the Catholic vote' it had once taken for granted.

A week later the Prime Minister, as usual, warned the electors that Labor was open to Communist influence and hence not to be trusted to deal sagaciously with the North West Cape agreement, with the threat to Malaysia or indeed with any part of Australia's foreign policy and defence. He then denounced what he called Labor's attempt to buy the voters — as a preliminary to making some spirited bids himself. He did not quite match Calwell's offer on child endowment but outbid him in most other areas. Government payments to medical benefits funds would be increased, young married couples would be given up to £250 each to help them buy their own houses, and secondary-school students would have scholarships to match the Labor offer but in addition the Government would give £5,000,000 a year for science teaching to public and private schools. The D.L.P. urged that national expenditure on defence should be doubled. During the campaign the party lost its most fervent and influential sponsor in the Catholic hierarchy. Dr Daniel Mannix, Archbishop of Melbourne from 1917 to 1963, champion of the left and leading anti-conscriptionist in World War I, had become a pro-conscriptionist and a hero of the far right when he died in his ninety-ninth year. One immediate consequence was that his successor ended Mr Santamaria's regular news commentaries on a Victorian Catholic television network.

Few were surprised that the Coalition was returned to power though Menzies himself was surprised at the extent of his victory. The Liberals won 52 seats, the Country Party 20 and the A.L.P. fifty. The Ministry was enlarged to twenty-five of whom only eleven were members of the inner Cabinet. Menzies consulted McEwen about the allocation of portfolios, but there were few changes and none in the really important positions. The premature election for the House of Representatives necessitated a separate election for half the Senate seats a year later. This campaign underlined the basic differences between the parties, especially on foreign policy. Sir Robert stood smugly, as well he might, on the Government's record and promised more of the same. Calwell bitterly denounced conscription, recently introduced by Menzies under the National Service Act, as 'the lottery of death', while Senator G. Cole for the D.L.P. called for Australia to develop a nuclear deterrent to fend off what he saw as a threat from China and Indonesia. The Government polled very slightly better than at the previous Senate election but lost a seat to the D.L.P., giving a deadlocked Chamber — 30 Liberal and Country Party senators, 27 A.L.P., 2 D.L.P. and one Independent. However the Government could rely on the D.L.P. for support in most issues.

During the last two years of Sir Robert Menzies' reign fortune smiled on the Government, at least in the sphere of home affairs. The state of the economy continued to improve and the Government proceeded, at a somewhat leisurely pace, to implement its 'welfare state' election promises without, of course, any serious opposition or even criticism from the Labor benches. The only cloud on the financial horizon was that world wool prices were falling. The Government proposed a wool reserve price stabilisation scheme, similar in principle to that operating in the wheat industry, but it sagaciously refrained from imposing it. In the past, even in wartime, wool-growers had always been hostile to any marketing scheme which savoured of compulsion, collectivism or, most horrid, 'socialism'. So the Commonwealth arranged for a referendum among wool-growers, who for some months passionately abused each other instead of 'those ---s in Canberra'. In December 1965 they voted and turned down the plan by a very small majority. A few months earlier in September the Vernon Committee made its report on the state of the national economy. Expert economists were very impressed with its recommendations, but the Government was not. It incurred some criticism for ignoring them.

More troublesome was the last and worst of a number of naval accidents which occurred on the night of 11 February 1964 off Jervis Bay. During manoeuvres the aircraft-carrier H.M.A.S. *Melbourne* rammed and sank, with the loss of eighty-two lives, the destroyer H.M.A.S. *Voyager*. Ashamed, perhaps, of the gross professional incompetence thus revealed, the Navy tried to hush the matter up for many hours. Menzies immediately announced the appointment of a Royal Commission of inquiry which, after protracted public sittings, apportioned blame fairly evenly between the two commanders, one living and the other among the *Voyager*'s dead. However the matter was not allowed to rest there. Friends of the *Melbourne*'s commander discovered evidence suggesting that the dead man had been deeply addicted to alcohol and there were suggestions that fellow officers, and the Government, had conspired to say nothing but good of the dead to the manifest detriment of the living. The matter was never really satisfactorily resolved.

In September 1965, only a few months before his retirement from politics, Sir Robert Menzies appointed R. G. Casey, Baron Casey since 1960, Governor-General of Australia, thereby following the precedent set by a Labor Prime Minister, James Scullin, thirty-five years earlier. Many, including the new Governor-General, were astounded that the greatest of Australian Anglophiles should have been the first non-Labor Prime Minister to recommend an Australian for the position. Besides it was an open secret that Casey had resigned from Parliament five years earlier, largely because he could not tolerate Menzies' domination of Cabinet and interference in his (Casey's) Ministry of External

Affairs. When Menzies sounded him out before the official announcement, he told friends of his astonishment. Others, more acute or perhaps only more cynical, believed that Menzies was simply preparing the way for his own appointment as Casey's successor: though that was not to be.

In May 1964 the Government's campaign promise to give money for the building of science laboratories to 'independent' as well as government schools was implemented. Public reaction, or rather the relative lack of it, showed that anti-Catholic bigotry was no longer, as it had previously always been, a sentiment that flourished in the breasts of most Australians. In Australia state aid to church schools had always meant, mainly, state aid to Catholic schools simply because, while nearly all Catholic parents sent their children to Catholic schools, nearly all Protestant or agnostic parents, except for the wealthier among them, sent their children to the secular government schools. For nearly a hundred years majority Protestant bigotry had ensured that 'state aid' was an unthinkable thought for any government. As we have seen, however, to weld D.L.P. preferences to them and to widen the split in the Labor Party, Menzies and the Liberal-Country Party federal Coalition gradually, almost imperceptibly, re-introduced state aid in the 1960s. By 1964 it was apparent that, although official Protestant church organisations, rationalist societies and other such bodies would protest vigorously, most voters either simply did not care about the matter, or thought it only fair that Catholic taxpayers should get back some of their money for the schools to which, in conscience, they felt bound to send their children.

In the New South Wales election of May 1965, Robert Askin, leader of the Liberals who had been in Opposition for twenty-four years, promised a measure of state aid to non-state schools in his policy speech. Though the amount involved was only £200,000 a year, 'state aid' became a major issue in the campaign and one which certainly did no harm to the Opposition — which was sent to the treasury benches, though with a majority of only two seats. The new Government's most thorny problem was Joern Utzon's magnificent opera house, which had been building on Bennelong Point for eight years. The Cahill Labor Government had given the great architect a free hand, not merely with the design but with virtually every aspect of the project; and it was becoming apparent to some that he was less able to cope with quantity surveying, labour management, costs and other practical matters than he was with the grand concept. This however was not clear to the man and woman in the street or to thousands of artists and intellectuals. They only knew that one of the most beautiful buildings in the world was taking shape in their city, that Utzon was its inspired creator and that no grubby politician must be permitted to sully his vision. The nettle was firmly grasped by Askin's Minister for Public Works. Davis Hughes, Country Party member for the Armidale seat and the most able man in the Coalition. He took control of the business side of the work and, when Utzon resigned, appointed a panel of Australian architects to supervise the execution of Utzon's design. He was mightily abused for his efforts, but the great building was finished in October 1973.

A less creditable act of the Askin Government deserves some attention because it illustrates graphically the extraordinary weakness of local government throughout Australia. The elected council of the City of Sydney had long had a majority of Labor aldermen. On 14 November 1967 the Liberal-Country Party State Government simply gazetted an Act which removed the City Council from office and appointed three commissioners to administer the city and to make arrangements for new elections after they had decided on the boundaries for a much smaller city area. There were no charges of misconduct or corruption against the old elected council, and no reasons were given for the change in boundaries imposed by the Government. The real reason, of course, was to ensure that the new, reduced city's boundaries would be such as to ensure that it would usually elect a Council with an anti-Labor majority. The commissioners deliberated for nearly two years during which time they ruled the city in a completely arbitrary, though doubtless efficient, manner. The strangest part of the story, to anyone unfamiliar with Australian local government, is that the whole operation caused scarcely more than a ripple of protest and apparently did no electoral harm to the Government.

The government of South Australia also changed hands in March, 1965 — after thirty-two years of continuous Liberal-Country Party rule, for the last twenty-seven years of which the Premier had been Sir Thomas Playford, grandson of a colonial premier of the same name, an orchardist in the Mount Lofty Ranges on the outskirts of Adelaide, and a liberal with a small 'l'. All Australian governments irrespective of party labels, tend to manipulate the electoral laws in such a way as to favour the return of their own candidates. The South Australian Liberal-Country Party Governments between 1933 and 1965 had the distinction of producing the most notorious gerrymander in Australian history. By 1965 one vote in some country electorates carried as much weight as three or more votes in some city electorates. The following tables show the extent of the gerrymander in both the New South Wales and South Australian elections in 1965. In both cases the D.L.P. vote has been added somewhat simplistically to the Liberal and Country Party votes to produce a consolidated conservative or anti-Labor figure. In South Australia the Liberal and Country Party were subsumed under the title Liberal and Country League.

N.S.W. State Election 1965
Party vote as percentage of total formal vote

				Seats Won	
A.L.P.	43.4	A.L.P.	43.4	45	
Lib.	39.6	Anti-		31	
C.P.	10.2	Labor	52.0	16	47
D.L.P.	2.1			—	
Independents, minor parties, etc.	4.7		4.6	2	

S.A. State Election 1965
Party vote as percentage of total formal vote

				Seats Won
A.L.P.	55.0		55.0	21
L.C.L.	35.9	Anti-		17
D.L.P.	4.4	Labor	40.3	
Independents, minor parties, etc.	4.7			1

The South Australian Labor Government thus elected by an immense majority of the voters, lost power again in 1968, naturally, since the gerrymander remained unaltered. However, electoral boundaries were re-drawn, so as not to favour the Liberal and Country Parties quite so brazenly, before the election of 1970. Labor then won power again, and retained office at subsequent general elections in 1972 and 1975. During these years the nature of South Australian society was transformed, largely owing to the energy, idealism and consummate political skill of one man. Donald Dunstan, Q.C. LL.B., became Attorney-General when Labor was elected in 1965, but on the retirement of his leader in 1967, added to this portfolio that of Housing, the Treasuryship, and the Premiership. A middle-class radical by nature and conviction, rather than a typical Labor man of working-class, trade-union antecedents, Dunstan was the main driving force in the Government and the Labor movement of the State. Capital and corporal punishment were expunged from the statute book, a female judge was appointed to the Bench for the first time in Australian history, liquor laws and the educational system were reformed, the arts were encouraged as never before, racial discrimination was made a criminal offence, and nude bathing beaches demarcated for those who cared to use them. For generations South Australia had been incomparably the most socially and politically conservative, Anglophile, 'wowserish' State in the Commonwealth, where respectability was held nearer even than cleanliness to Godliness. In ten years the State's character was transformed, in many respects, almost into a mirror-image of what it had been. Its citizens had always liked to think that 'culture' flourished in Adelaide as in no other Australian city. 'A.D.' (after Dunstan), as some put it, cultural pursuits no longer had to fend off constant attacks from the wowsers. The 'city of dreadful Knights', as cynics had punningly characterised Adelaide, became the city of democracy, intellectual freedom, 'progress' and permissiveness.

EMBROILMENT WITH VIETNAM AND INDONESIA

After the Commonwealth election of November 1963 Parliament, press and public were even more preoccupied with external issues than they had been before it. Sukarno continued with his 'confrontation' of Malaysia and in April 1964 the Malaysian Government formally asked for, and was given, more assistance. Australian naval units patrolled the sea approaches to Sarawak and Sabah (North Borneo) and a squadron of engineers and a few helicopters were sent to help the Malaysian and British forces there with road-making and transport of supplies; but they were ordered to defend themselves only if fired upon by Indonesian troops. Meanwhile the Government still kept in full diplomatic contact with the Indonesians and E. G. Whitlam, deputy-leader of the A.L.P., continued to urge that a formal treaty should supersede the informal arrangements and understandings with Malaysia. He also reiterated — what was obvious but little noticed by the Government — that Indonesian charges of neo-colonialism would be generally believed in Asia, so long as Malaysia's only allies were 'white' Anglo-Saxon powers.

In the same month there was a political storm in Canberra over Sir Garfield Barwick's resignation from the Ministry of External Affairs and the Government to become Chief Justice of the High Court, a position just rendered vacant by Sir Owen Dixon's retirement. At a SEATO conference in Manila Barwick stated publicly that an Indonesian attack on Australian forces in Malaysia would, under the terms of the ANZUS Pact, automatically bring United States forces into the fighting. In the next few days American spokesmen seemed to be denying that this was the U.S.

view of its obligations under ANZUS — a state of affairs lending strong colour to the old Labor contention that ANZUS was worth very little. So the Government appeared embarrassed at its great ally's apparent embarrassment, and people generally believed that Barwick had been 'kicked upstairs' as punishment for his gaffe. It is possible, however, that popular belief was wrong on this occasion: that what Barwick said was in fact endorsed by both the Australian and American Governments, and that Menzies was disappointed when Barwick chose to accept his offer of the Chief Justiceship.[2]

The Prime Minister moved Hasluck from Defence to replace Barwick at External Affairs. He was generally considered to be more hard-headed and perhaps less idealistic than his predecessor. One of his first actions, little noticed at the time because people's attention was focused on the Malaysian situation, was to agree to an American request for more help in its undeclared war on North Vietnam. On 8 June the new Defence Minister, Senator Paltridge, announced the Australian military presence of thirty 'advisers' in South Vietnam would be doubled to sixty. Another event, less remarked in Australia than its future consequences warranted, was the attack by North Vietnamese patrol-boats on the U.S. destroyer *Maddox*, in the Gulf of Tonkin in the first days of August. This 'unprovoked attack' was used by President Johnson to begin open land warfare against North Vietnam, although in fact U.S. Forces had been waging clandestine warfare against the country for many months. The American account of the incident seems to have been taken at face value by Australian politicians in the governing parties and by Australian diplomats who, at least, should have known better.[3]

On the same day that the Australian Army team in South Vietnam was doubled, Papua New Guinea's newly elected Assembly met for the first time, but the rate of change in the territory was far slower than that in world opinion. The new Minister for Territories, G. E. Barnes, a conservative old Queensland grazier and Country Party member, was continually bombarded by complaints from the U.N. Trusteeship Council. The Assembly had hardly met before the Council demanded encouragement of political parties and elimination from the Assembly of the ten elected Europeans and ten nominated 'official' members.

[2] Kevin Perkins, *Menzies, Last of the Queen's Men*, Adelaide, 1968, pp. 212-19.

[3] Evan Whitton, in *National Times*, Canberra, 28 April-3 May, 1975.

Events abroad at this time included one from which most Australians could take some comfort — the growing rift between the two great Communist powers, China and Russia. It became increasingly obvious that they were at least as likely to make war on each other, as either or both were to attack 'the West'. Nevertheless most of those in Washington, Canberra and elsewhere, who had long believed in the monolithic nature of the 'World Communist conspiracy', continued to act as though it were a fact. The Russo-Chinese split provided comfort for conservatives at home also. The Australian Communist Party, already weakened by mass defections following Khrushchev's denunciations of Stalinism in 1956, split into bitterly feuding factions drawing their doctrinal inspiration from Moscow and Peking mainly, but also from Belgrade and even, for a time, from Rome. Nevertheless secret policemen and other right-thinking persons continued to use 'Communist' as a blanket description of many disparate left-wing groups and individuals.

In the first half of 1965 the man who had declined to enlist in the A.I.F. during World War I sent Australian soldiers into action both in Malaysia and Vietnam. On New Year's Day Indonesia formally withdrew from the United Nations Organisation and, not surprisingly, Dr Sukarno announced, a few months later, that as a non-member of the United Nations Indonesia no longer felt obliged to allow the people of West Irian their 'act of self-determination'. Indonesian troop numbers were built up along the border of the North Bornean member-states of Malaysia and guerilla raids on the peninsula itself increased in frequency. Malaysia formally asked for help and the Government decided that the Australian battalion in Malaya would thenceforth serve at 'the front' in Borneo, in rotation with British and Malaysian units. Additional air and ground support was also provided. By June three diggers (and several times as many Indonesian soldiers) had been killed in action in Borneo, and yet the two Governments maintained correct, even cordial, diplomatic relations. Moreover, serious though 'confrontation' with Malaysia was becoming, by March attention was focused on Vietnam.

In that month Hasluck, as Minister for External Affairs, said that the Government opposed peace negotiations if they involved a prior withdrawal of U.S. troops. Implicit in this statement was the very essence of what was, and remained for the next seven years, the position of conservative Australian Governments: everything, including truth and the lives of Australian conscripts, must be sacrificed to what they saw as the necessity for placating American opinion so that, they hoped, a grateful United States would one day protect Australia from a possible Asian invasion. Vigorous dissent was at once manifest. A group of Anglican bishops, headed by an old radical, the Right Rev. J. S. Moyes, Bishop of Armidale, engaged in a public correspondence with the Prime Minister who had, on balance, the worst of the encounter. This did not, of course, prevent him from crossing the Rubicon on 29 April when he announced that a battalion of Australians would be sent to Vietnam. His stated reason was:

> The takeover of South Vietnam would be a direct military threat to Australia . . . It must be seen as part of a thrust by Communist China between the Indian and Pacific Oceans.[4]

Both parts of the statement were palpable nonsense. No sane man could think one or all of the Indo-Chinese states a *direct* military threat to Australia in the then foreseeable future, and China was so far from making a thrust to the south that she did not send a single soldier across her southern border to help the North Vietnamese, even when upwards of half a million American soldiers, sailors and airmen were engaged on the southern side. However there is no doubt that majority opinion at this stage favoured the Government decision, though probably for the real, and not the stated, reasons for it.

Early in June President Johnson announced that U.S. ground forces would openly be used in direct combat with the Viet Cong, and of course Australia immediately followed suit. Debate on the war became more embittered. One notable contribution on the conservative side was made by the Anglican Primate of Australia and Archibishop of Sydney, the Right Rev. H. R. Gough. On his return from a visit to Vietnam in November this inspired servant of the Prince of Peace told the press that:

> Australian troops . . . in Vietnam really had their tails up . . . Where six months ago there was doubt, there is not doubt now that the Communists have had it.[5]

Much more frequently his public speeches were concerned with denouncing the morals and manners of young people, and warning against indulgence in the 'sins of the flesh'. Early in 1966, to avoid figuring as co-respondent in a divorce case involving one of his female parishioners, he returned hastily to his native land to become Rector of Freshford near Bath. Since then the Anglican Church in Australia has been less prone to follow its ancient tradition of appointing Englishmen to sees. The Government tried

[4] T. B. Millar 'Problems of Australian Foreign Policy', *A.J.P.H.*, December, 1965, vol. 11, no. 3, p. 273.

[5] *Sunday Telegraph*, 21 November 1965.

to compensate for the intellectual weakness of such support by issuing a series of pamphlets setting out the arguments in favour of the undeclared war. Prepared by the Department of External Affairs, and sent to a wide range of prominent citizens, including school headmasters, these, though a great inprovement on the thoughts of the Primate, probably did the Government more harm than good, if only by exposing it to the charge of using public funds to indoctrinate children. As the war dragged on those who supported it tended more and more to avoid debate, as far as possible, because any agitation of the pros and cons tended to swell the volume of dissent.

As the Government embroiled itself more deeply in Vietnam, its 'confrontation' with Indonesia began to be resolved, though not because of its own efforts. First the Malaysian Federation began to show signs of breaking up just as quickly as it had been formed, and this development perhaps encouraged Indonesia to think its objectives might be attainable without fighting or even 'confrontation'. On 9 August 1965 it was announced that, by agreement between Tunku Abdul Rahman and Lee Kuan Yew, its Prime Minister, Singapore became an independent, sovereign state, pledged to collaborate with Malaysia in defence, foreign and economic policies. This example, plus the Tunku's high-handed attitude to them, made the Bornean states of the federation waver in their commitment to it; but on 30 September a *coup d'etat* in Djakarta transformed the whole situation, though in ways which were at first not at all clear.

It seems that a relatively small band of soldiers, inspired by the Indonesian Communist Party, suddenly assassinated a few generals known for their anti-Communist views. Within hours right-wing soldiers, led by Major-General Suharto, had assassinated the assassins and established themselves as the real rulers of the country, though Sukarno remained President and nominally its ruler. Such, at any rate, was the account given by the victors. It will probably never be known whether it is substantially true or whether the first coup was staged by the Suharto forces to provide cover, or excuse, for their own violent deeds. Certain it is that there followed an army-directed blood-bath in which countless Communists, alleged Communists and leftists of all kinds were murdered. The official figure for the pogrom, given by the new government, was 87 000: other estimates range up to over a million. The Australian Department of External Affairs treated these developments with some reserve, simply because for some months it was unclear just who was in charge of the country. Meanwhile 'confrontation' continued, but in a much muted form.

HOLT SUCCEEDS MENZIES

In the latter part of 1965 there were continual rumours that Menzies was about to retire. In July he underwent surgery for what was rumoured to be cancer of the bowel. At 71 he told friends that he was 'slowing down' and observed that it had been sad to see Winston Churchill, whose funeral he had attended on 30 January, deteriorating publicly in front of Parliament and the world. Once Sir Robert nodded off to sleep on the front bench, for him an incredible lapse. He had always been a great actor, one who enjoyed the spotlight and the crowd's plaudits, and who knew how to make the very most of an entrance or an exit, even from a typist's office. Yet his departure from public life was conspicuously undramatic. At the end of a Cabinet meeting on 20 January 1966 he said, 'Well, gentlemen, this is the last time I shall be with you . . .', spoke a few more sentences, and the thing was done.

Tributes to his work poured in, but relatively more copiously from Britain, the United States and Europe than from Australia. The *Washington Post* called him 'probably the most completely successful public man of his time'.[6] This was just, but like other human beings Menzies wanted to be loved, particularly by his own countrymen. It was his tragedy that few even of his greatest admirers felt for him any personal warmth, that most regarded him as more English than Australian, and that not a few considered him a great anachronism — the most capable and unscrupulous defender of nineteenth century values who ever lived in the Antipodes. It must have been his consolation that, if not loved, he was missed. People marvelled at the sheer quantity of time, space and action which he had occupied. For twenty years past, on festive occasions, friend and foe alike had sung:

The balls of Bob Menzies
Are wrinkled and crinkled
Curvaceous, capacious
As the dome of St. Paul's.
The crowds they all muster
To gape at that cluster
And gaze on the size of
Those bloody great balls!

Like a great national monument 'Pig Iron Bob' had been there so long, and so continuously, that it seemed impossible political life should carry on without him — as of course it did.

[6] Perkins, p. 228.

Australian, 1966

THAT WAS THE WEEK THAT WAS

The Liberals met immediately and elected Harold Holt, unopposed, to the leadership of the party. William McMahon, Minister for Labour, defeated Hasluck for the deputy-leadership. By 26 January, Australia Day, the new Ministry had been sworn in by one of their old colleagues, Lord Casey, the recently appointed Governor-General. There were only two new faces in the Cabinet, though Holt shuffled some of the portfolios, most notably by replacing himself at the Treasury with his new deputy, McMahon. 'Young Harold', as Menzies called him, had been the latter's *protégé* and heir-apparent for many years. The whole operation was carried through in as dignified and urbane a manner as the old master could have wished.

The new Prime Minister was born in New South Wales in 1908 and was educated at Wesley College in Melbourne some years after the young Menzies had left. As a school prefect he acquired the nickname 'Puss', probably on account of the broad grin which, throughout life, came so readily to his face. He studied law at the University of Melbourne but practised only briefly as a solicitor before being elected to the Commonwealth Parliament for the U.A.P. when he was only 27 years old in 1935. More than something of a playboy in private life, almost fanatical about physical fitness, affable and friendly to everybody, Holt was less conservative and more flexible than his chief, though by no means devoid of great ability and considerable integrity. Menzies was sagacious enough to place him in positions where his gift for getting on well with people was of maximum use to the Government. He was Minister for Labour and National Service and Immigration from 1949 to 1956, when he dropped the last portfolio. In 1958, as we have seen, he was moved to the Treasury.

It was soon obvious that Holt would carry on with most lines of policy established by Menzies. He made few innovations. On 14 February he presided over the introduction of decimal currency, a move begun but inwardly deplored by Sir Robert. He announced an easing of conditions under which some Asians might be naturalised, and this pointed to another difference between him and his predecessor. Though aware of Asia's importance to Australia, Menzies had always treated it as a place to be flown over or sailed past as quickly as possible on his way to London or New York. One of Holt's first acts was to arrange visits to meet the governmental heads in South Vietnam, Malaysia, Singapore and Thailand. He *liked* Asians, as he liked other people and conducted a great deal of personal diplomacy, on the American model, with friendly Asian countries. On the other hand his total commitment to American policy was as great as Menzies' after Suez. Only the style was different. Holt behaved more obsequiously towards Australia's 'great and powerful friend', even allowing himself to be patronised by President Johnson in a way that Menzies would never have done.

During Holt's brief tenure of office foreign relations loomed larger than ever before. With a general election due at the end of the year, the Prime Minister took even more responsibility for what happened in this area than Menzies had done, whether the nominal Minister, Hasluck, liked it or not. From the point of view of the Government, events in Indonesia sorted themselves out very satisfactorily. 'Confrontation' disappeared from the headlines and peace talks between Indonesia and Malaysia resulted in its official abandonment in August, when Hasluck visited Djakarta and invited his opposite-number, Mr Malik, to visit Australia. However, neither the Vietnamese Communists/Nationalists nor the Americans would just go away from South Vietnam in the same manner. In February 1966 Hubert Humphrey, Vice-President of the United States, visited Australia to ask for more support and on 8 March Holt promptly and obediently announced that Australia's contribution would be trebled to a force of 4500 men, including conscripted national servicemen. The sting of the announcement was in the tail. To old Labor men and women and to the large minority of younger people, who thought this undeclared war was harming Australia's best interests, to conscript young men for service and perhaps death in Vietnam was wicked folly to be fought at all costs. The Labor Party reacted accordingly, though most of its parliamentary members did not at this time oppose the war itself. Communists, radicals, most intellectuals, some churchmen and a good many others did however. Protests, demonstrations and teach-ins multiplied. Holt, unintentionally, added to them by his behaviour on a visit to Washington.

From Deakin to Menzies most Australian prime ministers had felt that London was the centre of the world, the forum in which their political stature would finally be judged. Holt and his successors in office seemed to feel the same way about the United States. On a visit there at the end of June, Holt wound up a speech to President Johnson with the ringing declaration 'All the way with L.B.J.!' — which had been the Democratic party's campaign slogan at the previous U.S. presidential election. The remark was meant to express total, uncritical support for U.S. policy in Vietnam but, of course, implied the same kind of support for Johnson personally and for his party, as opposed to the American opposition Republicans. Many, among them even some of the strongest proponents of the war, were appalled by the syncophantic tone of the Prime Minister's speech: but worse was to come.

From 20 to 24 October, at Holt's invitation, Johnson became the first U.S. President to visit Australia while in office. In his train came 400 American journalists and photographers plus an unknown number of bodyguards and secret policemen. The Prime Minister obviously exulted in the visit and was photographed everywhere with the visitor. Calwell, leader of the A.L.P. Opposition, charged that the whole exercise was a political propaganda stunt, timed to influence the result of the Commonwealth general election to be held only a month later on 22 November. Perhaps it was. Huge crowds of pro- and anti-war demonstrators, sometimes brought the presidential cavalcade to a halt. On one such occasion the Liberal Premier of New South Wales earned some lasting notoriety by loudly urging his chauffeur to 'drive over the bastards'; but most of the demonstrators had come to echo the sentiments implied by Holt's remark in Washington. The poet, Dorothy Auchterlonie, compared the Melbourne procession with an imperial Roman triumph in tributary territory. On many occasions Johnson turned aside, from acknowledging the crowd's plaudits, long enough to draw the grinning Holt forward with one patronising hand on his shoulder. 'Look' he said, 'this is your Prime Minister!'[7]

The following election was fought substantially over the war, or more accurately over conscription for it. The D.L.P. advocated two years compulsory service for *all* young men, not just some chosen by lot. Holt promised massive increases in state aid to public and private education, especially the latter, but his major emphasis was on what he saw as the necessity for backing the United States in Vietnam. Calwell promised a wide range of pension increases and welfare-state measures, but again his emphasis was on the war. If elected, Labor would abolish conscription forthwith and, in consultation with the Americans, bring home Australian regular troops at the earliest opportunity. The result was an overwhelming victory for the Government, the greatest since the election of 1949. The Liberal and Country Party candidates came within an ace (49.98 per cent) of winning an absolute majority of all valid first preference votes cast, without counting the D.L.P.'s 7 per cent. The new House contained 61 Liberals, 21 Country Party and only 41 Labor members plus one Independent.

Holt was naturally delighted but he was above all a team man and he made few changes in his Ministry. The most significant was the removal of Mr Billy Snedden from the Attorney-General's Department to Immigration and to the additional position of leader

[7] *Australian*, 21 October 1966.

Look, this is your Prime Minister

of the Government in the House of Representatives. Mr Nigel Bowen replaced him as Attorney-General. Very much more drastic changes occurred in the Labor camp. The ageing Calwell had undertaken to retire from the leadership of federal parliamentary Labor if the party were again unsuccessful at the election. He did so, though not without a good deal of bitter recrimination. The Labor Caucus elected to succeed him E. G. Whitlam, previously deputy-leader, and long seen as the ablest right-of-centre man in the federal parliamentary party.

UNPARALLELED PROSPERITY

While the politicians fought for place and power, and sometimes even for principle, the bankers, merchants and manufacturers became richer than ever before and the majority of the people who worked for them gained a better share of creature comforts. Harold Holt's great win at the polls perhaps reflected the voters' entire satisfaction with full employment and expanding prosperity, as much as with his war policy in Indo-China. After the minor recession caused by the 'credit-squeeze', the long economic boom continued and reached its peak in the 1960s. In *The Affluent Society*, the great American economist J. K. Galbraith seemed to describe Australia almost as justly as he described the U.S.A., but a great many Australian writers published works anatomising the state of the nation or congratulating themselves and their countrymen upon it. One of the best was Donald Horne's *The Lucky Country*, whose ironic overtones were not always noticed. The title was such an apt short description of Australia in the 1960s that it passed into common speech as an accepted cliché.

Manufacturing industry continued to expand, to diversify and to provide jobs for a greater proportion of the workforce than ever before. It became difficult to think of any product in common use that was not made locally. Between 1941 and 1966 the number of factory employees increased from about 650 000 to 1 309 000 and the total value of factory output from £1,290,000,000 to £14,690,000,000. A growing export trade in manufactured goods lessened somewhat the dangerous dependence on wheat and wool which had for so long been the hallmark of the economy. Even so, primary products continued to account for the bulk of Australian exports and foreign exchange. In the decade 1938 to 1948 pastoral, agricultural and dairy products together amounted to 74 per cent of Australian exports and manufactured goods to 14.5 per cent. In 1967 the equivalent percentages were 68.7 per cent and 20 per cent. Of course wool and wheat still comprised the great bulk of exports. Throughout the 1960s world wheat prices held up better than those for wool and so wheat became steadily more important, relative to wool, in the national economy. At the same time demand for wheat and wool in the traditional British and European markets began to fall off. To some extent this was offset by a steadily rising demand from Japan, but again and again the state purchasing agencies of Communist China and the U.S.S.R. bought bulk supplies of grain and wool, sufficiently large to keep Australian farmers and pastoralists in business, if rarely in such wealth as they had known in the early 1950s. Most farmers and graziers were among the most fervent supporters of the Coalition Governments which continued to denounce the Russian Government at every opportunity and to refuse recognition of the Government of mainland China, but the irony of the situation was quite lost upon them.

The lucky country's greatest good fortune was the discovery of rich mineral resources at this time. The most exciting finds occurred during the 1960s just as the difficulties of the wool industry were increasing. By the mid-1970s mineral exports had replaced wool as the major source of foreign exchange. Australia had for a century or more been blessed with gold and silver and abundant supplies of the commoner base metals — lead, zinc, copper, tin, iron, and so on, to say nothing of coal: but the twentieth century's major source of power and wealth, oil, had eluded her. Even more important for the future than oil was uranium, the readiest source of nuclear energy. Rich deposits of uranium ore were discovered at Rum Jungle in the Northern Territory in 1949 and many new discoveries followed. In the mid-1950s the Government established the Atomic Energy Commission and by the 1970s it was clear that Australia was like to become one of the major world sources of this metal.

In December 1953 oil gushed from an exploratory drill for the first time in Australian history. This strike was made at Exmouth Gulf, not far from the future site of the U.S. 'communications centre' in Western Australia about 1100 kilometres north of Perth. There was great excitement and speculation on the share market, but this field proved to be not commercially worthwhile. Eight years later the Moonie field about 300 kilometres west of Brisbane produced good quality oil and further discoveries of oil and natural gas followed, most notably in Bass Strait, in the vicinity of Barrow Island off the north-west coast of Western Australia, and in the desolate country to the east of Lake Eyre in South Australia. By

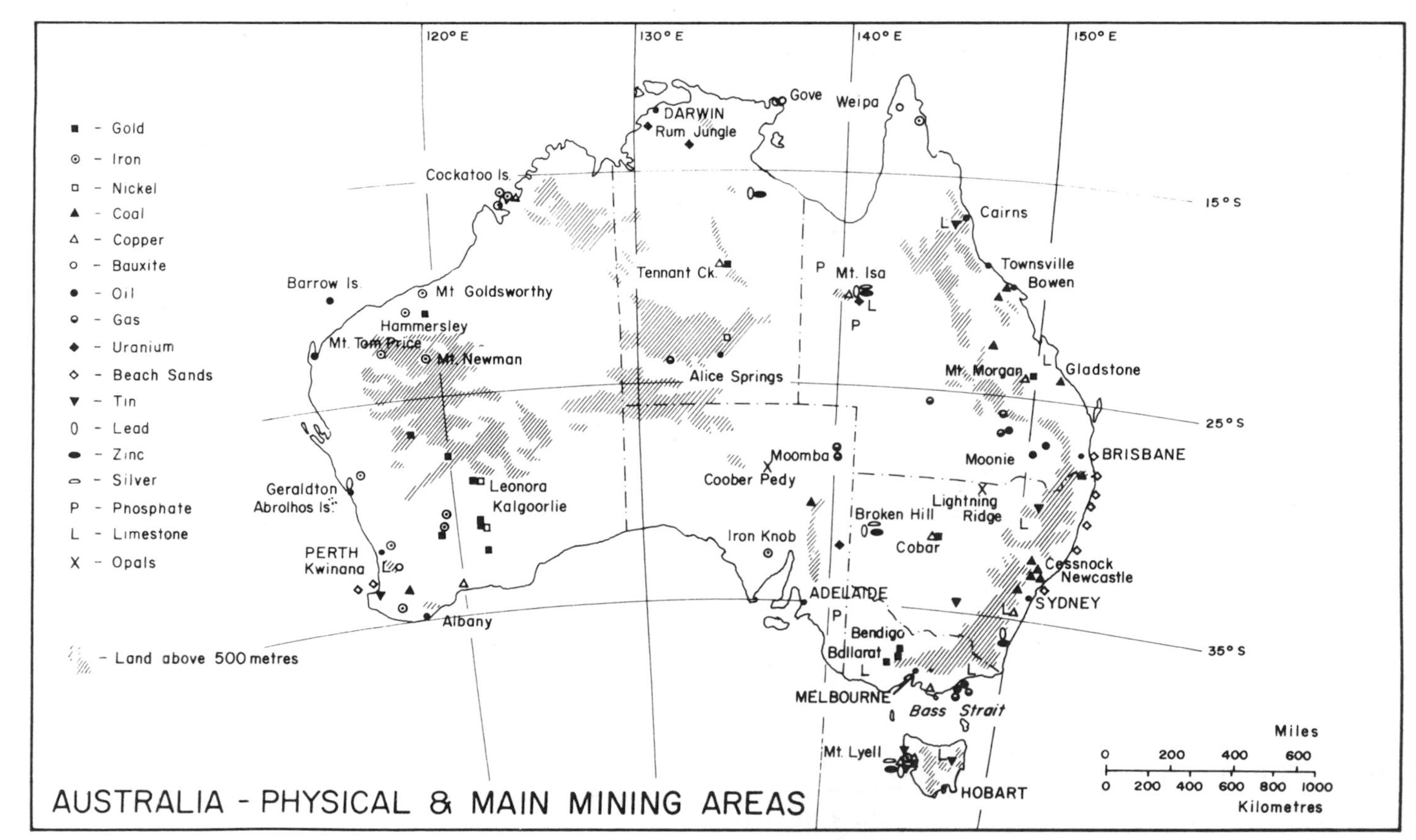

AUSTRALIA - PHYSICAL & MAIN MINING AREAS

1969 Melbourne, Brisbane and Adelaide had all been supplied with natural gas and most of the oil used in Australia was being produced and refined locally.

A great many other minerals used by modern industry but previously unknown or unexploited locally, were found in the 1960s. During this decade Australia became the major world supplier of mineral sands — rutile, ilmenite, zircon and monazite. Tungsten and manganese mining also became important. At Weipa on the western coast of Cape York Peninsula a new port was built and full scale production and export of bauxite (for the production of aluminium) began in 1963. In the following year large deposits of phosphate rock were discovered in North West Queensland. In time these should replace imports for the manufacture of superphosphate manures, so important for the wheat industry. The peak of the metal boom was reached in 1968 and 1969 when a great many inexperienced investors burnt their fingers, particularly over share-dealings in new nickel mines not far from Kalgoorlie. Nevertheless the nickel sulphide ore bodies, 27 million tons of them averaging 3 per cent nickel, were real enough, and comparable supplies were later discovered at Greenvale and Maryborough in Queensland.

Most significant of all as earners of foreign exchange were immense newly-developed deposits of iron ore and coal. In the remote Pilbara region of Western Australia new towns, railways and ports were built to extract, process and export the iron ore, mainly to Japan. The ore is of excellent quality and can, for the most part, be got by open-cut surface mining. Both old and new coal-mining fields shared in the mining boom. Ever since the early years of the twentieth century, when oil began to provide more and more of the world's power, Australia's coal exporting industry had been in the doldrums. The steeply rising price of oil fuels caused many industrialists, especially in Japan, to turn to coal again from the mid 1960s onwards.

It should not be thought that the export of minerals replaced that of wool, wheat, sugar, beef, wine and all the other traditionally hallowed primary products. On the contrary Australia produced and exported more, and a wider range, of these things than ever: but, as we have seen, she became as well a major exporter of minerals and a highly industrialised and urbanised modern state. By the end of the 1960s the volume of Australian import and export trade was among the twelve greatest in the world. Per head of population it was greater than Britain's and more than three times greater than that of the United States. Between 1960 and 1970 the total annual value of overseas trade rose from about $4,000,000,000 to over $8,000,000,000.

An ever higher proportion of the population lived in the capital cities and was employed in tertiary, as opposed to primary and secondary industries. The skyline of the cities was transformed. At the end of World War II no building in the continent numbered more than ten or twelve stories. By 1970, particularly in Sydney and Melbourne, thirty and forty-storey 'skyscrapers' were commonplace. Seven new universities and many more colleges of advanced education were built. The arts and sciences flourished as never before. Private persons, public companies and even such notoriously philistine bodies as suburban and town councils actually bought pictures and commissioned the creation of murals and statues. Serious, scholarly journals multiplied almost as rapidly as popular illustrated magazines. Some expatriate artists and writers, like Patrick White, began to return to a land where their work might be appreciated as such things rarely had been in former days. The quality, quantity and complexity of Australian creative work and of its appreciation were much greater than ever before, and this reflected a much more sophisticated, cosmopolitan society. Many, particularly among the older generation, doubted that all these changes were for the good.

Emancipation from the spiritual apron-strings of the mother country meant, for many, acceptance of a more material domination by the United States and participation in its neo-imperialist wars. The unprecedented affluence of Australian society was built largely on massive investment by foreigners, mostly Americans but, increasingly, Japanese. Ownership of so much of Australia by British capital had not seemed to matter. It was, many felt, all in the family: but ownership, and so an increasing measure of control, by Americans and Japanese was another matter. Prosperity might be bought too dearly. By 1970 American news, views, attitudes, and even accents among some Australian entertainers, had largely displaced British and Australian ones in newspapers, T.V. programmes and film shows. The more affluent, sophisticated, civilised, diversified cultural life of the 1960s was splendid no doubt, but many regretted the demise of the simple image of Lawson's and Paterson's barbarous and heroic bushman, with which most Australians had liked to identify up until about 1960.

Similarly many felt that the affluent society of Sir Robert Menzies and 'Young Harold' was a poor substitute for the aspiring society of Alfred Deakin and Andrew Fisher. In the early Commonwealth a drive towards social reform and a better life for all citizens had stood at the very heart of Australian nationality. In the 1960s social reforms came haphazardly, if at all, and

ART SPELT WITH A CAPITAL OUTLAY

'A man to watch! Bought Nolan in '45, Drysdale in '36, B.H.P. in '22, Colonial Sugar in '16. A real connoisseur!'

Sydney Morning Herald, 1966

competition ensured that the 'tall poppies' grew taller. The gap between salaries of people in white-collar, executive-type positions and the wages of manual workers, which had been narrowing for a century and a half, actually grew slightly wider again. And yet the aspirations of the early Commonwealth had been strictly confined to white Australians of British descent and, in some important ways, to male ones at that. In the Australia of Harold Holt, if not of Bob Menzies, Europeans, brown, black and yellow people, and even women and Aboriginal Australians were beginning to be recognised as fully human beings.

The founding fathers of the Commonwealth had specifically excluded Aboriginals from its responsibilities. Section 127 stated:

> In reckoning the numbers of the people of the Commonwealth, or of a State or other part of the Commonwealth, aboriginal natives shall not be counted.

The State governments dealt variously with Aboriginals but in general Paul Hasluck's description of their situation was just:

> a legal status that has more in common with that of a born idiot than of any other class of British subject.[8]

One of the newly elected Holt Government's first acts was to pass a Bill, long delayed in Menzies' days of power, authorising a referendum to alter the Constitution to give the Commonwealth power to count and to legislate for Aboriginals. Another Bill provided for a referendum to abolish the 'nexus' between the number of senators and of members of the House of Representatives, fixed by the Constitution at approximately one half. Neither was a party measure and both commanded general support in Canberra and among politically aware citizens. The second measure would, in the long run, have reduced the number of federal politicians without altering in the slightest the balance of power between parties or States. Yet it was rejected by the people when they voted on both questions on 27 May 1967. As usual most voted 'No' because they were unsure of the precise implications of voting 'Yes' — except that to do so would possibly be 'to give the Government more power'.

The same voters, however, voted overwhelmingly 'Yes' to the request for Commonwealth power over Aboriginals. Though many were equally unsure of the precise implications of a 'Yes' vote, they knew that Aboriginals had never had 'a fair go' since the arrival of

[8] Paul Hasluck, *Black Australians*, Melbourne, 1942, pp.160-1.

the first European fleet in 1788, and that the Commonwealth wished, belatedly, to begin remedying this position. For the first time in history every electorate in every State returned a 'Yes' majority, though pessimists noted that the margin was lowest in those States which contained the highest proportion of Aboriginal people. In Papua-New Guinea the first eight indigenes to be appointed assistant district-officers began duty.

Holt gained some credit at this time for bestowing his blessing on the revival of a Senate procedure which had fallen into disuse. Although the Government had no unquestioned control of the Upper House, it encouraged the creation of select committees, consisting generally of senators from all parties, to study and report upon politically contentious questions. Another event, this one overseas, which gave the Government more delight than it was wise to manifest publicly was the total eclipse of Dr Sukarno, for so long the populist left-wing President of Indonesia. In March the Indonesian Congress ingeniously appointed General Suharto, leader of the right-wing military coup, acting-president without formally dismissing Sukarno. Australian relations with Indonesia became much warmer thenceforth, but nothing else at home or abroad gave much comfort to the Government. Rumours that Britain intended to withdraw its armed forces from Singapore and Malaysia were confirmed in July, and further it seemed that there would be a phased withdrawal from the whole Indian Ocean area. That the planned withdrawal was connected with a renewed British attempt to enter the European Common Market did nothing to make it more palatable in Australia, especially in conservative circles.

In January 1967 at Holt's invitation, Air Vice-Marshal Ky, Premier of South Vietnam, visited Australia — to be met by 6000-strong protest marches in Sydney and Melbourne and a good deal of friendly and hostile demonstrating elsewhere. Calwell, still leader of the Opposition, called him among other things a 'quisling gangster', a 'butcher' and a 'social and moral leper'.[9] Ky proved to be a suaver diplomat than his Australian supporters had feared he might be. Nevertheless the visit, by concentrating attention on the Vietnam war, had the overall effect of swelling the ranks of those opposed to it. Dissent increased steadily throughout the year, as indeed it was doing in the United States: but this only made the Government more stubborn. On 17 October the Prime Minister announced that another 1700 men would be sent to Vietnam plus a tank squadron and more helicopters, bringing the total Australian

[9] *A.J.P.H.*, vol. 13, no. 2, August 1967, p.254.

military presence to about eight thousand. Even the conservative *Sydney Morning Herald* suspected that the move was simply a gesture by the Government to give some support to President Johnson's crumbling credibility on the Vietnam issue in the United States. Hasluck, the Minister for External Affairs, returned from a visit to Saigon to assure his countrymen, like all Government visitors before him, that the diggers and the Americans were steadily winning the war which opponents had declared from the outset to be unwinnable.

At home also troubles for the Government multiplied throughout the year. The most intractable of them was a bitter running fight within its own ranks. The formidable 'Black Jack' McEwen, deputy Prime Minister, leader of the Country Party and Minister for Trade, was at daggers drawn with the Liberal Party Treasurer, McMahon. McEwen accused a group of Liberal politicians with rural interests, of being behind a body known as the Basic Industries Group which, he thundered, was out to destroy him and the Country Party. On the other side McMahon and a great many other Liberal parliamentarians, whether or no they gave clandestine support to the Basic Industries Group, certainly thought McEwen and his public servants in the Department of Trade exercised a great deal too much influence on Government policies. The Prime Minister exerted all his tact and charm to pour oil on the troubled waters, but the storm continued with lulls from time to time. Generally McEwen seems to have had the better of McMahon and the Liberals, except for one major engagement in November when Britain devalued the pound sterling. To the fury of the Country Party and its supporters, Cabinet, led on this issue by Holt and McMahon, decided not to follow Britain's lead. The A.L.P. and most business interests applauded the decision, but it bore very heavily on the immediate financial welfare of most primary producers.

In the latter part of the year the Government got into more trouble over Number 34 Squadron of the Royal Australian Air Force, the unit which for many years had had the special task of ferrying about the country Cabinet ministers, official guests of the Government and other very important persons such as the Leader of Her Majesty's Opposition. Newspapers revealed that some flights were being made to carry members' wives and children about the country for purely personal purposes. The Opposition quickly asked searching questions about the cost of the 'V.I.P. Flight' (No. 34 Squadron), and asked for the tabling of records of individual flights. Responsible ministers replied that this could not be done since no such records were kept, only to have the lie given them by one of their own colleagues, the Liberal Senator Gorton, who tabled the supposedly non-existent records. The Opposition naturally redoubled its attack with the claim that ministers who had deceived the Parliament, notably Mr Howson, Minister for Air, should resign. He offered to do so but Cabinet decided not to accept the offer. As the Melbourne *Age* pointed out, Howson's resignation would inevitably have raised the question of whether the Prime Minister should follow suit, since he too had said the records did not exist.

Another minor but continuous source of embarrassment to the Government was the young Liberal member for Adelaide, Mr Andrew Jones, the cross Harold Holt had to bear in atonement for the landslide which had endorsed his stewardship at the last election. Since Adelaide was regarded as a safe Labor seat no one had worried about the calibre of the endorsed Liberal candidate; but Mr Jones won the seat and proved to be perhaps the most brash and ingenuous person ever elected to the House of Representatives. His innocent statements to the press kept him constantly in the news and his Liberal and Country Party comrades constantly on tenterhooks. In one press interview he rashly expressed his disappointment with Parliament House because, he said, so many members were intoxicated for so much of the time. He was forced to apologise for this indiscretion, and was soon afterwards arrested and deprived of his driving-licence for speeding. Needless to say, he proved to be what Australian parliamentarians term a 'oncer'. Not surprisingly his constituents failed to send him back to enliven the House for a second time.

Mr Jones was the least of the Coalition's worries, however, just as growing unease and resentment at its pursuit of the undeclared Vietnam war was the greatest. The Government lost by-elections in Corio, a seat centring on Geelong in Victoria and in Capricornia, centring on Rockhampton in Queensland, the former exhibiting a massive 'swing' toward Labor. Then, owing to Menzies' 'premature' dissolution of the Representatives when the auspices had favoured his Government in 1963, there was an election for half the members of the Senate on 27 November 1967. The major issues were foreign policy and the credibility of the Government, which had been severely shaken by its Vietnam policies as well as by the *Voyager* and V.I.P. planes controversies. The vote for Coalition candidates fell sharply from its peak only a year earlier and, in Victoria, Queensland and Tasmania to its lowest point since World War II. The Government lost one seat so that, after 1 July 1968, the A.L.P. and D.L.P. together could defeat the Government in the Senate without the help of the Independent

Tasmanian, Senator Turnbull, whereas previously he had held the balance of power.

The Prime Minister was deeply worried by the result, and by the declining popularity of his policies which it reflected: but he was young for a first-rank politician and he had always kept himself physically fit, working hard and playing hard. At 60 he was still a keen and active spear-fisherman, a strong swimmer and an expert at 'body-surfing'. How successfully he might have coped with his deteriorating political fortunes we shall never know. On 19 December, with a wild surf running, he went for a walk along the ocean beach near Portsea, Victoria, with four friends. While they watched, he entered the water and was never seen again.

Absurd rumours went the rounds. Some people believed he had been 'kidnapped' by the personnel of a Russian submarine; others, even more implausibly, that his death had been 'arranged' by the ubiquitous United States' Central Intelligence Agency in conjunction with A.S.I.O., the Australian Security Intelligence Organisation. Like some primitive tribesmen, many people found it difficult to believe that the head of the national Government could simply have drowned — as he clearly had. Others again were shocked that he should have been alone with a few friends, un-guarded by secret or other policemen, and unattended by a train of secretaries, servants or henchmen; but most perhaps, thought the manner of his death some measure of the good fortune of the 'lucky country'. Like Deakin travelling to work on a cable tram sixty years before, or Chifley standing in the queue for *Rusty Bugles* twenty years earlier, an Australian Prime Minister still had relatively little need to guard against physical assault or assassination by even his bitterest domestic political opponents, and he could still live his own private life when off duty. At Christmas 1967, except for New Zealand, there were few other countries on earth of which as much could be said. And yet the lucky country was less domestically peaceful than it had once been. With increasing affluence and sophistication came, it seemed, increasing violence. In 1960 the whole country was deeply shocked by the first case of kidnapping, involving murder, in its history. During the 1966 election campaign a young girl spat in the Prime Minister's face and a young madman shot at Calwell, the leader of the Opposition. Crimes of violence increased rapidly, both absolutely and per head of population, although the figures were still far behind those for the United States.

Chapter 12

RECESSION AND REFORM
c. 1969—1975

The new Prime Minister and Vietnam — Party opposition to Gorton's leadership — McMahon's difficulties — Labor's reforms — A forced election — Return of the Coalition Government

THE NEW PRIME MINISTER AND VIETNAM

On 22 December 1967 the memorial service for Harold Holt was attended by Prince Charles as the Queen's representative, Harold Wilson the British Prime Minister, President Johnson and a good many other heads of state. The Christmas holiday period was further enlivened by remarkably public manoeuvring for the vacant leadership of the Liberal Party, and so for the Prime Ministership. The six most favoured candidates, McMahon, Hasluck, Senator Gorton, Bury, Fairhall and Snedden appeared on T.V. shows, gave press interviews freely and generally behaved as though they were soliciting votes from the public rather than from their parliamentary party colleagues. The position was complicated by the action of the Country Party leader, the dour 'Black Jack' McEwen who, as Deputy Prime Minister when Holt died, automatically became Prime Minister while the Liberal power-struggle proceeded.

He announced that he and his Country Party colleagues would not serve in any government led by 'Billy' McMahon, deputy-leader of the Liberals, should he be chosen as their leader; and he refused to give any reason for his stand. However on 6 January 1968 the *Australian* newspaper revealed that McEwen objected to McMahon's close association with one of its former editors, Mr Maxwell Newton, and to their association with the Basic Industries Group. Since the Liberals had no hope of governing without Country Party support, McMahon dropped out of the contest. Fairhall withdrew because of doubts about his health and Snedden's candidature was taken seriously by hardly anyone but himself. He was relatively inexperienced, quite brash and had not even achieved Cabinet rank. In the Liberal Party Caucus on 9 January it was reported that, on the final ballot, Gorton, by 51 votes to 30, beat the able but colourless Hasluck, who had scorned to canvass support during the hectic three weeks since Holt's disappearance.

Born in Melbourne in 1911 and educated at Geelong Grammar School and an Oxford college famed for its sporting achievements, Brasenose, the new Prime Minister had a distinguished Air Force career during World War II, flying in Britain, Singapore, Darwin and the Battle of Milne Bay. He was severely wounded and carried the scars for the rest of his life. Reconstructed by plastic surgery, his rather lop-sided face conveyed the impression of toughness, good humor, self-confidence and a devil-may-care recklessness. Six foot two inches (188 centimetres) tall, with a somewhat gangling gait, he was a good mixer in club or pub with a genuinely egalitarian, unaffected attitude to his fellow creatures. His earthy grip on life was so strong that he was quite unruffled by references to the circumstance of his illegitimacy. To a journalist employed by Sir Frank Packer, who wrote that he was 'a bastard by birth', 'Jolly John' Gorton amiably replied that:

> there are many who believe that Mr. Reid, by applying himself assiduously to that task for many years, has achieved a status through his own efforts which I hold through action, not by me, but by my parents.[1]

The Liberal caucus was right to think that such a man would, as Prime Minister, wield far more electoral appeal than any other of its members: yet some supported him only with deep misgivings. He seldom expressed himself as clearly as in his considered remark about Alan Reid. There was a broad, larrikin streak in his nature which often caused him to act impulsively, wilfully, even irresponsibly: and, as time was to make clear, he was nearer to the A.L.P. than to most of his Liberal Party colleagues in two important respects. He was a convinced centralist who wanted more power for the Commonwealth Government at the expense of those of the States, and he was a fervent Australian nationalist. A few days after his election to the Liberal leadership, on a nation-wide T.V. programme he consciously contrasted himself with Menzies in this latter respect by saying, 'Well, you might say I am Australian to my boot-heels'. In little more than three years his promotion of these two cherished sentiments, quite as much as his personal weaknesses, had destroyed his standing, not with the electors, but with decisively important sections of his own party.

[1] C. A. Hughes, 'Australian Political Chronicle, May-August 1971', *A.J.P.H.*, December 1971, vol. 17, no. 3, p.426.

Thus in January 1968 Gorton became the first Prime Minister with a seat in the Senate. At the end of the month he resigned in order to stand as Liberal candidate for Holt's vacant, blue-ribbon seat of Higgins in the Melbourne suburbs. Only after his election to the House of Representatives did he reconstruct Holt's Cabinet and then he made surprisingly few changes. The brilliant but eccentric W. C. Wentworth, kept on the back benches for nineteen years by Menzies and Holt, had worked hard in the party for Gorton's election and was rewarded with the portfolio of Social Services and Aboriginal Affairs. The young and very modestly endowed P. R. Lynch, an M.H.R. only since the previous election of 1966, had worked equally hard for Gorton. To everyone's surprise he became Minister for the Army. J. M. (Malcolm) Fraser, Minister for the Army under Holt, was transferred by Gorton to his own old position as Minister for Education and Science. Despite the fact that most of Holt's ministers remained at their old posts it at once became clear that the country was to experience a very different style of government. Holt had been a great party man who liked to rule by consensus. Gorton believed the Prime Minister's will should prevail in all important matters and he usually saw that it did — often enough in despite of majority feeling in his own party.

Politics were still dominated by external affairs and these in turn were still dominated by the Vietnam war. To the D.L.P., and most members of the Coalition parties, the issue was as simple as it had always been. Australia was an affluent, capitalist society to which Communism was opposed. The North Vietnamese and the insurgents in South Vietnam were Communists, backed with arms and moral support by Red China and Red Russia. Therefore they must be fought to the death lest they take over the whole of Vietnam and Indo-China and so strengthen world Communism. Even more importantly, Australia must fight shoulder to shoulder with her great ally, the United States, so that, in the event of a future attack, a grateful America would be more disposed to protect her. Moreover we were fighting at the request of the Vietnamese, under the SEATO arrangements to protect the democratic people of the country from a Communist takeover.

Those opposed to the war agreed with the proposition that the North Vietnamese and southern 'rebel' forces were Communist-led, but with nothing else. They held that the Vietnamese Communists were leading a broadly-based war of national liberation from exploiting powers, first the French, then the Japanese, the French again and finally the Americans; and for evidence they pointed to President Eisenhower's statement in his memoirs that if genuinely free elections had been held throughout

Vietnam in the middle 1950s up to 80 per cent of the population would have voted for the Communist nationalist leader, Ho-Chi-Minh, rather than for the French-backed chief-of-state, Bao Dai. Further they held that a Communist Vietnam would be likely to oppose China as the two countries had been enemies for thousands of years. In any case, they believed, it was utterly immoral to wage war upon a country thousands of kilometres away simply because that country, or its supposed friends, might on some future occasion attack Australia. Finally they believed that the recent history of Vietnam no less than that of Indonesia, Algeria and the rest of the ex-colonial world, showed that the war was un-winnable from the start; and that Australian intervention could have no other effect than to undermine national security by arousing deep resentment in Vietnam and South-East Asia generally. Moreover Australian ministers were simply lying to the Parliament and the people when they reiterated that Australia was bound to help South Vietnam under SEATO arrangements.[2]

During Gorton's Prime Ministership an increasing majority of the Australian electorate came to share the views of people like Dr J. F. Cairns the A.L.P. left-wing leader, who had resolutely opposed the war from the beginning: but the Government and millions of its supporters continued to maintain that they were still right and even, in the face of massive evidence to the contrary, that 'the Allies' were still winning. A few days after his election Gorton declared roundly that no more Australian troops would be sent to Vietnam, and that he would be opposed to the United States using its air power to destroy North Vietnam. Yet only a few days later he made a bellicose speech and continued thereafter, like most of his ministers, to sound more 'hawkish' than American spokesmen — indeed, embarrassingly so. In the last week of March Hasluck, Minister for External Affairs and Fairhall, Minister for Defence, vigorously defended bombing of the North as a necessary means of winning the war. Only a few days later on the 31st, President Johnson suddenly announced cessation of the bombing of most of North Vietnam and his decision not to stand again for the Presidency. Australia mattered so little in Washington, apparently, that the Government was informed of the bombing-halt only a day beforehand and had no warning at all of Johnson's retirement. The Prime Minister learnt of it from a radio broadcast and was furious, but could do little to remedy the situation or even to make sure Australia was consulted by her mighty ally in future.

[2] R. G. Neale, *Australia's Military Commitment to Vietnam*, Canberra, 1975, p. 22 *et passim*.

At home by 1968 there was probably more civil strife and open defiance of the law over Vietnam than there had been over conscription in World War I. In May the Government introduced legislation providing very much more severe penalties for youths who evaded their compulsory military service and for those who helped them to do so. Failure to answer a call-up notice or to serve might incur two years' imprisonment, imposed by a magistrate without the option of a jury trial. The only result was to swell the volume of protest. In the next few years more or less violent brawls between hundreds of student demonstrators and squads of policemen occurred in the capital cities and in some country towns. Every university experienced protests about the war. At the University of New England the Army headquarters on the campus was mysteriously burnt down one night. At the University of Sydney the State Governor, Sir Roden Cutler, a one-legged World War II V.C. winner, invited to address the Faculty of Arts, was jostled and pelted with fruit while 'left' and 'right' student factions fought about the war. Thousands of young men evaded the call-up by leaving the country or hiding from the police, and they were assisted to do so by millions of their elders who thought the war itself wrong or just felt it wrong to punish people for acting on their conscientious beliefs. Before the intervention stopped thousands of citizens, many of them prominent in the arts and education, had inserted in the newspapers signed advertisements urging young men to refuse service and inviting the Government to prosecute them for having thus broken the law. In fact few 'draft-resisters', as they were called, and practically none of those who aided and abetted them, were prosecuted. It seemed that the Government more and more sought to avoid the arrest of offenders, because each trial promoted discussion of the issues and so increased opposition to the war.

Student protesters were activated mainly, but not solely, by the war. As in France, Germany, the United States and the western world generally, however, the late 1960s in Australia saw a dramatic rise in the level of student militancy and political activity. For the most part their parents, unlike those of earlier generations of tertiary students, had not experienced the great Depression during their adult lives, but had grown up during and after World War II to take security of employment and rising living-standards for granted. Perhaps they failed to exhort their children to play safe and beware of 'politics' as so many older parents had done. Perhaps the young people asked more fundamental questions about the nature of society itself, because there was clearly no longer room for most of them to occupy *élite* positions in it as there had

Australian, 1966

THE RATBAG ELEMENT?

been for past generations of university students. Whatever the reasons, they behaved in a far more 'revolutionary' way than had earlier student radicals. Many of their teachers, who had complained for years about careerism, conformism and political apathy among students, suddenly found themselves complaining about indiscipline, rudeness and violence. Freed of the need to worry about jobs, and freed by the recently available contraceptive pill of the need to worry about unplanned children, young people lived far more free and less inhibited lives than ever before. Boys began to cultivate long hair and beards and girls to cut their hair short if they felt like it. Mini-skirts revealed the whole length of female thighs in a way that made the knee-length short skirts of the 1920s seem prudish. 'Jeans' became almost a uniform for the young of both sexes. Nakedness among young friends of different sex became socially acceptable. Consumption of marijuana, rather than alcohol or tobacco, became the symbol of sophistication and 'liberation'.

For many these things were merely fashionable, but for some they were outward signs of hostility to some of the fundamental values on which society seemed to be based. Competitiveness and acquisitiveness were strongly condemned. What, asked student radicals, was the point of affluent security in a world order which supported warfare, domestic police violence, greed and commercial pollution of the natural environment? Some joined Trotskyist, Maoist and other revolutionary organisations. More 'dropped out' of what they called the 'rat-race' to live the simple life in country or city communes. Nearly all of the 'New Left' believed passionately in 'confrontation' — something very like what the I.W.W. zealots long before had termed 'direct action'. Conventional political behaviour, such as the passing of resolutions at meetings, they thought accomplished little; but by simply sitting down in the street to protest, even a few score people could halt the traffic of a great city and thus compel many thousands to give some attention to their grievances; or by breaking into a vice-chancellor's office, even a dozen or two students might go far towards compelling a great university to abolish examinations, condone cheating and lower its academic standards. Many of these young radicals believed that such confrontations would hasten the inception of a complete social revolution. Few observers shared this belief, but the 'youth revolt' of the late 1960s and early 1970s did demonstrably accelerate the pace of reform, and in some respects of deterioration, within the existing social structure.

PARTY OPPOSITION TO GORTON'S LEADERSHIP

Apart from the festering Vietnam issue, the Government had little to worry about. There was some disquiet over another American base installed at Pine Creek near Alice Springs which, people believed, helped to guide spy-satellites over the U.S.S.R. and China, but as the North West Cape base already made Australia a potential nuclear target there seemed to be little point in agonising over further similar installations. In June and July 1968 Gorton's centralist policy and authoritarian manner infuriated the State premiers at his first Loan Council meeting, but the economy was flourishing and opinion polls showed that the new free-wheeling, folksy Prime Minister was popular with the electors. He decided to hold an early general election to confirm his authority and rumour fixed 30 November as the date for the poll. However the plan was vetoed by the Democratic Labor Party, which had done very well at the last election, much better it feared, than it might do again. Mr Santamaria, begetter and strategist of the D.L.P. though not a member of it, publicly threatened the Coalition parties that, if an election were held, the D.L.P. would switch its preferences to Labor in a number of selected seats. Gorton bowed to the inevitable. On 10 February 1969 Mr Hasluck ceased to be Minister for External Affairs and became Sir Paul Hasluck K.C.M.G., Governor-General of the Commonwealth in succession to Lord Casey. The *Sydney Morning Herald* regarded it as a good choice but a bad precedent, for never before had a serving federal politician stepped directly into the vice-regal mansion, Yarralumla. The second successive appointment of an Australian by an anti-Labor government made it unlikely that Englishmen would ever again fill the position.

On the same day a weekly news-sheet, published by the dreaded Mr Maxwell Newton, first referred somewhat cryptically to rumours that had been circulating for some time about the Prime Minister's personal life and drinking habits. A few weeks later on 19 March another scurrilous news-sheet published more detailed and sensational stories about 'Jolly John' Gorton's private affairs and then a fellow-Liberal, the somewhat 'wowserish' Mr Edward St. John, member for Warringah in New South Wales, broached the matter in Parliament. Specifically he charged that, in the early morning of the preceding 2 November, Gorton had behaved to the American Ambassador in such a rude and irresponsible manner as to show that he was unfit to be Prime Minister. St. John and other critics held that the incident at the U.S. Embassy was typical of Gorton's impulsive, and sometimes larrikinish, behaviour. The facts were these.

On 1 November 1968 President Johnson announced the cessation of all military action against North Vietnam. This time the Australian Government was apparently informed, though hardly consulted, about twenty-four hours beforehand. Gorton was furious at this cavalier treatment from Johnson whom, he thought, he had impressed with Australia's importance during a visit to Washington a few months previously. That night the Prime Minister was guest of honour at a dinner given by the Canberra Press Gallery. Soon after midnight he left with a young woman journalist, Miss Geraldine Willesee, and his press secretary, Mr T. Eggleton. The Prime Minister suggested they should take up a standing invitation to visit the American Embassy, which they did. Others present were the Ambassador and an attaché and Gorton's private secretary, Miss Ainsley Gotto.

During the whole visit of some two hours, despite Miss Gotto's pleading, Mr Gorton remained in private conversation at one end of the room with Miss Willesee, ignoring his host completely except for greetings on his arrival and departure. A furore raged for a few weeks. Some put forward the ingenious explanation that Gorton had purposely insulted the Ambassador by his behaviour, to demonstrate his displeasure over the lack of prior consultation; but it was difficult to produce similar explanations for other instances of recklessly unconventional actions. Nevertheless it was St. John who was isolated and forced out of the Liberal Party, not Gorton. To judge from public opinion polls it seemed that most voters positively approved his casual flouting of accepted social conventions. The 'wowser vote' was no longer so mighty a power in the land. From this time onward censorship by customs clerks, policemen, and other guardians of public morality was almost abandoned. Sexuality, nakedness and politically innovative ideas could be presented on the stage, in films, books and pictures as freely as in other civilised countries — except in Queensland. There the fundamentalist Country Party Premier, Mr Johannes Bjelke-Petersen, ensured that his State remained untainted by modernism, disturbing thoughts and depiction of pubic hair. On 8 July 1969, declaring that 'he could not but be struck by the poses depicted', a scholarly Brisbane magistrate confiscated a number of Aubrey Beardsley prints and fined the bookshop which had offered them for sale.[3]

Gorton's next major gaffe was perpetrated in Washington during a visit in May 1969 to pay his respects to the recently elected President Nixon. At a White House dinner he wound up his speech

[3] *A.J.P.H.*, vol. 15, no. 3, December 1969, p. 104.

with the ringing declaration, which must have at least puzzled his host, 'We will go a-waltzing Matilda with you' in resistance to aggression. Many Australians had no desire at all for personal friendship with the man who later became notorious as organiser of the Watergate 'break-in'. More felt the remark to be unduly obsequious, like the dead Harold Holt's unfortunate cry of 'All the way with L.B.J.!'. Even extremely conservative newspapers like the Brisbane *Courier-Mail* of 9 May, agreed that Mr Gorton's 'extraordinary remark' would be met with 'amazement and derision'.

The federal election, unwanted by the D.L.P., could not be postponed beyond the end of the year and was set down for 25 October. The Prime Minister announced that his Government would campaign strongly on defence and foreign policy, but it was in just these areas that it struck most trouble. On Hasluck's elevation to the Governor-Generalship at the beginning of the year, Gorton had appointed to replace him in the senior portfolio of External Affairs, a relatively young and inexperienced member for a Western Australian country seat, Mr Gordon Freeth. Conservative commentators were stunned and loudly cried, 'we told you so', when Freeth made a speech to the House in August suggesting new departures in foreign policy. Britain had announced she would withdraw from the Indian Ocean area by the end of 1971. In this context Freeth suggested that Australia might explore the possibility of some co-operation with the U.S.S.R. in the area as (though this was not openly stated) a counterbalance to China.

Ever since the election of the first post-war Menzies Government twenty years earlier, Australian foreign policy had been based on anti-Communism. That the Communist powers, particularly Russia, were totally menacing was the prime article of faith, transcending all rational discussion or considerations of *real-politik*. Freeth's modest and tentative proposal for the examination of reality raised bellows of pain and outrage from conservatives everywhere. There is every reason to think that the speech had at least tacit prime ministerial approval, but most Government members and the whole of the D.L.P. reacted so sharply that Gorton in effect disowned his Minister for External Affairs. The Western Australian secretary of the D.L.P. publicly threatened: 'John Gorton defends us or down the skids he goes'.[4] Fairhall, Minister for Defence, who had not been consulted, chose this time to announce his retirement from federal politics after the coming election. The whole affair probably lost some conservative votes for

[4] *Australian*, 23 August 1969.

the Government without, of course, gaining anything from the left and centre — if only because the proposal was still-born.

In his policy speech the chastened Prime Minister placed all the emphasis that even the D.L.P. could desire, on defence spending and on the Russian menace. He also promised radical reform of what was flatteringly called the national health scheme, tax reductions for lower and middle income earners, $100,000,000 for the development of water resources and a few specific benefits for 'swinging' electorates such as an institute of marine science for Townsville. For Labor E. G. Whitlam promised to withdraw all Australian forces from Vietnam by June 1970, massive grants for education and a range of increased social service benefits including a comprehensive health service. 'I firmly believe', said Mr McEwen, 'the Labor Party is under communist influence'[5] — hardly an original election campaign contribution from a leader of the Country Party.

The result showed a massive swing of popular support away from the Government coalition, which secured only 43.35 per cent of the votes cast for candidates for the Lower House as against 46.95 per cent for the A.L.P. However the D.L.P. preferences once again were sufficient to keep the Liberal and Country Parties in power with 46 and 20 seats respectively to Labor's fifty-nine. Two vacant Senate seats were filled on the same day, and the D.L.P. still held the balance of power in the Upper House with 4 seats to 27 held by the Government, 28 by the A.L.P. and one by an Independent. Freeth was punished for his disturbing thoughts by his rural electors, and soon afterwards compensated by Gorton with the Ambassadorship to Tokyo. Most people thought the swing towards Labor was the result of disillusionment with the Vietnam war and with the Prime Minister's impulsive and often self-contradictory policies, but a conservative scholar at the University of Melbourne, Dr Frank Knopfelmacher, gave a deeper and more general explanation:

> It would be wrong to regard Gorton and his team as the cause of the Liberal disaster. They are symptoms. The party of ex-colonial loyalists with no mother country to be loyal to is in a state of moral crisis and political paralysis. There is no non-Catholic conservative intelligentsia in Australia capable of arguing politics intelligently in public, and there seems to be nothing to replace the old, shrewd, imperial-colonial patriciate of the Menzies era.[6]

[5] *Australian*, 21 October 1969.

[6] *Australian*, 31 October 1969.

The election results had hardly been finalised when Mr David Fairbairn, a senior Cabinet member and Minister for National Development, resigned from the Government and challenged Gorton for the leadership of the Liberal Party. It was believed that Gorton survived by a bare majority of only one or two Caucus votes, and during 1970 his authority within his own party was further eroded, largely because of his strongly nationalist and centralist stance, but partly because of increasing evidence of personal weaknesses. He had developed an ungrammatical, convoluted way of speaking which had earned him the sobriquet of 'Bungles' and which had moved the North Sydney branch of the Liberal Party to resolve, even before the election:

> We are of the opinion that our party, which cherishes the right of all members to freely express their views, cannot afford to be led by one who neither expresses his views clearly, nor appears to accept the official platform.[7]

The last clause was an oblique reference to what many Liberals saw as Gorton's centralist, dictatorial attitude to the States. Their worst fears were confirmed by the Governor-General's speech to the new Parliament in March 1970. He promised the establishment of an Australian industry development corporation, a pet scheme of McEwen's for buying back from multi-national overseas corporations a measure of control over important Australian industries. The plan was naturally welcomed by Labor but was seen by large sections of the Liberal Party as rank socialism. A similar body was to be established in Papua-New Guinea. His excellency, Sir Paul Hasluck, also foreshadowed legislation to give the Commonwealth control of the sea-bed from low-water mark to the outer limits of the continental shelf. Since the discovery of oil in Bass Strait, off the north-west coast of Western Australia, and elsewhere, ownership of the sea-bed had become a matter of first rate importance. It was also one on which the Commonwealth Constitution, framed when mineral oil resources were only beginning to be developed and when national sovereignties were universally agreed to extend only to the 'three-mile limit', had nothing directly to say.

The State governments, naturally, were as keen to assert their claims to such a potentially rich source of revenue as the Commonwealth was to assert its. Opinion polls showed that most Australians agreed with Gorton's view that control of the sea-bed

[7] *S.M.H.*, 10 September 1969.

was clearly a matter for the national government. Probably the multi-national oil companies supported State claims in the belief that it would be easier for them to influence or manipulate relatively weak State governments, and even to play one off against another, than it would be to manipulate the Commonwealth. In the end, rather than split his party, the Prime Minister backed away from the issue and the Bill was shelved. Similarly at the annual Loan Council meeting on 26 June, Gorton restored some degree of harmony in Liberal ranks, at least temporarily, by agreeing to most of the demands for Commonwealth money made by the Premiers. To redeem his election promises about the national health scheme proved more difficult. Again he swore there would be no compromise and again, after implementing some improvements, he capitulated to pressure, this time from the powerful and intransigent medical profession.

While the Liberal Party was visibly losing authority and cohesion during Mr Gorton's Prime Ministership, important changes were taking place within the Labor and Country Parties. Whitlam, the new Federal Parliamentary Labor leader, possessed a great deal more electoral appeal than the old-fashioned Arthur Calwell had had. He was an extremely astute politician with considerable charisma who was seen, even by the anti-Labor press, as a likely 'alternative' Prime Minister. The party he led, however, was still divided against itself as a result of the splitting off of the D.L.P. faction in the middle 1950s. As we have seen, the work of B. A. Santamaria and Archbishop Mannix ensured that the schism was far deeper in Victoria than elsewhere. The fact that nearly all Catholic A.L.P. members and a great many non-Catholic right-wingers in that State were drawn, or pushed, into the D.L.P., left the official party open to a *de facto* takeover by extreme left-wing, militant trade union members. Thus for many years the Victorian branch of the A.L.P. sometimes defied federal policy directives and continually reminded the electorate of disunity and 'extremism' in Labor ranks. In September 1970 the A.L.P. Federal Executive, meeting by arrangement in Melbourne, voted by 10 to 7 to dissolve the Victorian branch of the party and to set up an advisory council of twelve (predominantly Victorian) members to plan its reconstruction with the A.L.P. federal president and secretary.

A retired left-wing Labor stalwart, Mr L. C. Haylen, for twenty years member for the New South Wales seat of Parkes and, incidentally, a good Catholic, lamented that the Victorian purge broke the 'last link of Labor with socialism', and that the A.L.P. was 'becoming a Kennedy-type party of millionaires, academics and careerists'.[8] Other observers could see no millionaires, and certainly no more careerists, in the new A.L.P. than in the Coalition parties, but it is true that from this time Labor appeared, more than ever before, as simply a nationalist bourgeois, liberal, reformist party which none but the self-deluded could think seriously committed to the general socialisation of society. By the same token it appealed more strongly to the 'swinging' voter, and seemed more likely to gain federal office, than at any time since the death of J. B. Chifley.

At the beginning of 1971 the seventy-year old John McEwen was knighted and announced his retirement from politics. He was succeeded by Douglas Anthony, son of a previous M.P. for the Richmond River district in Northern New South Wales. Born in 1929 Anthony had been educated at the King's School, Parramatta, and first elected to his father's old seat in 1957. Tall, well-built, fair-complexioned and quite extraordinarily handsome, Anthony was a shrewd, conservative, but only moderately intelligent politician, quite as capable as his former chief of driving hard bargains for his party. He was given McEwen's ministry of Trade and Industry and, of course, the Deputy Prime-Ministership, while Ian Sinclair, the Country Party's new deputy-leader, took over Anthony's old portfolio for Primary Industry. Meanwhile the Prime Minister's standing in the Liberal Party and the Government's standing in the country, continued to deteriorate.

On the same day that the Country Party smoothly reorganised itself after McEwen's departure, the Liberal caucus met for an acrimonious discussion of the election results. Members openly criticised the Prime Minister's propensity for making decisions without proper consultation with his colleagues or even with his Cabinet. A few days later he further embittered his relationship with the State Premiers, all of them Liberal or Country Party in politics except the Laborite Dunstan from South Australia, by telling them they could have nothing in the way of extra funds — except for a small grant for flood-relief to New South Wales. Even the hard-hearted Commonwealth Treasury officials, it was learned, had advised giving $40,000,000; but the Prime Minister alone decided that the States must bear the brunt of an anti-inflationary reduction in government spending. Gorton's exasperated colleagues finally rebelled early in March.

There was a public quarrel between Mr Malcolm Fraser, the Minister for Defence, and the Chief of the Army General Staff, Sir Thomas Daly, in which the soldier was said to have accused the

[8] *S.M.H.*, 16 September 1970.

Minister of 'disloyalty to the Army'. Without consulting Fraser the Prime Minister sent for Daly and then issued a denial of the story, but in such a way as to leave the impression that Fraser had acted wrongly. In the excitement no one seemed to notice how unquestionably wrong it was for a professional soldier to criticise in any way a minister of the government to which he was responsible. Fraser resigned from Cabinet and in a statement to the House of Representatives added:

> It should not be thought that this act alone has brought me to this point . . . The Prime Minister fought to prevent Cabinet discussion . . . The Prime Minister because of his unreasoned drive to get his own way, his obstinacy, impetuous and emotional reactions, has imposed strains upon the Liberal Party, the Government and the Public Service. I do not believe he is fit to hold the great office of Prime Minister, and I cannot serve in his Government.[9]

Whitlam gave notice that he would move a motion of no-confidence in the Government on the following day, but before the House met there was a meeting of the Liberal Party caucus at which two Victorian back-benchers moved confidence in Gorton's leadership. One member, a strong supporter of Gorton, was absent in hospital. Those present voted 33 for to 33 against the motion. With a grace very unusual in politics Gorton, as chairman of the meeting, gave his casting vote against — and ceased to be leader of the party and the nation. Caucus then elected McMahon as the new leader with Gorton as his deputy. Gorton asked McMahon for the Defence portfolio which, rashly, was granted him.

McMAHON'S DIFFICULTIES

Born in 1908 and educated at Sydney Grammar School and St. Paul's College in the University of Sydney, McMahon practised there as a solicitor until joining the army when war broke out in 1939. Ten years later he was elected to the House as member for the Sydney suburban seat of Lowe, which continued to return him to Parliament thereafter. Menzies gave him Cabinet rank as Minister for Navy and Air in 1951 only two years after his entry into politics. He made a competent, if not particularly distinguished minister in succeeding Liberal-Country Party governments, serving in an unusually wide range of posts. From 1966 to 1969 he won general praise for his work as Treasurer, but little for his subsequent performance as Minister for External Affairs. With the exception of the Labor defectors, Cook, Hughes and Lyons,

[9] *C.P.D.—H.R.*, 9 March 1971, pp. 679-84.

Sun, 1969

"Come on, fellas—don't you remember my friendly grin!"

McMahon was the only federal leader of the major non-Labor party, since Reid, to be based in New South Wales or indeed in any other State but Victoria, generally the citadel of the conservative political establishment in Australia. Only in 1965, when he was 57 years old, did he marry a beautiful and socially prominent young woman, Miss Sonia Hopkins. This showed, the wiseacres said, that he had prime-ministerial ambitions. Short and slightly built, McMahon was physically tough and something of a fitness fanatic whose face, like those of his partners in the game, often bore scars inflicted by a misdirected squash-racket. His baldness, huge ears, pointed nose and alert, beady eyes gave to his features a mouse-like appearance which was the delight of cartoonists. Slight deafness handicapped him in the cut and thrust of extempore debate.

Unlike his predecessor, the new Prime Minister was a shrewd, tactful, accommodating person who set out to reconcile the opposing factions in his party and to rule by consensus in Cabinet; but these qualities, which had served him so well in his climb to the pinnacle of power, proved quite inadequate when he had to exercise it. While Gorton had been too domineering to make a good leader, McMahon was too flexible and devious to give a firm lead to his colleagues. During his brief tenure of office the Government floundered from crisis to crisis while its leader sought to avoid hard decisions and to please everybody, with the result that he pleased almost nobody and dissension within the Government ranks became worse than ever. His strained relations with Gorton highlighted the personal hatreds which were tearing the party apart. Having made Gorton Minister for Defence in the new Cabinet, McMahon forced him to resign five months later for having published a series of newspaper articles attacking aspects of Government policy — and, by implication at least, aspects of McMahon's leadership. Specifically the Prime Minister charged that Gorton had broken the basic constitutional principle of the secrecy of, and collective responsibility for, Cabinet deliberations. Soon afterwards Gorton referred publicly to his leader as 'Billy the Leak'. It was reported that, in an effort to improve their relationship, McMahon approached Gorton in the House during a vote in May 1972 with the words, 'John, I'd like you to sit and talk to me during the division'. 'Go to buggery!' was Gorton's cordial reply. When asked about the incident by reporters, Gorton replied:

> Well — it was a bit of a journalistic beat-up, but it was near enough . . . He put his arm around me. And I don't like that. I don't like anyone putting their arm around me. And some are worse than others.[10]

[10] C. A. Hughes, 'Australian Political Chronicle, May-August 1972', *A.J.P.H.*, December 1972, vol. 18, no. 3, pp. 408-9.

The first major problem for the McMahon Government was the question of recognising Red, or mainland China. For twenty years the Coalition and the D.L.P. had represented that country as the greatest threat imaginable to Australia and had won elections partly by the vehemence of their denunciations. Yet by 1970 the diplomatically non-existent state was buying approximately one-third of Australia's wheat crop. The sales agreement expired in October 1970 and Peking showed no signs of renewing it, though the Red government pointedly made a large wheat purchase from Canada just after that country had negotiated an exchange of diplomats with it. With Australian farmers facing ruin, even the Country Party and, more remarkably, the D.L.P. began to talk of recognition but, as with so many other issues, McMahon procrastinated. Meanwhile Whitlam, as leader of the Opposition, in July 1971 visited China with an A.L.P. delegation and discussed trade and other matters with the Prime Minister, Chou-en-lai. The infuriated McMahon claimed that by his visit Whitlam had insulted practically all Australia's friends and allies in Asia and the Pacific, but he had hardly issued his denunciation when, like his predecessor in office, he was acutely embarrassed by another sudden American policy-switch of which, as Australian Prime Minister, he had had no warning. The world learnt that the American Secretary of State, Henry Kissinger, had in fact been in Peking at the time of the Whitlam visit, arranging for a meeting between Chou-en-lai and President Nixon. Whitlam announced that China would be recognised at once if Labor were returned to power at the next election. McMahon still talked of recognising China, but failed to do so.

Despite his diplomacy and his willingness to compromise, McMahon was no more able than Gorton had been to carry the Territorial Sea and Continental Shelf Bill through Parliament against the hostility of the States and of many of his own supporters. This legislation was shelved at the end of March 1972 in deference to the States. In October consideration of the measure was adjourned indefinitely, although the decision was carried by only one vote, Gorton and Killen having crossed the floor to vote with Labor.

The Government was divided also about how best to cope with a world currency crisis which inevitably affected Australia. McMahon was unlucky in having become Prime Minister just when the thirty-year long boom showed signs of ending. All over the world inflation and unemployment figures were rising in every affluent, industrialised, western country, even in West Germany and Japan where prosperity had been greatest. By the winter of

Age, 1971

'I'm after a Cabinet team — I just hope they're not after me.'

1971 unemployment was approaching 2 per cent of the workforce, a ridiculously low figure by North American standards but one which, post-war experience showed, was regarded as intolerably high by the Australian electorate. At the same time the inflation rate was more than 6 per cent per annum. Despite all that could be done, unemployment and inflation continued, with minor fluctuations, at a politically unacceptable level right up to the fall of the Coalition Government at the end of 1972.

The McMahon Government's greatest problems sprang from its old-fashioned attitude to various 'racial' questions. Since World War II the traditional Australian hatred and fear of foreigners, and particularly of black, yellow and brown people, had weakened enormously. Of course, some people, particularly in the over-40 age group, retained their prejudices, but even this minority usually felt inhibited about voicing them publicly. A tiny far-right-wing group styled the League of Rights, reinforced by a number of able white refugees from Black Africa, and a minute 'Australian Nazi Party' openly peddled racist propaganda, but by 1971 the community as a whole had become perhaps a little less racially bigoted than most others in the world.[11] Many young people, with all the zeal of converts compensating for the sins of their parents, demonstrated the militancy of their anti-racist feelings on every possible occasion.

The A.L.P. realised the extent of the change in feeling before the other major political parties did. At its 29th federal conference in June 1971 delegates voted 44 to 1 to amend the party's policy on immigration in such a way as to ensure that there could be no discrimination on racial grounds among aspiring immigrants. Donald Dunstan, the South Australian Premier, and Whitlam, the federal parliamentary leader, had long been prominent among those working for the change. At the end of the month the all-white, racially selected, Springbok football team arrived in Perth from the Union of South Africa. The old Australian passion for sport combined with the new-found hatred of racism to inspire massive demonstrations against apartheid whenever the team appeared. Mr Bob Hawke, newly elected president of the Australian Council of Trade Unions, promised that union boycotts would make it impossible for the South African team to move round Australia, and the Prime Minister promised, if necessary, to provide Royal Australian Air Force aircraft to transport it. Brawls, broken heads and bad language were most plentiful in Queensland where the Country Party Premier, Mr Bjelke-Petersen, declared a state of

[11] Alan Hughes, *Psychology and the Political Experience*, London, 1975, pp. 25-7 and *National Times*, 4-9 August 1975, pp. 26-7.

emergency and sent large numbers of aggressive policemen to the football matches.

McMahon toyed with the idea of calling an election to capitalise on what he thought would be general public hostility to the anti-apartheid demonstrators. By the time the tour was over he may have had doubts. At any rate when a (white) South African cricket tour was mooted later in the year, he sought to avoid a similar confrontation by asking the Chairman of the Australian Cricketing Board of Control, Sir Donald Bradman, to decide whether the tour should go ahead or not. The man whom most Australians devoutly believed to be the greatest cricketer of all time was a conservative stock-broker in private life. He consulted his Board and replied firmly that he agreed with the Prime Minister's slogan that politics should be kept out of sport but that, since this was notoriously not the case in South Africa, Australia should refuse to accept racially selected teams from that country.

The Government was further embarrassed by its gradualist approach to Aboriginal problems. In May 1972 a committee of inquiry, which it had appointed, recommended that land should be provided for Aboriginals forced off their customary hunting-grounds by pastoralists in the Northern Territory. Aboriginal leaders, recently counted as citizens for the first time, set up an 'Aboriginal Embassy' on the shaven lawns in front of Parliament House in Canberra and swore they would camp there until 'land rights' were granted their people. However the D.L.P. and Country Party ministers flatly opposed any action on the ground that granting land to Aboriginals would lead to apartheid. The Government gazetted a special ordinance enabling it to have police forcibly eject the Aboriginals and remove their tents, but others came back and remained to embarrass the Ministry.

The Vietnam war itself, by now thoroughly unpopular, was seen as a racial issue by many voters. Following President Nixon's announcement of a phased withdrawal of American troops, McMahon followed suit for Australia, but he received little credit for this move which had obviously been forced upon him by circumstances. In any case some Australian troops remained in the war-devastated country as long as the Liberal-Country Party Government remained in office in Canberra, and moratorium marches and other forms of protest continued. In the campaign for the general election, which could not be deferred beyond the end of the year, a young schoolteacher named Johnson stood as the A.L.P. candidate-in-hiding for the Victorian seat of Hotham. There was nothing to suggest that his evasion of national service did him or his party any harm with the voters.

As the election approached McMahon's leadership inspired despair in many conservative circles. On his pilgrimage to Washington he behaved so nervously and obsequiously that, according to press reports, American journalists were moved to open laughter. At a time when freedom of navigation in the Straits of Malacca was a major subject of discussion in the world's press, he told the Malaysian Prime Minister at a State Banquet that Australia's position on the issue was perfectly clear: it was that his Government had not yet made up its mind about the Straits of *Madagascar*. Some Liberals, forgetting the weaknesses which had been so glaring when he was Prime Minister, organised a 'Get Gorton Back' committee, but most feared to change leaders yet again so close to the election. McMahon finally set the date for the last possible moment, 2 December 1972. Early in the campaign he occasioned some hilarity among the vulgar by revealing to the nation that he frequently prayed to Almighty God, and that he thought a Liberal victory a proper subject for his supplications.

LABOR'S REFORMS

The first policy speech was given by Mr Gordon Barton, leader of the Australia Party, a recently formed political grouping which appealed strongly to middle-class intellectuals and radicals. In foreign policy and most other issues, except the most basic issue of all — trade unions versus employers, it stood somewhat to the left of the A.L.P. Senator Gair for the D.L.P. denounced the Australia Party for its policy of abortion on request and its permissive attitude to pornography. He warned that Labor was prepared to allow a free (non-party) parliamentary vote on such issues and would destroy the White Australia Policy. Whitlam for Labor promised to abolish military conscription immediately, to recognise China and to introduce a whole range of long overdue reforms, including a comprehensive free medical service and the provision of vastly more money for both public and private schools than the Coalition had ever given. The money for 'independent' schools was to be given on a 'needs' basis, however. This meant that rich and fashionable schools like the King's School or Melbourne Grammar, mostly Protestant, would get little or nothing, while poor and struggling private schools, mostly Catholic, would get a great deal more than before. Not surprisingly, a number of Catholic bishops welcomed this policy and made it clear that Catholics might vote for Labor in good conscience. Other Catholic prelates, however, like the Bishop of Bendigo, damned the A.L.P. for its leader's proposal to allow a 'conscience vote' on abortion.

As the campaign moved to its end, Country Party and Liberal politicians too placed more and more emphasis on the flood of pornography, promiscuity and immorality which, they held, would be bound to follow a Labor victory. They also sought to frighten the voters by reiterating that the 'moderate' Whitlam would in practice be manipulated behind the scenes by the sinister R. J. Hawke, President of the Australian Council of Trade Unions. Bob Hawke, however, was an unusual trade unionist. Born in 1929 in Bordertown, South Australia and educated at the Modern School in Perth, Hawke graduated in Arts and Law, won the Western Australian Rhodes Scholarship in 1952 and obtained a B.Litt. at Oxford. Nephew of a former Labor Premier of Western Australia, he was an extremely acute, personable and popular leader of the trade-union movement, so much so that Whitlam probably gained from the Coalition propaganda associating his name with Hawke's.

The Prime Minister's policy speech was brief and cool, produced with no audience but many technical advisers and aides in a T.V. studio. He appealed to the Government's record, and sought, rather unconvincingly, to match many of Labor's promises, but his main appeal was to fear of the unknown. After twenty-three years in the wilderness he suggested, Labor must necessarily lack the experience, the expertise and, above all, the stability to be trusted with the nation's destiny. Nevertheless, what was to many conservatives the unthinkable happened. By about eleven o'clock on that Saturday night it was clear to all that Australia had elected a Labor Government. McMahon bowed out before the T.V. cameras with a dignity he had lacked on so many other great occasions. The A.L.P. polled just short of 50 per cent of all valid first preference votes cast, the Liberals 32 per cent, the Country Party 9.4 per cent and the D.L.P. 5.3 per cent. Many observers proclaimed, somewhat prematurely, that the D.L.P. had ceased to be a national force. The Australia Party, which gave its preferences to Labor, polled about half the D.L.P. vote. In the new Parliament Labor had 67 seats to 58 held by the Opposition, 38 by the Liberals and 20 by the Country Party. In the Senate, however, the D.L.P. still held the balance of power. There were 26 Labor, 21 Liberal, 5 Country Party, 3 Independent and 5 D.L.P. senators.

The new Prime Minister, Edward Gough Whitlam, was born in Melbourne in 1916, the son of a senior Commonwealth civil servant. Educated at both private and government schools in Canberra and Sydney, he graduated with the B.A., and LL.B. degrees from the University of Sydney. In 1942 he married Margaret Dovey, daughter of a distinguished New South Wales judge. He served as a Flight-Lieutenant in the R.A.A.F. from

1941 to 1945 and was first elected to the Commonwealth Parliament as member for the outer Sydney suburban seat of Werriwa in 1952. As we have seen, he was elected to the leadership of the Federal Parliamentary Labor Party on Calwell's retirement in 1967. He was the seventh Labor Prime Minister and the first whose antecedents and upbringing were thoroughly middle class, rather than working class. Extremely intelligent and widely read, Whitlam stood six feet four (193 centimetres) in his socks. He carried himself well, had an impressive 'presence' and, it was said, looked the part of a Prime Minister. Indeed he established a kind of moral dominance in the House of Representatives while he was still leader of the Opposition, especially during the term of the McMahon Government. He spoke fluently and persuasively, was something of a classical and historical scholar, and had at his command a ready and devastating wit — as when he said of the Rev. Dr M. G. Mackay, Liberal member for a Sydney suburban seat from 1963 to 1972, that his career showed it was quite possible to serve both God and Mammon, though not necessarily in that order. With all these great gifts were joined two notable weaknesses. He was liable to sudden outbursts of temper in which he might say things which negated the work of hours or months; and like Menzies, with whom he was often compared, he too often appeared arrogant and domineering. Unlike Menzies, however, he could join in a laugh at his own expense over his arrogance. Indeed some of his apparently most vainglorious statements were made deliberately with tongue in cheek.

Such was the man sworn in as Prime Minister by Sir Paul Hasluck three days after the election in an unprecedented ceremony — unprecedented in that all twenty-seven portfolios were distributed between two men, Whitlam and the Deputy Prime Minister, Lance Barnard. While waiting for the declaration of the poll in doubtful seats and for all Labor members to assemble in Canberra to elect the Cabinet members, Whitlam and Barnard formed a perfectly constitutional Government of two, dubbed sourly by Opposition members the 'duumvirate'. In the two weeks before the full ministry was sworn in on 19 December, a host of changes was announced. It is safe to say that few Australians had previously realised how much governments can do by regulation without parliamentary discussion, and that it was thoroughly characteristic of the new Prime Minister thus to act decisively and immediately in the centre of the stage.

The duumvirate immediately abolished conscription, freed the seven imprisoned draft-resisters, dropped pending prosecutions of another 300 odd and issued pardons to 150 men absent without leave from the Army. It also announced substantially improved conditions for those who wanted to volunteer for the armed services. Negotiations were begun for an exchange of ambassadors with the People's Republic of China — and large orders for Australian wheat followed in due course. It re-opened the Arbitration Commission's hearing of the claim for equal pay for equal work for women. It announced plans for massive spending on Aboriginal welfare and suspended the granting of mining leases on Aboriginal reserves. Among other early measures were the abolition of British titles and of the sales tax or, as Mrs Whitlam happily put it, the entertainment tax, on contraceptives. Spending on education, the arts and culture was to be massively increased.

Most significant of all was the announcement that thenceforth 'race' or skin-colour would cease to be a criterion for admission to Australia and that racially selected sports teams would be banned from Australian soil. The formal ending of the White Australia Policy was not as sudden as it seemed to many conservatives. As we have seen, racist sentiment had declined sharply in the previous decade and in 1964 and 1966 the Coalition Governments of Menzies and Holt had quietly changed administrative practices in the Immigration Department so that about 6000 part-Europeans and non-Europeans were admitted annually; but previous Governments had been loath to proclaim the changes to the world or even to their electors. The new Labor Minister for Immigration, the flamboyant and able Al Grassby, gloried in his role and throve on publicity. About one-twelfth of all immigrants in 1973 were non-Europeans, although total assisted immigration declined sharply in that year to about only 25 000.

Caucus met to elect the ministry, all twenty-seven of them, on 18 December, a week before Christmas. Whitlam allotted portfolios immediately and the Cabinet was sworn in next day. Its unwieldy size was a continuing impediment to good government. The Coalition parties had solved this problem years before, by setting up an 'inner cabinet' of about ten members. Other ministers attended meetings only when matters directly relating to their portfolios were being discussed. Whitlam wanted to emulate this practice but could not secure Caucus approval for the change. If there had been an inner cabinet its members might have included, besides Whitlam and Barnard, Dr J. F. Cairns (Overseas Trade and Secondary Industry), W. G. Hayden (Social Security), Frank Crean (Treasurer), Clyde Cameron (Labour), Kim Beazley (Education), and R. F. X. ('Rex') Connor (Minerals and Energy). On the following day the Liberal caucus met to conduct a post-mortem on the election and refurbish its image. McMahon announced that he would not offer for the leadership and Mr Billy Snedden was chosen leader and Mr Phillip Lynch deputy, it is believed only by the narrowest of margins. Both men were Victorians so that the Liberal leadership returned to that State after its brief and disastrous sojourn with McMahon in New South Wales.

After its twenty-three years in the wilderness the Labor Government passed an unprecedented amount of legislation through the House of Representatives during its first eighteen months of office. During the Autumn sitting in 1973 alone, 114 Government bills were introduced and 103 passed, though many were held up in the hostile Senate. In retrospect many Labor men thought that too much was attempted at too fast a pace for the electorate, but during 1973 it seemed to radicals and nationalists that long overdue changes were coming too slowly because of Senate hostility but also, to some degree, because of sabotage in some sections of the public service. After such a long period in the service of conservative governments, some departmental heads appeared unhappy in the service of their new masters. Throughout its term of office the Whitlam Government was repeatedly embarrassed by the publication of confidential documents 'leaked' to Opposition politicians by venal civil servants, whose superior officers invariably proved unable or unwilling to identify and punish the malefactors. This was particularly — and predictably — true of A.S.I.O., the secret police intelligence organisation, nominally responsible only to the Prime Minister and the Attorney-General.

Under the previous governments there had been, within the Australian Yugoslav community, a long series of bombings and other outrages which culminated on 16 September 1972 in explosions outside Yugoslav tourist agencies in Sydney. Sixteen innocent passers-by were seriously injured. The criminals were generally believed to be members of the Ustashi, a secret right-wing Croat terrorist organisation whose members had collaborated with the Nazi conquerors of Yugoslavia during World War II, and were bitterly hostile to the current Communist Government of Yugoslavia led by Marshal Tito. However Senator Ivor Greenwood, the Liberal Party Attorney-General under McMahon, vehemently maintained that his A.S.I.O. spies denied that any Croatian terrorist organisation existed in Australia. Many felt this was because the Australian Ustashi elements were in fact being protected, if not helped, by elements within A.S.I.O.

On 2 March 1973 the new Attorney-General, Senator Murphy, discovered documentary evidence of a decision made by the heads of A.S.I.O., and certain other Commonwealth Government departments, that any statement on terrorism made by the Labor Government 'should not be at variance' with those made by Senator Greenwood.[12] With this evidence suggesting disloyalty to the Government, Murphy led a Commonwealth Police party in a 'raid' on A.S.I.O. headquarters in Melbourne to look for the files on Ustashi terrorism. There was tremendous excitement throughout the country with the Opposition claiming that the 'raid' had undermined Australian security. The Country Party leader, Anthony, made the astonishing statement that A.S.I.O. ought not to be accountable to any government. In the upshot the spying organisation was rather heavily discredited, but so was Senator Murphy whose methods had alarmed most people. The Government appointed a well-known judge to enquire into A.S.I.O.'s workings and to make recommendations for its reorganisation.

Many conservatives became almost hysterical about Australia's new stance in international relations, even though the Government was merely implementing promises made in Whitlam's policy speech. Country Party politicians particularly never ceased to accuse the Government of destroying or undermining traditional alliances with Britain and the United States, because it sought good relations with other countries also, and because it adopted a more independent and less subservient style in its relations with the great republic. For instance, when President Nixon ordered the resumption of bombing on Hanoi late in December 1972, three Australian ministers publicly denounced the move while Whitlam, who held the Foreign Affairs portfolio in addition to the Prime Ministership, wrote a strong, private note of protest. The Government continued to criticise aspects of U.S. policy, such as the decision in 1975 to build up a naval base on the Indian Ocean Island of Diego Garcia, but at the same time it cherished the American alliance as the fundamental basis of Australian foreign policy.

In the same way basic cultural and material ties with Britain remained strong, while Australia adopted a more critical and self-reliant attitude. After the United Kingdom's entry into the European Economic Community on 1 January 1973 it was hardly possible to do anything else. The words 'British Subject' disappeared from Australian passports and 'Advance Australia Fair' replaced 'God Save the Queen' as the national anthem.

[12] C. A. Hughes 'Australian Political Chronicle, January-April 1973', *A.J.P.H.*, August 1973, vol. 19, no. 2, pp.249-50.

However the Queen remained as head of state and God would still be exhorted to save her when she was present in person at an Australian gathering. The old anthem was sung with immense fervour also at some meetings of older citizens and of the Liberal and Country Parties.

Under Whitlam's leadership the style of Australian relationships with the United States and Britain changed, but not the relationships themselves. Really new was the tremendous effort made to help in every possible way the development of *detente* between the super-powers and the cultivation of more friendly relations with other countries, particularly those of Asia and the 'Third World'. By November 1973 the Prime Minister and Foreign Minister had visited the capitals of all the major world powers except the Soviet Union, and of many smaller powers too. No man could have kept up this killing pace indefinitely and on the sixth of the month Whitlam handed over the Foreign Affairs portfolio to Senator Don Willesee. Nevertheless in 1974 the Prime Minister visited Moscow and many other European capitals. He incurred heavy press criticism and some loss of popularity for what was seen as the excessive amount of time he spent in journeys abroad, but there is no doubt that Australia was never before so well-regarded virtually everywhere overseas, except perhaps in the Union of South Africa, Rhodesia and fascist Portugal. The Government paid particular attention to the fostering of trade and friendship with China, Japan, Indonesia and the lesser states of South-East Asia. On his visits to Washington, Whitlam was the first Australian Prime Minister since Menzies to conduct himself and to represent his countrymen, with that seemly dignity which accords to and receives from others, a proper respect.

During the 1972 election campaign Whitlam had promised in the most explicit terms that Labor would do everything possible to expedite the independence of Papua New Guinea. The greatest danger to the emerging nation was that of fragmentation into separate and mutually hostile states. In Bougainville there appeared an especially strong secession movement inspired, some thought, by the multi-national interests engaged in mining the fantastically rich copper deposits there. Despite this and other difficulties, the Australian Government pressed ahead and Papua New Guinea attained full internal self-government on 1 December 1973. In 1975 the Chief Minister, Mr M. Somare, announced that the Queen would remain head of state, and the new nation was formally launched, with complete independence within the British Commonwealth on 16 September.

At home, during its first eighteen months in office, the

Government implemented or initiated a bewildering variety of reforms, some of which were seen as retrograde steps by its political opponents. There is space merely to mention some of the more important. Tuition fees were abolished in universities and other tertiary educational centres and living allowances for students increased. Commonwealth expenditure on primary and secondary education was massively stepped up. In an effort to control inflation a Prices Justification Tribunal was established. Another measure, which it was hoped would curb inflation, was taken in July 1973 when all tariffs on imported goods were cut by 25 per cent. The most vehement protests came from leaders of the Country Party — whose supporters stood to gain most from this move; but the conservative *Australian Financial Review* thought it 'undeniably one of the most forthright and courageous economic decisions' ever taken by an Australian government.[13] Similar reactions had greeted the Government's upward re-valuation of the Australian dollar by 7.05 per cent in the previous December. In the middle of the year Clyde Cameron, the Minister for Labour, announced that the Government would give extraordinarily good working conditions to its own public servants in order to make them the 'pace-setters' for industry generally. The 230 000 Commonwealth employees were given a standard 35-hour working week, at least four weeks' annual leave plus a holiday bonus payment, equal pay for equal work for women and paid maternity and paternity leave. In September Parliament abolished the death penalty in Commonwealth territories, some Liberals voting with the Government but the Country Party against, and in the following month on the motion of John Gorton, the House voted to legalise homosexuality between consenting adults, all parties being divided on this issue.

Early in the following year many country people were infuriated by the Government's decision to abolish a $50,000,000 subsidy on superphosphate manures. Like most forms of government assistance to primary producers, this subsidy had helped the rich more than the poor. A wealthy grazier who used perhaps twenty times as much superphosphate as a struggling farmer would receive precisely twenty times as much of the taxpayer's money. From this time onwards the Labor Government was anathema to most primary producers who, since the formation of the Country Party at the end of World War I, had come to regard as their right an ever-increasing measure of help from the public purse. For the period June 1971 to June 1973 for instance, it was calculated by the Commonwealth Bureau of Agricultural Economics that, of the

[13] *Australian Financial Review*, 19 July 1973.

average dairy farmer's nett annual income of $7,170, more than 43 per cent was provided by direct or indirect government subsidies.[14] At a Forrest Place meeting in the centre of Perth soon afterwards, the Prime Minister was abused, jostled and pelted with drink-cans by farmers who had travelled to the city for the purpose. Other citizens, however, had good reason to be pleased with the Government's performance. Australian writers, for instance, for the first time were paid royalties on copies of books on the shelves of public libraries throughout the country. Yet with all these things and many more to its credit, the Government was beset by two intractable problems, inflation and obstruction by the Senate.

A FORCED ELECTION

Despite the measures taken to curb it, and certainly at least in part because of lavish Government spending, inflation continued at the level it had reached under McMahon, between 3 and 4 per cent per quarter. Unemployment figures fell dramatically but inflation showed disquieting signs of rising. The Government correctly pointed out that it could not hope to curb inflation unless it had power to fix prices — a prerogative of the States, while the Opposition held of course that wages, not prices, must be fixed. A compromise was reached in the Senate whereby the Government asked the people for constitutional amendments to give the Commonwealth control over both wages and prices, but at a referendum held on 8 December 1973 both requests were turned down in every State. So inflation continued — as did Senate obstruction.

The Opposition majority in that chamber obstinately refused to pass four major pieces of legislation for which the Government had been given the clearest mandate at the election of 1972. There were bills aimed at reform of the arbitration system, the electoral system, the national health service, and a bill to give the Commonwealth control of the sea bed around the Australian coastline. The first sought to remove penal clauses from the existing law, to reform voting procedures within unions and to facilitate the amalgamation of small unions into larger bodies. The second batch of bills, bitterly opposed by the Country Party, sought to implement the principle of 'one vote one value' by making all electorates approximately equal in population. Under existing arrangements a vote in some rural electorates carried almost twice as much weight

[14] Industries Assistance Commission Report, *Dairy Industry*, Canberra, 1975, pp. 52, 198.

as one in some urban ones. Another of these bills sought to give electors in the Northern Territory and the A.C.T. a vote in Senate elections and in Commonwealth referenda — something which had been simply overlooked by those who framed the Constitution in 1901. The third sought to establish a comprehensive national health service along the lines of the Canadian scheme. It was bitterly resisted by most doctors and their professional organisations as well as by the Senate. The fourth, the Seas and Submerged Lands Bill of 1973, was substantially the same legislation as that defeated three years earlier under the Gorton Government and again under McMahon's leadership.

Early in 1974 Government strategists discussed the possibility of breaking the impasse by appealing to the people through a double dissolution of Parliament and another general election, but in the event this solution was forced on the Government by the Opposition. In April the Senate majority took the unprecedented step of refusing supply to a Government elected only seventeen months previously. More precisely the Opposition carried the threat of refusing supply through to the point of forcing the Prime Minister to ask the Governor-General for a double dissolution. Since federation no hostile Senate majority had ever used its powers in this irresponsible manner, not even during the great Depression when the situation of the country had been immeasurably worse. The date for the general election was fixed as 18 May 1974.

As usual in Australian elections, interest centred mainly on the Government's handling of the economy. Unemployment figures had fallen since McMahon's departure: on the other hand inflation had continued and amounted to some 14 per cent over the past year. During the campaign official figures showed that the rate had fallen to 2.1 per cent for the first quarter of the year as against 3.6 per cent for each of the two preceding quarters. This lucky chance probably ensured the re-election of the Government. In his policy speech the Prime Minister appealed for a 'fair go', arguing that the Government should be given a reasonable chance to carry out the programme of reform endorsed by the people in the preceding election. He made few new promises. He stressed that inflation was a problem common to all the industralised countries in the world and that official statistics showed that Australia was coping with it much better than most comparable countries. Snedden for the Liberals held that Government incompetence, not world economic conditions, was causing inflation. The Liberals would cure it by making cuts in income tax to the tune of $600,000,000. Since the deputy-Prime Minister elect, Anthony of the Country Party, seemed unwilling to endorse this remarkable prescription, Labor's ridiculing of Liberal monetary policies seemed justified. One clear difference between the major parties, however, was their attitude to foreign investment. Labor advocated careful control of it and the fostering of majority Australian ownership of all public companies. The Opposition wanted maximum encouragement of foreign investment even to the extent of re-introducing massive public subsidies, which had been abolished or severely pruned by Labor, to certain forms of foreign private enterprise, such as companies engaged in the search for more oilfields.

On the election day people were required to vote in four referenda for constitutional amendments in addition to casting a vote for their local member and for ten senators for the State in which they lived. All four constitutional amendments were sponsored by the Government and opposed by the Opposition parties. One sought to write into the federal Constitution a provision that all federal electorates, and all electorates in any one State, must contain approximately the same number of voters and that all State Upper Houses must be directly elected by the same voters. Another sought to have Senate elections held on the same day as general elections for the House of Representatives. A third sought to give citizens of the A.C.T. and the Northern Territory a vote in national referenda, and to enable federal constitutional changes to be made for the future by a majority of all votes and a majority in three, instead of four, of the six States. The fourth proposal sought to give the Commonwealth Government power to grant moneys directly to local government bodies instead of channelling such grants through the State governments. Naturally this last was seen as federal encroachment on State prerogatives and opposed by 'State-righters' everywhere. The other proposals were opposed by the conservative parties because they felt that more egalitarian electoral procedures might advantage the A.L.P.

In the event all four referenda were defeated, being carried by a majority of the voters in New South Wales but nowhere else. The same voters gave the Government a vote of confidence, though not of increased confidence: Labor polled 49.3 per cent of all valid votes cast for the House of Representatives as against 49.6 per cent at the previous election in 1972. When counting was finished the Government was left with only one seat fewer in the Representatives than in the previous Parliament. Labor improved its position in the Senate but not sufficiently to win control. There were 29 Labor and 29 Liberal and Country Party senators, plus one (ex-Liberal) Independent who almost invariably voted with his old colleagues and another, Senator Steele-Hall of the breakaway Liberal Movement who, it was thought, would do so only sometimes. The weeks of waiting for the final result to be known were enlivened for everybody by the defeated Liberal leader. Where McMahon had been a liability to his party, Mr Billy Snedden was a disaster. Having been actually christened 'Billy' by his fond Scottish immigrant parents, he announced soon after his succession to the Liberal leadership that he was thenceforth to be known as Bill, because ' "Billy" is a diminutive name and I am not a diminutive person'. Throughout the campaign he never managed to look as though he believed what he was saying, conveying the impression rather of a clockwork toy which had been wound up and programmed to exhibit indignation, confidence and other suitable emotions at calculated intervals. When the counting of votes was nearly over he announced that the Opposition parties under his leadership had not been defeated. Some thought he must be joking but the humour was entirely unintentional. For days he underlined the asinine statement to delighted reporters as in the *Age* of 30 May: 'we were not defeated. We didn't win enough seats to form a government, but I do not believe that what has occurred was in any sense a defeat'.

When the Labor Caucus reassembled on 10 June it replaced Mr Lance Barnard as deputy-leader of the party by Dr Jim Cairns and elected Senator Wheeldon to Cabinet in place of Mr Al Grassby, the popular Immigration Minister, who had been defeated for the seat of Riverina partly because of a 'racist' whispering campaign inspired, he believed, by the League of Rights. Cairns, whose doctorate was in Economics, was given responsibility for the Government's priorities review staff as well as for Overseas Trade and Secondary Industry. Cameron, Minister for Labour, added Immigration to his responsibilities, but at first there were few other changes.

During the first session of the new Parliament on 6 and 7 August 1974, there took place for the first time in history a joint sitting of the two Houses, as provided for in the Commonwealth Consitution. It will be remembered that the Senate had thrice rejected — or 'failed to pass' certain bills deemed vital by the Government, which had then secured a double dissolution. However the new Senate still refused to pass the legislation. The Constitution provides that in such a situation of deadlock there shall be a joint sitting at which the contentious bills may be brought forward and passed or negatived finally by a simple majority of all members of both Houses. Of course the Government had an assured majority of three in a joint sitting. The proceedings were televised live for the first time and so there were finally passed into law the three electoral bills, the two bills providing for a comprehensive national health scheme and the Petroleum and Minerals Authority Bill.

The extremely conservative General Practitioners' Society and the Australian Medical Association, backed by the great majority of doctors, promptly stepped up their intensive campaign of propaganda against the scheme which was the responsibility of two Queensland Labor ministers, W. G. Hayden (Social Security) and Dr Everingham (Health). Totally false rumours were spread that Hayden was a failed medical student, that he had suffered nervous breakdowns and was mentally unbalanced, and so on. The doctors threatened to sabotage the scheme by striking, if it were implemented. Hayden and Everingham, backed by the warm approval of most Australians, persisted and the scheme finally came into being on 1 July 1975 in all States except Queensland and New South Wales. The Liberal-Country Party Governments there held out for a time against accepting parts of the 'Medibank' arrangements, but by the end of the year it was working reasonably well throughout the continent. It was just thirty-seven years since the first effort to introduce a comprehensive national health scheme, forwarded by the young U.A.P. member R. G. Menzies, had foundered on the doctors' intransigence.

Early in 1975 Parliament passed another great measure, long planned by Senator Murphy who, however, had retired to the High Court Bench when it was finally enacted. The concept of 'guilt' was abolished from the marriage law and replaced by one sole ground for divorce — irretrievable breakdown of the marriage to be proved over a period of at least one year. However the successful launching of 'Medibank' and the great reform in the divorce law were the last and almost the only things on which the second Whitlam Government was able to congratulate itself.

RETURN OF THE COALITION GOVERNMENT

Many conservative citizens hated so much all that Labor stood for that they stopped at nothing, including the undermining of the democratic system itself, in order to bring the Government down. The Commonwealth Constitution states that a casual Senate vacancy must be filled until the next election by a substitute nominated by the Government of the State concerned. For many years all parties had observed the unwritten convention that State Governments, irrespective of their political complexion, nominated the person chosen by the same party as that to which the dead or retired senator had belonged. When Murphy retired to the High Court Bench early in 1975 the Liberal Premier of New South Wales, Tom Lewis, a nephew of the great Essington Lewis, dishonoured his name and weakened the democratic fabric by flatly refusing to appoint the Labor nominee. Press and public protests were strong enough to make him appoint to the Senate, instead of a Liberal Party member as he seemed to have planned, an ex-mayor of the border City of Albury, described by the Premier in illiterate language as 'a political neuter'. A few months later when a Queensland Labor Senator died, the wowser Country Party Premier of that State, Mr Joh Bjelke-Petersen, followed Lewis's subversive precedent by appointing to the Senate a bitterly anti-Government ex-Labor man, probably also the most inanely naive person ever to inhabit the federal Upper House. Most disgraceful of all was a scurrilous attack on the federal Government delivered quite gratuitously by Sir Colin Hannah, Governor of Queensland, whose first duty it was to preserve at least the appearance of political impartiality.

The Government's popularity declined, with few temporary upturns, almost from the day when it was elected in May 1974 and this basically for reasons beyond its, or any alternative Government's, control. It was perhaps ironical that another Labor Government should have been fated to preside over the Australian community during the onset of the second great depression, or financial crisis, of the capitalist world in the twentieth century, just as the Scullin Government had presided at the time of the first. The crisis was perhaps set off by inflationary pressures on the western economy rising from the United States' methods of financing its abortive intervention in Vietnam. From 1970 onwards trade recession with rising unemployment and inflation plagued the economies of all western industrialised countries. Signs of trouble in Australia were not wanting under Gorton and McMahon, when inflation and unemployment helped to end the long period of uninterrupted Liberal-Country Party rule. Massive expenditure on reform and welfare measures by the first Whitlam Government reduced unemployment in Australia but inevitably helped to accelerate the inflationary spiral.

At the same time the Arab sheikhs of the Middle East, and the rulers of other oil-exporting countries, dealt a devastating blow at the economies of the western world, which had become overwhelmingly dependent on cheap oil. By arbitrarily raising the world price of crude oil to undreamed of levels, they brought about steeply rising costs of production and further inflation in all industrialised nations. Since by 1970 Australia was producing about 70 per cent of her own requirements of crude oil, she was not as directly affected as Japan, Britain and many other countries, but the steep rise in the price of most imported goods, caused by the oil crisis, pressed heavily on her economic health. When Whitlam's new Cabinet met for the first time on 1 July 1974, it had to discuss

Australian, 1973. 'It's Time' was the A.L.P. campaign slogan in the 1972 election.

measures for the relief of unemployment which stood at 1.4 per cent of the workforce. The spectre of inflation showed no sign of departure. Now that of unemployment, which had nearly wrecked two Menzies governments when it briefly reached about 2 per cent of the workforce, had come to haunt the Whitlam Government also.

Cameron, the Minister for Labour, had Cabinet introduce a Regional Employment Development (R.E.D.) scheme, based on a Canadian plan, and a Structural Adjustment Board to help companies in trouble was also established. Dr Cairns, the Government's strongest advocate of subsidies and other help to private business to avoid further dismissals of staff, obtained more and more influence in the shaping of Government policy. On 12 September Mr Crean introduced a budget providing for a record increase in government spending, some taxation reductions and other measures designed to stimulate the economy. On 25 September there was a devaluation of 12 per cent against the American dollar and the tie between the two currencies was broken; but still unemployment increased. On 21 November, after weeks of rumours, the Prime Minister announced that Dr Cairns would replace Mr Crean as Treasurer. There followed further piecemeal measures designed to stimulate the flagging economy, but still unemployment increased. In May 1975 Cairns was brought down by the publication of confidential letters concerning loan negotiations, 'leaked' continuously to Opposition members by their undetected criminal friends in the public service departments, particularly the Treasury. Cairns, the only Commonwealth Treasurer never to have introduced a budget, was replaced by Hayden, the tough and hard-working Minister for Social Security. At the same time Caucus elected Frank Crean as deputy-leader of the party while Cairns became Minister for the Environment.

By the time Hayden introduced his first budget on 20 August, unemployment had risen to nearly 5 per cent and inflation showed signs of remaining at or above about 15 per cent for the coming year. Opinion polls showed that support for the Government was falling to an all-time low mark well below 40 per cent. They showed too that people thought inflation an even greater menace than unemployment: and so the general thrust of Hayden's budget was restrictive and deflationary, the very opposite of that of its predecessor. It made no immediate difference to the sick state of the economy. Nothing did. In March the Liberals had deprived Labor of its greatest electoral asset by deposing Snedden as their leader and replacing him with Malcolm Fraser, a wealthy grazier from the Victorian Western District. It was obvious that the Opposition could take over the Treasury benches whenever it cared to do so. At first their new leader seemed anxious to defer the day until it was quite clear that world economic conditions had reached rock bottom and recovery had begun, but most of his followers sought officiously to thrust greatness upon him.

Born in 1930 and educated at Melbourne Grammar School and Oxford, where he graduated with third-class honours, Fraser was often called 'the Prefect' or 'the Headmaster' by his party comrades and 'the crazy grazier' by his political enemies. An Oxford tutor remembered him as undoubtedly 'the greatest of all the Colonial drongoes' to have been one of his students.[15] Tall, lean and disdainful in manner, his pseudo-English, upper-class accent infuriated more ordinary Australians like the Minister for Minerals and Energy, R. F. X. (Rex) Connor, who complained in the House that the style of Fraser's speeches made them incomprehensible and an insult to all other members. In the Liberal Party Fraser was reputed to be both singularly idiosyncratic and an arch-conservative, not apparently a leader with great electoral appeal: but, following the 1974 election, Snedden's asininely disastrous leadership of the Opposition persuaded a majority of his colleagues that he had to be deposed at all costs.

Fraser seemed at first highly responsible, stating in the most unequivocal terms that a twice-elected government should be allowed to govern for its full term of three years and that he would never force an election, as Snedden had, by threatening to withhold supply — except under the most extraordinary and 'reprehensible' circumstances. With unemployment still rising and inflation undiminished, however, business circles, the Country Party and most Liberal members clamoured ever more loudly that the A.L.P. must be forced to the polls: and so Fraser spent the last months of 1975 searching frantically for a really 'reprehensible' circumstance while he prepared to withhold supply for the second time since 1901.

In the absence of anything more substantial the 'loans affair', which had already been used to discredit Cairns, was re-animated by the Opposition's corrupt friends in the Treasury and other Government departments. At the bottom of the 'affair' was 'Rex' Connor, septuagenarian member for Cunningham and Minister for Mines and Energy. An old-fashioned Laborite, inspired more by a fierce Australian nationalism than by socialist ideals, Connor was a big, forceful, blunt man nicknamed by his critics 'the Strangler'. His admirers thought him a visionary giant among pygmies. His great dream was to get back Australian control of Australian resources, particularly of oil and mineral rights so much of which

[15] *National Times*, 6-12 August 1976.

had been freely handed over to foreign corporations by previous conservative governments; but to buy out overseas interests would cost thousands of millions of dollars. With Cabinet approval Connor began inquiring about massive amounts of loan money rumoured to be most readily available from the newly-rich oil-sheikhs in the Middle East. Sums of $2,000 million and $4,000 million were mentioned by the Opposition's 'leaks' in the Treasury.

In fact no loan was ever raised and not a cent of public money ever changed hands, corruptly or otherwise. Connor was shown to have made inquiries about raising loans for the Government and that is all; but the Opposition and daily newspaper proprietors cried such a deal of stinking fish as to persuade most electors that something undefined but deeply reprehensible had taken place. Then the Treasury 'leaks' produced evidence showing that Connor had apparently continued to make loan inquiries after his authority to do so had been withdrawn by the Prime Minister. It was enough for Malcolm Fraser who instructed the Senate majority, not formally to refuse supply, but simply to 'defer' consideration of the supply bills before them. This manoeuvre, of course, had the same effect and the Government began to run out of money.

Seventy-five years of Commonwealth history furnished no directly applicable precedents, for in the previous year Whitlam had called for a double dissolution within hours of the threat to withhold supply, and before that no Opposition had ever dreamed of using a Senate majority to withold moneys necessary for carrying on the routine business of government. The Commonwealth Constitution seemed to confer on the Governor-General virtually unlimited — and undefined — emergency powers, but it was assumed by almost everybody that in solving the *impasse* he would be guided by unwritten British and Australian constitutional precedents, by the advice of his Prime Minister who of course commanded a majority in the Lower House, and by his overriding duty to maintain at least the appearance of political impartiality. Sir John Kerr, recently appointed by Whitlam, ignored all three obligations. He should first have asked the Senate to do its constitutional duty and consider the supply bills. If then the Senate formally rejected them he could have asked the Prime Minister's advice which would have been to call an election for half the Senate, which in any case had to be held within the next few months. Fraser publicly voiced his fear that such a course might solve the crisis by giving the A.L.P. a Senate majority, an eventuality which he said would distort the whole future of Australia — by allowing the Government actually to implement its new electoral distribution of seats based on the principle of one vote — one value.

Kerr in fact took neither step but had confidential talks with both Whitlam and Fraser as the crisis became more acute and opinion polls showed that the Senate's deferral of supply was overwhelmingly condemned by public opinion. Then on 11 November, Remembrance Day 1975, when Whitlam came to advise the Governor-General to call an election for half the Senate, he was curtly informed that his commission had been withdrawn, and that Fraser had been appointed as 'caretaker' Prime Minister pending a general election to follow a double dissolution of both Houses of Parliament. Within an hour or two the Senate passed the supply bills and the House of Representatives immediately passed a motion of no confidence in the 'caretaker' Prime Minister's Government. Kerr ignored the existence of this grossly unconstitutional situation and dissolved Parliament.

The Governor-General's whole course of action obviously took Whitlam and the Labor Government completely by surprise. So far from acting on the advice of his Prime Minister, the Governor-General had obviously and deliberately deceived him as to his real intentions. At the same time he appeared to have conspired with the Leader of the Opposition. Sir Garfield Barwick, the Chief Justice of the High Court and sometime Liberal Attorney-General, certified that Kerr's action was 'consistent with' the Constitution as it — or a vast range of other actions — was with the written legal document, though it was grossly inconsistent with every facet of the unwritten rules of precedent and practice on which Australian liberties chiefly depended.

Barwick apparently knew little and cared less about Australian constitutional history. Six months later he fecklessly contradicted himself at a National Press Club Luncheon in Canberra. He told the astounded journalists that his advice to the Governor-General had *not* been based on any part of the written Australian Constitution but on 'the local traditions of a responsible government'. This being so, in the absence of precedents in Commonwealth history, he should obviously have based his advice on directly applicable precedents from Colonial history. Three times between 1865 and 1878 popularly elected Victorian governments were denied supply by the Upper House, then elected on a restrictive property franchise. Each time the Premier of the day 'toughed it out' — with the full support of the British Governor — until the Upper House backed down and a compromise was reached.[16]

These actions of the Governor-General and the Chief Justice

[16] *S.M.H.*, 11 June 1976.

Age, 1975

were of a piece with the blows already struck at tradition by the Premier of New South Wales and the Premier and the Governor of Queensland. Inevitably they brought upon themselves personally and (though to a lesser extent), upon the two highest offices in the land the contempt of some, the adulation of others and the recognition by nearly all that traditional magisterial impartiality had departed from them. The two positions had been 'politicised' as never before. However, many conservative citizens, unconcerned with legal niceties and, on the principle that the 'King can do no wrong', assumed that Kerr's action had been correct. Most Labor people — and the weight of informed constitutional opinion — believed that the Liberal Party chiefs had procured the prostitution of the Constitution at the hands of its sworn guardian. The events of Remembrance Day became widely known as 'Kerr's coup'.

At the following general election of 13 December, the Liberal and Country Parties were returned with the greatest majority of seats held by any government since federation: 91 to 36 for the A.L.P. and with an absolute majority in the Senate. People were persuaded that retrenchment in government spending and massive 'incentives' or subsidies to farmers and businessmen would somehow cure inflation and unemployment. They voted overwhelmingly for the return of prosperity, not at all for Sir John Kerr's singular interpretation of the Commonwealth Constitution which, nevertheless, was legitimised by the result of the election. In the future it would be perfectly proper for governments in a minority position in the Senate to be refused supply and forced to a general election as often as twice a year, and Governors-General would wield more real power than any British monarch had held since Europeans first settled at Sydney Cove in the age of the American and French revolutions.

So Australia entered the last quarter of the twentieth century again governed, as she had been for most of its course, by a Coalition primarily concerned with resisting or minimising change and with preserving or maximising the possessions of the rich. One of the new Government's first actions was to restore the $50,000,000 superphosphate subsidy, a measure which had benefited Malcolm Fraser himself by about $5,000 in the last year before its abolition by Labor. There followed quickly massive cuts in money for Aborigines, the unemployed, the poor, women's causes, education and the arts and massive increases in defence-spending and allowances to business and farming interests. In the Fraser Government's first budget of August 1976 the only organisation to receive substantially increased government funds was A.S.I.O., the most notorious of several secret-police bodies, and the only person was Sir John Kerr whose salary as Governor-General rose by an astounding 171 per cent.[17] It seemed that the long reign of conformity and conservatism, sprung initially out of fear after the First World War and reinforced by success and affluence after the Second, was to resume and perhaps to continue indefinitely. And yet, with New Zealand, Australia remained in many important ways the most egalitarian country in the western world as she had been at the inception of the Commonwealth. In 1973 a scholarly survey showed that only 2.4 per cent of families had no assets at all compared with 20 per cent in Britain and the United States, while at the other end of the scale the richest 1 per cent of Australians controlled only 9 per cent of the nation's wealth compared with 33 per cent in Britain and 26 per cent in the United States.[18]

[17] *Nation Review*, 20-26 August 1976.

[18] *Australian*, 16 June 1973, p. 3.

BIBLIOGRAPHY

Works are listed under three headings:

1 BASIC REFERENCE WORKS AND GENERAL OR THEMATIC HISTORIES
2 ARTICLES IN LEARNED JOURNALS
3 BOOKS OR THESES DEALING MAINLY WITH MATTERS IN A SINGLE CHAPTER OR A FEW CHAPTERS ONLY

In sections 1 and 2 standard abbreviations used in this volume are given, for many works, in square brackets.

1 BASIC REFERENCE WORKS AND GENERAL OR THEMATIC HISTORIES

(a) BASIC REFERENCE WORKS

Australian Encyclopaedia, 10 vols, Angus & Robertson, Sydney, 1958 [*A.E.*].

Borchardt, D. L., *Australian Bibliography*, Pergamon Press, Sydney, 1976.

Commonwealth Acts (to 1976) [*C.A.*].

Commonwealth Parliamentary Debates (to 1961) [*C.P.D.*].

Commonwealth Parliamentary Debates (from 1962) — *House of Representatives* [*C.P.D. — H.R.*].

Commonwealth Parliamentary Debates (from 1962) — *Senate* [*C.P.D. — S.*].

Commonwealth Parliamentary Papers (from 1901) [*C.P.P.*].

Commonwealth Year Books 1908-1976 [*C.Y.B.*].

Crowley, F. K. (ed.), *Modern Australia in Documents 1901-1939*, Wren, Melbourne, 1973 [*M.A.D.* I].

Crowley, F. K. (ed.), *Modern Australia in Documents 1939-1970*, Wren, Melbourne, 1973 [*M.A.D.* II].

Hogan, T. P., Ward, Russel & Yarwood, A. T. (eds.), *Index to Journal Articles on Australian History*, University of New England, Armidale, 1976.

Hughes, C. A., *Mr. Prime Minister*, Oxford University Press, Melbourne, 1976.

Hughes, C. A. and Graham, B. D., *A Handbook of Australian Government and Politics 1890-1964*, Melbourne University Press, Melbourne, 1968 [*H. & G.*].

Hughes, C. A. and Graham, B. D., *Voting for the Australian House of Representatives 1901-1964*, A.N.U. Press, Canberra, 1974.

Journals of the Senate (from 1901) [*J.S.*].

Legge, J. S. (ed.), *Who's Who in Australia*, Herald & Weekly Times Ltd, Melbourne, annually to 1976.
Mayer, H., Bettison, M. & Keene, J., *A Research Guide to Australian Politics and Cognate Subjects*, Cheshire, Melbourne, 1976.
Sawer, G., *Australian Federal Politics and Law 1901-1929*, Melbourne University Press, Melbourne, 1956 [*S*.I].
Sawer, G., *Australian Federal Politics and Law 1929-1949*, Melbourne University Press, Melbourne, 1965 [*S*.II].
Serle, P., *Dictionary of Australian Biography*, 2 vols, Angus & Robertson, Sydney, 1949.
Stevens, F. S. (ed.), *Racism: The Australian Experience*, 3 vols, Australia and New Zealand Book Co., Sydney, 1971-72.
Votes and Proceedings of the House of Representatives (from 1901) [*V. & P.*].

(b) NEWSPAPERS

Advertiser (Adelaide).
Age (Melbourne).
Australian.
Australian Financial Review (Sydney).
Bulletin.
Canberra Times.
Courier-Mail (Brisbane).
Current Affairs Bulletin.
Mercury (Hobart).
Nation Review.
National Times.
Sydney Morning Herald [*S.M.H.*].
West Australian (Perth).

(c) GENERAL

Aitken, D., *The Country Party in New South Wales: A Study of Organisation and Survival*, A.N.U. Press, Canberra, 1972.
Alexander, F., *Australia Since Federation*, Nelson, Melbourne [c.1967].
Alexander, F., *From Curtin to Menzies and After: Continuity or Confrontation*, Nelson, Melbourne, 1973.
Baxter, J., *The Australian Cinema*, Pacific Books, Sydney, 1970.
Blainey, G., *The Rush That Never Ended: A History of Australian Mining*, Melbourne University Press, Melbourne, 1963.
Blainey, G., *The Tyranny of Distance: How Distance Shaped Australia's History*, Sun Books, Melbourne, 1966.
Boxer, A. H. (ed.), *Aspects of the Australian Economy*, Melbourne University Press, Melbourne, 1965.
Boyd, R., *Australia's Home: Its Origins, Builders and Occupiers*, Melbourne University Press, Melbourne, 1952.
Clark, M. H., *A Short History of Australia*, New American Library, New York, 1963.
Crawford, R. M., *Australia*, Hutchinson, London, 1958.
Crisp, L. F., *The Australian Federal Labour Party 1901-1951*, Longmans, London, 1955.

Crisp, L. F., *Australian National Government*, Longmans, Melbourne, 1965.

Crowley, F. K., *Australia's Western Third*, Macmillan, London, 1960.

Crowley, F. K. (ed.), *A New History of Australia*, William Heinemann, Melbourne, 1974.

Dixson, Miriam, *The Real Matilda: Woman and Identity in Australia 1788 to 1975*, Penguin Books, Melbourne, 1976.

Fitzpatrick, B., *A Short History of the Australian Labor Movement*, Rawson's Bookshop, Melbourne, 1940.

Fitzpatrick, B., *The Australian Commonwealth*, Cheshire, Melbourne, 1956.

Forster, C. (ed.), *Australian Economic Development in the Twentieth Century*, Allen & Unwin, London, 1970.

Forward, R. & Reece, B. (eds.), *Conscription in Australia*, University of Queensland Press, Brisbane, 1968.

Foster, H. W., *A Brief History of Australia's Basic Wage*, Australian Bank Officials Association, Melbourne, 1965.

Franklin, Margaret, *Black and White Australians 1788-1975*, Heinemann Educational Australia, Melbourne, 1976.

Gaby, Capt. James, *The Restless Waterfront*, Antipodean Publishers, Sydney, 1974.

Gollan, R., *Radical and Working Class Politics: a Study of Eastern Australia, 1850-1910*, Melbourne University Press, Melbourne, 1960.

Grattan, C. Hartley, *The South-West Pacific since 1900*, Michigan University Press, Ann Arbor, 1963.

Green, H. M., *A History of Australian Literature 1788-1950*, 2 vols, Angus & Robertson, Sydney, 1961.

Greenwood, G. (ed.), *Australia: a Social and Political Sketch*, Angus & Robertson, Sydney, 1955.

Griffin J. (ed.), *Essays in Economic History of Australia*, Jacaranda Press, Brisbane, 1967.

Hancock, W. K., *Australia*, Ernest Benn, London, 1930.

Hetherington, John, *Norman Lindsay: the Embattled Olympian*, Oxford University Press, Melbourne, 1973.

Hudson, W. J. (ed.), *Australia and Papua-New Guinea*, Sydney University Press, Sydney, 1971.

Hudson, W. J., *Australian Diplomacy*, Macmillan, Melbourne, 1970.

Hughes, H., *The Australian Iron and Steel Industry 1848-1962*, Melbourne University Press, Melbourne, 1964.

Iremonger, John, Merrit, John & Osborne, Graeme (eds.), *Strikes: Studies in Twentieth Century Australian Social History*, Angus & Robertson, Sydney, 1973.

Jones, M. A., *Housing and Poverty in Australia*, Melbourne University Press, Melbourne, 1972.

Kewley, T. H., *Social Security in Australia: The Development of Social Security and Health Benefits from 1900 to the Present*, Sydney University Press, Sydney, 1965.

Kewley, T. H., *Australia's Welfare State: The Development of Social Security Benefits*, Macmillan, Melbourne, 1969.

McLeod, A. L. (ed.), *The Pattern of Australian Culture*, Oxford University Press, Melbourne, 1963.

Mathews, P. D. & Ford, G. W. (eds.), *Australian Trade Unions: Their Development, Structure and Horizons*, Sun Books, Melbourne, 1968.

O'Farrell, Patrick, *The Catholic Church in Australia: a Short History 1788-1967*, Nelson, Melbourne, 1968.
Palfreyman, A. C., *The Administration of the White Australia Policy*, Melbourne University Press, Melbourne, 1967.
Phillips, A. A., *The Australian Tradition*, Cheshire, Melbourne, 1958.
Pike, Douglas, *Australia: the Quiet Continent*, Cambridge University Press, Cambridge, 1962.
Portus, J. H., *Australian Compulsory Arbitration 1900-1970*, Hicks Smith, Sydney, 1971.
Price, C. A., *The Great White Walls Are Built: Restrictive Immigration to North America and Australia 1836-1888*, A.N.U. Press, Canberra, 1974.
Quick, J. & Garran, R. R., *The Annotated Constitution of the Australian Commonwealth*, Angus & Robertson, Sydney, 1901.
Reese, T. R., *Australia in the Twentieth Century: a Political History*, Cheshire, Melbourne, 1964.
Reitsma, A. J., *Trade Protection in Australia*, Stenfert Kroese, Leiden, 1960.
Rowley, C., *Aboriginal Policy and Practice*, vol 1, *The Destruction of Aboriginal Society*, A.N.U. Press, Canberra, 1970.
Serle, G., *From Deserts the Prophets Come: the Creative Spirit in Australia 1788-1972*, William Heinemann, Melbourne, 1973.
Shaw, A. G. L., *The Story of Australia*, Faber, London, 1955.
Shaw, A. G. L., *Economic Development of Australia*, Longman, Melbourne, 1966.
Smith, Bernard, *Australian Painting 1788-1960*, Oxford University Press, Melbourne, 1971.
Summers, Anne, *Damned Whores and God's Police*, Penguin Books, Melbourne, 1975.
Wadham, S. M., *Australian Farming 1788-1965*, Cheshire, Melbourne, 1967.
Ward, Russel, *Australia: A Short History*, Ure Smith, Sydney, 1975.
Ward, Russel, *The Australian Legend*, Oxford University Press, Melbourne, 1976.
Watt, A., *The Evolution of Australian Foreign Policy 1938-1965*, Cambridge University Press, Cambridge, 1967.

2 ARTICLES IN LEARNED JOURNALS

The following fifty-five journals all contain articles on aspects of Australian History. Abbreviated journal titles are given after each. A detailed person and subject index to the content of 4020 articles is given in Hogan, T. P., Ward, Russel and Yarwood, A. T. (eds.), *Index to Journal Articles on Australian History*, University of New England, Armidale, 1976. Reference to this work will guide readers to research on topics of interest to them more readily than any possible select listing of the articles in this bibliography.

Arena
Armidale and District Historical Society Journal [*A.D.H.S.*]
Australian and New Zealand Journal of Sociology [*A.N.Z.J.O.S.*]
Australian Catholic Historical Society Journal [*J.A.C.H.S.*]

Australian Economic History Review (formerly *Business Archives*) [*A.E.H.R.*]
Australian Geographer [*A.G.*]
Australian Jewish Historical Society Journal [*A.J.H.S.J.*]
Australian Journal of Politics and History [*A.J.P.H.*]
Australian Left Review [*A.L.R.*]
Australian Literary Studies [*Aust. Lit. Stud.*]
Australian National University Historical Journal [*A.N.U.H.S.*]
Australian Outlook [*A.O.*]
Australian Quarterly [*A. Quart.*]
Business Archives (later *Australian Economic History Review*) [*Bus. Arch.*]
Canadian Historical Review [*Can. Hist. Rev.*]
Canberra and District Historical Society Journal [*C.D.H.S.*]
Dialogue
Early Days
Economic Record [*E.R.*]
Historian
Historical and Political Studies [*Hist. Pol. Stud.*]
Historical Studies Australia and New Zealand [*H.S.*]
History Today
Journal of British Studies [*Jou. Brit. Stud.*]
Journal of Commonwealth Political Studies [*J.C.P.S.*]
Journal of History [*J.H.*]
Journal of Imperial and Commonwealth History [*J.I.C.H.*]
Journal of Industrial Relations [*J.I.R.*]
Journal of Modern History [*J.M.H.*]
Journal of Pacific History [*J.P.H.*]
Journal of Religious History [*J.R.H.*]
Labour History [*L.H.*]
Latrobe Historical Studies [*L.T.H.S.*]
Latrobe Library Journal [*L.T.L.J.*]
Meanjin
Melbourne Historical Journal [*M.H.J.*]
New Zealand Journal of History [*N.Z.J.H.*]
Oceania
Overland
Pacific Historical Review [*Pac. Hist. Rev.*]
Politics
Public Administration [*P.A.*]
Queensland Heritage [*Q.H.*]
Queensland Historical Review [*Q.H.R.*]
Royal Australian Historical Society Journal [*R.A.H.S.*]
Royal Historical Society of Queensland Journal [*R.H.S.Q.*]
South Australiana [*S.A.*]
Tasmanian Historical Research Association Papers and Proceedings [*T.H.R.A.*]
Teaching History [*T.H.*]
Twentieth Century
University of Newcastle Historical Journal [*U.N.H.J.*]
University of N.S.W. Historical Journal [*U.N.S.W.H.J.*]
University of Queensland Papers [*Uni. of Qld. Papers*]
University Studies in Politics and History [*Uni. Studies*]
Victorian Historical Magazine [*V.H.M.*]

3 BOOKS DEALING MAINLY WITH MATTERS IN A SINGLE CHAPTER OR A FEW CHAPTERS ONLY

Many of the following books, e.g. J. A. La Nauze's biography of Alfred Deakin, are obviously relevant to several chapters. Nevertheless, to avoid repetition, each book is listed once only, in the chapter to which it is most relevant.

CHAPTER 1 (c.1900-1903)

Clark, V. S., *The Labour Movement in Australasia: a Study in Social Democracy*, Westminster, New York, 1906.

Deakin, A., *The Federal Story*, Robertson and Mullens, Melbourne, 1944.

Furphy, J., *Such is Life, Being Certain Extracts from the Diary of Tom Collins*, Bulletin Co., Sydney, 1903.

Groom, Jessie (ed.), *Nation Building in Australia: The Life and Work of Sir Littleton Ernest Groom*, Angus & Robertson, Sydney, 1941.

Jebb, R., *Studies in Colonial Nationalism*, Arnold, London, 1905.

La Nauze, J. A., *The Making of the Australian Constitution*, Melbourne University Press, Melbourne, 1972.

Lawson, H., *Prose Works*, 2 vols, Angus & Robertson, Sydney, 1940.

Lindsay, N., *Bohemians of the Bulletin*, Angus & Robertson, Sydney, 1965.

Moore, M. V., Unequal and Inferior: The White Australia Policy in the First Commonwealth Parliament, B.A. Hons thesis, University of New England, 1962.

Nairn, N. B., *Civilising Capitalism: the Labor Movement in New South Wales 1870-1900*, A.N.U. Press, Canberra, 1973.

O'Collins, G. G., *Patrick McMahon Glynn, A Founder of Australian Federation*, Melbourne University Press, Melbourne, 1965.

Palmer, V., *The Legend of the Nineties*, Melbourne University Press, Melbourne, 1954.

Paterson, A. B., *Collected Verse*, Angus & Robertson, Sydney, 1921.

Pearl, C., *Morrison of Peking*, Angus & Robertson, Sydney, 1967.

Reeves, W. P., *State Experiments in Australia and New Zealand*, 2 vols, Grant Richards, London, 1902.

Reynolds, J., *Edmund Barton*, Angus & Robertson, Sydney, 1948.

St. Ledger, A. J. J., *Australian Socialism: an Historical Sketch of Its Origin and Development*, Macmillan, London, 1909.

Willard, Myra, *History of the White Australia Policy to 1920*, Melbourne University Press, Melbourne, 1923.

Wise, B. R., *The Commonwealth of Australia: The Inner History of the Federal Cause*, Pitman, London, 1909.

Yarwood, A. T., *Asian Migration to Australia: The Background to Exclusion 1896-1923*, Melbourne University Press, Melbourne, 1964.

CHAPTER 2 (c.1904-1908)

Bailey, Thomas A., *A Diplomatic History of the American People*, Appleton-Century-Crofts, New York, 1955.

Brennan, N., *John Wren, Gambler: His Life and Times*, Hill of Content, Melbourne, 1971.

Dutton, G., *From Federation to War 1901-1914*, Cheshire, Melbourne, 1971.

Higgins, H. B., *A New Province for Law and Order: Being a Review by its Late President for Fourteen Years, of the Australian Court of Conciliation and Arbitration*, Workers Education Association of N.S.W., London and Sydney, 1922.

Hughes, W. M., *The Case for Labor*, Sydney University Press, Sydney, 1910.

Kendle, J. E., *The Colonial and Imperial Conferences 1887-1911: A Study in Imperial Organization*, Longmans, London, 1967.

La Nauze, J. A., *Alfred Deakin: A Biography*, 2 vols, Melbourne University Press, Melbourne, 1965.

Mawson, D., *The Home of the Blizzard, Being the Story of the Australasian Antarctic Expedition, 1911-1914*, Willian Heinemann, London, 1915.

Métin, A., *Le Socialisme sans Doctrines*, Felix Alcan, Paris, 1901. (Tr. and ed. Ward, Russel, Alternative Publishing Co., Sydney, 1977.)

Murdoch, W., *Alfred Deakin: a Sketch*, Constable, London, 1923.

Palmer, N., *Henry Bournes Higgins: A Memoir*, Harrap, London, 1931.

Reid, G. H., *My Reminiscences*, Cassell, London, 1917.

Spence, W. G., *Australia's Awakening: Thirty Years in the Life of an Australian Agitator*, Worker Trustees, Sydney, 1909.

Stone, L., *Jonah*, The Endeavour Press, Sydney, 1933.

Turner, H. G., *The First Decade of the Australian Commonwealth: A Chronicle of Contemporary Politics 1901-1910*, Mason, Firth McCutcheon, Melbourne, 1911.

CHAPTER 3 (c.1909-1913)

Atkin, G., The Introduction of Compulsory Voting in Queensland, 1914, B.A. Hons thesis, University of New England, 1967.

Atkinson, M. (ed.), *Trade Unionism in Australia*, Burrows, Sydney, 1915.

Bollen, J. D., *Protestantism and Social Reform in N.S.W. 1890-1910*, Melbourne University Press, Melbourne, 1972.

Catts, D., *King O'Malley: Man and Statesman*, Publicity Press, Sydney, 1957.

Child, J., *Unionism and the Labor Movement*, Macmillan, Melbourne, 1971.

Childe, V. G., *How Labour Governs: A Study of Workers' Representation in Australia*, Labour Publishing Co., London, 1923.

Coghlan, T. A., *Labour and Industry in Australia*, 4 vols, Oxford University Press, London, 1918.

Dale, G., *The Industrial History of Broken Hill*, Fraser and Jenkinson, Melbourne, 1918.

Dunstan, K., *Sports*, Cassell, Melbourne, 1973.

Dunstan, K., *Wowsers: Being an Account of the Prudery Exhibited by Certain Outstanding Men and Women in Such Matters as Drinking, Prostitution, Censorship and Gambling*, Cassell, Melbourne, 1968.

Evatt, H. V., *Liberalism in Australia: An Historical Sketch of Australian Politics Down to the Year 1915*, The Law Book Co. of Australasia, Sydney, 1918.

Evatt, H. V., *Australian Labour Leader: The Story of W. A. Holman and the Labour Movement*, Angus & Robertson, Sydney, 1940.

Fitzhardinge, L. F., *William Morris Hughes*, vol 1, Angus & Robertson, Sydney, 1964.

Ford, P. P., *Cardinal Moran and the A.L.P. A Study of the Encounter between Moran and Socialism 1899-1907: Its Effects upon the Australian Labor Party*, Melbourne University Press, Melbourne, 1966.

Gollan, R., *The Commonwealth Bank of Australia: Origins and Early History*, A.N.U. Press, Canberra, 1968.

Jauncey, L. C., *The Story of Conscription in Australia*, Allen & Unwin, London, 1935.

Joyner, C., *The Commonwealth and Monopolies*, Cheshire, Melbourne, 1963.

Mason, J., Catholics and the Labor Movement in New South Wales, 1890-1960, Litt.B. thesis, University of New England, 1963.

Murphy, D. J. (ed.), *Labor in Politics: The State Labor Parties in Australia 1880-1920*, University of Queensland Press, Brisbane, 1975.

Rickard, John, *Class and Politics: New South Wales, Victoria and the Early Commonwealth 1890-1910*, A.N.U. Press, Canberra, 1976.

Serle, Geoffrey, *The Rush to be Rich*, Melbourne University Press, Melbourne, 1971.

Tanner, T. W., The Introduction of Compulsory Military Training in Australia 1901-1914, Ph.D. thesis, University of New England, 1970.

CHAPTER 4 (c.1914-1919)

Bean, C. E. W., *The Official History of Australia in the War of 1914-1918*, 12 vols, Angus & Robertson, Sydney, 1938-42.

Bean, C. E. W., *Two Men I Knew: William Bridges and Brudenell White, Founders of the A.I.F.*, Angus & Robertson, Sydney, 1957.

Brennan, N., *Dr. Mannix*, Rigby, Adelaide, 1964.

Butler, A. G., *The Australian Army Medical Services in the War of 1914-1918*, Australian War Memorial, Canberra, 1943.

Butler, A. G., *The Digger: A Study in Democracy*, Angus & Robertson, Sydney, 1945.

Dennis, C. J., *The Moods of Ginger Mick*, Angus & Robertson, Sydney, 1916.

Gammage, W. L., *The Broken Years: Australian Soldiers in the Great War*, A.N.U. Press, Canberra, 1974.

Hughes, W. M., *The Splendid Adventure: A Review of Empire Relations within and without the Commonwealth of Britannic Nations*, Benn, London, 1929.

Main, J. M., *Conscription: the Australian Debate 1901-1970*, Cassell, Melbourne, 1970.

Mann, L., *Flesh in Armour: a Novel*, Robertson & Mullens, Melbourne, 1932.

Monash, J., *The Australian Victories in France*, Hutchinson, London, 1920.

Moorehead, A., *Gallipoli*, Hamilton, London, 1956.

Moynihan, M. (ed.), *People at War 1914-1918*, Wren, Melbourne, 1973.

Pearce, G. F., *Carpenter to Cabinet: Thirty Seven Years of Parliament*, Hutchinson, London, 1951.

Robson, L. L., *Australia and the Great War 1914-18*, Macmillan, Melbourne, 1969.

Robson, L. L., *The First A.I.F.: A Study of its Recruitment 1914-1918*, Melbourne University Press, Melbourne, 1970.

Smith, F. B., *The Conscription Plebiscites in Australia 1916-1917*, Victorian Historical Assoc., Melbourne, 1965.

Smithers, A. J., *Sir John Monash*, Angus & Robertson, Sydney, 1973.

Sutcliffe, J. T., (ed. Ford, G. W.), *A History of Trade Unionism in Australia*, Macmillan, Melbourne, 1967.

Turner, I. A. H., *Industrial Labour and Politics: The Dynamics of the Labour Movement in Eastern Australia, 1900-1921*, A.N.U. Press, Canberra, 1965.

Turner, I. A. H., *Sydney's Burning*, Heinemann, London, 1967.

Turner, L. C. F., *The Great War 1914-1918*, Cheshire, Melbourne, 1971.

Welfield, J., The Labor Party and the War 1914-15, B.A. Hons thesis, University of New England, 1965.

Whyte, W. F., *William Morris Hughes: His Life and Times*, Angus & Robertson, Sydney, 1957.

The Anzac Book: Written and Illustrated in Gallipoli by the Men of Anzac, Cassell, London, 1916.

CHAPTER 5 (c.1920-1928)

Bernays, C. A., *Queensland — Our Seventh Political Decade 1920-1930*, Angus & Robertson, Sydney, 1931.

Edwards, C., *Bruce of Melbourne: Man of Two Worlds*, Heinemann, London, 1965.

Fitzpatrick, B., *The British Empire in Australia: An Economic History, 1834-1939*, Melbourne University Press, Melbourne, 1941.

Forster, C., *Industrial Development in Australia 1920-1930*, A.N.U. Press, Canberra, 1964.

Graham, B. D., *The Formation of the Australian Country Party*, A.N.U. Press, Canberra, 1966.

Green, Frank C., *Servant of the House*, William Heinemann, Melbourne, 1969.

Johnston, G., *My Brother Jack*, Collins, London, 1964.

Kristianson, G. L., *The Politics of Patriotism: The Pressure Group Activities of the Returned Servicemen's League*, A.N.U. Press, Canberra, 1966.

Lang, J. T., *The Turbulent Years*, Alpha Books, Sydney, 1970.

Lawrence, D. H., *Kangaroo*, Heinemann, London, 1923.

Page, E., *Truant Surgeon: The Inside Story of Forty Years of Australian Political Life*, Angus & Robertson, Sydney, 1963.

Slessor, K., *One Hundred Poems 1919-1939*, Angus & Robertson, Sydney, 1944.

Wood, Thomas, *Cobbers*, Oxford University Press, London, 1934.

CHAPTER 6 (c.1929-1932)

Amos, K., *The New Guard Movement 1931-1935*, Melbourne University Press, Melbourne, 1976.

Bolton, G. C., *A Fine Country to Starve In*, University of Western Australia Press, Perth, 1972.

Campbell, E., *The Rallying Point: My Story of the New Guard*, Melbourne University Press, Melbourne, 1965.

Cooksey, T. (ed.), *The Great Depression in Australia*, Australian Society for the Study of Labour History, Canberra, 1970.

Cooksey, T., *Lang and Socialism: A Study of the Great Depression*, A.N.U. Press, Canberra, 1971.

Copland, D. B., *Australia in the World Crisis 1923-33*, Cambridge University Press, Cambridge, 1934.

Cowan, Z., *Isaac Isaacs*, Oxford University Press, Melbourne, 1967.

Denning, W., *Caucus Crisis: The Rise and Fall of the Scullin Government*, Cumberland Argus, Parramatta, 1937.

Evatt, H. V., *The King and his Dominion Governors*, Oxford University Press, London, 1936.

Foott, B., *Dismissal of a Premier: The Philip Game Papers*, Morgan, Sydney, 1968.

Lang, J. T., *The Great Bust: The Depression of the Thirties*, Angus & Robertson, Sydney, 1962.

Lang, J. T., *Why I Fight*, Labor Daily Ltd, Sydney, 1934.

Louis, L. J. & Turner, I. (eds.), *The Depression of the 1930s*, Cassell, Melbourne, 1968.

May, A. L., *The Battle for the Banks*, Sydney University Press, Sydney, 1968.

Robertson, J., *J. H. Scullin: a Political Biography*, University of Western Australia Press, Perth, 1974.

Schedvin, C. B., *Australia and the Great Depression: A Study of Economic Development and Policy in the 1920s and 1930s*, Sydney University Press, Sydney, 1970.

Tennant, K., *The Battlers*, Sirius, Sydney, 1945.

Tennant, K., *Foveaux*, Sirius, Sydney, 1946.

Young, I., *Theodore: His Life and Times*, Alpha Books, Sydney, 1971.

CHAPTER 7 (c.1933-1938)

Aitken, D., *The Colonel: A Political Biography of Sir Michael Bruxner*, A.N.U. Press, Canberra, 1969.

Andrews, E. M., *Isolationism and Appeasement in Australia: Reactions to the European Crises 1935-1939*, A.N.U. Press, Canberra, 1970.

Ball, W. Macmahon (ed.), *Press, Radio and World Affairs: Australia's Outlook*, Melbourne University Press, Melbourne, 1938.

Brodgen, S., *The History of Australian Aviation*, Hamilton Press, Melbourne, 1960.

Coleman, P., *Obscenity, Blasphemy, Sedition: Censorship in Australia*, Jacaranda Press, Brisbane, 1962.

Drummond, D. H., *Australia's Changing Constitution: No States or New States*, Angus & Robertson, Sydney, 1943.

Esthus, R. A., *From Enmity to Alliance: U.S.—Australian Relations 1931-1941*, Melbourne University Press, Melbourne, 1965.

Ingamells, R. C., *Conditional Culture*, F. W. Preece, Adelaide, 1938.

Kisch, E. E., *Australian Landfall*, (ed. A. T. Yarwood), Australasian Book Society, Sydney, 1969.

Lang, J. T., *I Remember*, Invincible Press, Sydney, 1956.

Lyons, E., *So We Take Comfort*, Heinemann, London, 1965.

Maclaurin, W. R., *Economic Planning in Australia 1929-1936*, P. S. King, London, 1939.

Shepherd, J., *Australia's Interests and Policies in the Far East*, Institute of Pacific Relations, New York, 1970.

Stephensen, P. R., *The Foundation of Culture in Australia: An Essay Towards National Self Respect*, W. J. Miles, Sydney, 1936.

Waten, J., *The Depression Years 1929-1939*, Cheshire, Melbourne, 1971.

CHAPTER 8 (c.1939-1944)

Bateson, C., *The War with Japan: A Concise History*, Ure Smith, Sydney, 1968.

Blainey, G., *The Steel Master: A Life of Essington Lewis*, Macmillan, Melbourne, 1971.

Casey, R. G., *Personal Experience 1939-1946*, Constable, London, 1962.

Chester, A., *John Curtin*, Angus & Robertson, Sydney, 1943.

Dowsing, I., *Curtin of Australia*, Acacia Press, Melbourne, 1969.

Fadden, A. W., *They Called Me Artie: The Memoirs of Sir Arthur Fadden*, Jacaranda Press, Brisbane, 1969.

Hasluck, P., *The Government and the People, 1939-1941*, Australian War Memorial, Canberra, 1952.

Hasluck, P., *The Government and the People, 1942-1945*, Australian War Memorial, Canberra, 1970.

Havighurst, Alfred F., *Twentieth Century Britain*, Row, Peterson, New York, 1966.

Hetherington, J., *Blamey: A Biography of Field-Marshal Sir Thomas Blamey*, Australian War Memorial, Canberra, 1973.

Lambert, Eric, *The Twenty Thousand Thieves*, Frederick Muller, London, 1952.

Lambert, Eric, *The Veterans*, Frederick Muller, London, 1954.

Long, G. (ed.), *Australia in the War of 1939-1945*, 22 vols, Australian War Memorial, Canberra, (various dates).

Long, G., *The Six Years War: A Concise History of Australia in the 1939-1945 War*, Australian War Memorial, Canberra, 1973.

Muirden, B., *The Puzzled Patriots: The Story of the Australia First Movement*, Melbourne University Press, Melbourne, 1968.

Ross, Lloyd, *John Curtin for Labor and for Australia*, A.N.U. Press, Canberra, 1971.

Walker, E. R., *The Australian Economy in War and Reconstruction*, Oxford University Press, New York, 1947.

CHAPTER 9 (c.1945-1949)

Ball, W. Macmahon, *Japan: Enemy or Ally?*, Cassell, Melbourne, 1948.

Bolton, G. C., *Dick Boyer: An Australian Humanist*, A.N.U. Press, Canberra, 1967.

Crisp, L. F., *Ben Chifley, A Biography*, Longmans, London, 1961.

Dalziel, A., *Evatt, the Enigma*, Lansdowne Press, Melbourne, 1967.

Davidson, A., *The Communist Party of Australia, A Short History*, Hoover Institution Press, Stanford, 1969.

Evatt, H. V., *Australia in World Affairs*, Angus & Robertson, Sydney, 1946.

Howard, F. *Kent-Hughes: a Biography of Colonel the Hon. Sir Wilfred Kent-Hughes*, Macmillan, Melbourne, 1972.

Hudson, W. J., *Australian Diplomacy*, Macmillan, Melbourne, 1970.

May, A. L., *The Battle for the Banks*, Sydney University Press, Sydney, 1965.

Mitchell, B., *Teachers, Education and Politics*, University of Brisbane Press, Brisbane, 1976.

Spender, P. C., *Politics and a Man*, Collins, Sydney, 1972.

Spratt, E., *Eddie Ward: Firebrand of East Sydney*, Rigby, Adelaide, 1965.

Tennant, K., *Evatt: Politics and Justice*, Angus & Robertson, Sydney, 1970.

CHAPTER 10 (c.1950-1960)

Alexander, F., *From Curtin to Menzies and After*, Nelson, Melbourne, 1973.

Brown, W. G., *The Petrov Conspiracy*, Current Book Distributors, Sydney, 1956.

Coleman, P. (ed.), *Australian Civilization: A Symposium*, Cheshire, Melbourne, 1962.

Davies, A. F. and Encel, S. (eds.), *Australian Society: A Sociological Introduction*, Cheshire, Melbourne, 1967.

Encel, S., *Cabinet Government in Australia*, Melbourne University Press, Melbourne, 1962.

Haylen, L., *Twenty Years Hard Labor*, Macmillan, Melbourne, 1969.

Jupp, J., *Australian Party Politics*, Melbourne University Press, Melbourne, 1964.

Mackenzie, N., *Women in Australia*, Cheshire, Melbourne, 1962.

Menzies, R. G., *Afternoon Light: Some Memories of Men and Events*, Cassell, Melbourne, 1967.

Murray, P., *The Split: Australian Labor in the Fifties*, Cheshire, Melbourne, 1970.

Ormonde, P., *The Movement*, Thomas Nelson, Melbourne, 1972.

Overacker, L., *Australian Parties in a Changing Society 1945-67*, Cheshire, Melbourne, 1968.

Perkins, K., *Menzies: Last of the Queen's Men*, Rigby, Adelaide, 1968.

Price, C. A., *Southern Europeans in Australia*, Oxford University Press, Melbourne, 1963.

Pringle, J. D., *Australian Accent*, Chatto, London, 1958.

Santamaria, B. A., *The Price of Freedom: The Movement After Ten Years*, Campion, Melbourne, 1964.

Truman, T., *Catholic Action and Politics*, Georgian House, Melbourne, 1959.

Watt, A., *The Evolution of Australian Foreign Policy 1938-1965*, Cambridge University Press, Cambridge, 1967.

Webb, L. C., *Communism and Democracy in Australia: A Survey of the 1951 Referendum*, Cheshire, Melbourne, 1954.

West, K., *Power in the Liberal Party: A Study in Australian Politics*, Cheshire, Melbourne, 1965.

White, P., *The Tree of Man*, Eyre & Spottiswoode, London, 1956.

Whitington, Don, *The House Will Divide: a Review of Australian Federal Politics*, Lansdowne Press, Melbourne, 1954.

Whitlam, N. & Stubbs, J., *Nest of Traitors — the Petrov Affair*, Jacaranda, Brisbane, 1974.

CHAPTER 11 (c.1960-1968)

Albinski, H. S., *Politics and Foreign Policy in Australia: The Impact of Vietnam and Conscription*, Duke University Press, Durham, N.C., 1970.

Ball, W. Macmahon, *Australia and Japan*, Nelson, Melbourne, 1969.

Calwell, A. A., *Be Just and Fear Not*, Lloyd O'Neil, Melbourne, 1972.

Campbell, E. & Whitmore, H., *Freedom in Australia*, Sydney University Press, Sydney, 1966.

Davidson, F. G., *The Industrialization of Australia*, Melbourne University Press, Melbourne, 1957.

Dutton, G. (ed.), *Australia and the Monarchy: a Symposium*, Sun Books, Melbourne, 1966.

Encel, S., *Equality and Authority: A Study of Class, Status and Power in Australia*, Cheshire, Melbourne, 1970.

Fitzpatrick, B. & Wheelwright, E. L., *The Highest Bidder: A Citizen's Guide to Problems of Foreign Investment in Australia*, Lansdowne, Melbourne, 1962.

Gelber, H. G., *The Australian-American Alliance: Costs and Benefits*, Penguin, Melbourne, 1968.

Gordon, R. (ed.), *The Australian New Left: Critical Essays and Strategy*, William Heinemann, Melbourne, 1970.

Hasluck, P., *Black Australians*, Melbourne University Press, Melbourne, 1942.

Henderson, R. F., Harcourt, A. & Harper, R. J. A., *People in Poverty: A Melbourne Survey*, Melbourne University Press, Melbourne, 1970.

Horne, D., *The Lucky Country: Australia in the Sixties*, Angus & Robertson, Sydney, 1969.

Joske, P. E., *Australian Federal Government*, Butterworth, Sydney, 1967.

McFarlane, B., *Economic Policy in Australia: The Case for Reform*, Cheshire, Melbourne, 1960.

Mayer, H. (ed.), *Australian Politics: A Reader*, Cheshire, Melbourne, 1966.

Mayer, H. (ed.), *Australian Politics: A Second Reader*, Cheshire, Melbourne, 1969.

McGregor, C., *Profile of Australia*, Hodder & Stoughton, London, 1966.

Menzies, R. G., *The Measure of the Years*, Cassell, London, 1970.

Millar, T. B., *Australia's Defence*, Melbourne University Press, Melbourne, 1965.

Moore, J. H. (ed.), *The American Alliance: Australia, New Zealand and the United States, 1940-1970*, Cassell, Melbourne, 1970.

Neale, R. G., *Australia's Military Commitment to Vietnam*, Department of Foreign Affairs, Canberra, 1975.

Partridge, P. H., *Society, Schools and Progress in Australia*, Pergamon Press, Oxford, 1968.

Teichmann, M (ed.), *New Directions in Australian Foreign Policy: Ally, Satellite or Neutral?*, Penguin, Melbourne, 1969.

Wheelwright, E. L. & Miskelly, J., *Anatomy of Australian Manufacturing Industry: The Ownership and Control of 300 of the Largest Manufacturing Companies in Australia*, Law Book Company, Sydney, 1967.

CHAPTER 12 (c.1969-1975)

Conway, R., *The Great Australian Stupor*, Sun Books, Melbourne, 1971.

Evans, G. (ed.), *Labor and the Constitution, 1972-1975: The Whitlam Years in Australian Government*, Heinemann Educational Australia, Melbourne, 1977.

Harris, S., *Political Football*, Gold Star Publications, Melbourne, 1972.

Horne, D., *Death of the Lucky Country*, Penguin, Melbourne, 1976.

Horsfall, J. C., *The Liberal Era: a Political and Economic Analysis*, Sun Books, Melbourne, 1974.

Kelly, P., *The Unmaking of Gough*, Angus & Robertson, Sydney, 1976.

Lloyd, C. & Clark, A., *Kerr's King Hit*, Cassell, Melbourne, 1976.

Lloyd, C. & Reid, G. S., *Out of the Wilderness: The Return of Labor*, Cassell, Melbourne, 1974.

Mayer, H. & Nelson, H. (eds.), *Australian Politics: A Third Reader*, Cheshire, Melbourne, 1973.

Mol, J. J., *Religion in Australia: A Sociological Investigation*, Nelson, Melbourne, 1971.

Oakes, L. & Solomon, D., *The Making of an Australian Prime Minister*, Cheshire, Melbourne, 1973.

Playford, J. & Kirsner, D. (eds.), *Australian Capitalism: Towards a Socialist Critique*, Penguin Books, Melbourne, 1972.

Reid, A., *The Power Struggle*, Shakespeare Head Press, Sydney, 1969.

Spigelman, J., *Secrecy: Political Censorship in Australia*, Angus & Robertson, Sydney, 1972.

St. John, E., *A Time to Speak*, Sun Books, Melbourne, 1969.

Stevenson, A. M., Martin, E. M. & O'Neill, J. A., *High Living: A Study of Family Life in Flats*, Melbourne University Press, Melbourne, 1967.

Trengove, A., *John Grey Gorton: An Informal Biography*, Cassell, Melbourne, 1969.

APPENDICES

I GOVERNORS-GENERAL: COMMONWEALTH OF AUSTRALIA

Rt. Hon. JOHN ADRIAN LOUIS, EARL OF HOPETOUN (afterwards MARQUIS OF LINLITHGOW), P.C., K.T., G.C.M.G., G.C.V.O. From 1 January 1901 to 9 January 1903.

Rt. Hon. HALLAM, BARON TENNYSON, P.C., G.C.M.G. From 17 July 1902 to 9 January 1903 (Acting).

Rt. Hon. HALLAM, BARON TENNYSON, P.C., G.C.M.G. From 9 January 1903 to 21 January 1904.

Rt. Hon. HENRY STAFFORD, BARON NORTHCOTE, P.C., G.C.M.G., G.C.I.E., C.B. From 21 January 1904 to 9 September 1908.

Rt. Hon. WILLIAM HUMBLE, EARL OF DUDLEY, P.C., G.C.B., G.C.M.G., G.C.V.O. From 9 September 1908 to 31 July 1911.

Rt. Hon. THOMAS, BARON DENMAN, P.C., G.C.M.G., K.C.V.O. From 31 July 1911 to 18 May 1914.

Rt. Hon. SIR RONALD CRAUFURD MUNRO-FERGUSON (afterwards VISCOUNT NOVAR OF RAITH), G.C.M.G. From 18 May 1914 to 6 October 1920.

Rt. Hon. HENRY WILLIAM, BARON FORSTER OF LEPE, P.C., G.C.M.G. From 6 October 1920 to 8 October 1925.

Rt. Hon. JOHN LAWRENCE, BARON STONEHAVEN (afterwards 1st VISCOUNT STONEHAVEN), P.C., G.C.M.G., D.S.O. From 8 October 1925 to 22 January 1931.

Rt. Hon. SIR ISAAC ALFRED ISAACS, G.C.B., G.C.M.G., K.C. From 22 January 1931 to 23 January 1936.

Brigadier-General the Rt. Hon. ALEXANDER GORE ARKWRIGHT HORE-RUTHVEN, BARON GOWRIE (afterwards 1st EARL OF GOWRIE), V.C., P.C., G.C.M.G., C.B., D.S.O., K.G.St.J. From 23 January 1936 to 30 January 1945.

His Royal Highness PRINCE HENRY WILLIAM FREDERICK ALBERT, DUKE OF GLOUCESTER, EARL OF ULSTER AND BARON CULLODEN, K.G., P.C., K.T., K.P., G.C.B., G.C.M.G., G.C.V.O., General in the Army, Air Chief Marshal in the Royal Air Force, One of His Majesty's Personal Aides-de-Camp. From 30 January 1945 to 11 March 1947.

Rt. Hon. SIR WILLIAM JOHN McKELL, G.C.M.G., Q.C. From 11 March 1947 to 8 May 1953.

Field Marshal SIR WILLIAM JOSEPH SLIM (afterwards VISCOUNT SLIM OF YARRALUMLA), K.G., G.C.B., G.C.M.G., G.C.V.O., G.B.E., D.S.O., M.C., K.St.J. From 8 May 1953 to 2 February 1960.

Rt. Hon. WILLIAM SHEPHERD, VISCOUNT DUNROSSIL, P.C., G.C.M.G., M.C., K.St.J., Q.C. From 2 February 1960 to 3 February 1961.

Rt. Hon. WILLIAM PHILIP, VISCOUNT DE LISLE, V.C., P.C., G.C.M.G., G.C.V.O., K.St.J. From 3 August 1961 to 22 September 1965.

Rt. Hon. RICHARD GARDINER, BARON CASEY, K.G., P.C., G.C.M.G., C.H., D.S.O., M.C., K.St.J. From 22 September 1965 to 30 April 1969.

Rt. Hon. SIR PAUL HASLUCK, G.C.M.G., G.C.V.I., K.St.J. From 30 April 1969 to 11 July 1974.

Rt. Hon. SIR JOHN KERR, K.C.M.G., K.St.J., Q.C. From 11 July 1974.

II MINISTRIES: COMMONWEALTH OF AUSTRALIA

1 BARTON MINISTRY, 1 January 1901 to 24 September 1903.
2 DEAKIN MINISTRY, 24 September 1903 to 27 April 1904.
3 WATSON MINISTRY, 27 April 1904 to 18 August 1904.
4 REID-McLEAN MINISTRY, 18 August 1904 to 5 July 1905.
5 DEAKIN MINISTRY, 5 July 1905 to 13 November 1908.
6 FISHER MINISTRY, 13 November 1908 to 2 June 1909.
7 DEAKIN MINISTRY, 2 June 1909 to 29 April 1910.
8 FISHER MINISTRY, 29 April 1910 to 24 June 1913.
9 COOK MINISTRY, 24 June 1913 to 17 September 1914.
10 FISHER MINISTRY, 17 September 1914 to 27 October 1915.
11 HUGHES MINISTRY, 27 October 1915 to 14 November 1916.
12 HUGHES MINISTRY, 14 November 1916 to 17 February 1917.
13 HUGHES MINISTRY, 17 February 1917 to 10 January 1918.
14 HUGHES MINISTRY, 10 January 1918 to 9 February 1923.
15 BRUCE-PAGE MINISTRY, 9 February 1923 to 22 October 1929.
16 SCULLIN MINISTRY, 22 October 1929 to 6 January 1932.
17 LYONS MINISTRY, 6 January 1932 to 7 November 1938.
18 LYONS MINISTRY, 7 November 1938 to 7 April 1939.
19 PAGE MINISTRY, 7 April 1939 to 26 April 1939.
20 MENZIES MINISTRY, 26 April 1939 to 14 March 1940.
21 MENZIES MINISTRY, 14 March 1940 to 28 October 1940.
22 MENZIES MINISTRY, 28 October 1940 to 29 August 1941.
23 FADDEN MINISTRY, 29 August 1941 to 7 October 1941.
24 CURTIN MINISTRY, 7 October 1941 to 21 September 1943.
25 CURTIN MINISTRY, 21 September 1943 to 6 July 1945.
26 FORDE MINISTRY, 6 July 1945 to 13 July 1945.
27 CHIFLEY MINISTRY, 13 July 1945 to 1 November 1946.
28 CHIFLEY MINISTRY, 1 November 1946 to 19 December 1949.
29 MENZIES MINISTRY, 19 December 1949 to 11 May 1951.
30 MENZIES MINISTRY, 11 May 1951 to 11 January 1956.
31 MENZIES MINISTRY, 11 January 1956 to 10 December 1958.
32 MENZIES MINISTRY, 10 December 1958 to 18 December 1963.
33 MENZIES MINISTRY, 18 December 1963 to 26 January 1966.
34 HOLT MINISTRY, 26 January 1966 to 14 December 1966.
35 HOLT MINISTRY, 14 December 1966 to 19 December 1967.
36 McEWEN MINISTRY, 19 December 1967 to 10 January 1968.
37 GORTON MINISTRY, 10 January 1968 to 28 February 1968.
38 GORTON MINISTRY, 28 February 1968 to 12 November 1969.
39 GORTON MINISTRY, 12 November 1969 to 10 March 1971.
40 McMAHON MINISTRY, 10 March 1971 to 5 December 1972.

41 WHITLAM MINISTRY, 5 December 1972 to 19 December 1972.
42 WHITLAM MINISTRY, 19 December 1972 to 12 June 1974.
43 WHITLAM MINISTRY, 12 June 1974 to 11 November 1975.
44 FRASER MINISTRY, 11 November 1975.

III COMMONWEALTH REFERENDA (and PLEBISCITES)

Date Held	Powers Sought	'Yes' Voters		Result
		States	% of Total	
12.12.06	Alteration of beginning of of senators' terms of office from January to July	All	82.65	Yes
13.4.10	To make *per caput* payments to the States	Qld., W.A., Tas.	49.04	No
,,	To take over State public debts	All but N.S.W.	54.95	Yes
26. 4.11	Control of trade and commerce, financial corporations, employment and monopolies	W.A.	39.42	No
,,	Nationalization of monopolies	W.A.	39.89	No
31. 5.13	Control of trade and commerce except for intra-State trade	Qld., S.A., W.A.	49.38	No
,,	Control of financial corporations	Qld., S.A., W.A.	49.33	No
,,	Control of employment, unemployment, industrial disputes etc.	Qld., S.A., W.A.	49.33	No
,,	Control of arbitration in State railways	Qld., S.A., W.A.	49.13	No
,,	Control of monopolies including 'trusts'	Qld., S.A., W.A.	49.78	No
,,	Nationalization of monopolies except for State enterprises	Qld., S.A., W.A.	49.33	No
28.10.16	Popular opinion on military conscription for overseas service	Vic., W.A., Tas.	48.38	No
20.12.17	Popular opinion on military conscription for overseas service	W.A., Tas.	46.21	No
13.12.19	To prolong wartime powers over trade, corporations and industrial matters	Vic., Qld. W.A.	49.65	No
,,	To prolong wartime powers to nationalize monopolies	Vic., Qld., W.A.	48.64	No

Date Held	Powers Sought	'Yes' Voters		Result
		States	% of Total	
4. 9.26	To control corporations, trusts, industrial disputes etc.	N.S.W, Qld.	43.50	No
,,	To protect 'the public interest' in the maintenance of essential services	N.S.W., Qld.	42.80	No
17.11.28	To validate the Commonwealth-States financial agreement on State debts and loan-raising	All	74.30	Yes
6. 3.37	Control of air navigation and aircraft	Vic., Qld.	53.56	No
,,	Control of marketing without being subject to section 92 (absolute freedom of inter-State trade)	None	36.26	No
19. 8.44	Extension for five years of wartime powers over rehabilitation of service personnel, employment, marketing, company law, monopolies, profits and prices, production and distribution of goods, overseas exchange, air transport, railway gauges, national works, national health and social services, Aborigines	S.A., W.A.	45.99	No
28. 9.46	Control of social services and pensions	All	54.39	Yes
,,	Control of marketing primary products without restriction by section 92	N.S.W., Vic., W.A.	50.57	No
,,	Control of conditions of industrial employment	N.S.W., Vic., W.A.	50.30	No
29. 5.48	Control of rents and prices	None	40.66	No
22. 9.51	Control of Communists and Communism	Qld., W.A., Tas.	49.44	No

Date Held	Powers Sought	'Yes' Voters		Result
		States	% of Total	
27. 5.67	Abolition of nexus (membership of 2:1) between House of Representatives and Senate	N.S.W.	40.25	No
,,	Power to count Aboriginals in censuses and to make laws with respect to them	All	90.77	Yes
8.12.73	Control of prices	None	43.09	No
,,	Control of incomes	None	34.42	No
18. 5.74	To hold Senate elections simultaneously with those for the House of Representatives	N.S.W.	49.67	No
,,	To validate constitutional changes by a majority of all votes cast and a majority in three (not four) of the States	N.S.W.	47.99	No
,,	To ensure that members of both Houses in the Commonwealth and the States be elected directly from constituencies approximately equal in population	N.S.W.	47.20	No
,,	To grant moneys directly (not through State governments) to local government bodies	N.S.W.	46.85	No

IV Election Results — Commonwealth of Australia

House of Representatives

PARTIES	1901		1903		1906		1910		1913	
	% total valid vote	Seats	% total valid vote	Seats	% total valid vote	Seats	% total valid vote	Seats	% total valid vote	Seats
Labor (A.L.P.)	18.72	14	30.96	23	36.64	26	49.97	43	48.47	37
Protectionist	43.65	31	29.69	26	21.28	20				
Liberal							45.09	31	48.94	38
Freetrade Anti-Socialist	35.66	28	34.37	25	38.17	27				
Independents	1.97	2	4.98	1	3.91	2	4.94	1	2.59	1

PARTIES	1914		1917		1919		1922		1925	
	% total valid vote	Seats	% total valid vote	Seats	% total valid vote	Seats	% total valid vote	Seats	% total valid vote	Seats
Labor (A.L.P.)	50.89	42	43.94	22	42.49	26	42.95	29	45.04	23
Liberal	47.22	32								
Nationalist			54.22	53	46.78	38	35.23	26	42.46	37
Country					9.26	11	12.56	14	10.74	14
Liberal							4.70	5		
Independents	1.89	1	1.84	—	1.47	—	4.56	1	1.76	1

PARTIES	1928		1929		1931		1934		1937	
	% total valid vote	Seats	% total valid vote	Seats	% total valid vote	Seats	% total valid vote	Seats	% total valid vote	Seats
Labor (A.L.P.)	44.64	31	48.84	46	27.09	14	26.82	18	43.18	29
Nationalist	39.09	29	37.78	17						
U.A.P.					36.09	34	32.98	33	34.41	29
Country	12.08	14	11.25	11	12.26	16	16.62	14	15.55	16
NSW (Lang) Labor					10.58	4	14.37	9		
Independents	4.19	1	2.13	1	13.98	7	9.21	—	6.86	—

PARTIES	1940		1943		1946		1949		1951	
	% total valid vote	Seats	% total valid vote	Seats	% total valid vote	Seats	% total valid vote	Seats	% total valid vote	Seats
Labor (A.L.P.)	40.16	32	49.94	49	49.71	43	45.98	47	47.63	52
U.A.P.	30.22	23								
U.A.P. and Allied Groups			19.7	13	32.97	18				
Liberal							39.39	55	40.62	52
Country	13.71	14			10.69	11	10.87	19	9.73	17
Country and Allied Groups			12.48	11						
Non-Communist Labor (Lang L.)	5.23	4			1.59	1	0.71	—		
Independents	10.68	1	16.97	1	5.04	1	3.05	—	2.02	—

PARTIES	1954		1955		1958		1961		1963	
	% total valid vote	Seats	% total valid vote	Seats	% total valid vote	Seats	% total valid vote	Seats	% total valid vote	Seats
Labor (A.L.P.)	50.03	57	44.63	47	42.81	45	47.91	60	45.47	50
Liberal	38.54	47	39.73	57	37.23	58	33.58	45	37.09	52
Country	8.52	17	7.91	18	9.32	19	8.52	17	8.94	20
Anti-Communist Labor (D.L.P.)			5.17	—	9.41	—	8.71	—	7.45	—
Independents	2.91	—	2.56	—	1.23	—	1.28	—	1.05	—

PARTIES	1966		1969		1972		1974		1975	
	% total valid vote	Seats	% total valid vote	Seats	% total valid vote	Seats	% total valid vote	Seats	% total valid vote	Seats
Labor (A.L.P.)	40.44	41	46.95	58	49.60	67	49.3	66	42.8	36
Liberal	40.24	61	34.80	46	32.06	38	34.95	40	41.98	68
Country	9.74	21	8.55	19	9.42	20	9.96	21	11.02	23
Anti-Communist Labor (D.L.P.)	7.33	—	6.01	—	5.24	—	1.42	—	1.36	—
Independents	2.25	1	3.69	—	3.68	—	4.37	—	2.84	—

Sources: C. A. Hughes & B. D. Graham, *A Handbook of Australian Government & Politics 1890-1964*, A.N.U. Press, Canberra, 1968.
Commonwealth Parliamentary Handbook
Commonwealth Parliamentary Debates
Commonwealth Year Books

V Election Results — Commonwealth of Australia

Senate

PARTIES	1901		1903		1906		1910		1913	
	% total valid vote	Seats	% total valid vote	Seats	% total valid vote	Seats	% total valid vote	Seats	% total valid vote	Seats
Labor (A.L.P.)	13.50	8	29.75	14	38.73	15	50.29	22	48.73	29
Protectionist	44.86	11	17.53	9	12.42	4				
Fusion							45.56	14		
Liberal									49.38	7
Freetrade	39.45	17	34.33	13						
Anti-Socialist					46.53	17				
Independents	2.19	—	18.38	1	2.32	—	4.15	—	1.89	—

PARTIES	1914		1917		1919		1922		1925	
	% total valid vote	Seats	% total valid vote	Seats	% total valid vote	Seats	% total valid vote	Seats	% total valid vote	Seats
Labor (A.L.P.)	52.15	31	43.73	12	42.85	1	45.70	12	45.03	7
Liberal	47.77	5								
Nationalist			55.37	24	46.39	35	36.24	23	45.35	25
Country					8.78	—	12.99	1	9.45	4
Liberal S.A.							2.79	—		
Independents	0.08	—	090	—	1.98	—	2.28	—	0.17	—

PARTIES	1928		1931		1934		1937		1940	
	% total valid vote	Seats	% total valid vote	Seats	% total valid vote	Seats	% total valid vote	Seats	% total valid vote	Seats
Labor (A.L.P.)	48.95	7	29.26	8	28.08	3	48.48	16	37.52	17
Nationalist	39.28	23								
U.A.P./Country			55.42	26	53.22	33	46.71	20	50.40	19
Country	11.18	6								
NSW (Lang) Labor			12.11	2	13.23	—				
Non-Communist Labor									7.56	—
Independents	59	—	3.21	—	5.47	—	4.81	—	4.52	—

PARTIES	1943		1946		1949		1951		1953	
	% total valid vote	Seats	% total valid vote	Seats	% total valid vote	Seats	% total valid vote	Seats	% total valid vote	Seats
Labor (A.L.P.)	55.09	22	52.06	33	44.89	34	45.89	28	50.61	29
U.A.P./Country	39.12	14								
Liberal/Country			43.32	3	50.41	26	49.69	32	44.43	31
Independents	5.79	—	4.62	—	4.70	—	4.42	—	4.96	—

PARTIES	1955		1958		1961		1964		1967	
	% total valid vote	Seats	% total valid vote	Seats	% total valid vote	Seats	% total valid vote	Seats	% total valid vote	Seats
Labor (A.L.P.)	40.61	29	42.78	27	44.71	28	44.66	25	45.03	28
Liberal/Country	48.67	30	45.19	32	42.09	32	45.71	33	42.77	29
Anti-Communist Labor	6.10	1								
D.L.P.			8.42	1	9.82	—	8.39	2	9.77	2
Independents	4.62	—	3.61	—	3.38	—	1.24	—	2.43	1

PARTIES	1970		1974		1975					
	% total valid vote	Seats	% total valid vote	Seats	% total valid vote	Seats				
Labor (A.L.P.)	42.22	26	47.29	29	40.94	27				
Liberal/Country	38.17	27	43.04	30	51.76	35				
Liberal Movnt.			1.17	1	1.09	1				
D.L.P.	11.11	5	3.56	—	2.71	1				
Independents	8.50	2	4.94	—	3.50	—				

Sources: C. A. Hughes & B. D. Graham, *A Handbook of Australian Government & Politics 1890-1964*, A.N.U. Press, Canberra, 1968.
Commonwealth Parliamentary Handbook
Commonwealth Parliamentary Debates
Commonwealth Year Books

VI POPULATION 1900-1975 (COMMONWEALTH & STATES)

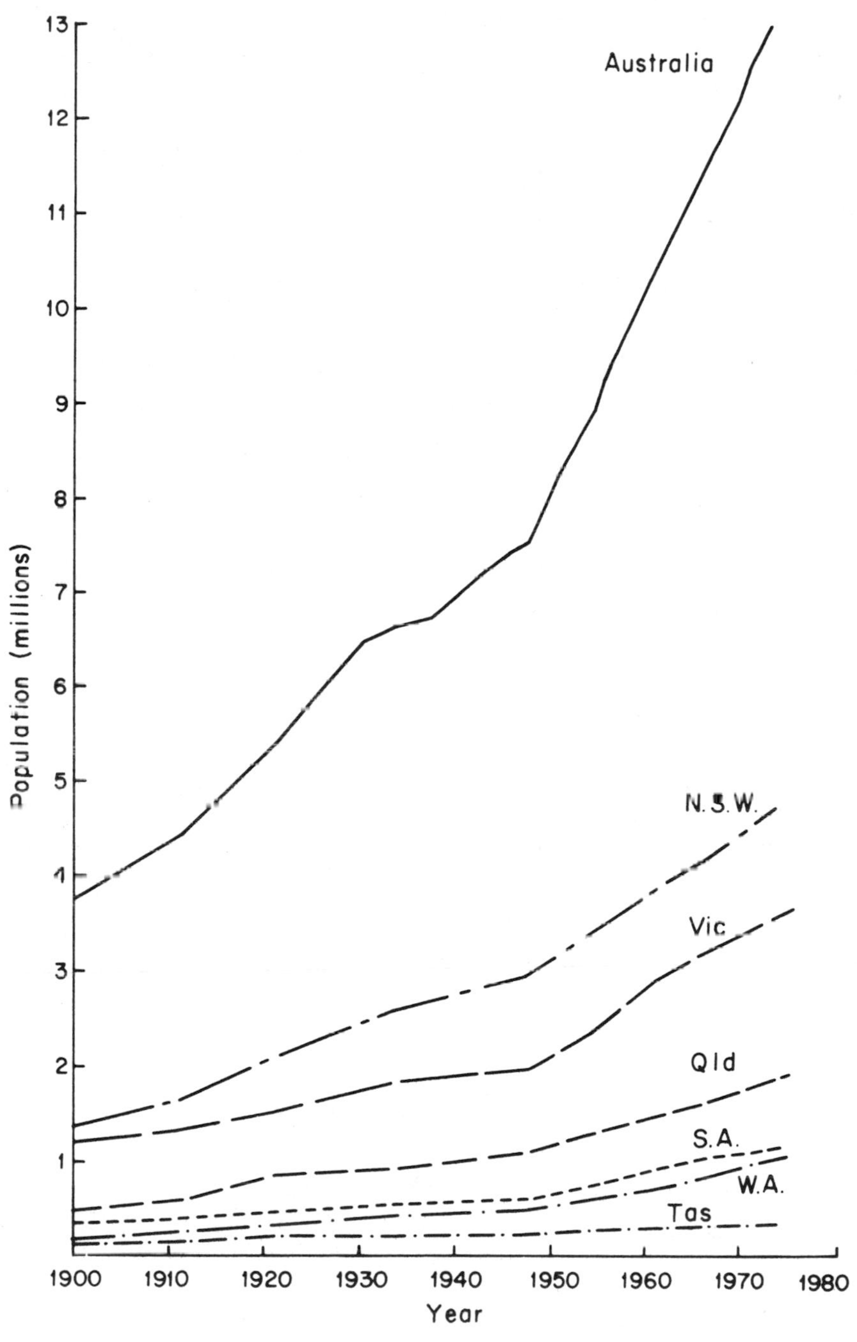

VII POPULATION OF AUSTRALIAN STATES AND CAPITAL CITIES WITH PERCENTAGES OF STATE POPULATIONS LIVING IN METROPOLITAN AREAS OF CAPITAL CITIES

STATE AND METRO. AREA	1901	%	1911	%	1921	%	1933	%
N.S.W. Sydney	1,354,846 481,830	35.55	1,646,734 651,800	38.97	2,100,371 899,059	42.80	2,600,847 1,235,267	47.50
VIC. Melbourne	1,201,070 535,008	44.54	1,315,551 600,200	44.04	1,531,280 766,465	50.05	1,820,261 991,934	54.49
QLD. Brisbane	498,129 103,756	20.1	605,813 143,500	23.07	755,972 209,946	27.77	947,534 299,748	31.63
S.A. Adelaide	358,346 175,641	45.76	408,558 192,400	46.01	495,160 255,375	51.57	580,949 312,619	53.81
W.A. Perth	184,124 53,800	20.55	282,114 111,400	37.86	332,732 154,873	46.55	438,852 207,440	47.27
TAS. Hobart	172,475 34,657	19.42	191,211 40,200	20.78	213,780 52,361	24.49	227,599 60,406	26.54
A.C.T. Canberra	— —		1,714 —		2,572 —		8,947 7,325	81.87
N.T.	—		—		3,867		4,850	
AUSTRALIA	3,773,801		4,455,005		5,435,734		6,629,839	
Capital City Population	1,462,094	35.44	1,739,500	38.12	2,338,079	43.01	3,107,414	46.87

Sources: *Official Year Books of Australia.*
Official Year Books of the States.

1947	%	1954	%	1961	%	1966	%	1971*	%
2,984,838 1,484,004	49.72	3,423,529 1,863,161	54.42	3,917,013 2,183,388	55.74	4,233,822 2,446,345	57.78	4,601,180 3,176,980	69.05
2,054,701 1,226,409	59.69	2,452,341 1,524,111	62.98	2,930,113 1,911,895	65.25	3,219,526 2,110,168	65.54	3,502,351 2.509,298	71.65
1.106,415 402,030	36.34	1,318,259 502,320	39.45	1,518,828 621,550	40.92	1,663,685 718,822	43.21	1,827,065 818,423	44.79
646,073 382,454	59.20	797,094 483,508	60.66	969,340 587,957	60.66	1,091,875 727,916	66.67	1,178,707 809,482	68.97
502,480 272,528	54.24	639,771 348,647	54.50	736,629 420,133	57.03	836,673 499,969	59.76	1,030,469 641,800	62.28
257,078 76,534	29.77	308,752 95.206	30.91	350,340 115,932	33.09	371,435 119,469	32.16	390,413 129.928	33.28
16,905 15,156	89.65	30,315 28,277	93.28	58,828 56,449	95.96	96,013 92,308	96.14	144,063 140,864	97.78
10,868		16,469		27,095		37,433		86,390	
7,579,358		8,986,530		10,508,186		11,550,462		12,755,638	
3,843,959	50.72	4,845,230	54.21	5,897,304	56.12	6,714,997	58.14	8,226,775	64.50

*Includes Aborigines for the first time.

VIII

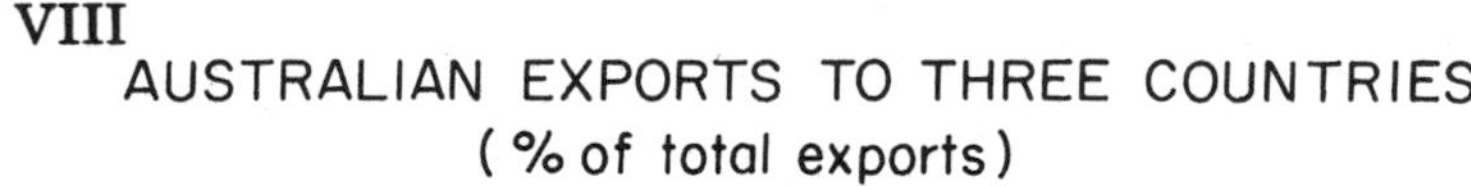

AUSTRALIAN EXPORTS TO THREE COUNTRIES
(% of total exports)

(%)
60
50
40
30
20
10
U. K.
U. S.
Japan
1900
1910
1920
1930
1940
1950
1960
1970
1980
Year

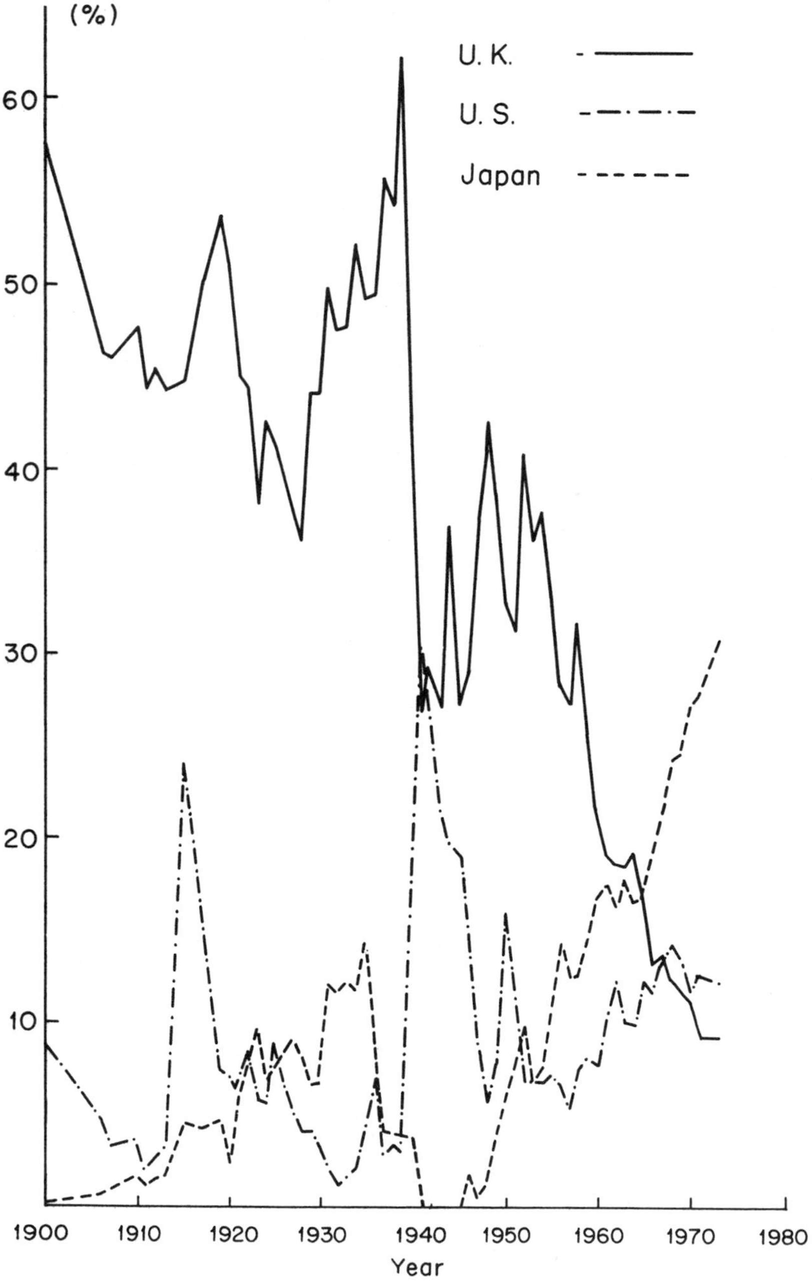

XI

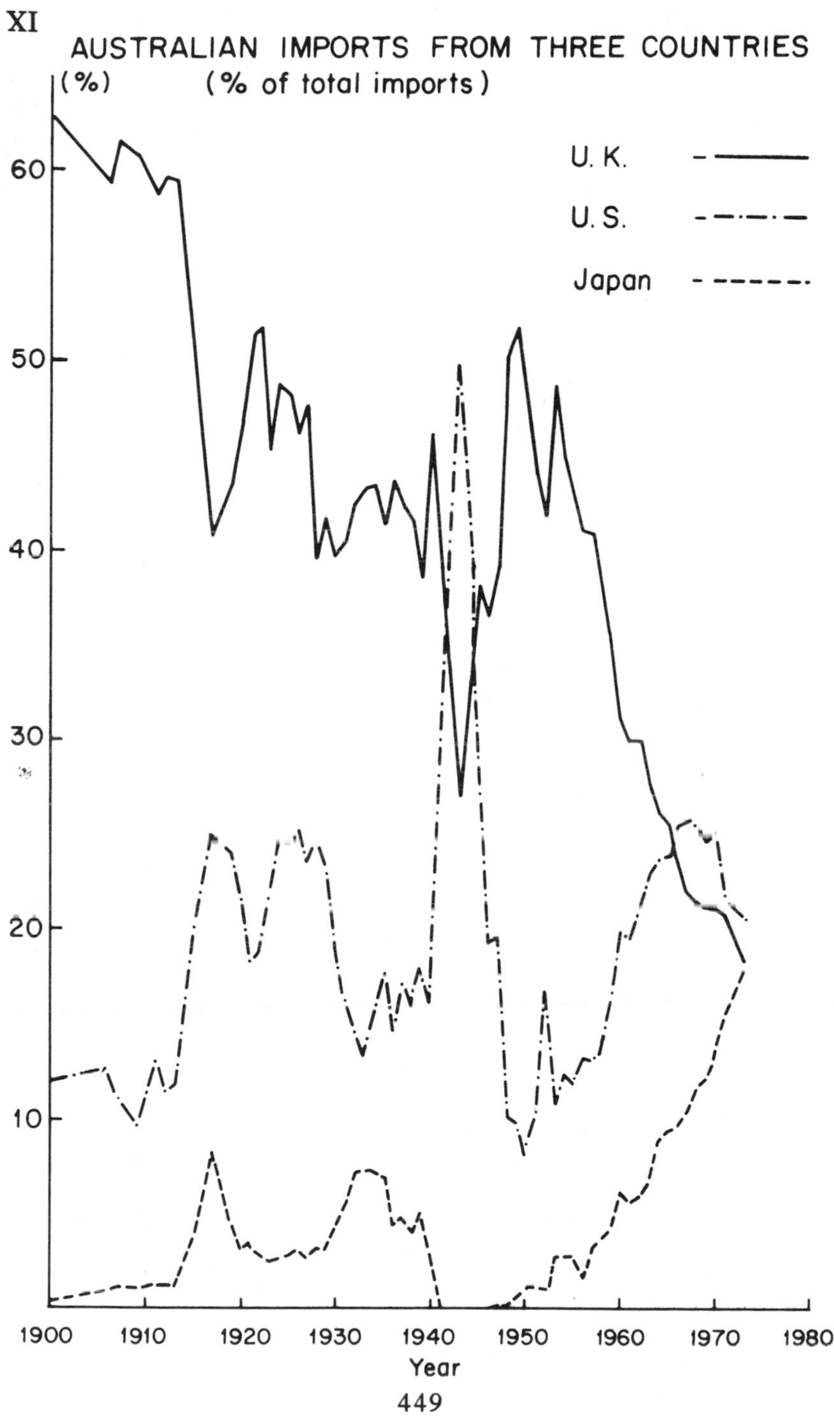
AUSTRALIAN IMPORTS FROM THREE COUNTRIES
(% of total imports)
(%)
U. K.
U. S.
Japan
60
50
40
30
20
10
1900
1910
1920
1930
1940
1950
1960
1970
1980
Year

X UNEMPLOYMENT IN AUSTRALIA SINCE FEDERATION

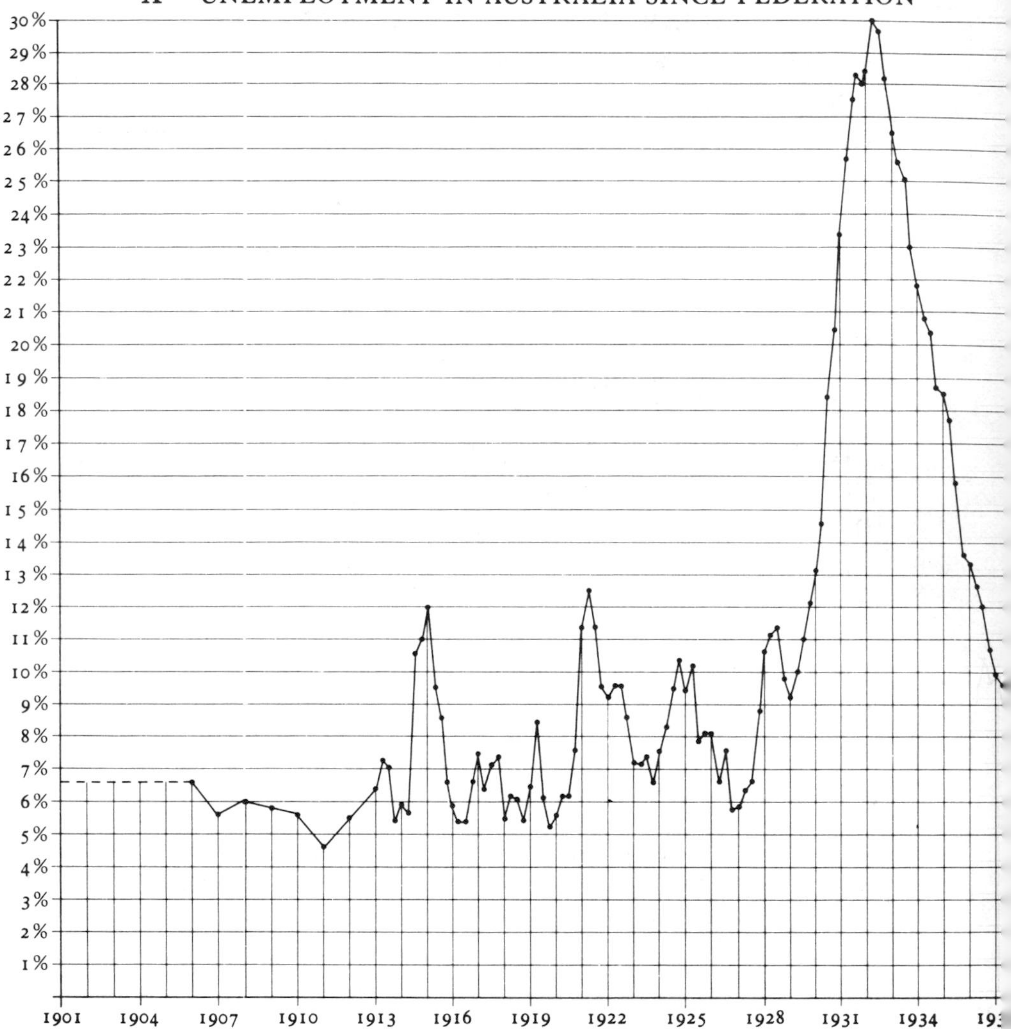

1913-1953: Percentage of Unemployed Trade Union Members.
(Source: *Official Year Books of the Commonwealth of Australia.*)

1953-1961: Registered Unemployed as Percentage of the Labour Force.
(Source: *Labour Market Studies No. 2* supplied by Commonwealth Bureau of Census and Statistics.)

1961-1973: All Persons Unemployed as Percentage of the Labour Force.
(Source: 1961-64, *Labour Report 1964*; 1964-1973, *The Labour Force*, Commonwealth Bureau of Census and Statistics.)

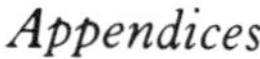

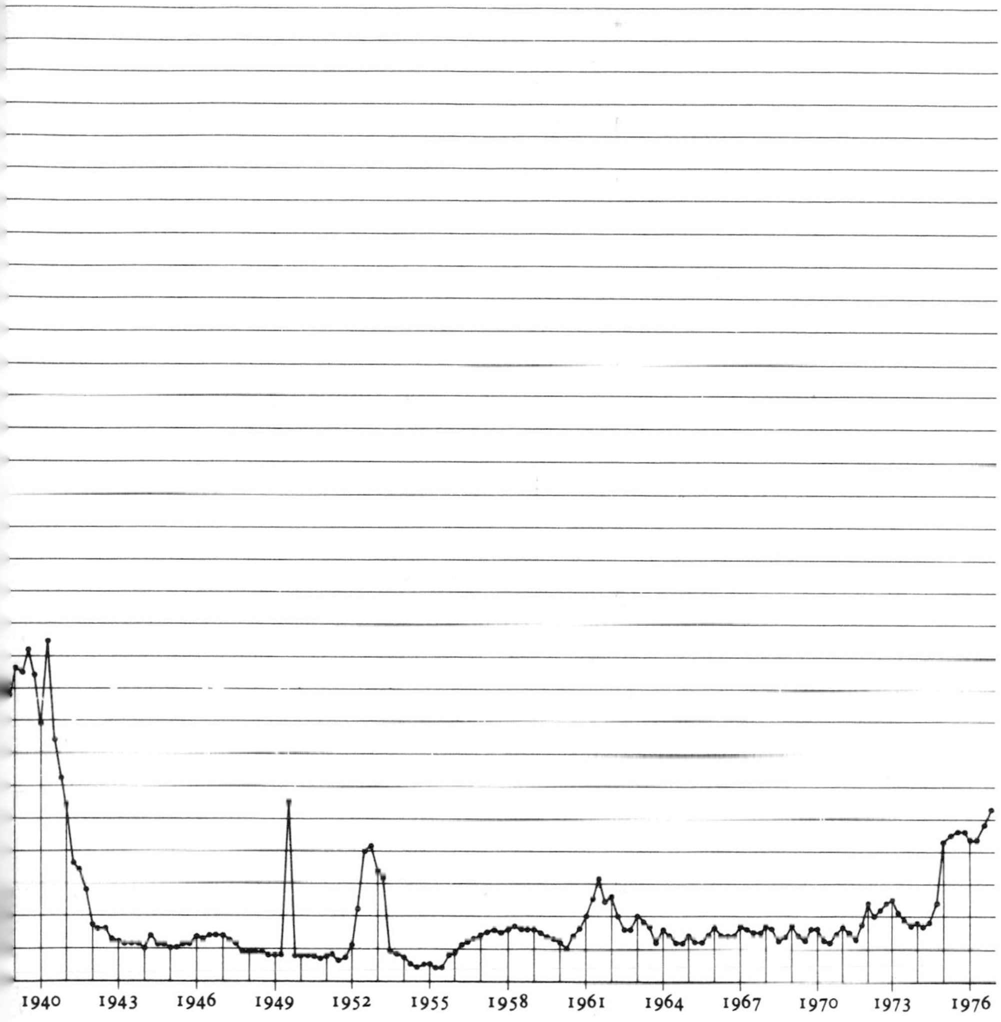

1940 1943 1946 1949 1952 1955 1958 1961 1964 1967 1970 1973 1976

INDEX